Auction Theory

Auction Theory

Vijay Krishna

Department of Economics
Pennsylvania State University
University Park, Pennsylvania

ACADEMIC PRESS

An Imprint of Elsevier

San Diego   San Francisco   New York   Boston   London   Sydney   Tokyo

This book is printed on acid-free paper. ∞

Academic Press

An Imprint of Elsevier

525 B Street, Suite 1900, San Diego, California 92101-4495, USA
http://www.academicpress.com

Academic Press
84 Theobalds Road, London WC1X 8RR, UK
http://www.academicpress.com

Library of Congress Catalog Card Number: 2001098962
ISBN-13: 978-0-12-426-297-3
ISBN-10: 0-12-426297-X

PRINTED IN THE UNITED STATES OF AMERICA
08 09 10 11 12   14 13 12 11 10

Contents

Preface

The analysis of auctions as games of incomplete information originates in the work of William Vickrey (1961). In this book I discuss the theory of auctions in this tradition. The goal is to give an account of developments in the field in the 40 years since Vickrey's pioneering paper.

I do not attempt to provide a comprehensive survey of auction theory. The field has burgeoned, especially in the past couple of decades, and a comprehensive survey would be nearly impossible—the Econ Lit database has more than a thousand entries with the word "auction" or "auctions" in their titles, and about one-half of these papers are theoretical. Instead I have opted to concentrate on selected themes that I consider to be central to the theory. I adopt the point of view that a detailed consideration of a few basic models is more fruitful than a perfunctory discussion of a large number of variations. I can only hope that my choice of themes is not too arbitrary.

The models that are considered are discussed in some detail and, with a few minor exceptions, complete proofs of all propositions are provided. It is my contention that the strengths and weaknesses of the theory can be appreciated only by examining the inner workings of the propositions with some care.

Game Theory. The theory of games, especially concerning games of incomplete information, constitutes the basic apparatus of the book. Most modern graduate texts in microeconomics now have a substantial emphasis on game theory (see Kreps, 1990 or Mas-Colell *et al.*, 1995); any of these can acquaint the reader with the basic notions needed to follow the material in this book. More advanced texts on game theory include Fudenberg and Tirole (1991) and Osborne and Rubinstein (1994). To assist the reader, Appendix F contains the basic game theoretic definitions used in this book but is by no means an adequate substitute for consulting one of the texts mentioned.

Appendices. Auxiliary matters are relegated to a series of appendices. In particular, Appendices A through D contain some essential material concerning continuous probability distributions.

Notational Conventions. The notation is more or less standard. Real-valued random variables are denoted by uppercase letters, say X or Y, and their realizations by the corresponding lowercase letters, x or y. Sets are denoted by scripted letters, $\mathcal{X}$ or $\mathcal{Y}$. Thus, for instance, the random variable X takes on values $x \in \mathcal{X}$.

Boldface characters denote vectors, so that $\mathbf{x} = (x_1, x_2, \ldots, x_N)$ is an N-vector whose ith component is x_i. If $\mathbf{x}$ and $\mathbf{y}$ are N-vectors, then $\mathbf{x} \geq \mathbf{y}$ denotes that for all i, $x_i \geq y_i$, and $\mathbf{x} \gg \mathbf{y}$ denotes that for all i, $x_i > y_i$. The vector $\mathbf{x}_{-i}$ is obtained from $\mathbf{x}$ by omitting the ith component—that is, $\mathbf{x}_{-i} = (x_1, \ldots, x_{i-1}, x_{i+1}, \ldots, x_N)$ and we identify $(x_i, \mathbf{x}_{-i})$ with $\mathbf{x}$.

Vector valued random variables are denoted by bold uppercase letters, $\mathbf{X}$ or $\mathbf{Y}$.

The symbol ■ denotes the end of a proof and ▲ denotes the end of an example.

Definitions of recurring symbols—for example, the symbol m is used throughout the book to denote a monetary payment—can be found via the index.

References. At the end of each chapter is a section titled "Chapter Notes." This contains bibliographic references to the works on which the material in the chapter is based. So as to not interrupt the flow, the body of the chapter itself contains no bibliographic references.

Acknowledgments. Much of this book was conceived and written while I was on sabbatical leave from Penn State University during the 1999–2000 academic year. I am grateful to my home institution for giving me this opportunity and to the Institute of Economics at the University of Copenhagen and the Center for Rationality at the Hebrew University of Jerusalem for hosting me during that year. Both provided wonderful environments for this project.

Jean-Pierre Benoît, Kala Krishna, Bob Marshall, and Bob Rosenthal read most of the book, asked a lot of tough questions, and offered much useful advice. I am also grateful to John Morgan, Motty Perry, Phil Reny, Hal Varian, and a fine group of anonymous reviewers for their comments.

In writing this book I benefited greatly from the efforts of Sergei Iz-malkov. He read the whole manuscript meticulously and made numerous valuable suggestions regarding both substance and exposition. Every author should be so fortunate as to have the assistance of someone like him.

Scott Bentley of Academic Press, apart from being a wonderful editor, very graciously allowed me to miss every deadline I had committed to.

Pronouns. Although there is a single author, the remainder of the book uses the plural "we"—as in "we see that ..."—rather than the singular "I." This is not to indicate any royal lineage, but only that the book is intended to be a conversation between the author and the reader.

To my parents, Raj and Kamla Krishna,
who taught only by example

1

Introduction

In 193 A.D., having killed the Emperor Pertinax, in a bold move the Præ-
torian Guard proceeded to sell off the entire Roman Empire by means of an
auction. The winning bid was a promise of 25,000 sesterces per man to the
Guard. The winner, Didius Julianus, was duly declared emperor but lasted
for only two months before suffering from what is perhaps the earliest and
most extreme instance of the "winner's curse"—he was beheaded.

Auctions have been used since antiquity for the sale of a variety of objects. Herodotus reports that auctions were used in Babylon as early as
500 B.C. Today both the range and the value of objects sold by auction
has grown to staggering proportions. Art objects and antiques have always
been sold at the fall of the auctioneer's hammer. But now numerous kinds
of commodities ranging from tobacco, fish, and fresh flowers to scrap metal
and gold bullion are sold by means of auctions. Bond issues by public utili-
ties are usually auctioned off to investment banking syndicates. Long-term
securities are sold in weekly auctions conducted by the U.S. Treasury to
finance the borrowing needs of the government. Perhaps the most important use of auctions has been to facilitate the transfer of assets from public to private hands—a worldwide phenomenon in the past two decades.
These have included the sale of industrial enterprises in Eastern Europe
and the former Soviet Union and transportation systems in Britain and
Scandinavia. Traditionally, the rights to use natural resources from public
property—such as timber rights and off-shore oil leases—have been sold by
means of auctions. In the modern era, auctions of rights to use the electro-
magnetic spectrum for communication are also a worldwide phenomenon.

Finally, there has been a tremendous growth in both the number of Internet auction websites, where individuals can put up items for sale under common auction rules, and the value of goods sold there.

The process of procurement via competitive bidding is nothing but an auction except that in this case the bidders compete for the right to sell their products or services. Billions of dollars of government purchases are almost exclusively made in this way, and the practice is widespread, if not endemic, in business. In what follows, an auction will be understood to include the process of procurement via competitive bidding. Of course, in this case it is the person bidding lowest who wins the contract.

What is the reason that auctions and competitive bidding are so prevalent? Are there situations to which an auction is particularly suited as a selling mechanism as opposed to, say, a fixed, posted price? From the point of view of the bidders, what are good bidding strategies? From the point of view of the sellers, are particular forms of auctions likely to bring greater revenues than others? These and other questions form the subject matter of this book.

Some Common Auction Forms

The open ascending price or *English* auction is the oldest and perhaps most prevalent auction form. The word "auction" itself is derived from the Latin *augere*, which means "to increase" (or "augment"), via the participle *auctus* ("increasing"). In one variant of the English auction, the sale is conducted by an auctioneer who begins by calling out a low price and raises it, typically in small increments, as long as there are at least two interested bidders. The auction stops when there is only one interested bidder. One way to formally model the underlying game is to postulate that the price rises continuously and each bidder indicates an interest in purchasing at the current price in a manner apparent to all by, say, raising a hand. Once a bidder finds the price to be too high, he signals that he is no longer interested by lowering his hand. The auction ends when only a single bidder is still interested. This bidder wins the object and pays the auctioneer an amount equal to the price at which the second-last bidder dropped out.

The *Dutch* auction is the open descending price counterpart of the English auction. It is not commonly used in practice but is of some conceptual interest. Here the auctioneer begins by calling out a price high enough so that presumably no bidder is interested in buying the object at that price. This price is gradually lowered until some bidder indicates her interest. The object is then sold to this bidder at the given price.

The sealed-bid *first-price* auction is another common form. Its workings are rather straightforward: bidders submit bids in sealed envelopes; the person submitting the highest bid wins the object and pays what he bid.

Finally, there is the sealed-bid *second-price* auction. As its name suggests, once again bidders submit bids in sealed envelopes; the person submitting the highest bid wins the object but pays not what he bid, but the second-highest bid.

Valuations

Auctions are used precisely because the seller is unsure about the values that bidders attach to the object being sold—the maximum amount each bidder is willing to pay. If the seller knew the values precisely, he could just offer the object to the bidder with the highest value at or just below what this bidder is willing to pay. The uncertainty regarding values facing both sellers and buyers is an inherent feature of auctions.

If each bidder knows the value of the object to himself at the time of bidding, the situation is called one of privately known values or *private values*. Implicit in this situation is that no bidder knows with certainty the values attached by *other* bidders and knowledge of other bidders' values would not affect how much the object is worth to a particular bidder. The assumption of private values is most plausible when the value of the object to a bidder is derived from its consumption or use alone. For instance, if bidders assign different values to a painting, a stamp, or a piece of furniture only on the basis of how much utility they would derive from possessing it, perhaps viewing it purely as a consumption good, then the private values assumption is reasonable. On the other hand, if bidders assign values on the basis of how much the object will fetch in the resale market, viewing it as an investment, then the private values assumption is not a good one.

In many situations, how much the object is worth is unknown at the time of the auction to the bidder himself. He may have only an estimate of some sort or some privately known signal—such as an expert's estimate or a test result—that is correlated with the true value. Indeed, other bidders may possess information, say additional estimates or test results, that if known, would affect the value that a particular bidder attaches to the object. Thus, values are unknown at the time of the auction and may be affected by information available to other bidders. Such a specification is called one of *interdependent values* and is particularly suited for situations in which the object being sold is an asset that can possibly be resold after the auction. A special case of this is a situation in which the value, though unknown at the time of bidding, is the same for all bidders—a situation described as being one of a pure *common value*.[1] A common value model is most appropriate when the value of the object being auctioned is derived from a market

---

[1]Sometimes the term "common values" is itself used to label what we have called "interdependent values." We use the latter term, as it more accurately describes the situation.

price that is unknown at the time of the auction. An archetypal example is the sale of a tract of land with an unknown amount of oil underground. Bidders may have different estimates of the amount of oil, perhaps based on privately conducted tests, but the final value of the land is derived from the future sales of the oil, so this value is, to a first approximation, the same for all bidders.

Note that the term "interdependence" refers only to the structure of values and how these are affected by information held by other bidders. It does not refer to any statistical properties of this information—that is, how the signals observed by the bidders are distributed. Thus, we could have a situation in which values are interdependent, so that a particular bidder's value depends on a signal observed by another bidder, but at the same time, the signals themselves are statistically independent. Similarly, we could have a situation in which the values are not interdependent, so that a particular bidder's value depends only on his own signal, but the signals themselves are correlated.

Equivalent Auctions

Four auction formats have been outlined here. Two were open auctions—the English and the Dutch—while two were sealed-bid auctions—the first- and second-price formats. These seem very different institutions, and certainly, they differ in the way that they are implemented in the real world. Open auctions require that the bidders collect in the same place, whereas sealed bids may be submitted by mail, so a bidder may observe the behavior of other bidders in one format and not in another. For rational decision makers, however, some of these differences are superficial.

First, observe that the Dutch open descending price auction is strategically equivalent to the first-price sealed-bid auction.[2] In a first-price sealed-bid auction, a bidder's strategy maps his private information into a bid. Although the Dutch auction is conducted in the open, it offers no useful information to bidders. The only information that is available is that some bidder has agreed to buy at the current price; but that causes the auction to end. Bidding a certain amount in a first-price sealed-bid auction is equivalent to offering to buy at that amount in a Dutch auction, provided the item is still available. For every strategy in a first-price auction there is an equivalent strategy in the Dutch auction and vice versa.

Second, when values are private, the English open ascending auction is also equivalent to the second-price sealed-bid auction, but in a weaker sense than noted earlier. The English auction offers information about when

---

[2]Two games are strategically equivalent if they have the same normal form except for duplicate strategies. Roughly this means that for every strategy in one game, a player has a strategy in the other game, which results in the same outcomes.

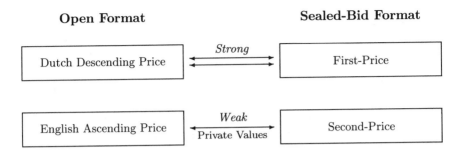

FIGURE 1.1. Equivalence of Open and Sealed-Bid Formats

other bidders drop out, and by observing this, it may be possible to infer something about their privately known information. With private values, however, this information is of no use. In an English auction, it clearly cannot be optimal to stay in after the price exceeds the value—this can only cause a loss—or to drop out before the price reaches the value—thus forgoing potential gains. Likewise, in a second-price auction it is best to bid the value (this is discussed in more detail later). Thus, with private values, the optimal strategy in both is to bid up to or stay in until the value.

This equivalence between the English and second-price auction is *weak* in two senses. First, the two auctions are not strategically equivalent. Second, and more important, the optimal strategies in the two are the same only if values are private. With interdependent values, the information available to others is relevant to a particular bidder's evaluation of the worth of the object. Seeing some other bidder drop out early may bring bad news that may cause a bidder to reduce his own estimate of the object's value. Thus, if values are interdependent, the two auctions need not be equivalent from the perspective of the bidders. Figure 1.1 depicts the equivalences between the open and sealed-bid formats introduced here.

Revenue versus Efficiency

The main questions that guide auction theory involve a comparison of the performance of different auction formats as economic institutions. These are evaluated on two grounds and the relevance of one or the other criterion depends on the context. From the perspective of the seller, a natural yardstick in comparing different auction forms is the *revenue*, or the expected selling price, that they fetch. From the perspective of society as a whole, however, *efficiency*—that the object end up in the hands of the person who values it the most *ex post*—may be more important. This is especially true when the auction concerns the sale of a publicly held asset to the private sector, so the seller, in this case a government, may want to choose a format that ensures that the object is allocated efficiently, even if the revenue from some other, inefficient format is higher.

But should efficiency be a criterion at all? Why can we not rely on "the market" to reallocate the object efficiently, even if the auction does not do so? After all, if there are unrealized gains from trade, the person who wins the auction can resell the object to someone who attaches a higher value. We will argue that this argument is suspect for many reasons. First, post-auction transactions will typically involve a small number of agents, especially in the context of privatization, and so will result in some bargaining about the resale price. Such bargaining is unlikely to result in efficient outcomes since it will typically take place under conditions of incomplete information. Second, resale may involve significant transaction costs, so it may not take place even when it should. In Chapter 4 we take up the question of whether resale will lead to efficiency more formally. In short, we find that even in the best circumstances—with no transaction costs or bargaining delays—the answer is no. Resale cannot guarantee efficiency, so a policy maker interested in achieving efficiency would do well to choose the auction format carefully.

Of course, revenue and efficiency are not the only criteria that should guide the choice of an auction format. The common auction forms discussed thus far have the virtue of simplicity—the rules of the auction are transparent—and this may be an important practical consideration. Another important factor may be the potential for collusion among bidders. As we will see later, auction formats differ in their susceptibility to such collusion.

What Is an Auction?

A wide variety of selling institutions fall under the rubric of "an auction." There are hybrid Dutch-English auctions in which the price is lowered until there is an interested bidder and then other bidders are allowed to outbid this amount. There are what may be called "deadline" auctions— commonly used by Internet auction sites—in which the person with highest standing bid before a fixed stopping time, say, noon on Sunday, is declared the winner. There are "candle" auctions, with a random stopping time, in which the person with the highest bid standing before the wick of a candle burns out wins. One may conceive of a third-price auction or an auction in which the winner pays the average of all other bids. The range of possibilities is rather wide and even more so when sales of multiple objects are considered. Without adopting a rigid view as to what may be called an auction and what may not, we seek to identify some important features that such institutions have in common.

A common aspect of auction-like institutions is that they elicit information, in the form of bids, from potential buyers regarding their willingness to pay and the outcome—that is, who wins what and pays how much—is determined solely on the basis of the received information. An implication of this is that auctions are *universal* in the sense that they may be used to sell any good. A valuable piece of art and a second-hand car can both be sold by means of an English auction under the same basic set of rules. Alternatively, both can be sold by means of a first-price sealed-bid auction. The auction form does not depend on any details specific to the item at hand.

A second important aspect of auction-like institutions is that they are *anonymous*. By this we mean that the identities of the bidders play no role in determining who wins the object and who pays how much. So if bidder 1 wins with a bid of b_1 and pays some amount p, then keeping all other bids fixed, if some other bidder, say 2, were to bid b_1 and bidder 1 were to bid b_2, then bidder 2 would win and pay p also. Every bidder other than 1 and 2, say bidder 3, is completely unaffected if bidders 1 and 2 exchange their bids in the manner described above.

In later chapters we place auctions in a larger class of institutions, called *mechanisms*. Mechanisms differ from auctions in that they are not necessarily universal or anonymous.

Outline of Part I

In Part I of the book, we study situations where a *single* indivisible object is sold to one of many potential buyers.

Chapter 2 introduces the basic theory of auctions with *private values* beginning with the case where these are symmetrically and independently distributed. It derives equilibrium strategies in first- and second-price auctions and compares their performance. Chapter 3 concerns the benchmark "revenue equivalence principle," in its simplest form. Chapter 4 is then concerned with amendments to the revenue equivalence principle necessitated by various extensions to the basic model including asymmetries, risk aversion, and budget constraints. Chapter 5 examines the problem of mechanism design with private values, considering both optimal and efficient mechanisms.

Chapter 6 introduces the model of auctions with *interdependent values* and affiliated signals, again deriving equilibrium strategies in the common auction forms. The main goal here is to rank the common auction forms in terms of the expected selling price. Chapter 7 derives the "revenue ranking principle" and explores some of its implications. Chapter 8 again explores some extensions and qualifications to the basic model necessitated by asymmetries among bidders. Chapter 9 considers the problem of allocating efficiently when bidders are asymmetric, focusing on the efficiency properties of the English auction. Chapter 10 studies mechanism design

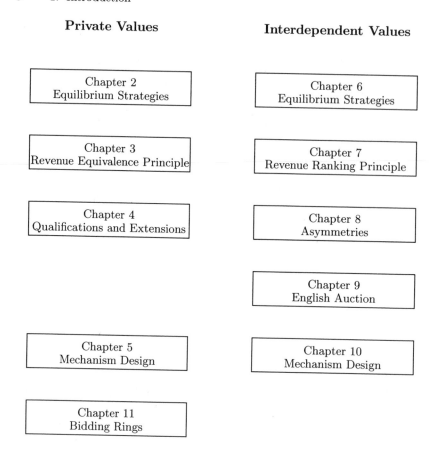

Private Values   **Interdependent Values**

| Chapter 2
Equilibrium Strategies | | Chapter 6
Equilibrium Strategies |

| Chapter 3
Revenue Equivalence Principle | | Chapter 7
Revenue Ranking Principle |

| Chapter 4
Qualifications and Extensions | | Chapter 8
Asymmetries |

| | | Chapter 9
English Auction |

| Chapter 5
Mechanism Design | | Chapter 10
Mechanism Design |

| Chapter 11
Bidding Rings | |

FIGURE 1.2. Outline of Part I

with interdependent values, again considering both optimal and efficient mechanisms.

Finally, Chapter 11 is concerned with collusive behavior among bidders and the formation of bidding cartels. The models here are with private values.

Figure 1.2 shows the organization of Part I, emphasizing the more or less parallel development of the subject matter in the private value and the interdependent value cases.

Part II of the book concerns *multiple* object auctions. Chapter 12 serves as an introduction to this part.

Chapter Notes

Cassady (1967) provides a panoramic view of real-world auction institutions, past and present, that is both colorful and insightful.

Second-price auctions are also referred to as Vickrey auctions. It was commonly believed that the second-price auction was a purely theoretical construct proposed by Vickrey (1961) as a sealed-bid counterpart of the open ascending-price format. Lucking-Reiley (2000) points out, however, that many stamp auctions have been conducted under second-price rules since the nineteenth century. In this context, they originated as a means of allowing bidders who could not be present at the actual, open ascending-price auction, to submit bids by mail.

Many Internet auction websites have adopted what are effectively second-price rules. For instance, at the popular auction site *eBay*, goods are sold by means of what appears to be an English auction. Bidders can, however, make use of *proxy bidding* wherein they employ a computer program, sometimes called an "elf," to bid on their behalf. The computer program raises rival bids by the minimum increment as long as it is below some limit set by the bidder. It is easy to see that this is effectively a second-price auction in which the amount bid is the same as the limit set by a bidder. Again see the paper by Lucking-Reiley (2000).

There have been many excellent surveys of auction theory. These vary in both content and emphasis reflecting, as does this book, the interests of the authors and the state of theory at the time they were written. We mention some of the prominent ones. Milgrom (1985) gives a cogent account of the theory of symmetric single object auctions and shows how the theory may be extended to situations in which there are multiple objects but each bidder wants at most one. McAfee and McMillan (1987a) also concentrate on the symmetric single object case but emphasize many extensions and applications of the theory. Milgrom (1987) attempts to answer the question of when auctions are appropriate and why they are so prevalent. He places auctions in the larger context of general institutions of economic exchange and evaluates their performance in different environments. The survey by Wilson (1993), again largely concerning single object auctions, offers a wide range of examples in which equilibrium bidding strategies can be computed in closed form. Technical aspects of the symmetric private values model are carefully treated by Matthews (1995). Klemperer (2000) emphasizes that many aspects of auction theory have interesting applications to other branches of economic theory.

There is now a substantial and rapidly growing literature concerning empirical work on auctions and the development of associated econometric tools. A detailed discussion would take us too far afield, so we only mention a representative sample of the work. The papers by Hendricks *et al.* (1994),

Hendricks and Paarsch (1995) and Laffont *et al.* (1995) serve as useful introductions to the area.

Auctions have also been the subject of a now large body of work in experimental economics. Kagel (1995) has written a thoughtful survey of the area.

Part I

Single Object Auctions

2

Private Value Auctions: A First Look

We begin the formal analysis by considering equilibrium bidding behavior in the four common auction forms in an environment with independently and identically distributed private values. In the previous chapter we argued that the open descending price (or Dutch) auction is strategically equivalent to the first-price sealed-bid auction. When values are private, the open ascending price (or English) auction is also equivalent to the second-price sealed-bid auction, albeit in a weaker sense. Thus, for our purposes, it is sufficient to consider the two sealed-bid auctions.

This chapter introduces the basic methodology of auction theory. We postulate an informational environment consisting of (i) a valuation structure for the bidders—in this case, that of private values—and (ii) a distribution of information available to the bidders—in this case, it is independently and identically distributed. We consider different auction formats—in this case, first- and second-price sealed-bid auctions. Each auction format now determines a game of incomplete information among the bidders and, keeping the informational environment fixed, we determine a Bayesian-Nash equilibrium for each resulting game. When there are many equilibria, we usually select one on some basis—dominance, perfection, or symmetry—but make sure that the criterion is applied uniformly to all formats. The relative performance of the auction formats on grounds of revenue or efficiency is then evaluated by comparing the equilibrium outcomes in one format versus another.

2.1   The Symmetric Model

There is a single object for sale and N potential buyers are bidding for the object. Bidder i assigns a value of X_i to the object—the maximum amount a bidder is willing to pay for the object. Each X_i is independently and identically distributed on some interval $[0, \omega]$ according to the increasing distribution function F. It is assumed that F admits a continuous density $f \equiv F'$ and has full support. We allow for the possibility that the support of F is the nonnegative real line $[0, \infty)$ and if that is so, with a slight abuse of notation, write $\omega = \infty$. In any case, it is assumed that $E[X_i] < \infty$.

Bidder i knows the realization x_i of X_i and only that other bidders' values are independently distributed according to F. Bidders are risk neutral—they seek to maximize their expected profits. All components of the model other than the realized values are assumed to be commonly known to all bidders. In particular, the distribution F is common knowledge, as is the number of bidders.

Finally, it is also assumed that bidders are not subject to any liquidity or budget constraints—each bidder i has sufficient resources so that, if necessary, he or she can pay the seller up to his or her value x_i. Thus, each bidder is both willing and able to pay up to his or her value.

We emphasize that the distribution of values is the same for all bidders and we will refer to this situation as one involving *symmetric* bidders.

In this framework, we will examine two major auction formats:

I. A first-price sealed-bid auction, where the highest bidder gets the object and pays the amount he bid.

II. A second-price sealed-bid auction, where the highest bidder gets the object and pays the second highest bid.

Each of these auction formats determines a game among the bidders. A strategy for a bidder is a function $\beta_i : [0, \omega] \to \mathbb{R}_+$, which determines his or her bid for any value. We will typically be interested in comparing the outcomes of a symmetric equilibrium—an equilibrium in which all bidders follow the same strategy—of one auction with a symmetric equilibrium of the other. Given that bidders are symmetric, it is natural to focus attention on symmetric equilibria. We ask the following questions:

(i) What are symmetric equilibrium strategies in a first-price auction (I) and a second-price auction (II)?

(ii) From the point of view of the seller, which of the two auction formats yields a higher expected selling price in equilibrium?

2.2   Second-Price Auctions

Although the first-price auction format is more familiar and even natural, we begin our analysis by considering second-price auctions. The strategic problem confronting bidders in second-price auctions is much simpler than that in first-price auctions, so they constitute a natural starting point. Also recall that in the private values framework, second-price auctions are equivalent to open ascending price (or English) auctions.

In a second-price auction, each bidder submits a sealed bid of b_i, and given these bids, the payoffs are:

$$\Pi_i = \begin{cases} x_i - \max_{j \neq i} b_j & \text{if } b_i > \max_{j \neq i} b_j \\ 0 & \text{if } b_i < \max_{j \neq i} b_j \end{cases}$$

We also assume that if there is a tie, so that $b_i = \max_{j \neq i} b_j$, the object goes to each winning bidder with equal probability.

Bidding behavior in a second-price auction is straightforward.

Proposition 2.1 *In a second-price sealed-bid auction, it is a weakly dominant strategy to bid according to $\beta^{II}(x) = x$.*

Proof. Consider bidder 1, say, and suppose that $p_1 = \max_{j \neq 1} b_j$ is the highest competing bid. By bidding x_1, bidder 1 will win if $x_1 > p_1$ and not if $x_1 < p_1$ (if $x_1 = p_1$, bidder 1 is indifferent between winning and losing). Suppose, however, that he bids an amount $z_1 < x_1$. If $x_1 > z_1 \geq p_1$, then he still wins and his profit is still $x_1 - p_1$. If $p_1 > x_1 > z_1$, he still loses. However, if $x_1 > p_1 > z_1$, then he loses whereas if he had bid x_1, he would have made a positive profit. Thus, bidding less than x_1 can never increase his profit but in some circumstances may actually decrease it. A similar argument shows that it is not profitable to bid more than x_1. ∎

It should be noted that the argument in Proposition 2.1 relied neither on the assumption that bidders' values were independently distributed nor the assumption that they were identically so. Only the assumption of private values is important and Proposition 2.1 holds as long as this is the case.

With Proposition 2.1 in hand, let us ask how much each bidder expects to pay in equilibrium. Fix a bidder, say 1, and let the random variable $Y_1 \equiv Y_1^{(N-1)}$ denote the highest value among the $N-1$ remaining bidders. In other words, Y_1 is the highest order statistic of $X_2, X_3, \ldots, X_N$ (see Appendix C). Let G denote the distribution function of Y_1. Clearly, for all y, $G(y) = F(y)^{N-1}$. In a second-price auction, the expected payment by a bidder with value x can be written as

$$
\begin{aligned}
m^{\mathrm{II}}(x) &= \mathrm{Prob[Win]} \times E[\text{2nd highest bid} \mid x \text{ is the highest bid}] \\
&= \mathrm{Prob[Win]} \times E[\text{2nd highest value} \mid x \text{ is the highest value}] \\
&= G(x) \times E[Y_1 \mid Y_1 < x]
\end{aligned}
\tag{2.1}
$$

2.3 First-Price Auctions

In a first-price auction, each bidder submits a sealed bid of b_i, and given these bids, the payoffs are

$$
\Pi_i = \begin{cases} x_i - b_i & \text{if } b_i > \max_{j \neq i} b_j \\ 0 & \text{if } b_i < \max_{j \neq i} b_j \end{cases}
$$

As before, if there is more than one bidder with the highest bid the object goes to each such bidder with equal probability.

In a first-price auction, equilibrium behavior is more complicated than in a second-price auction. Clearly, no bidder would bid an amount equal to his or her value since this would only guarantee a payoff of 0. Fixing the bidding behavior of others, at any bid that will neither win for sure nor lose for sure, the bidder faces a simple trade-off. An increase in the bid will increase the probability of winning while, at the same time reducing the gains from winning. To get some idea about how these effects balance off, we begin with a heuristic derivation of symmetric equilibrium strategies.

Suppose that bidders $j \neq 1$ follow the symmetric, increasing and differentiable equilibrium strategy $\beta^{\mathrm{I}} \equiv \beta$. Suppose bidder 1 receives a signal, $X_1 = x$, and bids b. We wish to determine the optimal b.

First, notice that it can never be optimal to choose a bid $b > \beta(\omega)$ since in that case, bidder 1 would win for sure and could do better by reducing his bid slightly so that he still wins for sure but pays less. So we need only consider bids $b \leq \beta(\omega)$. Second, a bidder with value 0 would never submit a positive bid since he would make a loss if he were to win the auction. Thus, we must have $\beta(0) = 0$.

Bidder 1 wins the auction whenever he submits the highest bid—that is, whenever $\max_{i \neq 1} \beta(X_i) < b$. Since β is increasing, $\max_{i \neq 1} \beta(X_i) = \beta(\max_{i \neq 1} X_i) = \beta(Y_1)$, where, as before, $Y_1 \equiv Y_1^{(N-1)}$, the highest of $N-1$ values. Bidder 1 wins whenever $\beta(Y_1) < b$ or equivalently, whenever $Y_1 < \beta^{-1}(b)$. His expected payoff is therefore

$$
G\left(\beta^{-1}(b)\right) \times (x - b)
$$

where, again, G is the distribution of Y_1. Maximizing this with respect to b yields the first-order condition:

$$\frac{g\left(\beta^{-1}(b)\right)}{\beta'\left(\beta^{-1}(b)\right)}\left(x-b\right) - G\left(\beta^{-1}(b)\right) = 0 \qquad (2.2)$$

where $g = G'$ is the density of Y_1.

At a symmetric equilibrium, $b = \beta(x)$, and thus (2.2) yields the differential equation

$$G\left(x\right)\beta'\left(x\right) + g\left(x\right)\beta\left(x\right) = xg(x) \qquad (2.3)$$

or equivalently,

$$\frac{d}{dx}\left(G\left(x\right)\beta\left(x\right)\right) = xg(x)$$

and since $\beta\left(0\right) = 0$, we have

$$\begin{aligned}\beta\left(x\right) &= \frac{1}{G\left(x\right)}\int_0^x yg(y)\,dy \\ &= E[Y_1 \mid Y_1 < x]\end{aligned}$$

The derivation of β is only heuristic because (2.3) is merely a necessary condition—we have not formally established that if the other $N-1$ bidders follow β, then it is indeed optimal for a bidder with value x to bid $\beta\left(x\right)$. The next proposition verifies that this is indeed correct.

Proposition 2.2 *Symmetric equilibrium strategies in a first-price auction are given by*

$$\beta^{\mathrm{I}}(x) = E[Y_1 \mid Y_1 < x] \qquad (2.4)$$

where Y_1 is the highest of $N-1$ independently drawn values.

Proof. Suppose that all but bidder 1 follow the strategy $\beta^{\mathrm{I}} \equiv \beta$ given in (2.4). We will argue that in that case it is optimal for bidder 1 to follow β also. First, notice that β is an increasing and continuous function. Thus, in equilibrium the bidder with the highest value submits the highest bid and wins the auction. It is not optimal for bidder 1 to bid a $b > \beta\left(\omega\right)$. The expected payoff of bidder 1 with value x if he bids an amount $b \leq \beta\left(\omega\right)$ is calculated as follows. Denote by $z = \beta^{-1}(b)$ the value for which b is the equilibrium bid—that is, $\beta(z) = b$. Then we can write bidder 1's expected

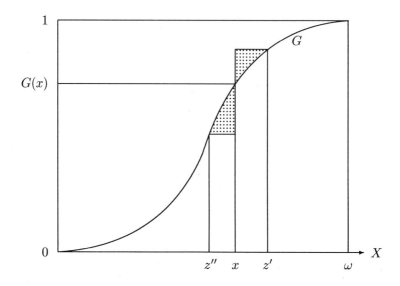

FIGURE 2.1. Losses from Over- and Under-Bidding in a First-Price Auction

payoff from bidding $\beta(z)$ when his value is x as follows:

$$
\begin{aligned}
\Pi(b, x) &= G(z)[x - \beta(z)] \\
&= G(z)x - G(z)E[Y_1 \mid Y_1 < z] \\
&= G(z)x - \int_0^z yg(y)\,dy \\
&= G(z)x - G(z)z + \int_0^z G(y)\,dy \\
&= G(z)\,(x - z) + \int_0^z G(y)\,dy
\end{aligned}
$$

where the fourth equality is obtained as a result of integration by parts. (Alternatively, see formula (A.2) in Appendix A.)

We thus obtain that

$$
\Pi(\beta(x), x) - \Pi(\beta(z), x) = G(z)\,(z - x) - \int_x^z G(y)\,dy \geq 0
$$

regardless of whether $z \geq x$ or $z \leq x$.

(The preceding argument shows that bidding an amount $\beta(z') > \beta(x)$ rather than $\beta(x)$ results in a loss equal to the shaded area to the right in Figure 2.1; similarly, bidding an amount $\beta(z'') < \beta(x)$ results in a loss equal to the area to the left.)

We have thus argued that if all other bidders are following the strategy β, a bidder with a value of x cannot benefit by bidding anything other than $\beta(x)$; and this implies that β is a symmetric equilibrium strategy. ∎

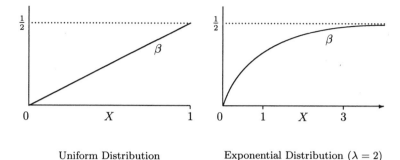

FIGURE 2.2. Equilibria of Two-Bidder Symmetric First-Price Auctions

The equilibrium bid can be rewritten as

$$\beta^I(x) = x - \int_0^x \frac{G(y)}{G(x)}\, dy$$

by using (A.2) in Appendix A again. This shows that the bid is, naturally, less than the value x. Since

$$\frac{G(y)}{G(x)} = \left[\frac{F(y)}{F(x)}\right]^{N-1}$$

the degree of "shading" (the amount by which the bid is less than the value) depends on the number of competing bidders and as N increases, approaches 0. Thus, for fixed F, as the number of bidders increases, the equilibrium bid $\beta^I(x)$ approaches x.

It is instructive to derive the equilibrium strategies explicitly in a few examples.

Example 2.1 *Values are uniformly distributed on* $[0,1]$.

If $F(x) = x$, then $G(x) = x^{N-1}$ and

$$\beta^I(x) = \frac{N-1}{N} x$$

In this case, the equilibrium strategy calls upon a bidder to bid a constant fraction of his value. For the case of two bidders, the equilibrium bidding strategy is depicted in the left-hand panel of Figure 2.2. ▲

Example 2.2 *Values are exponentially distributed on* $[0,\infty)$ *and there are only two bidders.*

If $F(x) = 1 - \exp(-\lambda x)$, for some $\lambda > 0$, and $N = 2$, then

$$\begin{aligned}
\beta^{\mathrm{I}}(x) &= x - \int_0^x \frac{F(y)}{F(x)} \, dy \\
&= \frac{1}{\lambda} - \frac{x \exp(-\lambda x)}{1 - \exp(-\lambda x)}
\end{aligned}$$

As a particular instance, consider the case where $\lambda = 2$ so that $E[X] = \frac{1}{2}$. The equilibrium bidding strategy in this case is depicted in the right-hand panel of Figure 2.2. The figure highlights the fact that with the exponentially distributed values, even a bidder with a very high value, say $1 million, will not bid more than 50 cents! This seems counterintuitive at first—the bidder is facing the risk of a big loss by not bidding higher—but is explained by the fact that the probability that the bidder with a high value will lose in equilibrium is infinitesimal. Indeed, for a bidder with a value of $1 million, it is smaller than $10^{-400000}$. This fact, together with the assumption that bidders are risk neutral, implies that bidders with high values are willing to bid very small amounts. Formally, the fact that no bidder bids more than $\frac{1}{2}$ is a consequence of the property that for all x,

$$\beta^{\mathrm{I}}(x) = E[Y_1 \mid Y_1 < x] \leq E[Y_1]$$

and when there are only two bidders, the latter is the same as $E[X]$. ▲

2.4   Revenue Comparison

Having derived symmetric equilibrium strategies in both the second- and first-price auctions, we can now compare the selling prices—the revenues accruing to the seller—in the two formats.

In a first-price auction, the winner pays what he or she bid and thus the expected payment by a bidder with value x is

$$m^{\mathrm{I}}(x) = \text{Prob[Win]} \times \text{Amount bid} = G(x) \times E[Y_1 \mid Y_1 < x] \qquad (2.5)$$

which is the same as in a second-price auction (see (2.1)). Figure 2.3 depicts both the expected payment and the expected payoff of a bidder with value x in either auction. Because the expected revenue of the seller is just the sum of the *ex ante* (prior to knowing their values) expected payments of the bidders, this also implies that the expected revenues in the two auctions are the same. Let us see why.

The *ex ante* expected payment of a particular bidder in either auction is

$$\begin{aligned}
E[m^A(X)] &= \int_0^\omega m^A(x) f(x) \, dx \\
&= \int_0^\omega \left(\int_0^x y g(y) \, dy \right) f(x) \, dx
\end{aligned}$$

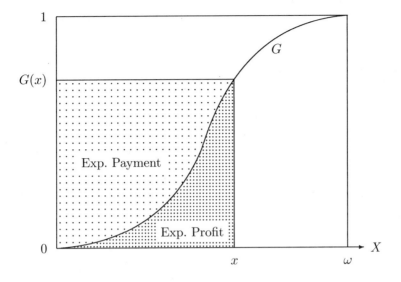

FIGURE 2.3. Payments and Profits in First- and Second-Price Auctions

where $A = $ I or II. Interchanging the order of integration we obtain that

$$
\begin{aligned}
E\left[m^A\left(X\right)\right] &= \int_0^\omega \left(\int_y^\omega f(x)\, dx\right) y g(y)\, dy \\
&= \int_0^\omega y\left(1 - F(y)\right) g(y)\, dy
\end{aligned}
\tag{2.6}
$$

The expected revenue accruing to the seller $E\left[R^A\right]$ is just N times the *ex ante* expected payment of an individual bidder, so,

$$
\begin{aligned}
E\left[R^A\right] &= N \times E\left[m^A\left(X\right)\right] \\
&= N \int_0^\omega y\left(1 - F(y)\right) g(y)\, dy
\end{aligned}
$$

But now notice that the density of $Y_2^{(N)}$, the second highest of N values, $f_2^{(N)}(y) = N\left(1 - F(y)\right) f_1^{(N-1)}(y)$ (see Appendix C) and since $f_1^{(N-1)}(y) = g(y)$, we can write

$$
\begin{aligned}
E\left[R^A\right] &= \int_0^\omega y f_2^{(N)}(y)\, dy \\
&= E\left[Y_2^{(N)}\right]
\end{aligned}
\tag{2.7}
$$

In either case, the expected revenue is just the expectation of the second-highest value. Thus, we conclude that *the expected revenues of the seller in the two auctions are the same.* For future reference, we record this fact in the following proposition.

Proposition 2.3 *With independently and identically distributed private values, the expected revenue in a first-price auction is the same as the expected revenue in a second-price auction.*

The fact that the expected selling prices in the two auctions are equal is all the more striking because in specific realizations of the values the price at which the object is sold may be greater in one auction or the other. With positive probability, the revenue R^{I} in a first-price auction exceeds R^{II}, the revenue in a second-price auction, and vice versa. For instance, when values are uniformly distributed and there are only two bidders, the equilibrium strategy in a first-price auction is $\beta^{\mathrm{I}}(x) = \frac{1}{2}x$. If the realized values are such that $\frac{1}{2}x_1 > x_2$, then the revenue in a first-price auction is greater than that in a second-price auction. On the other hand, if $\frac{1}{2}x_1 < x_2 < x_1$, the opposite is true. Thus, while the revenue may be greater in one auction or another depending on the realized values, we have argued that *on average* the revenue to the seller will be the same.

Actually, we can say more about the distribution of prices in the two auctions. It is clear that the revenues in a second-price auction are more variable than in its first-price counterpart. In the former, the prices can range between 0 and ω; in the latter, they can only range between 0 and $E[Y_1]$. A more precise result can be formulated along the following lines. Let L^{I} denote the distribution of the equilibrium price in a first-price auction and likewise, let L^{II} be the distribution of prices in a second-price auction. Then L^{II} is a *mean-preserving spread* of L^{I}—from the perspective of the seller, a second-price auction is *riskier* than a first-price auction (see Appendix B). Every risk-averse seller prefers the latter to the former (assuming, of course, that bidders are risk-neutral).[1] Figure 2.4 depicts the two distributions in the case of uniformly distributed values with two bidders. Since the two distributions have the same mean, the two shaded regions are, as they must be, equal in area.

Proposition 2.4 *With independently and identically distributed private values, the distribution of equilibrium prices in a second-price auction is a mean-preserving spread of the distribution of equilibrium prices in a first-price auction.*

Proof. The revenue in a second-price auction is just the random variable $R^{\mathrm{II}} = Y_2^{(N)}$; the revenue in a first-price auction is the random variable $R^{\mathrm{I}} = \beta(Y_1^{(N)})$, where $\beta \equiv \beta^{\mathrm{I}}$ is the symmetric equilibrium strategy from

---

[1]This is also equivalent to the statement that L^{I} dominates L^{II} in the sense of *second-order stochastic dominance*. Again, see Appendix B.

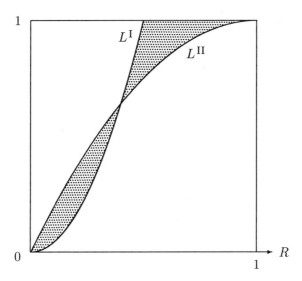

FIGURE 2.4. Distribution of Prices in First- and Second-Price Auctions

Proposition 2.2. So we can write

$$E\left[R^{\mathrm{II}} \mid R^{\mathrm{I}} = p\right] = E\left[Y_2^{(N)} \mid Y_1^{(N)} = \beta^{-1}(p)\right]$$

But for all y,

$$E\left[Y_2^{(N)} \mid Y_1^{(N)} = y\right] = E\left[Y_1^{(N-1)} \mid Y_1^{(N-1)} < y\right] \qquad (2.8)$$

This is because the only information regarding the second-highest of N values, $Y_2^{(N)}$, that the event that the highest of N values $Y_1^{(N)} = y$ provides is that the highest of $N - 1$ values, $Y_1^{(N-1)}$, is less than y. (See (C.6) in Appendix C for a formal demonstration.)

Using (2.8), we can write

$$\begin{aligned}
E\left[R^{\mathrm{II}} \mid R^{\mathrm{I}} = p\right] &= E\left[Y_1^{(N-1)} \mid Y_1^{(N-1)} < \beta^{-1}(p)\right] \\
&= \beta\left(\beta^{-1}(p)\right) \\
&= p
\end{aligned}$$

recalling (2.4).

Since $E\left[R^{\mathrm{II}} \mid R^{\mathrm{I}} = p\right] = p$, there exists a random variable Z such that the distribution of R^{II} is the same as that of $R^{\mathrm{I}} + Z$ and $E\left[Z \mid R^{\mathrm{I}} = p\right] = 0$. Thus, L^{II} is a mean-preserving spread of L^{I}. ∎

2.5   Reserve Prices

In the analysis so far, the seller has played a passive role. Indeed, we have implicitly assumed that the seller parts with the object at whatever price it will fetch. In many instances, sellers reserve the right to not sell the object if the price determined in the auction is lower than some threshold amount, say $r > 0$. Such a price is called the *reserve price*. We now examine what effect such a reserve price has on the expected revenue accruing to the seller.

Reserve Prices in Second-Price Auctions

Suppose that the seller sets a "small" reserve price of $r > 0$. Since the price at which the object is sold can never be lower than r, no bidder with a value $x < r$ can make a positive profit in the auction. In a second-price auction, a reserve price makes no difference to the behavior of the bidders—it is still a weakly dominant strategy to bid one's value. The expected payment of a bidder with value r is now just $rG(r)$, and the expected payment of a bidder with value $x \geq r$ is

$$m^{\text{II}}(x, r) = rG(r) + \int_r^x yg(y)\, dy \qquad (2.9)$$

since the winner pays the reserve price r whenever the second-highest bid is below r.

Reserve Prices in First-Price Auctions

Now consider a first-price auction with a reserve price $r > 0$. Once again, since the price is at least r, no bidder with a value $x < r$ can make a positive profit. Furthermore, if β^{I} is a symmetric equilibrium of the first-price auction with reserve price r, it must be that $\beta^{\text{I}}(r) = r$. This is because a bidder with value r wins only if all other bidders have values less than r and, in that case, can win with a bid of r itself. In all other respects, the analysis of a first-price auction is unaffected, and in a manner analogous to Proposition 2.2 we obtain that a symmetric equilibrium bidding strategy for any bidder with value $x \geq r$ is

$$\begin{aligned}
\beta^{\text{I}}(x) &= E\left[\max\{Y_1, r\} \mid Y_1 < x\right] \\
&= r\frac{G(r)}{G(x)} + \frac{1}{G(x)} \int_r^x yg(y)\, dy
\end{aligned}$$

The expected payment of a bidder with value $x \geq r$ is

$$\begin{aligned}
m^{\text{I}}(x, r) &= G(x) \times \beta^{\text{I}}(x) \\
&= rG(r) + \int_r^x yg(y)\, dy \qquad (2.10)
\end{aligned}$$

which is the same as in (2.9).

Thus, once again, the expected payments and hence the expected revenues in the first- and second-price auctions are the same—Proposition 2.3 generalizes so as to accommodate reserve prices.

Revenue Effects of Reserve Prices

How do reserve prices affect the seller's expected revenue? As before, let A denote either the first- or second-price auction. In both, the expected payment of a bidder with value r is $rG(r)$. A calculation similar to that in (2.6) shows that the *ex ante* expected payment of a bidder is now

$$
\begin{aligned}
E\left[m^A\left(X,r\right)\right] &= \int_r^\omega m^A\left(x,r\right)f(x)\,dx \\
&= r\left(1-F(r)\right)G(r) + \int_r^\omega y\left(1-F(y)\right)g(y)\,dy
\end{aligned}
$$

What is the optimal, or revenue maximizing, reserve price from the perspective of the seller? Suppose that the seller attaches a value $x_0 \in [0,\omega)$. This means that if the object is left unsold, the seller would derive a value x_0 from its use. Clearly, the seller would not set a reserve price r that is lower than x_0. Then the overall expected payoff of the seller from setting a reserve price $r \geq x_0$ is

$$
\Pi_0 = N \times E\left[m^A\left(X,r\right)\right] + F(r)^N x_0
$$

Differentiating this with respect to r, we obtain

$$
\frac{d\Pi_0}{dr} = N\left[1-F(r)-rf(r)\right]G(r) + NG(r)f(r)x_0
$$

Now recall that the *hazard rate* function associated with the distribution F is defined as $\lambda\left(x\right) = f(x)/\left(1-F(x)\right)$. Thus, we can write

$$
\frac{d\Pi_0}{dr} = N\left[1-(r-x_0)\lambda\left(r\right)\right]\left(1-F(r)\right)G(r) \tag{2.11}
$$

First, notice that if $x_0 > 0$, then the derivative of Π_0 at $r = x_0$ is positive, implying that the seller should set a reserve price $r > x_0$. If $x_0 = 0$, then derivative of Π_0 at $r = 0$ is 0, but as long as $\lambda\left(r\right)$ is bounded, the expected payment attains a local minimum at 0, so a small reserve price leads to an increase in revenue. Thus, *a revenue maximizing seller should always set a reserve price that exceeds his or her value.* Why does a reserve price that exceeds x_0 lead to an increase in revenue? Consider a second-price auction with two bidders and suppose $x_0 = 0$. By setting a positive reserve price r the seller runs the risk that if the highest value among the bidders, Y_1, is smaller than r, the object will remain unsold. This potential loss is offset,

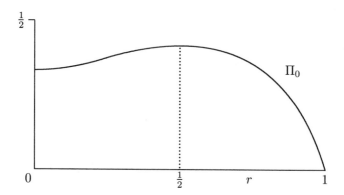

FIGURE 2.5. Optimal Reserve Price with Uniformly Distributed Values

however, by the possibility that while the highest value Y_1 exceeds r, the second-highest value, Y_2, is smaller than r (in all other cases, the reserve price has no effect). Now the application of the reserve price means that the object will be sold for r rather than Y_2. The probability of the first event is $F(r)^2$ and the loss is at most r. So for small r, the expected loss is at most $rF(r)^2$. The probability of the second event is $2F(r)(1 - F(r))$, and for small r, the gain is of order r, so the expected gain is of order $2rF(r)(1 - F(r))$. Thus, the expected gain from setting a small reserve price exceeds the expected loss. This fact is sometimes referred to as the *exclusion principle* since it implies, in effect, that it is optimal for the seller to exclude some bidders, those with values below the reserve price, from the auction even though their values exceed x_0.

Second, the relevant first-order condition implies that the optimal reserve price r^* must satisfy

$$(r^* - x_0)\,\lambda\,(r^*) = 1$$

or equivalently,

$$r^* - \frac{1}{\lambda\,(r^*)} = x_0 \qquad (2.12)$$

If $\lambda\,(\cdot)$ is increasing, this condition is also sufficient and it is remarkable that the optimal reserve price does not depend on the number of bidders. Roughly, the reason is that a reserve price comes into play only in instances when there is a single bidder with a value that exceeds the reserve price. So when a marginal change in the reserve price matters, it affects revenues in the same way as if there were a single bidder. Figure 2.5 depicts the expected revenue as a function of the reserve price r when F is the uniform distribution on $[0, 1]$, there are only two bidders, and $x_0 = 0$. As is clear from the figure, the optimal reserve price $r^* = \frac{1}{2}$. The resulting expected revenue is $\frac{5}{12}$.

Entry Fees

A positive reserve price r results in bidders with low values, lying below r, being excluded from the auction—since their equilibrium payoffs are zero, such bidders are indifferent between participating in the auction and not. An alternative instrument that the seller can also use to exclude buyers with low values is an *entry fee*—a fixed and nonrefundable amount that bidders must pay the seller prior to the auction in order to be able to submit bids. An entry fee is, as it were, the price of admission to the room in which the auction is being conducted.

A reserve price of r excludes all bidders with values $x < r$. The same set of bidders can be excluded by asking each bidder to pay an entry fee e such that

$$e = \int_0^r G(y)\,dy$$

Notice that e equals the expected payoff of a bidder with value r in either a first- or second-price auction (see Figure 2.4), so a bidder with value $x < r$ would not find it worthwhile to pay e in order to participate in the auction. The exclusion effect of a reserve price r can be replicated with an entry fee of e as determined earlier. Conversely, the exclusion effect of an entry fee e can be duplicated with a reserve price of r, again, as determined earlier.

Efficiency versus Revenue

A reserve price (or equivalently, an entry fee) raises the revenue to the seller but may have a detrimental effect on efficiency. Suppose that the value that the seller attaches to the object is 0. In the absence of a reserve price, the object will always be sold to the highest bidder and in the symmetric model studied here, that is also the bidder with the highest value. Thus, both the first- and second-price auctions allocate efficiently in the sense that the object ends up in the hands of the person who values it the most. If the seller sets a reserve price $r > 0$, however, there is a positive probability that the object will remain in the hands of seller and this is inefficient. This simple observation implies that there may be a trade-off between efficiency and revenue.

Commitment Issues

There are two practical considerations that we have neglected. First, we have implicitly assumed that the seller can credibly commit to not sell the object if it cannot be sold at or above the reserve price. This commitment is particularly important because by setting a reserve price the seller is giving up some gains from trade. Without such a commitment, buyers may anticipate that the object, if durable, will be offered for sale again in a later auction and perhaps with a lower reserve price. These expectations may affect their bidding behavior in the first auction. Indeed, in the absence of a credible "no sale" commitment, the problem confronting a seller is analogous to that of a durable goods monopoly. In both, a potential future sale may cause buyers to wait for lower prices and this may reduce demand today. In effect, potential future sales may compete with current sales. In response, the seller may have to set lower reserve prices today than would be optimal in a one-time sale or if the good were perishable.

A second and not unrelated issue concerns secret reserve prices. We have assumed that the reserve price is publicly announced prior to the auction. In many situations, especially in art auctions, it is announced that there is a reserve price, but the level of the reserve price is not disclosed. In effect, the seller can opt to not sell the object after learning all the bids and hence the price. But this is rational only if the seller anticipates that in a future sale the price will be higher. Once again, buyers' expectations regarding future sales may affect the bidding in the current auction.

Chapter Notes

The basic model of auctions with independent private values was introduced by Vickrey (1961). He derived equilibrium bidding strategies in a first-price auction when values are drawn from the uniform distribution (Example 2.1) and observed that the expected revenues in the first- and second-price auctions were the same. He recognized that this equivalence held more generally—that is, for arbitrary distributions—and formally established this in a subsequent paper, Vickrey (1962).

The symmetric independent private values model was analyzed in more detail by Riley and Samuelson (1981). The treatment of reserve prices follows that in Myerson (1981) and in Riley and Samuelson (1981). Milgrom (1987) discusses the problem of commitment in connection with reserve prices.

3

The Revenue Equivalence Principle

In the previous chapter we saw that regardless of the distribution of values, the expected selling price in a symmetric first-price auction is the same as that in a second-price auction. As a result a risk-neutral seller is indifferent between the two formats. The fact that the expected selling prices in the two auctions are equal is quite remarkable. The two auctions are not strategically equivalent as defined in Chapter 1, and in particular instances, the price in one or the other auction may be higher. This chapter explores the reasons underlying the equality of expected revenues in Proposition 2.3. In the process, we will discover that this equality extends beyond first- and second-price auctions to a whole class of auction forms.

3.1 Main Result

The auction forms we consider all have the feature that buyers are asked to submit *bids*—amounts of money they are willing to pay. These bids alone determine who wins the object and how much the winner pays. We will say that an auction is *standard* if the rules of the auction dictate that the person who bids the highest amount is awarded the object. Both first- and second-price auctions are, of course, standard in this sense but so, for instance, is a *third-price auction*, discussed later in this chapter, in which the winner is the person bidding the highest amount but he or she pays the third-highest bid. An example of a nonstandard method is a *lottery* in which the chances that a particular bidder wins is the ratio of his or her bid to the total amount bid by all. Such a lottery is nonstandard since the person who bids the most is not necessarily the one who is awarded the object.

Given a standard auction form, A, and a symmetric equilibrium β^A of the auction, let $m^A(x)$ be the equilibrium *expected payment* by a bidder with value x. It turns out, quite remarkably, that provided that the expected payment of a bidder with value 0 is 0, the expected payment function $m^A(\cdot)$ does not depend on the particular auction form A. As a result, the expected revenue in any standard auction is the same, a fact known as the revenue equivalence principle.

Proposition 3.1 *Suppose that values are independently and identically distributed and all bidders are risk neutral. Then any symmetric and increasing equilibrium of any standard auction, such that the expected payment of a bidder with value zero is zero, yields the same expected revenue to the seller.*

Proof. Consider a standard auction form, A, and fix a symmetric equilibrium β of A. Let $m^A(x)$ be the equilibrium expected payment in auction A by a bidder with value x. Suppose that β is such that $m^A(0) = 0$.

Consider a particular bidder, say 1, and suppose other bidders are following the equilibrium strategy β. It is useful to abstract away from the details of the auction and consider the expected payoff of bidder 1 with value x and when he bids $\beta(z)$ instead of the equilibrium bid $\beta(x)$. Bidder 1 wins when his bid $\beta(z)$ exceeds the highest competing bid $\beta(Y_1)$, or equivalently, when $z > Y_1$. His expected payoff is

$$\Pi^A(z, x) = G(z)x - m^A(z)$$

where as before $G(z) \equiv F(z)^{N-1}$ is the distribution of Y_1. The key point is that $m^A(z)$ depends on the other players' strategy β and z but is independent of the true value, x.

Maximization results in the first-order condition,

$$\frac{\partial}{\partial z}\Pi^A(z, x) = g(z)x - \frac{d}{dz}m^A(z) = 0$$

At an equilibrium it is optimal to report $z = x$, so we obtain that for all y,

$$\frac{d}{dy}m^A(y) = g(y)y \tag{3.1}$$

Thus,

$$
\begin{aligned}
m^A(x) &= m^A(0) + \int_0^x yg(y)\,dy \\
&= \int_0^x yg(y)\,dy \\
&= G(x) \times E[Y_1 \mid Y_1 < x] \tag{3.2}
\end{aligned}
$$

since, by assumption, $m^A(0) = 0$. Since the right-hand side does not depend on the particular auction form A, this completes the proof. ∎

For the specification in Example 2.1, the expected payment function can be easily calculated.

Example 3.1 *Values are uniformly distributed on* $[0, 1]$.

If $F(x) = x$, then $G(x) = x^{N-1}$ and for any standard auction satisfying $m^A(0) = 0$, (3.2) implies that

$$m^A(x) = \frac{N-1}{N} x^N$$

and

$$E\left[m^A(X)\right] = \frac{N-1}{N(N+1)}$$

while the expected revenue is

$$E\left[R^A\right] = N \times E\left[m^A(X)\right] = \frac{N-1}{N+1}$$

▲

3.2   Some Applications of the Revenue Equivalence Principle

The revenue equivalence principle is a powerful and useful tool. In this section we show how, with judicious use, it can be used to derive equilibrium bidding strategies in alternative, unusual auction forms. We then show how it can be extended and applied to situations in which bidders are unsure as to how many other, rival bidders they face.

3.2.1   Unusual Auctions

We consider two unusual formats: an all-pay auction and a third-price auction. Although neither is used as a real-world auction to sell objects, the former is a useful model of other auction-like contests—some examples are offered next—while the latter is a useful theoretical construct.

Equilibrium of All-Pay Auctions

Consider an *all-pay* auction with the following rules. Each bidder submits a bid and, as in the standard auctions discussed earlier, the highest bidder wins the object. The unusual aspect of an all-pay auction is that all bidders pay what they bid. The all-pay auction is a useful model of lobbying activity. In such models, different interest groups spend money—their "bids"—in order to influence government policy and the group spending the most—the highest "bidder"—is able to tilt policy in its favored direction, thereby "winning the auction." Since money spent on lobbying is a sunk cost borne by all groups regardless of which group is successful in obtaining its preferred policy, such situations have a natural all-pay aspect. We are interested in symmetric equilibrium strategies in an all-pay auction with symmetric, independent private values.

Suppose for the moment that there is a symmetric, increasing equilibrium of the all-pay auction such that the expected payment of a bidder with value 0 is 0. In other words, the assumptions of Proposition 3.1 are satisfied. Then we know that the expected payment in such an equilibrium must be the same as in (3.2). Now in an all-pay auction, the expected payment of a bidder with value x is the *same* as his bid—he forfeits his bid regardless of whether he wins or not—and so if there is a symmetric, increasing equilibrium of the all-pay auction β^{AP}, it must be that

$$\begin{aligned} \beta^{\mathrm{AP}}(x) &= m^A(x) \\ &= \int_0^x yg(y)\,dy \end{aligned}$$

To verify that this indeed constitutes an equilibrium of the all-pay auction, suppose that all bidders except one are following the strategy $\beta \equiv \beta^{\mathrm{AP}}$. If he bids an amount $\beta(z)$, the expected payoff of a bidder with value x is

$$G(z)x - \beta(z) = G(z)x - \int_0^z yg(y)\,dy$$

and integrating the second term by parts, this becomes

$$G(z)(x-z) + \int_0^z G(y)\,dy$$

which is the same as the payoff obtained in a first-price auction by bidding $\beta^{\mathrm{I}}(z)$ against other bidders who are following β^{I}. For the same reasons as in Proposition 2.2, this is maximized by choosing $z = x$. Thus, β^{AP} is a symmetric equilibrium.

Equilibrium of Third-Price Auctions

Suppose that there are at least three bidders. Consider a sealed-bid auction in which the highest bidder wins the object but pays a price equal to the third-highest bid. A *third*-price auction, as it is called, is a purely theoretical construct: there is no known instance of such a mechanism actually being used. It is an interesting construct nevertheless—equilibria of such an auction display some unusual properties—and leads to a better understanding of the workings of the standard auction forms. Here we show how the revenue equivalence principle can once again be used to derive equilibrium bidding strategies.

Again, suppose for the moment that there is a symmetric, increasing equilibrium of the third-price auction, say β^{III}, such that the expected payment of a bidder with value 0 is 0. Once again, since the assumptions of Proposition 3.1 are satisfied, we must have that for all x, the expected payment in a third-price auction is

$$m^{\text{III}}(x) = \int_0^x yg(y)\,dy \qquad (3.3)$$

On the other hand, consider bidder 1 and suppose that he wins in equilibrium when his value is x. Winning implies, of course, that his value x exceeds the highest of the other $N - 1$ values—that is, $Y_1 < x$. The price bidder 1 pays is the random variable $\beta^{\text{III}}(Y_2)$, where, Y_2 is the second-highest of the $N - 1$ other values. The density of Y_2, conditional on the event that $Y_1 < x$, can be written as

$$f_2^{(N-1)}(y \mid Y_1 < x) = \frac{1}{F_1^{(N-1)}(x)}(N-1)(F(x) - F(y))\,f_1^{(N-2)}(y)$$

where $(N-1)(F(x) - F(y))$ is the probability that Y_1 exceeds $Y_2 = y$ but is less than x and $f_1^{(N-2)}(y)$ is the density of the highest of $N - 2$ values. The expected payment in a third-price auction can then be written as

$$
\begin{aligned}
m^{\text{III}}(x) &= F_1^{(N-1)}(x)\,E\left[\beta^{\text{III}}(Y_2) \mid Y_1 < x\right] \\
&= \int_0^x \beta^{\text{III}}(y)(N-1)(F(x) - F(y))\,f_1^{(N-2)}(y)\,dy \quad (3.4)
\end{aligned}
$$

Equating (3.3) and (3.4), we obtain that

$$\int_0^x \beta^{\text{III}}(y)(N-1)(F(x) - F(y))\,f_1^{(N-2)}(y)\,dy = \int_0^x yg(y)\,dy$$

and differentiating with respect to x, this implies that

$$
\begin{aligned}
(N-1)f(x)\int_0^x \beta^{\text{III}}(y)f_1^{(N-2)}(y)\,dy &= xg(x) \\
&= x \times (N-1)f(x)F(x)^{N-2}
\end{aligned}
$$

since $G(x) \equiv F(x)^{N-1}$. This can be rewritten as

$$\int_0^x \beta^{\text{III}}(y)f_1^{(N-2)}(y)\,dy = xF_1^{(N-2)}(x)$$

since, $F_1^{(N-2)}(x) \equiv F(x)^{N-2}$. Differentiating once more with respect to x,

$$\beta^{\mathrm{III}}(x) f_1^{(N-2)}(x) = x f_1^{(N-2)}(x) + F_1^{(N-2)}(x)$$

and rearranging this we get

$$
\begin{aligned}
\beta^{\mathrm{III}}(x) &= x + \frac{F_1^{(N-2)}(x)}{f_1^{(N-2)}(x)} \\
&= x + \frac{F(x)}{(N-2) f(x)}
\end{aligned}
$$

This derivation, however, is valid only if β^{III} is increasing and from the preceding equation it is clear that a sufficient condition for this is that the ratio F/f is increasing. This condition is the same as requiring that $\ln F$ is a concave function or equivalently that F is *log-concave*.

Proposition 3.2 *Suppose that there are at least three bidders and F is log-concave. Symmetric equilibrium strategies in a third-price auction are given by*

$$\beta^{\mathrm{III}}(x) = x + \frac{F(x)}{(N-2) f(x)} \tag{3.5}$$

An important feature of the equilibrium in a third-price auction is worth noting: the equilibrium bid *exceeds* the value. To better understand this phenomenon, first, notice that for much the same reason as in a second-price auction, it is dominated for a bidder to bid below his value in a third-price auction. Unlike in a second-price auction, however, it is not dominated for a bidder to bid above his value. Fix some equilibrium bidding strategies of the third-price auction, say β, and suppose that all bidders except 1 follow β. Suppose bidder 1 with value x bids an amount $b > x$. If $\beta(Y_2) < x < \beta(Y_1) < b$, this is better than bidding x since it results in a profit, whereas bidding x would not. If, however, $x < \beta(Y_2) < \beta(Y_1) < b$, then bidding b results in a loss. When $b - x \equiv \varepsilon$ is small, the gain in the first case is of order ε^2, whereas the loss in the second case is of order ε^3. Thus, it is optimal to bid higher than one's value in a third-price auction.

Comparing equilibrium bids in first-, second-, and third-price auctions in case of symmetric private values, we have seen that

$$\beta^{\mathrm{I}}(x) < \beta^{\mathrm{II}}(x) = x < \beta^{\mathrm{III}}(x)$$

(assuming, of course, that the distribution of values is log-concave).

3.2.2   Uncertain Number of Bidders

In our analysis so far, each bidder knows his or her own value but is uncertain about the values of others. All other aspects of the situation—the number of bidders, the distribution from which they draw their values—are assumed to be common knowledge. In many auctions—particularly in those of the sealed-bid variety—a bidder may be uncertain about how many other interested bidders there are. In this section we show how the standard model may be amended to include this additional uncertainty.

Let $\mathcal{N} = \{1, 2, \ldots, N\}$ denote the set of *potential* bidders and let $\mathcal{A} \subseteq \mathcal{N}$ be the set of *actual* bidders—that is, those that participate in the auction. All potential bidders draw their values independently from the same distribution F.

Consider an actual bidder $i \in \mathcal{A}$ and let p_n denote the probability that any participating bidder assigns to the event that he is facing n other bidders. Thus, bidder i assigns the probability p_n that the number of actual bidders is $n + 1$. The exact process by which the set of actual bidders is determined from the set of potential bidders is not important. What is important is that the process be symmetric so that every actual bidder holds the *same* beliefs about how many other bidders he faces—the probabilities p_n do not depend on the identity of the bidder nor on his value. It is also important that the set of actual bidders does not depend on the realized values.

As long as bidders hold the same beliefs about the likelihood of meeting different numbers of rivals, the conclusion of Proposition 3.1 obtains in a straightforward manner. Consider a standard auction A and a symmetric and increasing equilibrium β of the auction. Note that since bidders are unsure about how many rivals they face, β does not depend on n. Consider the expected payoff of a bidder with value x who bids $\beta(z)$ instead of the equilibrium bid $\beta(x)$. The probability that he faces n other bidders is p_n. In that case, he wins if $Y_1^{(n)}$, the highest of n values drawn from F, is less than z and the probability of this event is $G^{(n)}(z) = F(z)^n$. The overall probability that he will win when he bids $\beta(z)$ is therefore

$$G(z) = \sum_{n=0}^{N-1} p_n G^{(n)}(z)$$

His expected payoff from bidding $\beta(z)$ when his value is x is then

$$\Pi^A(z, x) = G(z)x - m^A(z)$$

and the remainder of the argument is the same as in Proposition 3.1. Thus, we conclude that the revenue equivalence principle holds even if there is uncertainty about the number of bidders.

Suppose that the object is sold using a second-price auction. Even though the number of rival buyers that a particular bidder faces is uncertain, it is still a dominant strategy for him to bid his value. The expected payment in a second-price auction of an actual bidder with value x is therefore

$$m^{\mathrm{II}}(x) = \sum_{n=0}^{N-1} p_n G^{(n)}(x) E\left[Y_1^{(n)} \mid Y_1^{(n)} < x\right]$$

Now suppose that the object is sold using a first-price auction and that β is a symmetric and increasing equilibrium. The expected payment of an actual bidder with value x is

$$m^{\mathrm{I}}(x) = G(x)\beta(x)$$

where $G(x)$ is as defined earlier. The revenue equivalence principle implies that for all x, $m^{\mathrm{I}}(x) = m^{\mathrm{II}}(x)$, so

$$\begin{aligned}
\beta(x) &= \sum_{n=0}^{N-1} \frac{p_n G^{(n)}(x)}{G(x)} E\left[Y_1^{(n)} \mid Y_1^{(n)} < x\right] \\
&= \sum_{n=0}^{N-1} \frac{p_n G^{(n)}(x)}{G(x)} \beta^{(n)}(x)
\end{aligned}$$

where $\beta^{(n)}$ is the equilibrium bidding strategy in a first-price auction in which there are exactly $n+1$ bidders for sure (see Proposition 2.2 on page 17). Thus, the equilibrium bid for an actual bidder with value x when he is unsure about the number of rivals he faces is a weighted average of the equilibrium bids in auctions when the number of bidders is known to all.

Chapter Notes

The revenue equivalence principle was established by Riley and Samuelson (1981) and Myerson (1981), showing, in effect, that the phenomenon noticed by Vickrey (1961, 1962) was quite general.

For a model of interest group lobbying modeled as an all-pay auction, albeit in a complete information setting, see Baye et al. (1993). Third-price auctions were first analyzed by Kagel and Levin (1993) who pointed out the over-bidding phenomenon . The explicit derivation of equilibrium strategies is due to Wolfstetter (2001).

Auctions with an uncertain number of bidders have been considered by McAfee and McMillan (1987b), Matthews (1987), and Harstad et al. (1990). The first two papers are particularly interested in how risk-averse bidders— considered in the next chapter—are affected by uncertainty regarding the number of competitors they face. Harstad et al. (1990) derive equilibrium bidding strategies in different auctions under number uncertainty when bidders are risk neutral.

4

Qualifications and Extensions

The revenue equivalence principle derived in the previous chapter, Proposition 3.1, is a simple yet powerful result. It constitutes a benchmark of the theory of private value auctions—all other results in the area constitute a departure from the revenue equivalence principle and can be measured against it. Because of its central nature, it is worthwhile to recount the key assumptions underlying the principle:

1. *Independence*—the values of different bidders are independently distributed.

2. *Risk neutrality*—all bidders seek to maximize their expected profits.

3. *No budget constraints*—all bidders have the ability to pay up to their respective values.

4. *Symmetry*—the values of all bidders are distributed according to same distribution function F.

In this chapter we investigate how the revenue equivalence principle is affected when some of these assumptions are relaxed. We first explore the consequences of risk aversion on the part of bidders. We then study the effects of the assumption that bidders have sufficient financial resources to pay any price up to their values. We ask how the revenue equivalence principle holds up in an augmented model in which bidders are subject to budget constraints. Finally, we delve into the important issue of *ex ante* heterogeneity among the bidders. In each case, to isolate the effects of each assumption, we retain the others. For instance, we examine the consequences of risk aversion, retaining the assumptions regarding the independence of values, the lack of budget constraints, and symmetry among the bidders. In the same vein, we examine the consequences of budget constraints in a model with risk-neutral, symmetric bidders with independently distributed values, and we explore the consequences of bidder asymmetries, retaining the independence of the values, and the risk neutrality of the bidders.

An exploration of the consequences of relaxing the first assumption—the independence of the values—is postponed for the moment. It is the focus of Chapter 6, where we consider a more general model that simultaneously relaxes both this assumption and the assumption of private values.

4.1   Risk-Averse Bidders

We now argue that if bidders are risk-averse, but all other assumptions are retained, the revenue equivalence principle no longer holds. In particular, we retain all our other assumptions: independence of values, symmetry among bidders, and the absence of budget constraints.

Risk neutrality implies that the expected payoff of a bidder is additively separable—it is just the difference between his or her expected gain and his expected payment, so the payoff is linear in the payments. This quasi-linearity of a bidder's payoff is crucial in the derivation of the revenue equivalence result and is lost when bidders are not risk neutral.

To examine the consequences of risk aversion, suppose that each bidder has a von-Neumann-Morgenstern utility function $u : \mathbb{R}_+ \to \mathbb{R}$ that satisfies $u(0) = 0$, $u' > 0$ and $u'' < 0$. Each bidder now seeks to maximize his or her expected utility rather than expected profits. The main finding is as follows:

Proposition 4.1 *Suppose that bidders are risk-averse with the same utility function. With symmetric, independent private values, the expected revenue in a first-price auction is greater than that in a second-price auction.*

Proof. First, notice that risk aversion makes no difference in a second-price auction: it is still a dominant strategy for each bidder to bid his or her value. Thus, in a second-price auction, the expected price is the same as it would be if bidders were risk neutral.

Let us now examine a first-price auction. Suppose that when bidders are risk averse and have the utility function u, the equilibrium strategies are given by an increasing and differentiable function $\gamma : [0, \omega] \to \mathbb{R}_+$ satisfying $\gamma(0) = 0$. If all but bidder 1, say, follow this strategy, then bidder 1 will never bid more than $\gamma(\omega)$. Given a value x, each bidder's problem is to choose $z \in [0, \omega]$ and bid an amount $\gamma(z)$ to maximize his or her expected utility—that is,

$$\max_{z} G(z)u(x - \gamma(z)) \tag{4.1}$$

where, as before, $G \equiv F^{N-1}$ is the distribution of the highest of $N - 1$ values. The first-order condition for this problem is

$$g(z) \times u(x - \gamma(z)) - G(z) \times \gamma'(z) \times u'(x - \gamma(z)) = 0.$$

In a symmetric equilibrium, it must be optimal to choose $z = x$. Hence, we get

$$\frac{g(x)u(x - \gamma(x))}{\gamma'(x)} = G(x)u'(x - \gamma(x))$$

which is the same as

$$\gamma'(x) = \frac{u(x - \gamma(x))}{u'(x - \gamma(x))} \times \frac{g(x)}{G(x)} \tag{4.2}$$

With risk neutrality, $u(x) = x$, and (4.2) then yields

$$\beta'(x) = (x - \beta(x)) \times \frac{g(x)}{G(x)} \tag{4.3}$$

where $\beta(\cdot)$ denotes the equilibrium strategy with risk-neutral bidders.

Next notice that if u is strictly concave and $u(0) = 0$, for all $y > 0$, $[u(y)/u'(y)] > y$. Using this fact, from (4.2) we can derive that

$$\gamma'(x) = \frac{u(x - \gamma(x))}{u'(x - \gamma(x))} \times \frac{g(x)}{G(x)} > (x - \gamma(x)) \times \frac{g(x)}{G(x)} \tag{4.4}$$

Now if $\beta(x) > \gamma(x)$, we have $(x - \gamma(x)) \times g(x)/G(x) > (x - \beta(x)) \times g(x)/G(x)$, and because of (4.4) this implies that $\gamma'(x) > \beta'(x)$.

To summarize, if $\beta(\cdot)$ and $\gamma(\cdot)$ are the equilibrium strategies with risk-neutral and risk-averse bidders, respectively,

$$\beta(x) > \gamma(x) \text{ implies that } \beta'(x) < \gamma'(x) \tag{4.5}$$

It is also easy to check that

$$\beta(0) = \gamma(0) = 0 \tag{4.6}$$

(4.5) and (4.6) imply that for all $x > 0$,

$$\gamma(x) > \beta(x)$$

Thus, in a first-price auction, risk aversion causes an increase in equilibrium bids. Since bids have increased, the expected revenue has also increased. Using Proposition 3.1 and the fact that the expected revenue in a second-price auction is unaffected by risk aversion, we deduce that the expected revenue in a first-price auction is higher than that in a second-price auction. ∎

Why does risk aversion lead to higher bids in a first-price auction? Consider a particular bidder, say 1, with value x. Fix the strategies of all other bidders and suppose bidder 1 bids the amount b. Now suppose that this bidder considers decreasing his bid slightly from b to $b - \Delta$. If he wins the auction with this lower bid, this leads to a gain of Δ. A lowering of his bid could, however, cause him to lose the auction. For a risk-averse bidder, the effect of a slightly lower winning bid on his wealth level has a smaller utility consequence than does the possible loss if this lower bid were, in fact, to result in his losing the auction. Compared to a risk-neutral bidder, a risk-averse bidder will thus bid higher. Put another way, by bidding higher, a risk-averse bidder will, as it were, "buy" insurance against the possibility of losing.

Example 4.1 *Constant relative risk aversion (CRRA) utility functions.*

Consider a situation with two bidders who display constant relative risk aversion—their utility functions are of the form $u(z) = z^\alpha$, where α satisfies $0 < \alpha < 1$, so that the coefficient of relative risk aversion, $-zu''(z)/u'(z)$, is $1 - \alpha$. Suppose that both values are drawn from the distribution F. It is convenient to define $F_\alpha \equiv F^{1/\alpha}$ and notice that F_α is also a distribution function with the same support as F. The symmetric equilibrium bidding strategy in a first-price auction is the solution to the differential equation in (4.2). With the specified utility function, (4.2) becomes

$$\gamma'(x)F(x) + \frac{1}{\alpha}\gamma(x)f(x) = \frac{1}{\alpha}xf(x)$$

together with the boundary condition $\gamma(0) = 0$. Using $F(x)^{(1/\alpha)-1}$ as the integrating factor, the solution to this is easily seen to be

$$\gamma(x) = \frac{1}{F_\alpha(x)} \int_0^x y f_\alpha(y)\, dy$$

where $f_\alpha = F_\alpha'$. This, of course, is of the same form as derived in Proposition 2.2 on page 17.

Thus, we conclude that the equilibrium bidding strategy with two bidders with CRRA utility functions $u(z) = z^\alpha$ whose values are drawn from the distribution F is the *same* as the equilibrium bidding strategy with two risk-neutral bidders whose values are drawn from the distribution F_α. Since $F_\alpha \leq F$, the expected revenue in a first-price auction with risk-averse bidders is greater than with risk-neutral bidders. The expected revenue in a second-price auction is, of course, unchanged. ▲

Example 4.2 *Constant absolute risk aversion (CARA) utility functions.*

Consider a situation with bidders who exhibit constant absolute risk aversion—their utility functions are of the form $u(z) = 1 - \exp(-\alpha z)$, where $\alpha > 0$ is the coefficient of absolute risk aversion, $-u''(z)/u'(z)$. Suppose that values are independently distributed according to the function F and let G denote, as usual, the distribution of the highest of $N - 1$ values. First, consider a second-price auction. Consider a bidder with value x who bids z and wins the auction. In a second-price auction, such a bidder faces some uncertainty about the price he or she will pay since that is determined by the second-highest bid. Suppose that the other bidders are following their equilibrium (and weakly dominant) strategy of bidding their values so that the second-highest bid is Y_1. Let $\rho(x, z)$ be the *risk premium* associated with the "price gamble"—it is the certain amount the bidder would forgo in order to remove the associated uncertainty. Formally,

$$u(x - \rho(x, z)) = E[u(x - Y_1) \mid Y_1 < z] \tag{4.7}$$

and CARA implies that we can write $\rho(z) \equiv \rho(x, z)$ since the risk premium depends only on the gamble being faced—which is entirely determined by z—and not on the "wealth level" x. It is optimal for bidder 1 to bid his or her true value and thus

$$x \in \arg\max_z G(z)E[u(x - Y_1) \mid Y_1 < z]$$

Using (4.7) this can be rewritten as

$$x \in \arg\max_z G(z)u(x - \rho(z))$$

But this is the same as bidder 1's maximization problem in a *first*-price auction if all other bidders follow the bidding strategy $\gamma = \rho$ (see (4.1)). This implies that for CARA bidders, the equilibrium bidding strategy in a first-price auction is to bid the risk premium associated with "price gamble" in a second-price auction. Finally, since

$$G(x)u(x - \gamma(x)) = G(x)E[u(x - Y_1) \mid Y_1 < x]$$

the equilibrium expected utility of a CARA bidder in a first-price auction is the same as his expected utility in a second-price auction. ▲

A key feature of the standard auction model with risk-neutral bidders is that the payoff functions are separable in money. In particular, they are *quasi-linear*—linear in the payments that bidders make—and bidders maximize their expected profits, which are just

Expected Value − Expected Payment

This separation between the expected value and the expected payment is crucial for revenue equivalence principle. Specifically, in the proof of Proposition 3.1 on page 30, this separation leads to equation (3.1) and hence to the conclusion that the expected payments are the same in any standard auction. Risk-averse bidders, on the other hand, maximize

$$\text{Expected Utility of (Value } - \text{ Payment)}$$

and since utility is nonlinear—it is concave—the maximand is no longer linear in the payments that bidders make. The fact that bidders' objective functions are no longer linear in their payments is the reason for the failure of the revenue equivalence principle.

4.2 Budget Constraints

Until now we have implicitly assumed that bidders face no cash or credit constraints—that is, bidders are able to pay the seller up to amounts equal to their values. In many situations, however, bidders may face financial constraints of one sort or another. In this section we ask how the presence of financial constraints affects equilibrium behavior in first- and second-price auctions and what effect they have on the revenue from these auctions.

We continue with the basic symmetric independent private value setting introduced in the previous chapter. There is a single object for sale and N potential buyers are bidding for the object. As before, bidder i assigns a value of X_i to the object. But now, in addition, each bidder is subject to an absolute *budget* of W_i. In no circumstances can a bidder with value-budget pair (x_i, w_i) pay more than w_i. We also suppose that if bidder i were to bid more than w_i and *default*, then a (small) penalty would be imposed.

Each bidder's value-budget pair (X_i, W_i) is independently and identically distributed on $[0, 1] \times [0, 1]$ according to the density function f.[1] Bidder i knows the realized value-budget pair (x_i, w_i) and only that other bidders' budget-value pairs are independently distributed according to f. As before, bidders are assumed to be risk neutral and again we compare first- and second-price auctions. In a substantive departure from the models studied so far, the private information of the bidders is two-dimensional. We will refer to the pair (x_i, w_i) as the *type* of bidder i.

In any auction A (say, a first- or second-price auction), a bidder's strategy is a function of the form $B^A : [0, 1] \times [0, 1] \to \mathbb{R}$ that determines the amount bid depending on both his value and his budget.

---

[1] The independence holds only across bidders. The possibility that for each bidder the values and budgets are correlated is admitted.

4.2.1   Second-Price Auctions

We begin our analysis by considering second-price auctions. In this case, bidders' equilibrium strategies are straightforward.

Proposition 4.2 *In a second-price auction, it is a dominant strategy to bid according to* $B^{\mathrm{II}}(x, w) = \min\{x, w\}$.

Proof. First, notice that it is dominated to bid above one's budget. Suppose bidder i wins by bidding above his budget. If the second highest bid is below his budget, then he would have also won by bidding w_i. If the second highest bid is above his budget, he has to renege, does not get the object, and pays the fine, resulting in a negative surplus.

Second, if $x_i \le w_i$, then the budget constraint does not bind and the same argument as in the unconstrained situation implies that it is a weakly dominant strategy to bid x_i. If $x_i > w_i$, then the same argument shows that bidding w_i dominates bidding less. ∎

For every type (x, w), define $x'' = \min\{x, w\}$ and consider the type $(x'', 1)$. Notice that since values never exceed 1, a bidder of type $(x'', 1)$ effectively never faces a financial constraint. But since $\min\{x'', 1\} = x'' = \min\{x, w\}$, we have that $B^{\mathrm{II}}(x, w) = B^{\mathrm{II}}(x'', 1)$. Thus, in a second-price auction the type $(x'', 1)$ would submit a bid identical to that submitted by type (x, w). The type $(x'', 1)$ is, as it were, the richest member of the family with types (x, w) such that $\min\{x, w\} = x''$. Figure 4.1 depicts the set of types who bid the same in a second-price auction as does type (x, w). This consists of all types on the thin-lined right angle "Leontief iso-bid" curve whose corner lies on the diagonal.

As before, let $m^{\mathrm{II}}(x, w)$ denote the expected payment of a bidder of type (x, w) in a second-price auction. Since $B^{\mathrm{II}}(x, w) = B^{\mathrm{II}}(x'', 1)$, we have that

$$m^{\mathrm{II}}(x, w) = m^{\mathrm{II}}(x'', 1) \tag{4.8}$$

Now define

$$\mathcal{L}^{\mathrm{II}}(x'') = \{(X, W) : B^{\mathrm{II}}(X, W) < B^{\mathrm{II}}(x'', 1)\} \tag{4.9}$$

to be the set of types who bid less than type $(x'', 1)$ in a second-price auction.

Define

$$F^{\mathrm{II}}(x'') = \int_{\mathcal{L}^{\mathrm{II}}(x'')} f(X, W)\, dX dW \tag{4.10}$$

to be the probability that a type $(x'', 1)$ will out-bid *one* other bidder. Notice that this is indeed the distribution function of the random variable $X'' = \min\{X, W\}$. The probability that a type $(x'', 1)$ will actually win the auction is just $(F^{\mathrm{II}}(x''))^{N-1} \equiv G^{\mathrm{II}}(x'')$. In Figure 4.1, $F^{\mathrm{II}}(x'')$ is the

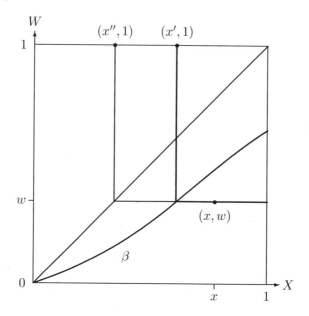

FIGURE 4.1. First- and Second-Price Auctions with Budget Constraints

probability mass attached to the set of types lying below the lighter of the two right angles.

Now notice that we can write the expected utility of a type $(x'', 1)$ when bidding $B^{II}(z, 1)$ as

$$G^{II}(z)x'' - m^{II}(z, 1)$$

In equilibrium, it is optimal to bid $B^{II}(x'', 1)$ when the true type is $(x'', 1)$, so in a manner completely analogous to the arguments in Chapter 2 (specifically, Proposition 3.1), we have that

$$m^{II}(x'', 1) = \int_0^{x''} y g^{II}(y) \, dy \qquad (4.11)$$

where g^{II} is the density function associated with G^{II}. The *ex ante* expected payment of a bidder in a second-price auction with financial constraints can then be written, in manner completely analogous to (2.7), as

$$
\begin{aligned}
R^{II} &= \int_0^1 m^{II}(x'', 1) f^{II}(x'') \, dx'' \\
&= E\left[Y_2^{II(N)}\right] \qquad (4.12)
\end{aligned}
$$

where $Y_2^{II(N)}$ is the second-highest of N draws from the distribution F^{II}.

4.2.2   First-Price Auctions

First, suppose that in a first-price auction, the equilibrium strategy is of the form

$$B^{\mathrm{I}}(x,w) = \min\{\beta(x), w\} \qquad (4.13)$$

for some increasing function $\beta(x)$. In this case, it must be that $\beta(x) < x$, otherwise a bidder of type $x < w$ would deviate by bidding slightly less. Although sufficient conditions in terms of the primitives of the model that guarantee the existence of such an equilibrium can be provided, here we content ourselves with directly assuming that such an equilibrium exists.

As in the case of a second-price auction, for every type (x, w) define x' to be a value such that $\beta(x') = \min\{\beta(x), w\}$ and consider the type $(x', 1)$. As before, a bidder of type $(x', 1)$ effectively never faces a financial constraint. But since $\min\{\beta(x'), 1\} = \beta(x') = \min\{\beta(x), w\}$, we have that $B^{\mathrm{I}}(x, w) = B^{\mathrm{I}}(x', 1)$. Thus, in a first-price auction the type $(x', 1)$ would submit a bid identical to that submitted by type (x, w). Figure 4.1 also depicts the set of types who bid the same in a first-price auction as does type (x, w). This consists of all types on the thick line right-angle "Leontief iso-bid" curve whose corner lies on the curve β.

Now define

$$\mathcal{L}^{\mathrm{I}}(x') = \{(X, W) : B^{\mathrm{I}}(X, W) < B^{\mathrm{I}}(x', 1)\} \qquad (4.14)$$

and define m^{I}, F^{I}, and G^{I} in a fashion completely analogous to the corresponding objects for a second-price auction. Exactly the same reasoning shows that

$$E\left[R^{\mathrm{I}}\right] = E\left[Y_2^{\mathrm{I}(N)}\right] \qquad (4.15)$$

where $Y_2^{\mathrm{I}(N)}$ is the second-highest of N draws from the distribution F^{I}.

4.2.3   Revenue Comparison

To compare the expected payments in the two auctions, notice that since for all x, $\beta(x) < x$, the definitions of $\mathcal{L}^{\mathrm{II}}(x)$ and $\mathcal{L}^{\mathrm{I}}(x)$ in (4.9) and (4.14), respectively, imply that $\mathcal{L}^{\mathrm{I}}(x) \subset \mathcal{L}^{\mathrm{II}}(x)$. See Figure 4.1. Now (4.10) implies that for all x, $F^{\mathrm{I}}(x) \le F^{\mathrm{II}}(x)$ and a strict inequality holds for all $x \in (0, 1)$. We have thus argued that F^{I} stochastically dominates F^{II}. This implies that

$$E\left[Y_2^{\mathrm{I}(N)}\right] > E\left[Y_2^{\mathrm{II}(N)}\right]$$

Thus, we have shown the following:

Proposition 4.3 *Suppose that bidders are subject to financial constraints. If the first-price auction has a symmetric equilibrium of the form $B^{\mathrm{I}}(x, w) =$*

$\min \{\beta(x), w\}$, *then the expected revenue in a first-price auction is greater than the expected revenue in a second-price auction.*

At an intuitive level, Proposition 4.3 results from the fact that budget constraints are "softer" in first-price auctions than in second-price auctions. Given a situation with budget constraints, consider a hypothetical situation in which each bidder's value is $Z_i = \min \{X_i, W_i\}$ and there are no budget constraints. Since value-budget pairs are independently and identically distributed across bidders, the revenue equivalence principle applies to the hypothetical situation, so the second-price and first-price auctions yield the same expected revenue, say R. Now returning to the original situation with budget constraints, Proposition 4.2 implies that the revenue from the second-price auction in the original situation is also R—bids in the two are identical for every realization. The revenue in a first-price auction is greater than R because the comparison is between a situation in which bidders have values $X_i \geq Z_i$ and budgets $W_i \geq Z_i$ and a hypothetical situation in which they have values Z_i but no budget constraints.

4.3   Asymmetries among Bidders

In this section, we consider situations in which bidders are *ex ante* asymmetric: different bidders' values are drawn from different distributions. Asymmetries among bidders do not affect bidding behavior in second-price auctions—it is still a weakly dominant strategy for each bidder to bid his or her value. In a first-price auction, however, asymmetries lead to numerous complications. First, although an equilibrium exists (see Appendix G), unlike in the case of symmetric bidders, a closed form expression for the bidding strategies is not available, making a comparison with the second-price auction rather difficult. Second, the allocations under the two auctions are quite different—the second-price auction is efficient whereas the first-price auction is not—and as a result, the two are no longer revenue equivalent. Indeed, as we will see, no general ranking of the revenues can be obtained.

We begin by exploring the nature of equilibrium bidding behavior in first-price auctions. To keep the analysis at a relatively simple level, we concentrate on the case of two bidders.

4.3.1   Asymmetric First-Price Auctions with Two Bidders

Suppose there are two bidders with values X_1 and X_2, which are independently distributed according to the functions F_1 on $[0, \omega_1]$ and F_2 on $[0, \omega_2]$, respectively. Suppose for the moment that there is an equilibrium of the first-price auction in which the two bidders follow the strategies β_1 and β_2, respectively. Further suppose that these are increasing and differentiable and have inverses $\phi_1 \equiv \beta_1^{-1}$ and $\phi_2 \equiv \beta_2^{-1}$, respectively.

It is clear that $\beta_1(0) = 0 = \beta_2(0)$, since it would be dominated for a bidder to bid more than the value. Moreover, $\beta_1(\omega_1) = \beta_2(\omega_2)$ since otherwise, if say, $\beta_1(\omega_1) > \beta_2(\omega_2)$, then bidder 1 would win with probability 1 when his value is ω_1 and would pay more than he needs to—he could increase his payoff by bidding slightly less than $\beta_1(\omega_1)$. Let

$$\bar{b} \equiv \beta_1(\omega_1) = \beta_2(\omega_2) \tag{4.16}$$

be the common highest bid submitted by either bidder.

Given that bidder $j = 1,2$ is following the strategy β_j, the expected payoff of bidder $i \neq j$ when his value is x_i and he bids an amount $b < \bar{b}$ is

$$\begin{aligned} \Pi_i(b, x_i) &= F_j\big(\phi_j(b)\big)(x_i - b) \\ &= H_j(b)(x_i - b) \end{aligned}$$

where $H_j(\cdot) \equiv F_j\big(\phi_j(\cdot)\big)$ denotes the distribution of bidder j's bids.

The first-order condition for bidder i requires that for all $b < \bar{b}$,

$$h_j(b)(\phi_i(b) - b) = H_j(b) \tag{4.17}$$

where $j \neq i$ and, as usual, $h_j(b) \equiv H_j'(b) = f_j\big(\phi_j(b)\big)\phi_j'(b)$ is the density of j's bids. This can be rearranged so that

$$\phi_j'(b) = \frac{F_j\big(\phi_j(b)\big)}{f_j\big(\phi_j(b)\big)} \frac{1}{(\phi_i(b) - b)} \tag{4.18}$$

A solution to the system of differential equations in (4.18)—one for each bidder—together with the relevant boundary conditions constitutes an equilibrium of the first-price auction. Unfortunately, an explicit solution can be obtained only in some special cases—an example is given later—and so instead, we deduce some properties of the equilibrium strategies indirectly. To do this, we make some assumptions regarding the specific nature of the asymmetries.

Weakness Leads to Aggression

Suppose that bidder 1's values are "stochastically higher" than those of bidder 2. In particular, we will make the stronger assumption that the distribution F_1 *dominates* F_2 *in terms of the reverse hazard rate*—that is, $\omega_1 \geq \omega_2$ and for all $x \in (0, \omega_2)$,

$$\frac{f_1(x)}{F_1(x)} > \frac{f_2(x)}{F_2(x)} \tag{4.19}$$

Reverse hazard rate dominance is further discussed in Appendix B where it is also shown that it implies that F_1 stochastically dominates F_2—that is, $F_1(x) \leq F_2(x)$. If (4.19) holds, we will call bidder 1 the "strong" bidder and bidder 2 the "weak" bidder.

(A simple class of examples in which the two distributions can be ordered according to the reverse hazard rate consists of distributions satisfying $F_1(x) = (F_2(x))^\theta$ for some $\theta > 1$.)

We now show that the weak bidder will bid more aggressively than the strong bidder in the sense that for any fixed value, the bid of the weak bidder will be higher than the bid of the strong bidder.

Proposition 4.4 *Suppose that the value distribution of bidder 1 dominates that of bidder 2 in terms of the reverse hazard rate. Then in a first-price auction, the "weak" bidder 2 bids more aggressively than the "strong" bidder 1—that is, for any $x \in (0, \omega_2)$,*

$$\beta_1(x) < \beta_2(x)$$

Proof. First, notice that if there exists a c such that $0 < c < \bar{b}$ and $\phi_1(c) = \phi_2(c) \equiv z$, then (4.18) and (4.19) imply that

$$\phi_2'(c) = \frac{F_2(z)}{f_2(z)} \frac{1}{(z-c)} > \frac{F_1(z)}{f_1(z)} \frac{1}{(z-c)} = \phi_1'(c)$$

Since $\phi_i'(c) = 1/\beta_i'(z)$, this is equivalent to saying that if there exists a z such that $\beta_1(z) = \beta_2(z)$, then $\beta_1'(z) > \beta_2'(z)$. In other words, if the curves β_1 and β_2 ever intersect, the former is steeper than the latter and this implies that they intersect at most once.

We will argue by contradiction. So suppose that there exists an $x \in (0, \omega_2)$ such that $\beta_1(x) \geq \beta_2(x)$. Then either β_1 and β_2 do not intersect at all so that $\beta_1 > \beta_2$ everywhere; or they intersect only once at some value $z \in (0, \omega_2)$ and for all x such that $z < x < \omega_2$, $\beta_1(x) > \beta_2(x)$. In either case, for all x close to ω_2, $\beta_1(x) > \beta_2(x)$.

Now notice that if $\omega_1 > \omega_2$, then from (4.16) $\beta_1(\omega_1) = \beta_2(\omega_2)$, so $\beta_1(\omega_2) < \beta_2(\omega_2)$. This contradicts the fact that for all x close to ω_2, $\beta_1(x) > \beta_2(x)$.

Next suppose $\omega_1 = \omega_2 \equiv \omega$. If we write $\beta_1(\omega) = \beta_2(\omega) = \bar{b}$, then in terms of the inverse bidding strategies we have that for all b close to $\bar{b}$, $\phi_1(b) < \phi_2(b)$. This implies that for all b close to $\bar{b}$,

$$H_1(b) = F_1(\phi_1(b)) \leq F_2(\phi_2(b)) = H_2(b)$$

and since $H_1(\bar{b}) = 1 = H_2(\bar{b})$, it must be that $h_1(b) > h_2(b)$. Now using (4.17) we obtain that for all b close enough to $\bar{b}$,

$$\phi_1(b) = \frac{H_2(b)}{h_2(b)} + b > \frac{H_1(b)}{h_1(b)} + b = \phi_2(b)$$

which is a contradiction. ■

We know that F_1 stochastically dominates F_2 so that bidder 1's values are stochastically higher. At the same time, Proposition 4.4 shows that for any given value, bidder 2 bids higher than does bidder 1. What can be said about the distributions of bids, H_1 and H_2? Notice that since for all $b \in (0, \bar{b})$, $\phi_1(b) > \phi_2(b)$ it now follows from (4.17) and (4.18) that

$$\frac{H_2(b)}{h_2(b)} = \phi_1(b) - b > \phi_2(b) - b = \frac{H_1(b)}{h_1(b)}$$

so that the distribution of bids of the strong bidder H_1 dominates the distribution of bids of the weak bidder H_2 in terms of the reverse hazard rate. Thus, under the hypotheses of Proposition 4.4, H_1 also stochastically dominates H_2.

Why is it that the weak bidder bids more aggressively than does the strong bidder? To gain some intuition, it is useful to see why the opposite is impossible—that is, it cannot be that the strong bidder bids more aggressively than does the weak bidder. If for all x, $\beta_1(x) > \beta_2(x)$, then certainly the distribution H_1 of competing bids facing the weak bidder is stochastically higher than the distribution H_2 of competing bids facing the strong bidder. It is easy to see that all else being equal, a bidder who faces a stochastically higher distribution of bids—in the sense of reverse hazard rate dominance—will bid higher. It is also true that for a particular bidder, all else being equal, a higher realized value will lead to a higher bid. Now consider a particular bid b and suppose that $\beta_1(x_1) = \beta_2(x_2) = b$. Since by assumption, the strong bidder bids more aggressively, it must be that the value at which the strong bidder bids b is lower than the value at which the weak bidder bids b—that is, $x_1 < x_2$. This means that, relative to the strong bidder, the weak bidder faces *both* a stochastically higher distribution of competing bids—H_1 versus H_2—and has a higher value—x_2 versus x_1. Since both forces cause bids to be higher, if it were optimal for the strong bidder to bid b when his value is x_1, it cannot be optimal for the weak bidder to bid b when his value is x_2. Thus, we have a contradiction.

Put another way, in equilibrium the two forces must balance each other. The weak bidder faces a stochastically higher distribution of competing bids than does the strong bidder, but the value at which any particular bid b is optimal for the weak bidder is lower than it is for the strong bidder.

Asymmetric Uniform Distributions

Equilibrium bidding strategies in asymmetric first-price auctions can be explicitly derived if the two value distributions are uniform but with differing supports. Specifically, suppose bidder 1's value X_1 is uniformly distributed on $[0, \omega_1]$ and bidder 2's value X_2 is uniformly distributed on $[0, \omega_2]$ and that $\omega_1 \geq \omega_2$. Then $F_i(x) = x/\omega_i$ and $f_i(x) = 1/\omega_i$ so that the first-order condition (4.17) can be simplified as follows: for $i = 1, 2$ and $j \neq i$, for all $b \in (0, \bar{b})$,

$$\phi_i'(b) = \frac{\phi_i(b)}{\phi_j(b) - b} \tag{4.20}$$

which is equivalent to

$$\left(\phi_i'(b) - 1\right)\left(\phi_j(b) - b\right) = \phi_i(b) - \phi_j(b) + b$$

Adding the two equations for $i = 1, 2$ results in

$$\frac{d}{db}\left((\phi_1(b) - b)(\phi_2(b) - b)\right) = 2b$$

and integrating this, we obtain

$$(\phi_1(b) - b)(\phi_2(b) - b) = b^2 \tag{4.21}$$

(The constant of integration is zero since $\phi_i(0) = 0$.) Since $\phi_i(\bar{b}) = \omega_i$,

$$\left(\omega_1 - \bar{b}\right)\left(\omega_2 - \bar{b}\right) = \bar{b}^2$$

so that

$$\bar{b} = \frac{\omega_1 \omega_2}{\omega_1 + \omega_2} \tag{4.22}$$

Now using (4.21), the equations in (4.20) can be rewritten as follows: for $i = 1, 2$,

$$\phi_i'(b) = \frac{\phi_i(b)(\phi_i(b) - b)}{b^2} \tag{4.23}$$

with the advantage that in this form they are separable in the variables.

We now undertake a change of variables by defining $\xi_i(b)$ implicitly by

$$\phi_i(b) - b = \xi_i(b)b \tag{4.24}$$

so that

$$\phi_i'(b) - 1 = \xi_i'(b)b + \xi_i(b)$$

With this substitution, the differential equation (4.23) becomes

$$\xi_i'(b)b + \xi_i(b) + 1 = \xi_i(b)(\xi_i(b) + 1)$$

or

$$\frac{\xi_i'(b)}{\xi_i(b)^2 - 1} = \frac{1}{b}$$

the solution to which is easily verified to be

$$\xi_i(b) = \frac{1 - k_i b^2}{1 + k_i b^2}$$

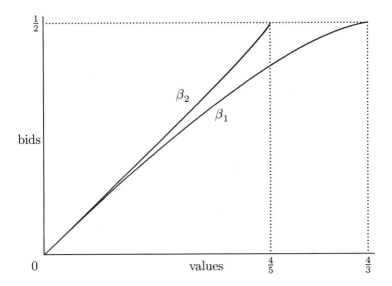

FIGURE 4.2. Equilibrium of an Asymmetric First-Price Auction

where k_i is a constant of integration. Using (4.24) this becomes

$$\phi_i(b) = \frac{2b}{1 + k_i b^2} \qquad (4.25)$$

and since $\phi_i(\bar{b}) = \omega_i$, where $\bar{b}$ is defined in (4.22), we obtain that the constant of integration

$$k_i = \frac{1}{\omega_i^2} - \frac{1}{\omega_j^2} \qquad (4.26)$$

The bidding strategies, obtained by inverting (4.25), are

$$\beta_i(x) = \frac{1}{k_i x}\left(1 - \sqrt{1 - k_i x^2}\right) \qquad (4.27)$$

It is routine to verify that these form an equilibrium.[2]

Figure 4.2 depicts the equilibrium bidding strategies when $\omega_1 = \frac{4}{3}$ and $\omega_2 = \frac{4}{5}$.

4.3.2 Revenue Comparison

We first use the equilibrium strategies derived above to show that for some distributions, the revenue from a first-price auction may exceed that from a second-price auction.

---

[2] Although we do not verify this here, it can be shown that this is the only equilibrium.

Example 4.3 *With asymmetric bidders, the expected revenue in a first-price auction may exceed that in a second-price auction.*

As a special case of the example with values drawn from different uniform distributions, let $\alpha \in [0, 1)$ and suppose that bidder 1's value X_1 is uniformly distributed on the interval $[0, 1/(1 - \alpha)]$ whereas bidder 2's value X_2 is uniformly distributed on the interval $[0, 1/(1 + \alpha)]$. (In the example depicted in Figure 4.2, $\alpha = 1/4$.)

We will compare the expected revenues accruing from a second-price auction to those from a first-price auction when $\alpha > 0$. Notice that when $\alpha = 0$, the situation is symmetric and the two auctions yield the same expected revenue.

Revenue in the Second-Price Auction

It is a dominant strategy to bid one's value in a second-price auction and hence the distribution of the selling price in a second-price auction is

$$L_\alpha^{II}(p) = \text{Prob}\left[\min\{X_1, X_2\} \le p\right]$$

where $p \in \left[0, \frac{1}{1+\alpha}\right]$. We have

$$
\begin{aligned}
L_\alpha^{II}(p) &= F_1(p) + F_2(p) - F_1(p) F_2(p) \\
&= (1 - \alpha)p + (1 + \alpha)p - (1 - \alpha)(1 + \alpha)p^2 \\
&= 2p - (1 - \alpha^2)p^2
\end{aligned}
$$

which is *increasing* in α. Thus, in a second-price auction the expected selling price when $\alpha > 0$ is *lower* than the expected selling price when $\alpha = 0$.

Revenue in the First-Price Auction

Since $\omega_1 = 1/(1 - \alpha)$ and $\omega_2 = 1/(1 + \alpha)$, from (4.22) it follows that the highest amount that either bidders bids is $\bar{b} = \frac{1}{2}$. Moreover, the constants of integration in (4.26) are $k_1 = -4\alpha$ and $k_2 = 4\alpha$. Using (4.25) the inverse bidding strategies in equilibrium are: for all $b \in \left[0, \frac{1}{2}\right]$,

$$
\begin{aligned}
\phi_1(b) &= \frac{2b}{1 - 4\alpha b^2} \\
\phi_2(b) &= \frac{2b}{1 + 4\alpha b^2}
\end{aligned}
$$

The distribution of the equilibrium prices in a first-price auction is thus

$$L_\alpha^{I}(p) = \text{Prob}\left[\max\{\beta_1(X_1), \beta_2(X_2)\} \le p\right]$$

where $p \in \left[0, \frac{1}{2}\right]$. We have

$$
\begin{aligned}
L_\alpha^{\mathrm{I}}(p) &= F_1(\phi_1(p)) \times F_2(\phi_2(p)) \\
&= (1-\alpha)\frac{2p}{1-4\alpha p^2} \times (1+\alpha)\frac{2p}{1+4\alpha p^2} \\
&= \frac{\left(1-\alpha^2\right)(2p)^2}{1-\alpha^2(2p)^4}
\end{aligned}
$$

which is *decreasing* in α. Thus, in a first-price auction the expected selling price when $\alpha > 0$ is *higher* than the expected selling price when $\alpha = 0$.

For $\alpha = 0$, the expected selling price in the two auctions is the same. An increase in α leads to a decrease in the expected price in the second-price auction and an increase in the expected price in a first-price auction.

We have thus shown that in this example, for all $\alpha > 0$, the expected selling price in a first-price auction is *greater* than that in a second-price auction. (More generally, it can be shown that with asymmetric uniformly distributed values, the first-price auction is revenue superior for all ω_1 and ω_2.) ▲

A second example shows that the opposite ranking is also possible.

Example 4.4 *With asymmetric bidders, the expected revenue in a second-price auction may exceed that in a first-price auction.*

This example is of a different nature from the preceding one. It involves a situation in which the distribution of values is not continuous; in other words, the values are chosen from a finite set. We saw in the previous example that the derivation of equilibrium strategies in asymmetric first-price auctions is somewhat involved. The discreteness of the values makes it easier to find an equilibrium.

Suppose that there is no uncertainty about bidder 1's value: $X_1 = 2$ always. Bidder 2's value, X_2, is equally likely to be 0 or 2.

In a second-price auction, the expected revenue is $2 \times \mathrm{Prob}\,[X_2 = 2] = 1$.

In a first-price auction, bidder 1 can guarantee a payoff of 1 by bidding just above 0 since by doing this he is sure to win with probability no less than $\frac{1}{2}$. By bidding more than 1 his payoff is less than 1. Thus, bidder 1 will never bid more than 1. This implies that if bidder 2 were to bid $1 + \varepsilon$ when her value is 2, her *ex ante* expected payoff would be at least $\frac{1}{2}(2-(1+\varepsilon)) = \frac{1}{2} - \varepsilon$. Since ε is arbitrary her *ex ante* expected payoff is at least $\frac{1}{2}$. Thus, the sum of the expected payoffs of the two bidders in a first-price auction is at least $1\frac{1}{2}$ and consequently, the seller's expected revenue is no greater than $\frac{1}{2}$.

Thus, in this example, the expected selling price in a first-price auction is *less* than that in a second-price auction. ▲

4.3.3 Efficiency Comparison

As noted earlier, it is a weakly dominant strategy for a bidder to bid his or her value in a second-price auction—recall that this is true even when bidders are asymmetric—so the winning bidder is also the one with the highest value. Thus, the second-price auction is always *ex post* efficient under the assumption of private values.

In contrast, asymmetries inevitably lead to inefficient allocations in a first-price auction. Suppose that there are two bidders and (β_1, β_2) is an equilibrium of the first-price auction such that both strategies are continuous and increasing. Because the bidders are asymmetric—their values are drawn from different distributions—it will be the case that $\beta_1 \neq \beta_2$. Without loss of generality, suppose that $\beta_1(x) < \beta_2(x)$ and since both the strategies are continuous, for small enough $\varepsilon > 0$, it is also the case that $\beta_1(x + \varepsilon) < \beta_2(x - \varepsilon)$. This, of course, means that with positive probability the allocation is inefficient since bidder 2 would win the auction even though he has a lower value than does bidder 1.

For future reference we record these observations as follows:

Proposition 4.5 *With asymmetrically distributed private values, a second-price auction always allocates the object efficiently, whereas with positive probability, a first-price auction does not.*

4.4 Resale and Efficiency

In the previous section we saw that asymmetries among bidders lead to inefficient allocations in first-price auctions—with positive probability the winner of the auction is not the person who values the object the most. Achieving an efficient allocation may well be an important, or even primary, policy goal of the seller, especially if the seller is a government undertaking the privatization of some public asset. This seems to imply that such a seller should use an efficient auction—with private values, say a second-price auction—even if, as we have seen, it may bring lower revenues than an inefficient one, say a first-price auction. An argument against this point of view, in the Chicago school vein, is that even if the outcome of the auction is inefficient, post-auction transactions among buyers—resale—will result in an efficient final allocation. Absent any transaction costs, the asset will be transferred into the hands of the person who values it the most. The conclusion is that the choice of the auction form is irrelevant to the efficiency question and one may as well select the auction format on other grounds, say revenue. In this section we ask whether this is indeed the case. Does resale automatically lead to efficiency?

To examine the resale question in the simplest possible setting, consider the basic setup of the previous section. There are two bidders with values

X_1 and X_2, which are independently distributed according to the functions F_1 and F_2, respectively, and for notational ease suppose that these have a common support $[0, \omega]$. The bidders are asymmetric, so $F_1 \neq F_2$. Suppose in addition that $E[X_1] \neq E[X_2]$, a condition that will hold generically.

In this context, let us first put forward the argument that a first-price auction followed by resale will lead to efficiency. Suppose β_1 and β_2 are equilibrium bidding strategies in the first-price auction and we know that these are increasing. Further, suppose that at the conclusion of the auction, both the bids—winning and losing—are publicly announced. This means that if the bids were b_1 and b_2, then at the conclusion of the auction, it would be commonly known that the buyers have values $x_1 = \beta_1^{-1}(b_1)$ and $x_2 = \beta_2^{-1}(b_2)$, respectively. If $b_1 > b_2$ but $x_1 < x_2$, the outcome of the auction would be inefficient but since the values would be commonly known, so would the fact that there are some unrealized gains from trade. In particular, knowing that $x_1 < x_2$, bidder 1 could offer to resell the object to bidder 2 at some price between the two values. This would mean that ultimately the object ends up in the right hands.

This line of reasoning seems so simple as to be beyond question. It fails, however, to take into account that rational buyers will behave differently during the auction once they correctly foresee future resale possibilities. Let us see why.

To model the situation outlined above carefully, we need to be more specific about how resale actually takes place—that is, how the buyer and the seller settle on a price. Suppose that after learning what the losing bid was, the winner of the auction—and the new owner of the object—may, if he so wishes, resell the object to the other bidder by making a one-time take-it-or-leave-it offer. Notice that all bargaining power in this transaction resides with the (new) seller—that is, the winner of the auction. In particular, if bidder 1 wins the auction and subsequently learns that $x_1 < x_2$, then he can offer to sell the object to bidder 2 at a price $p = x_2$ (or just below) and this offer will be accepted. Bidder 1 will then make a profit of $x_2 - b_1$, whereas bidder 2's profit will be 0 (or just above). Of course, this is one of many possible ways in which the price may be determined. It is particularly simple and has the virtue that it ensures efficiency if the values are commonly known, so in some sense, it makes the best case for resale since there are no underlying transaction costs or delays. As an alternative, one could consider a situation in which the buyer makes a take-it-or-leave-it offer to the seller without affecting any of what follows.

Our main finding is that there cannot be an equilibrium of a first-price auction with resale in which the outcome of the auction completely reveals the values. Thus, the prospects of post-auction resale make an efficient allocation impossible.

Suppose to the contrary that the first-price auction with resale has an efficient equilibrium. The equilibrium must specify both how bidders bid in the auction and what they do in the post-auction resale stage. Let β_1 and β_2 denote the bidding strategies in the first-price auction, and suppose that these are *increasing* with inverses $\phi_1 \equiv \beta_1^{-1}$ and $\phi_2 \equiv \beta_2^{-1}$. In the resale stage, if the announced bids b_1 and b_2 are such that $b_i > b_j$ but $x_i < \phi_j(b_j)$, then i makes a take-or-leave-it offer to sell the object to j at a price of $\phi_j(b_j)$. This is accepted if and only if $x_j \geq \phi_j(b_j)$. Otherwise, no offer is made.

The assumption that β_1 and β_2 are invertible means that after the winning and losing bids are announced, the values will become commonly known. Thus, if there are any unrealized gains from trade, resale will take place and the object will be allocated efficiently.

As a first step, notice that, as in the previous section, the bidding strategies must agree both at the lower and the upper end of the support of values—that is, $\beta_1(0) = 0 = \beta_2(0)$ and for some $\bar{b}$,

$$\beta_1(\omega) = \bar{b} = \beta_2(\omega) \tag{4.28}$$

Now suppose bidder 2 behaves according to the prescribed equilibrium strategy. Suppose bidder 1 has value x_1 but behaves as if his value were z_1—that is, he bids an amount $\beta_1(z_1)$ in equilibrium and in the resale stage also follows the given equilibrium strategy as if his value were z_1. Bidder 1's overall expected payment in equilibrium when he behaves as if his value is z_1 is[3]

$$
\begin{aligned}
m_1(z_1) \;=\; & F_2\left(\phi_2\beta_1(z_1)\right)\beta_1(z_1) \\
& - \int_{z_1}^{\phi_2\beta_1(z_1)} \max\{z_1, x_2\}\, f_2(x_2)\, dx_2
\end{aligned} \tag{4.29}
$$

The first term is bidder 1's expected payment to the seller. The second term is the result of monetary transfers between the bidders in the event that resale takes place. If $z_1 < X_2 < \phi_2\beta_1(z_1)$, then bidder 1 wins the auction and resells the object to bidder 2 at a price of $X_2 = \max\{z_1, X_2\}$. On the other hand, if $\phi_2\beta_1(z_1) < X_2 < z_1$, then bidder 1 loses the auction but purchases the object from bidder 2 at a price of $z_1 = \max\{z_1, X_2\}$.

The final allocation is efficient, so if bidder 1 behaves as if his value is z_1, the probability that he will get the object is just $F_2(z_1)$. Following the reasoning in the proof of the revenue equivalence principle (Proposition 3.1 on page 30), the expected payoff to bidder 1 from behaving as if his value is z_1 when it is actually x_1 is

$$F_2(z_1)x_1 - m_1(z_1)$$

---

[3] We write $\phi_2\beta_1(z_1)$ to denote $\phi_2(\beta_1(z_1))$.

In equilibrium, it is not optimal for bidder 1 to deviate, so we must have

$$F_2(x_1) x_1 - m_1(x_1) \geq F_2(z_1) x_1 - m_1(z_1)$$

The first-order condition for this optimization results in the differential equation

$$m_1'(x_1) = x_1 f_2(x_1)$$

and since $m_1(0) = 0$, it follows that

$$m_1(x_1) = \int_0^{x_1} x_2 f_2(x_2)\, dx_2 \qquad (4.30)$$

Setting $z_1 = x_1$ in (4.29) and equating this with (4.30), we obtain that a necessary condition for a first-price auction followed by resale to be efficient is that for all x_1,

$$F_2(\phi_2\beta_1(x_1))\beta_1(x_1) - \int_{x_1}^{\phi_2\beta_1(x_1)} \max\{x_1, x_2\} f_2(x_2)\, dx_2$$
$$= \int_0^{x_1} x_2 f_2(x_2)\, dx_2 \qquad (4.31)$$

Equation (4.31) says that the expected payment of bidder 1 in an equilibrium of the first-price auction with resale that is efficient—the expression on the left-hand side—is the same as that in an efficient *second*-price auction—the expression on the right-hand side. Indeed, it is just a version of the revenue equivalence principle extended to the asymmetric case: since the equilibrium outcomes of a first-price auction with resale are the same as those of a second-price auction, the expected payments in the two must be the same.[4]

Now $\beta_1(\omega) = \bar{b}$, so $\phi_2\beta_1(\omega) = \omega$. Setting $x_1 = \omega$ in (4.31), we obtain

$$\bar{b} = E[X_2]$$

But interchanging the roles of bidder 1 and 2, we similarly obtain that

$$\bar{b} = E[X_1]$$

and since $E[X_1] \neq E[X_2]$, this is a contradiction. We have thus argued that in an asymmetric first-price auction followed by resale, the bidding strategies β_1 and β_2 *cannot* be increasing everywhere. Bidders' equilibrium behavior in the auction cannot reveal their values completely, so resale transactions must take place under incomplete information.

---

[4] A general revenue equivalence principle for asymmetric situations is derived in Chapter 5 and can also be used to deduce equation (4.31).

From here it is a short step to see that because of this incomplete information, reaching an efficient allocation in all circumstances is impossible. In the interests of space, we only sketch the argument. Suppose the equilibrium strategies β_1 and β_2 are continuous but only nondecreasing—we have already ruled out the possibility that they are increasing. In other words, the strategies involve some "pooling"—that is, for at least one of the bidders, say bidder 2, there is an interval of values $[x_2', x_2'']$ such that for all $x_2 \in [x_2', x_2'']$, the equilibrium bid $\beta_2(x_2)$ is the same, say b_2. We will now argue that pooling is also incompatible with efficient resale.

We first claim that there exists an $x_1 \in (x_2', x_2'')$ such that $\beta_1(x_1) \geq b_2$. Otherwise, for all x_1 such that $\beta_1(x_1) \geq b_2$, $x_1 \geq x_2''$. Let x_1'' be the smallest value for bidder 1 such that $\beta_1(x_1) = b_2$, and we know that $x_1'' \geq x_2''$. Now we must have $b_2 < x_1''$ since otherwise bidder 2 with value x_2'' would never bid b_2—the most that she can gain from winning the auction is $\max\{x_2'', x_2''\} = x_1''$, so she would never bid more than this amount. Since $b_2 < x_1''$, for ε small enough, $b_2 < x_1'' - \varepsilon$. But now notice that by bidding $b_2 + \varepsilon$ instead of below b_2, bidder 1 with value $X_1 = x_1'' - \varepsilon$ would gain a discrete amount—winning against all values X_2 in $[x_2', x_2'']$ to which he was losing previously—at an infinitesimal cost. This is a profitable deviation, so we have reached a contradiction.

Thus, there exists an $x_1 \in (x_2', x_2'')$ such that $\beta_1(x_1) \geq b_2$. If the realized values are x_1 and some $x_2 \in (x_1, x_2'']$, then bidder 1 wins the auction but $x_1 < x_2$. The announcement of b_2 reveals to bidder 1 only that $X_2 \in [x_2', x_2'']$. He would then make a take-it-or-leave-it offer p that maximizes his expected profit. But such an offer would of necessity satisfy $p > x_1$ and so would be rejected with positive probability even though efficiency dictates that the object be transferred from bidder 1 to bidder 2. Thus, any equilibrium with pooling is inefficient.

If the resale price is determined instead by the buyer making a take-it-or-leave-it offer, the argument is virtually the same as that above, except that the resale price is $\min\{X_1, X_2\}$ instead of $\max\{X_1, X_2\}$. All the other steps are identical.

We have thus argued the following:

Proposition 4.6 *With asymmetric bidders, a first-price auction followed by resale (at a take-it-or-leave-it price offered by one of the parties) does not result in efficiency.*

Proposition 4.6 casts doubt on the argument that resale will inevitably lead to efficiency. A seller whose goal is to ensure that the object ends up in the hands of the person who values it the most cannot rely on the "market" to do the job. The appropriate choice of an auction format remains very relevant—in order to assure efficiency, it is best to use an efficient auction.

Chapter Notes

The result that with symmetric risk-averse bidders the revenue from the first-price auction is greater than that in a second-price auction is due to Holt (1980), who studied the analogous problem in the context of bidding for procurement contracts. The key to Proposition 4.1, of course, is the fact that in a first-price auction, risk aversion causes bidders to increase their bids. A simple generalization of this is available: In a first-price auction, bidders with utility functions $\varphi \circ u$ will bid higher than bidders with the utility function u, where φ is a concave transformation such that $\varphi(0) = 0$. Thus, an *increase* in risk aversion will cause bidders in a first-price auction to bid higher. The result that CARA bidders are indifferent between the first- and second-price auctions is due to Matthews (1987).

The material on auctions with budget constraints is based on Che and Gale (1998). This paper provides a sufficient condition on the primitives that guarantees that the first-price auction has an equilibrium of the sort hypothesized in Proposition 4.3. It also considers situations where the financial constraints need not be in the form of an absolute budget but may be somewhat more flexible. For instance, it may be that bidders face borrowing constraints so that they can borrow larger amounts only at higher marginal costs.

Vickrey (1961) himself pointed out that asymmetries among bidders may lead to inefficient allocations in a first-price auction. He studied a two-bidder asymmetric example in which bidder 1's value, a, was commonly known and bidder 2's value was uniformly distributed on $[0, 1]$. In this case, an equilibrium of the first-price auction involves randomization on the part of bidder 1, and Vickrey (1961) showed that depending on the value of a, the revenue from a first-price auction could be better or worse than that from a second-price auction. The derivation of equilibrium bidding strategies in first-price auctions with asymmetric uniformly distributed values is due to Griesmer *et al.* (1967). Plum (1992) has extended this to the more general class of asymmetric "power" distributions. It can be shown that an equilibrium exists in general under weak conditions on the distributions of values. Appendix G outlines some results in this direction. With a view to applications, Marshall *et al.* (1994) have developed numerical techniques to compute bidding strategies in asymmetric auctions.

Maskin and Riley (2000a) have studied the equilibrium properties of asymmetric first-price auctions in more detail and have derived some sufficient conditions for one or the other auction to be revenue superior. Examples 4.3 and 4.4, which together demonstrate that no general revenue ranking is possible, are taken from their paper.

Gupta and Lebrun (1999) have also studied a model of a first-price auction with resale but reach very different conclusions from those reached here. In particular, they do not find that resale will lead to inefficiency.

This discrepancy is easily accounted for. Gupta and Lebrun (1999) assume that regardless of the outcome, at the conclusion of the auction the *values* of the bidders are publicly announced. Since after the auction is over, bidders are completely informed of each other's values, resale is inevitably efficient. The auctioneer, however, has no direct knowledge of bidders' values, so it is not clear how this is to be implemented. In contrast, in our model, we assumed that only that the *bids* were announced and showed that if bidders take this into account, the bids would not reveal the values completely. Haile (2000) studies a model of resale in which, at the time of bidding, buyers have only partial information regarding the true value. After the auction is over they receive a further signal that determines their actual values. The discrepancy between the estimated values at the time of the auction and the true values realized after the auction creates a motive for resale.

5

Mechanism Design

An auction is one of many ways that a seller can use to sell an object to potential buyers with unknown values. In an auction, the object is sold at a price determined by competition among the buyers according to rules set out by the seller—the auction format—but the seller could use other methods. The seller could post a fixed price and sell the object to the first arrival. Or the seller could negotiate with one of the buyers, say one chosen at random. The seller could also hold an auction and then negotiate with the winner. The range of options is virtually unlimited. This chapter considers the underlying allocation problem by abstracting away from the details of any particular selling format and asking the question: What is the best way to allocate an object?

As before, a seller has one indivisible object to sell and there are N risk-neutral potential buyers (or bidders) from the set $\mathcal{N} = \{1, 2, \ldots, N\}$. Again, buyers have private values and these are independently distributed. Buyer i's value X_i is distributed over the interval $\mathcal{X}_i = [0, \omega_i]$ according to the distribution function F_i with associated density function f_i. Notice that, as in Section 4.3, we allow for asymmetries among the buyers: the distributions of values need not be the same for all buyers.

For the sake of simplicity, we suppose that the value of the object to the seller is 0.

Let $\mathcal{X} = \times_{j=1}^{N} \mathcal{X}_j$ denote the product of the sets of buyers' values, and for all i, let $\mathcal{X}_{-i} = \times_{j \neq i} \mathcal{X}_j$. Define $f(\mathbf{x})$ to be the joint density of $\mathbf{x} = (x_1, x_2, \ldots, x_N)$. Since the values are independently distributed, $f(\mathbf{x}) =$

$f_1(x_1) \times f_2(x_2) \times \ldots \times f_N(x_N)$. Similarly, define $f_{-i}(\mathbf{x}_{-i})$ to be the joint density of $\mathbf{x}_{-i} = (x_1, \ldots, x_{i-1}, x_{i+1}, \ldots, x_N)$.

5.1   Mechanisms

A selling *mechanism* $(\mathcal{B}, \boldsymbol{\pi}, \boldsymbol{\mu})$ has the following components: a set of possible *messages* (or "bids") $\mathcal{B}_i$ for each buyer; an *allocation rule* $\boldsymbol{\pi} : \mathcal{B} \to \Delta$, where Δ is the set of probability distributions over the set of buyers $\mathcal{N}$; and a *payment rule* $\boldsymbol{\mu} : \mathcal{B} \to \mathbb{R}^N$. An allocation rule determines, as a function of all N messages, the probability $\pi_i(\mathbf{b})$ that i will get the object. A payment rule determines, again as a function of all N messages, for each buyer i, the expected payment $\mu_i(\mathbf{b})$ that i must make.

Notice that both first- and second-price auctions are mechanisms. The set of possible bids $\mathcal{B}_i$ in both can be safely assumed to be $\mathcal{X}_i$. Assuming that there is no reservation price, the allocation rule for both is $\pi_i(\mathbf{b}) = 1$ if $b_i > \max_{j \neq i} b_j$ and $\pi_j(\mathbf{b}) = 0$ for $j \neq i$. They differ only in the associated payment rules. For a first-price auction, $\mu_i^{\mathrm{I}}(\mathbf{b}) = b_i$ if $b_i > \max_{j \neq i} b_j$ and $\mu_j^{\mathrm{I}}(\mathbf{b}) = 0$ for $j \neq i$. For a second-price auction, $\mu_i^{\mathrm{II}}(\mathbf{b}) = \max_{j \neq i} b_j$ if $b_i > \max_{j \neq i} b_j$ and $\mu_j^{\mathrm{II}}(\mathbf{b}) = 0$ for $j \neq i$. If there are ties, each winning bidder has an equal likelihood of being awarded the object, so the π_j have to take account of this.

Every mechanism defines a game of incomplete information among the buyers. An N-tuple of strategies $\beta_i : [0, \omega_i] \to \mathcal{B}_i$ is an *equilibrium* of a mechanism if for all i and for all x_i, given the strategies $\boldsymbol{\beta}_{-i}$ of other buyers, $\beta_i(x_i)$ maximizes i's expected payoff.

5.1.1   The Revelation Principle

A mechanism could, in principle, be quite complicated since we have made no assumptions on the sets $\mathcal{B}_i$ of "bids" or "messages." A smaller and simpler class consists of those mechanisms for which the set of messages is the same as the set of values—that is, for all i, $\mathcal{B}_i = \mathcal{X}_i$. Such mechanisms are called *direct* since, in effect, every buyer is asked to directly report a value. Formally, a *direct mechanism* $(\mathbf{Q}, \mathbf{M})$ consists of a pair of functions $\mathbf{Q} : \mathcal{X} \to \Delta$ and $\mathbf{M} : \mathcal{X} \to \mathbb{R}^N$ where $Q_i(\mathbf{x})$ is the probability that i will get the object and $M_i(\mathbf{x})$ is the expected payment by i. If it is an equilibrium for each buyer to reveal his or her true value, then the direct mechanism is said to have a truthful equilibrium. We will refer to the pair $(\mathbf{Q}(\mathbf{x}), \mathbf{M}(\mathbf{x}))$ as the *outcome* of the mechanism at $\mathbf{x}$.

The following result, referred to as the *revelation principle*, shows that the outcomes resulting from any equilibrium of any mechanism can be replicated by a truthful equilibrium of some direct mechanism. In this sense, there is no loss of generality in restricting attention to direct mechanisms.

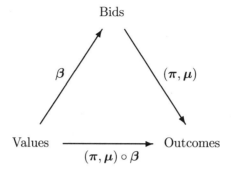

FIGURE 5.1. The Revelation Principle

Proposition 5.1 (Revelation Principle) *Given a mechanism and an equilibrium for that mechanism, there exists a direct mechanism in which (i) it is an equilibrium for each buyer to report his or her value truthfully and (ii) the outcomes are the same as in the given equilibrium of the original mechanism.*

Proof. Let $\mathbf{Q} : \mathcal{X} \rightarrow \mathbf{\Delta}$ and $\mathbf{M} : \mathcal{X} \rightarrow \mathbb{R}^N$ be defined as follows: $\mathbf{Q}(\mathbf{x}) = \boldsymbol{\pi}(\boldsymbol{\beta}(\mathbf{x}))$ and $\mathbf{M}(\mathbf{x}) = \boldsymbol{\mu}(\boldsymbol{\beta}(\mathbf{x}))$. In other words, as depicted in Figure 5.1, the direct mechanism $(\mathbf{Q}, \mathbf{M})$ is a composition of $(\boldsymbol{\pi}, \boldsymbol{\mu})$ and $\boldsymbol{\beta}$. Conclusions (i) and (ii) can now be verified routinely. ∎

The idea underlying the revelation principle is very simple. Fix a mechanism and an equilibrium $\boldsymbol{\beta}$ of the mechanism. Now instead of having the buyers submit messages $b_i = \beta_i(x_i)$ and then applying the rules of the mechanism in order to determine the outcome—who gets the object and who pays what—we could directly ask the buyers to "report" their values x_i and then make sure that the outcome is the same as if they had submitted bids $\beta_i(x_i)$. Put another way, a direct mechanism does the "equilibrium calculations" for the buyers automatically. Now suppose that some buyer finds it profitable to be untruthful and report a value of z_i when his true value is x_i. Then in the original mechanism the same buyer would have found it profitable to submit a bid of $\beta_i(z_i)$ instead of $\beta_i(x_i)$. But since the β_i constitute an equilibrium, this is impossible.

5.1.2 Incentive Compatibility

Given a direct mechanism $(\mathbf{Q}, \mathbf{M})$, define

$$q_i(z_i) = \int_{\mathcal{X}_{-i}} Q_i(z_i, \mathbf{x}_{-i}) f_{-i}(\mathbf{x}_{-i}) \, d\mathbf{x}_{-i} \tag{5.1}$$

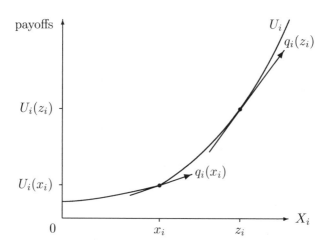

FIGURE 5.2. Implications of Incentive Compatibility

to be the probability that i will get the object when he reports his value to be z_i and all other buyers report their values truthfully. Similarly, define

$$m_i(z_i) = \int_{\mathcal{X}_{-i}} M_i(z_i, \mathbf{x}_{-i}) f_{-i}(\mathbf{x}_{-i}) \, \mathbf{dx}_{-i} \tag{5.2}$$

to be the expected payment of i when his report is z_i and all other buyers tell the truth. It is important to note that because the values are independently distributed, both the probability of getting the object and the expected payment depend only on the *reported* value z_i and not on the *true* value, say x_i. The expected payoff of buyer i when his true value is x_i and he reports z_i, again assuming that all other buyers tell the truth, can then be written as

$$q_i(z_i) x_i - m_i(z_i) \tag{5.3}$$

The direct revelation mechanism $(\mathbf{Q}, \mathbf{M})$ is said to be *incentive compatible* (IC) if for all i, for all x_i and for all z_i,

$$U_i(x_i) \equiv q_i(x_i) x_i - m_i(x_i) \geq q_i(z_i) x_i - m_i(z_i) \tag{5.4}$$

We will refer to U_i as the *equilibrium payoff function*.

Incentive compatibility has some simple but powerful implications. First, for each reported value z_i, the expected payoff $q_i(z_i) x_i - m_i(z_i)$ is an affine function of the true value x_i. Incentive compatibility implies that

$$U_i(x_i) = \max_{z_i \in \mathcal{X}_i} \{q_i(z_i) x_i - m_i(z_i)\}$$

that is, U_i is a maximum of a family of affine functions, therefore U_i *is a convex function.*

Second, we can write for all x_i and z_i,

$$
\begin{aligned}
q_i(x_i)z_i - m_i(x_i) &= q_i(x_i)x_i - m_i(x_i) + q_i(x_i)(z_i - x_i) \\
&= U_i(x_i) + q_i(x_i)(z_i - x_i)
\end{aligned}
$$

so incentive compatibility is equivalent to the requirement that for all x_i and z_i,

$$U_i(z_i) \geq U_i(x_i) + q_i(x_i)(z_i - x_i) \tag{5.5}$$

This implies that for all x_i, $q_i(x_i)$ is the slope of a line that supports the function U_i at the point x_i. (See Figure 5.2.) A convex function is absolutely continuous[1] and thus it is differentiable almost everywhere in the interior of its domain (in Figure 5.2, U_i is not differentiable at x_i). Thus, at every point that U_i is differentiable,

$$U_i'(x_i) = q_i(x_i) \tag{5.6}$$

Since U_i is convex, this implies that q_i *is a nondecreasing function.*

Third, every absolutely continuous function is the definite integral of its derivative, so we have

$$U_i(x_i) = U_i(0) + \int_0^{x_i} q_i(t_i)\, dt_i \tag{5.7}$$

which implies that up to an additive constant, the expected payoff to a buyer in an incentive compatible direct mechanism $(\mathbf{Q}, \mathbf{M})$ depends *only* on the allocation rule $\mathbf{Q}$. If $(\mathbf{Q}, \mathbf{M})$ and $(\mathbf{Q}, \overline{\mathbf{M}})$ are two incentive compatible mechanisms with the same allocation rule $\mathbf{Q}$ but different payment rules, then the expected payoff functions associated with the two mechanisms, U_i and $\overline{U}_i$, respectively, differ by at most a constant—the two mechanisms are *payoff equivalent.* Put another way, the "shape" of the expected payoff function is completely determined by the allocation rule $\mathbf{Q}$ alone. The payment rule $\mathbf{M}$ only serves to determine the constants $U_i(0)$. See Figure 5.3 where, despite appearances to the contrary, $\overline{U}_i - U_i$ is a constant.

Finally, note that a mechanism is incentive compatible if and only if the associated q_i is nondecreasing. We have already argued that incentive compatibility implies that q_i is nondecreasing. To see the converse, note that (5.5) can be rewritten as

$$\int_{x_i}^{z_i} q_i(t_i)\, dt_i \geq q_i(x_i)(z_i - x_i)$$

by using (5.7) and this certainly holds if q_i is nondecreasing.

---

[1] For a definition of an absolutely continuous function, see the notes at the end of this chapter (page 82).

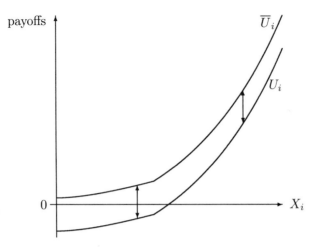

FIGURE 5.3. Payoff Equivalence

Revenue Equivalence (Redux)

The payoff equivalence derived here immediately implies a general form of the revenue equivalence principle.

Proposition 5.2 (Revenue Equivalence) *If the direct mechanism* $(\mathbf{Q}, \mathbf{M})$ *is incentive compatible, then for all* i *and* x_i *the expected payment is*

$$m_i(x_i) = m_i(0) + q_i(x_i)\,x_i - \int_0^{x_i} q_i(t_i)\ dt_i \qquad (5.8)$$

Thus, the expected payments in any two incentive compatible mechanisms with the same allocation rule are equivalent up to a constant.

Proof. Since $U_i(x_i) = q_i(x_i)\,x_i - m_i(x_i)$ and $U_i(0) = -m_i(0)$, the equality in (5.7) can be rewritten as (5.8). ∎

Proposition 5.2 generalizes the revenue equivalence principle from Chapter 3, Proposition 3.1, to situations where buyers may be asymmetric. To see this, note that if buyers are symmetric and there is an increasing symmetric equilibrium, then the object is allocated to the buyer with the highest value; thus, for all such auctions, the allocation rule is the same. The remaining hypothesis in Proposition 3.1 pins down the expected payments completely by supposing that $m_i(0) = 0$.

At first glance, Proposition 5.2 seems to contradict the finding in the previous chapter that with asymmetric buyers, revenue equivalence between the first- and second-price auctions did not hold. Notice, however, that Proposition 5.2 implies only that, given the possible asymmetries, if there are two auctions with the *same* allocation rule, then they are revenue equivalent. When buyers are asymmetric, the first- and second-price auctions allocate differently—a second-price auction allocates efficiently, whereas a first-price auction typically does not. This accounts for differences in the resulting payments and revenues in the two auctions when buyers are not symmetric.

The general revenue equivalence principle can be usefully restated as follows: In any incentive compatible mechanism the expected payment of a buyer depends, up to an additive constant, on the allocation rule alone.

5.1.3 Individual Rationality

A mechanism in which the payments are so high that a buyer is better off by not participating will not attract this potential buyer. Specifically, we will say that a direct mechanism $(\mathbf{Q}, \mathbf{M})$ is *individually rational* if for all i and x_i, the equilibrium expected payoff $U_i(x_i) \geq 0$. We are implicitly assuming here that by not participating, a buyer can guarantee himself or herself a payoff of zero.

If the mechanism is incentive compatible, then from (5.7) individual rationality is equivalent to the requirement that $U_i(0) \geq 0$, and since $U_i(0) = -m_i(0)$, this is equivalent to the requirement that $m_i(0) \leq 0$.

5.2 Optimal Mechanisms

In this section we view the seller as the designer of the mechanism and examine mechanisms that maximize the expected revenue—the sum of the expected payments of the buyers—among all mechanisms that are incentive compatible and individually rational. We reiterate that when carrying out this exercise, the revelation principle guarantees that there is no loss of generality in restricting attention to direct mechanisms.

We will refer to a mechanism that maximizes expected revenue, subject to the incentive compatibility and individual rationality constraints, as an *optimal mechanism*.

5.2.1 Setup

Suppose that the seller uses the direct mechanism $(\mathbf{Q}, \mathbf{M})$. The expected revenue of the seller is

$$E[R] = \sum_{i \in \mathcal{N}} E[m_i(X_i)]$$

where the *ex ante* expected payment of buyer i is

$$
E\left[m_i\left(X_i\right)\right] = \int_0^{\omega_i} m_i\left(x_i\right) f_i\left(x_i\right) \, dx_i
$$

$$
= m_i\left(0\right) + \int_0^{\omega_i} q_i\left(x_i\right) x_i f_i\left(x_i\right) \, dx_i
$$

$$
- \int_0^{\omega_i} \int_0^{x_i} q_i\left(t_i\right) f_i\left(x_i\right) \, dt_i dx_i
$$

by substituting from (5.8). Interchanging the order of integration in the last term results in

$$
\int_0^{\omega_i} \int_0^{x_i} q_i\left(t_i\right) f_i\left(x_i\right) \, dt_i dx_i = \int_0^{\omega_i} \int_{t_i}^{\omega_i} q_i\left(t_i\right) f_i\left(x_i\right) \, dx_i dt_i
$$

$$
= \int_0^{\omega_i} \left(1 - F_i\left(t_i\right)\right) q_i\left(t_i\right) \, dt_i
$$

Thus, we can write

$$
E\left[m_i\left(X_i\right)\right] = m_i\left(0\right) + \int_0^{\omega_i} \left(x_i - \frac{1 - F_i\left(x_i\right)}{f_i\left(x_i\right)}\right) q_i\left(x_i\right) f_i\left(x_i\right) \, dx_i
$$

$$
= m_i\left(0\right) + \int_{\mathcal{X}} \left(x_i - \frac{1 - F_i\left(x_i\right)}{f_i\left(x_i\right)}\right) Q_i\left(\mathbf{x}\right) f\left(\mathbf{x}\right) \, d\mathbf{x}
$$

using the definition of $q_i\left(x_i\right)$ from (5.1).

The seller's objective therefore is to find a mechanism that maximizes

$$
\sum_{i \in \mathcal{N}} m_i\left(0\right) + \sum_{i \in \mathcal{N}} \int_{\mathcal{X}} \left(x_i - \frac{1 - F_i\left(x_i\right)}{f_i\left(x_i\right)}\right) Q_i\left(\mathbf{x}\right) f\left(\mathbf{x}\right) \, d\mathbf{x} \qquad (5.9)
$$

subject to the constraint that the mechanism is

IC. incentive compatible, which is equivalent to the requirement that q_i be nondecreasing; and

IR. individually rational, which is equivalent to the requirement that $m_i\left(0\right) \le 0$.

5.2.2 Solution

We now make a simplification that allows an explicit derivation of the optimal selling mechanism. Define

$$
\psi_i\left(x_i\right) \equiv x_i - \frac{1 - F_i\left(x_i\right)}{f_i\left(x_i\right)} \qquad (5.10)
$$

to be the *virtual valuation* of a buyer with value x_i. It is routine to verify that for all i,

$$E\left[\psi_i(X_i)\right] = 0 \tag{5.11}$$

The design problem is said to be *regular* if for all i, the virtual valuation $\psi_i(\cdot)$ is an increasing function of the true value x_i. Since

$$\psi_i(x_i) = x_i - \frac{1}{\lambda_i(x_i)}$$

where $\lambda_i \equiv f_i/(1 - F_i)$ is the hazard rate function associated with F_i, a sufficient condition for regularity is that for all i, $\lambda_i(\cdot)$ is increasing. In what follows, we will assume that the design problem is regular.

Thus, the seller should choose $(\mathbf{Q}, \mathbf{M})$ to maximize

$$\sum_{i \in \mathcal{N}} m_i(0) + \int_{\mathcal{X}} \left(\sum_{i \in \mathcal{N}} \psi_i(x_i) Q_i(\mathbf{x})\right) f(\mathbf{x}) \, d\mathbf{x} \tag{5.12}$$

Temporarily neglect the IC and IR constraints, and consider the expression

$$\sum_{i \in \mathcal{N}} \psi_i(x_i) Q_i(\mathbf{x}) \tag{5.13}$$

from the second term in (5.12). The function $\mathbf{Q}$ is then like a weighting function, and clearly it is best to give weight only to those $\psi_i(x_i)$ that are maximal, provided they are positive. This would maximize the function in (5.13) at *every* point $\mathbf{x}$ and so also maximize its integral.

With this in mind, consider a mechanism $(\mathbf{Q}, \mathbf{M})$ where

- the allocation rule $\mathbf{Q}$ is that the object goes to buyer i with positive probability if and only if $\psi_i(x_i) = \max_{j \in \mathcal{N}} \psi_j(x_j)$; thus,

$$Q_i(\mathbf{x}) > 0 \iff \psi_i(x_i) = \max_{j \in \mathcal{N}} \psi_j(x_j) \geq 0 \tag{5.14}$$

- the payment rule $\mathbf{M}$ is

$$M_i(\mathbf{x}) = Q_i(\mathbf{x}) x_i - \int_0^{x_i} Q_i(z_i, \mathbf{x}_{-i}) \, dz_i \tag{5.15}$$

We claim that (5.14) and (5.15) define an optimal mechanism.

First, notice that the resulting q_i is a nondecreasing function. Suppose $z_i < x_i$. Then by the regularity condition, $\psi_i(z_i) < \psi_i(x_i)$ and thus for all $\mathbf{x}_{-i}$, it is also the case that $Q_i(z_i, \mathbf{x}_{-i}) \leq Q_i(x_i, \mathbf{x}_{-i})$. Thus, q_i is a nondecreasing function.

Second, from (5.15), it is clear that $M_i(0, \mathbf{x}_{-i}) = 0$, for all $\mathbf{x}_{-i}$, and hence $m_i(0) = 0$.

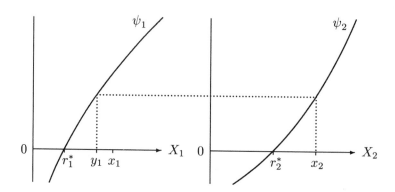

FIGURE 5.4. An Optimal Mechanism

Thus, the proposed mechanism is *both* incentive compatible and individually rational. It is optimal since it separately maximizes the two terms in (5.12) over all $\mathbf{Q}(\mathbf{x}) \in \mathbf{\Delta}$. In particular, it gives positive weight only to nonnegative and maximal terms in (5.13). This implies that the maximized value of the expected revenue (5.12) is

$$E\left[\max\left\{\psi_1\left(X_1\right), \psi_2\left(X_2\right), \ldots, \psi_N\left(X_N\right), 0\right\}\right] \tag{5.16}$$

In other words, it is the expectation of the highest virtual valuation, provided it is nonnegative.

A more intuitive formula may be obtained by writing

$$y_i\left(\mathbf{x}_{-i}\right) = \inf\left\{z_i : \psi_i\left(z_i\right) \geq 0 \text{ and } \forall j \neq i, \psi_i\left(z_i\right) \geq \psi_j\left(x_j\right)\right\}$$

as the smallest value for i that "wins" against $\mathbf{x}_{-i}$. Thus, we can rewrite (5.14) as

$$Q_i\left(z_i, \mathbf{x}_{-i}\right) = \begin{cases} 1 & \text{if } z_i > y_i\left(\mathbf{x}_{-i}\right) \\ 0 & \text{if } z_i < y_i\left(\mathbf{x}_{-i}\right) \end{cases}$$

which results in

$$\int_0^{x_i} Q_i\left(z_i, \mathbf{x}_{-i}\right) dz_i = \begin{cases} x_i - y_i\left(\mathbf{x}_{-i}\right) & \text{if } x_i > y_i\left(\mathbf{x}_{-i}\right) \\ 0 & \text{if } x_i < y_i\left(\mathbf{x}_{-i}\right) \end{cases}$$

and so (5.15) becomes

$$M_i\left(\mathbf{x}\right) = \begin{cases} y_i\left(\mathbf{x}_{-i}\right) & \text{if } Q_i\left(\mathbf{x}\right) = 1 \\ 0 & \text{if } Q_i\left(\mathbf{x}\right) = 0 \end{cases}$$

Thus, only the "winning" buyer pays anything; he pays the smallest value that would result in his winning.

Figure 5.4 illustrates the workings of mechanism when there are two buyers. The virtual valuation curves, ψ_1 and ψ_2, are depicted, and since these are different the two buyers are subject to different reserve prices of $r_1^* = \psi_1^{-1}(0)$ and $r_2^* = \psi_2^{-1}(0)$, respectively. With the given values x_1 and x_2, it is the case that $\psi_1(x_1) > \psi_2(x_2) > 0$ so that the reserve prices do not come into play. The object goes to buyer 1 who is asked to pay an amount y_1.

Thus, we obtain the main result:

Proposition 5.3 *Suppose the design problem is regular. Then the following is an optimal mechanism:*

$$Q_i(\mathbf{x}) = \begin{cases} 1 & \text{if } \psi_i(x_i) > \max_{j \neq i} \psi_j(x_j) \text{ and } \psi_i(x_i) \geq 0 \\ 0 & \text{if } \psi_i(x_i) < \max_{j \neq i} \psi_j(x_j) \end{cases}$$

and

$$M_i(\mathbf{x}) = \begin{cases} y_i(\mathbf{x}_{-i}) & \text{if } Q_i(\mathbf{x}) = 1 \\ 0 & \text{if } Q_i(\mathbf{x}) = 0 \end{cases}$$

The Symmetric Case

Suppose that we have a symmetric problem so that the distributions of values are identical across buyers. In other words, for all i, $f_i = f$, and hence for all i, $\psi_i = \psi$. Now we have that,

$$y_i(\mathbf{x}_{-i}) = \max\left\{\psi^{-1}(0), \max_{j \neq i} x_j\right\}$$

Thus, the optimal mechanism is a second-price auction with a reserve price $r^* = \psi^{-1}(0)$.

Proposition 5.4 *Suppose the design problem is regular and symmetric. Then a second-price auction with a reserve price $r^* = \psi^{-1}(0)$ is an optimal mechanism.*

Note that $\psi^{-1}(0)$ is the same as the optimal reserve price derived in Chapter 2 (see (2.12) on page 26).

5.2.3 Discussion and Interpretation

The optimal mechanism derived in Proposition 5.3 is typically inefficient, and there are two separate sources of inefficiency. First, the optimal mechanism calls on the seller to retain the object if the highest virtual valuation is negative. Since buyers' values are always nonnegative and the value to the seller is 0, this means that with positive probability the object is not allocated to one of the buyers even though there would be social gains from doing so. Second, even when the object is allocated, it is allocated to the

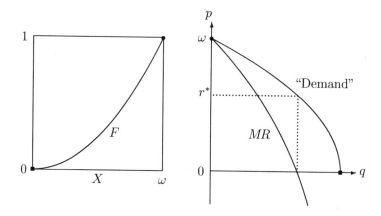

FIGURE 5.5. Virtual Valuations as Marginal Revenues

buyer with the highest *virtual* valuation and, in the asymmetric case, this need not be the buyer with the highest value.

Why is it optimal to allocate the object on the basis of virtual valuations and, more to the point, what are virtual valuations? Consider a particular buyer in isolation whose values are distributed according to the function F, say. Suppose the seller makes a take-it-or-leave-it offer to this buyer at a price of p. The probability that the buyer will accept the offer is just $1 - F(p)$, the probability that his or her value exceeds p. We can think of the probability of purchase as the "quantity" demanded by i and thus write the buyer's implied "demand curve" as $q(p) \equiv 1 - F(p)$. The inverse demand curve is then $p(q) \equiv F^{-1}(1 - q)$, where q is the "quantity" purchased (or equivalently, the probability of purchase). The resulting "revenue function" facing the seller is

$$p(q) \times q = qF^{-1}(1 - q)$$

and differentiating the revenue with respect to q

$$\frac{d}{dq}\left(p(q) \times q\right) = F^{-1}(1 - q) - \frac{q}{F'(F^{-1}(1 - q))}$$

Since $F^{-1}(1 - q) = p$ we have that

$$
\begin{aligned}
MR(p) &\equiv p - \frac{1 - F(p)}{f(p)} \\
&= \psi(p)
\end{aligned}
$$

the virtual valuation of i at $p(q) = p$. Thus, the virtual valuation of a buyer $\psi(p)$ can be interpreted as a *marginal revenue*, and recall that we have assumed that ψ is strictly increasing. Facing this buyer in isolation, the seller would set a "monopoly price" of r^* by setting $MR(p) = MC$, the marginal cost. Since the latter is assumed to be zero, $MR(r^*) = \psi(r^*) = 0$, or $r^* = \psi^{-1}(0)$.

Figure 5.5 depicts how the distribution function of a particular buyer can be rotated to obtain his or her "demand curve" by identifying corresponding points on the two curves. The associated "marginal revenue" curve and the "monopoly price," r^*, are also shown.

When facing many buyers, the optimal mechanism calls for the seller to set *discriminatory reserve prices* of $r_i^* = \psi_i^{-1}(0)$ for the buyers. If no buyer's value x_i exceeds his reserve price r_i^*, the seller keeps the object. Otherwise, it is allocated to the buyer with the *highest marginal revenue* and this "winning" buyer is asked to pay $p_i = y_i(\mathbf{x}_{-i})$, the smallest value such that he or she would still win.

In general, the optimal mechanism discriminates in favor of "disadvantaged" buyers in the following sense. Suppose that there are two buyers whose values are drawn from F_1 and F_2, respectively, with the same support $[0, \omega]$. Suppose further that for all x, the associated hazard rates satisfy $\lambda_1(x) \le \lambda_2(x)$. Then buyer 2 is relatively disadvantaged since his values are likely to be lower; in particular, F_1 stochastically dominates F_2. But given that both have the same realized value x, the virtual valuation of buyer 2 will be higher because

$$\psi_1(x) = x - \frac{1}{\lambda_1(x)} \le x - \frac{1}{\lambda_2(x)} = \psi_2(x)$$

Since the optimal mechanism awards the object on the basis of virtual valuations, buyer 2 will "win" more often than dictated by a comparison of actual values alone.

Finally, note that in the optimal mechanism, buyers whose values x are positive will walk away with some positive surplus. This is because the "winning buyer" pays an amount $y_i(\mathbf{x}_{-i})$ that is typically less than his value x_i. The expectation of the resulting surplus, $E[X_i - y_i(\mathbf{X}_{-i})]$, is sometimes referred to as the *informational rent* accruing to buyer i by virtue of the fact that he is the only one in the system who knows the value of X_i. The seller is therefore unable to perfectly price discriminate and extract all the surplus; buyers must be given some informational rents in order to get them to reveal their private information.

Auctions versus Negotiations

The characterization of an optimal mechanism as obtained above offers some insight into the value of competition. Specifically, suppose that a single seller confronts a single buyer in some sort of *negotiation* for the sale of an object. The buyer's value X_1 is drawn from a distribution F. The preceding analysis shows that the optimal mechanism involves a take-it-or-leave-it offer of $r_1^* = \psi^{-1}(0)$ on the part of the seller. All buyers with valuations X_1 above r^* accept the offer, and all those with valuations X_1 below r^* reject it. From (5.16), the expected revenue from the optimal mechanism can be written as

$$E\left[\max\left\{\psi(X_1), 0\right\}\right] \tag{5.17}$$

and this is an upper bound to the revenue from any negotiation or, for that matter, any other selling mechanism.

As an alternative to negotiating with a single buyer, suppose that the seller is able to attract the interest of another buyer whose value X_2 is also drawn from the same distribution F. Consider what happens if the seller were to sell an object by means of some standard *auction*, say of the second-price variety, without setting a reserve price. Following the reasoning underlying (5.16), it is easy to see that in the symmetric case the expected revenue from a second-price auction is

$$E\left[\max\left\{\psi(X_1), \psi(X_2)\right\}\right] \tag{5.18}$$

We now argue that (5.18) exceeds (5.17). First, consider the event that $X_1 \geq r^*$, that is, when buyer 1 would accept the seller's offer. Because of regularity, this is equivalent to the event that $\psi(X_1) \geq 0$, so we have

$$E\left[\max\left\{\psi(X_1), \psi(X_2)\right\} \mid \psi(X_1) \geq 0\right]$$
$$> E\left[\psi(X_1) \mid \psi(X_1) \geq 0\right]$$
$$= E\left[\max\left\{\psi(X_1), 0\right\} \mid \psi(X_1) \geq 0\right]$$

Next, consider the event that $X_1 < r^*$, so that buyer 1 would reject the seller's offer. Now since "max" is a convex function,

$$E\left[\max\left\{\psi(X_1), \psi(X_2)\right\} \mid \psi(X_1) < 0\right]$$
$$> \max\left\{E\left[\psi(X_1) \mid \psi(X_1) < 0\right], E\left[\psi(X_2) \mid \psi(X_1) < 0\right]\right\}$$

Since the X_1 and X_2 are independent, the right-hand side of the inequality above is the same as

$$\max\left\{E\left[\psi(X_1) \mid \psi(X_1) < 0\right], E\left[\psi(X_2)\right]\right\}$$
$$= \max\left\{E\left[\psi(X_1) \mid \psi(X_1) < 0\right], 0\right\}$$
$$= 0$$
$$= E\left[\max\left\{\psi(X_1), 0\right\} \mid \psi(X_1) < 0\right]$$

where we have used the fact that $E\left[\psi(X_2)\right] = 0$ (see (5.11)). Since in both the event $X_1 \geq r^*$ and the event $X_1 < r^*$ the conditional expectation of $\max\left\{\psi(X_1), \psi(X_2)\right\}$ exceeds the conditional expectation of $\max\left\{\psi(X_1), 0\right\}$, we deduce that (5.18) exceeds (5.17).

We have thus argued that no matter how the negotiations with a single buyer are conducted, it is better to invite a second buyer and hold an auction without a reserve price. The significance of this result stems from the fact that an auction without a reserve price is a "detail-free" mechanism—the seller need not know the exact distribution of values, only that both buyers' values come from the same distribution—while the optimal take-it-or-leave-it offer is not—finding r^* requires knowing F. Instead of worrying about what the optimal take-it-or-leave-it offer is, the seller is better off inviting a second interested buyer and letting competition do the work.

5.2.4 Auctions versus Mechanisms

In general, a mechanism may be tailored to a specific situation. For instance, the optimal mechanism identified in Section 5.2 depends on the specific distributions of buyers' values—that is, the F_i's. Both the allocation and the payment rules of the optimal auction depend on a comparison of virtual valuations, which, in turn, depend on buyers' value distributions. Moreover, as pointed out earlier, the optimal mechanism does not treat different buyers in the same way—buyers with different virtual valuations are treated differently. Thus, the optimal mechanism is neither universal (its rules are specific, via the value distributions, to the item for sale), nor is it anonymous (buyers' identities matter). The optimal mechanism does not satisfy the two important properties we set out in the Introduction as being characteristic of auctions.

From a practical standpoint, the restriction to mechanisms that satisfy these two properties is an important consideration. Any mechanism that depends on the fine details of buyers' distributions would be difficult to implement in practice. The admonition that we should primarily be concerned with mechanisms that do not depend on such fine detail has been called the "Wilson doctrine," named after the leading proponent of this point of view. In this book, we have defined auctions to be mechanisms that adhere to this doctrine.[2]

5.3 Efficient Mechanisms

In the context of a sale of an object to many potential buyers, we have already argued that a second-price auction (without a reserve price) will always allocate the object efficiently. This section concerns a generalization of the second-price auction that is applicable to other contexts. As an

---

[2]Notice that even determining the optimal reserve price depends on a detailed knowledge of the distributions of values.

example, in the next section we consider the possibility of efficient trade between a single seller with privately known costs of production and a single buyer with privately known values. (In the auction context, the value of the object to the seller is assumed to be commonly known.)

We first generalize our setup very slightly to allow the values of agents to lie in some interval $\mathcal{X}_i = [\alpha_i, \omega_i] \subset \mathbb{R}$, thereby allowing, when $\alpha_i < 0$, for the possibility of negative values (or positive costs).

An allocation rule $\mathbf{Q}^* : \mathcal{X} \to \mathbf{\Delta}$ is said to be *efficient* if it maximizes "social welfare"—that is, for all $\mathbf{x} \in \mathcal{X}$,

$$\mathbf{Q}^*(\mathbf{x}) \in \arg \max_{\mathbf{Q} \in \mathbf{\Delta}} \sum_{j \in \mathcal{N}} Q_j x_j \tag{5.19}$$

When there are no ties, an efficient rule allocates the object to the person who values it the most.[3] Any mechanism with an efficient allocation rule is said to be efficient. Given an efficient allocation rule $\mathbf{Q}^*$, define the maximized value of social welfare by

$$W(\mathbf{x}) \equiv \sum_{j \in \mathcal{N}} Q_j^*(\mathbf{x}) x_j \tag{5.20}$$

when the values are $\mathbf{x}$. Similarly, define

$$W_{-i}(\mathbf{x}) \equiv \sum_{j \neq i} Q_j^*(\mathbf{x}) x_j \tag{5.21}$$

as the welfare of agents other than i.

5.3.1   The VCG Mechanism

The Vickrey-Clarke-Groves, or *VCG mechanism* $(\mathbf{Q}^*, \mathbf{M}^V)$, is an efficient mechanism with the payment rule $\mathbf{M}^V : \mathcal{X} \to \mathbb{R}^N$ given by

$$M_i^V(\mathbf{x}) = W(\alpha_i, \mathbf{x}_{-i}) - W_{-i}(\mathbf{x}) \tag{5.22}$$

$M_i^V(\mathbf{x})$ is thus the difference between social welfare at i's lowest possible value α_i and the welfare of *other* agents at i's reported value x_i; assuming in both cases that the efficient allocation rule $\mathbf{Q}^*$ is employed.

In the context of auctions, $\alpha_i = 0$ and it is routine to see that the VCG mechanism is the same as a second-price auction. In the auction context, $M_i^V(\mathbf{x}) = W_{-i}(0, \mathbf{x}_{-i}) - W_{-i}(\mathbf{x})$, and this is positive if and only if $x_i \geq \max_{j \neq i} x_j$. In that case, $M_i^V(\mathbf{x})$ is equal to $\max_{j \neq i} x_j$, the second-highest value.

---

[3]There may be more than one efficient rule depending on how ties are resolved.

The VCG mechanism is incentive compatible. Indeed, it is easy to see that, as in the second-price auction, truth-telling is a weakly dominant strategy in the VCG mechanism. If the other buyers report values $\mathbf{x}_{-i}$, then by reporting a value of z_i, agent i's payoff is

$$Q_i^* (z_i, \mathbf{x}_{-i}) \, x_i - M_i^{\mathrm{V}} (z_i, \mathbf{x}_{-i}) = \sum_{j \in \mathcal{N}} Q_j^* (z_i, \mathbf{x}_{-i}) \, x_j - W (\alpha_i, \mathbf{x}_{-i})$$

by using (5.20) and (5.21). The definition of $\mathbf{Q}^*$ in (5.19) implies that for all $\mathbf{x}_{-i}$, the first term is maximized by choosing $z_i = x_i$; and since the second term does not depend on z_i, it is optimal to report $z_i = x_i$. Thus, i's equilibrium payoff when the values are $\mathbf{x}$ is

$$Q_i^* (\mathbf{x}) \, x_i - M_i^{\mathrm{V}} (\mathbf{x}) = W (\mathbf{x}) - W (\alpha_i, \mathbf{x}_{-i})$$

which is just the difference in social welfare induced by i when he reports his true value x_i as opposed to his lowest possible value α_i.

Since the VCG mechanism is incentive compatible, it has the properties derived in Section 5.1. In particular, the equilibrium expected payoff function U_i^{V} associated with the VCG mechanism,

$$U_i^{\mathrm{V}} (x_i) = E \left[W (x_i, \mathbf{X}_{-i}) - W (\alpha_i, \mathbf{X}_{-i}) \right]$$

is convex and increasing. Clearly, $U_i^{\mathrm{V}} (\alpha_i) = 0$ and the monotonicity of U_i^{V} now implies that the VCG mechanism is also individually rational.

If $(\mathbf{Q}^*, \mathbf{M})$ is some other efficient mechanism that is also incentive compatible, then by the revenue equivalence principle we know that for all i, the expected payoff functions for this mechanism, say U_i, differ from U_i^{V} by at most an additive constant, say c_i. If $(\mathbf{Q}^*, \mathbf{M})$ is also individually rational, then this constant must be nonnegative—that is, $c_i = U_i(x_i) - U_i^{\mathrm{V}}(x_i) \geq 0$. This is because otherwise we would have $U_i(\alpha_i) < U_i^{\mathrm{V}}(\alpha_i) = 0$, contradicting that $(\mathbf{Q}^*, \mathbf{M})$ was individually rational. Since the expected payoffs in $(\mathbf{Q}^*, \mathbf{M})$ are greater than in the VCG mechanism, and the two have the same allocation rule, the expected payments must be lower.

Proposition 5.5 *Among all mechanisms for allocating a single object that are efficient, incentive compatible, and individually rational, the VCG mechanism maximizes the expected payment of each agent.*

In many economic problems, it is desirable to consider mechanisms that do not require an injection of funds from the mechanism designer—that is, the mechanism designer's budget is exactly balanced *ex post*. While the VCG mechanism typically does not have this property, it is still an important guide in determining when this is feasible.

5.3.2   Budget Balance

In our notation, a mechanism is said to balance the budget if for every realization of values, the net payments from agents sum to zero—that is, for all $\mathbf{x}$,

$$\sum_{i \in \mathcal{N}} M_i(\mathbf{x}) = 0$$

The Arrow-d'Aspremont-Gérard-Varet or *AGV mechanism* (also called the "expected externality" mechanism) $(\mathbf{Q}^*, \mathbf{M}^A)$ is defined by

$$
M_i^{\mathrm{A}}(\mathbf{x}) \;=\; \frac{1}{N-1} \sum_{j \neq i} E_{\mathbf{X}_{-j}} \left[W_{-j}(x_j, \mathbf{X}_{-j}) \right]
$$
$$
- E_{\mathbf{X}_{-i}} \left[W_{-i}(x_i, \mathbf{X}_{-i}) \right] \tag{5.23}
$$

so that for all $\mathbf{x}$,

$$\sum_{i \in \mathcal{N}} M_i^{\mathrm{A}}(\mathbf{x}) = 0$$

To see that the AGV mechanism is incentive compatible, suppose that all other agents are reporting their values $\mathbf{x}_{-i}$ truthfully. The expected payoff to i from reporting z_i when his true value is x_i is

$$
E_{\mathbf{X}_{-i}} \left[Q_i^*(z_i, \mathbf{X}_{-i})\, x_i + W_{-i}(z_i, \mathbf{X}_{-i}) \right]
$$
$$
- E_{\mathbf{X}_{-i}} \left[\frac{1}{N-1} \sum_{j \neq i} E_{\mathbf{X}_{-j}} \left[W_{-j}(X_j, \mathbf{X}_{-j}) \right] \right]
$$

and since the second term is independent of z_i, this is maximized by setting $z_i = x_i$.

It is easy to see that the AGV mechanism may not satisfy the individual rationality constraint. The question of whether there are efficient, incentive compatible, individually rational mechanisms that, at the same time, balance the budget can also be answered by means of the VCG mechanism.

Proposition 5.6 *There exists an efficient, incentive compatible, and individually rational mechanism that balances the budget if and only if the VCG mechanism results in an expected surplus.*

Proof. The fact that it is necessary for the VCG mechanism to run an expected surplus follows from Proposition 5.5: If the VCG mechanism runs a deficit, then all efficient, incentive compatible, and individually rational mechanisms must run a deficit.

We now show that the condition is sufficient by explicitly constructing an efficient, incentive compatible mechanism that balances the budget and is individually rational.

First, consider the AGV mechanism $\mathbf{M}^A$ defined in (5.23). From the revenue equivalence principle we know that there exist constants c_i^A such that

$$U_i^A(x_i) = E\left[W(x_i, \mathbf{X}_{-i})\right] - c_i^A$$

Next, consider the VCG mechanism defined in (5.22). Again, from the revenue equivalence principle, there also exist constants c_i^V such that

$$U_i^V(x_i) = E\left[W(x_i, \mathbf{X}_{-i})\right] - c_i^V$$

Suppose that the VCG mechanism runs an expected surplus—that is,

$$E\left[\sum_{i \in \mathcal{N}} M_i^V(\mathbf{X})\right] \geq 0$$

Then

$$E\left[\sum_{i \in \mathcal{N}} M_i^V(\mathbf{X})\right] \geq E\left[\sum_{i \in \mathcal{N}} M_i^A(\mathbf{X})\right]$$

since the right-hand side is exactly 0. Equivalently,

$$\sum_{i \in \mathcal{N}} c_i^V \geq \sum_{i \in \mathcal{N}} c_i^A \tag{5.24}$$

For all $i > 1$, define $d_i = c_i^A - c_i^V$ and let $d_1 = -\sum_{i=2}^N d_i$. Consider the mechanism $\overline{\mathbf{M}}$ defined by

$$\overline{M}_i(\mathbf{x}) = M_i^A(\mathbf{x}) + d_i$$

Clearly, $\overline{\mathbf{M}}$ balances the budget. It is also incentive compatible since the payoff to each agent in the mechanism $\overline{\mathbf{M}}$ differs from the payoff from an incentive compatible mechanism, $\mathbf{M}^A$, by an additive constant. Thus, it is only necessary to verify that $\overline{\mathbf{M}}$ is individually rational.

For all $i \neq 1$,

$$\begin{aligned}
\overline{U}_i(x_i) &= U_i^A(x_i) + d_i \\
&= U_i^A(x_i) + c_i^A - c_i^V \\
&= U_i^V(x_i) \\
&\geq 0
\end{aligned}$$

By construction $\sum_{i=1}^N d_i = 0$ and observe from (5.24) that

$$d_1 = -\sum_{i>1} d_i = \sum_{i>1}\left(c_i^V - c_i^A\right) \geq \left(c_1^A - c_1^V\right)$$

Thus,

$$
\begin{aligned}
\overline{U}_1(x_1) &= U_1^A(x_1) + d_1 \\
&\geq U_1^A(x_1) + c_1^A - c_1^V \\
&= U_1^V(x_1) \\
&\geq 0
\end{aligned}
$$

so that $\overline{M}$ is also individually rational. ∎

While Proposition 5.5 results from a simple application of the revenue equivalence principle, it is nevertheless a very useful tool and can be used to consider a variety of problems—outside the realm of auction theory— concerning efficient allocations. As an example, we now turn to one such application.

5.3.3   An Application to Bilateral Trade

Suppose that there is a seller with a privately known cost $C \in [\underline{c}, \overline{c}]$ of producing a single indivisible good. Suppose also that there is a buyer with a privately known value $V \in [\underline{v}, \overline{v}]$ of consuming the good. The cost C and value V are independently distributed, and the prior distributions are commonly known and have full support on the respective intervals. Thus, there is incomplete information on both sides of the market. Finally, suppose that $\underline{v} < \overline{c}$ and $\overline{v} \geq \underline{c}$, so that the supports overlap and sometimes it is efficient not to trade. Is there some way to guarantee that trade will take place whenever it should? To answer this question, it is natural to adopt a mechanism design perspective.

A mechanism decides whether or not the good is traded. It also decides the amount P the buyer pays for the good and the amount R the seller receives. If the good is traded, the net gain to the buyer is $V - P$, and the net gain to the seller is $R - C$. At the moment, we do not restrict P or R to be positive or negative, nor do we assume that the budget is balanced—that is, $P = R$.

A mechanism is efficient if whenever $V > C$, the object is produced and allocated to the buyer.

Proposition 5.7 *In the bilateral trade problem, there is no mechanism that is efficient, incentive compatible, individually rational, and at the same time balances the budget.*

Proof. First, consider the VCG mechanism, whose operation in this context is as follows:

The buyer announces a valuation V and the seller announces a cost C.

1. If $V \leq C$, the object is not exchanged and no payments are made.

2. If $V > C$, the object is exchanged. The buyer pays $\max\{C, \underline{v}\}$ and the seller receives $\min\{V, \bar{c}\}$.

It is routine to verify that it is a weakly dominant strategy for the buyer to announce $V = v$ and the seller to announce $C = c$. This mechanism is efficient since, in equilibrium, the object is transferred whenever $v > c$.

A buyer with value $\underline{v}$ has an expected payoff of 0, and any buyer with value $v > \underline{v}$ has a positive expected payoff. Similarly, a seller with cost $\bar{c}$ has an expected payoff of 0, and any seller with cost $c < \bar{c}$ has a positive expected payoff. Thus, the mechanism is individually rational.

Whenever $V > C$, so there is trade, the fact that $\underline{v} < \bar{c}$ implies that the amount the seller receives $R = \min\{V, \bar{c}\}$ is *greater* than the amount buyer pays $P = \max\{C, \underline{v}\}$. The in this context, the VCG mechanism always runs a deficit. Indeed, for any realization of V and C such that $V > C$, the deficit $R - P = V - C$, which is exactly equal to the *ex post* gains that result from trade.

Now suppose that we have some other mechanism that is incentive compatible and efficient. By the revenue equivalence principle, there is a constant K such that the expected payment for any buyer with value v under this mechanism differs from his expected payment under the VCG mechanism by exactly K. Similarly, there is a constant L such that the expected receipts of any seller with cost c under this mechanism differ from her expected receipts under the VCG mechanism by exactly L.

Suppose the other mechanism is individually rational. Since in the VCG mechanism a buyer with value $\underline{v}$ gets an expected payoff of 0, we must have that $K \leq 0$. Similarly, since a seller with costs $\bar{c}$ gets an expected payoff of 0, we have $L \geq 0$. (This is just the same as the argument in Proposition 5.5.)

The expected deficit under the other mechanism is just the expected deficit under the VCG mechanism plus $L - K \geq 0$. But since the VCG mechanism runs a deficit, we have argued that every other mechanism also runs a deficit.

Thus, there does not exist an efficient mechanism that is incentive compatible, individually rational, and balances the budget. ∎

Chapter Notes

The formulation of the mechanism design problem is due to Myerson (1981) in a now classic paper. The revelation principle, general revenue equivalence, and the derivation of the optimal selling mechanism were all developed there. The interpretation of virtual valuations as "marginal revenues" and the analogy of the optimal mechanism design problem with the problem facing a discriminating monopolist was provided by Bulow and Roberts (1989).

The comparison of a two-bidder auction without a reserve price and optimal negotiations with a single buyer is based on the work of Bulow and Klemperer (1996). In this paper the authors show a more general result: From the seller's perspective, an $N + 1$ bidder English auction (without a reserve price) is superior to the mechanism which consists of an N bidder English auction followed by the seller, armed with information that is revealed during the auction, optimally negotiating with the winner.

The origins of the VCG mechanism can be traced to Vickrey (1961) who proposed the second-price auction and an extension to the case of multiple identical goods (see Chapter 12). Clarke (1971) proposed a similar mechanism in the context of public goods. These ideas were further generalized by Groves (1973). The balanced budget AGV mechanism was independently suggested by Arrow (1979) and d'Aspremont and Gérard-Varet (1979a, 1979b). Propositions 5.5 and 5.6 are due to Krishna and Perry (1998).

The result on the impossibility of efficient exchange in the bilateral trade problem, Proposition 5.7, is due to Myerson and Satterthwaite (1983). The treatment here follows that in Krishna and Perry (1998).

A real-valued function U defined on an interval $[0, \omega]$ is said to be *absolutely continuous* if for all $\varepsilon > 0$ there exists a $\delta > 0$ such that

$$\sum_{i=1}^{n} |U(x_i') - U(x_i)| < \varepsilon$$

for every finite collection $\{(x_i, x_i')\}$ of nonoverlapping intervals satisfying

$$\sum_{i=1}^{n} |x_i' - x_i| < \delta$$

Every convex function is absolutely continuous. An absolutely continuous function is differentiable almost everywhere and is the integral of its derivative. These are fairly standard results in real analysis and can be found, for instance, in Royden (1968).

6

Auctions with Interdependent Values

In this chapter we simultaneously relax two major assumptions regarding the nature of the information available to the bidders.

Interdependent Values

First, we relax the assumption of private values—that each bidder knows the value of the object to himself—by allowing for the possibility that bidders have only partial information regarding the value, say in the form of a noisy signal. Indeed, other bidders may possess information that would, if known to a particular bidder, affect the value he assigns to the object. The resulting information structure is called one of *interdependent values*. We assume that each bidder has some private information concerning the value of the object. Bidder i's private information is summarized as the realization of the random variable $X_i \in [0, \omega_i]$, called i's *signal*. It is assumed that the value of the object to bidder i, V_i, can be expressed as a function of all bidders' signals and we will write

$$V_i = v_i(X_1, X_2, \ldots, X_N)$$

where the function v_i is bidder i's *valuation* and is assumed to be nondecreasing in all its variables and twice continuously differentiable. In addition, it is assumed that v_i is strictly increasing in X_i.

This specification supposes that the value is completely determined by the signals—that is, there is no remaining uncertainty. This need not be the case, however, and more general formulations can also be accommodated. In a more general setting, suppose that $V_1, V_2, \ldots, V_N$ denote the N (unknown) values to the bidders; $X_1, X_2, \ldots, X_N$ denote the N signals available to the bidders; and S denotes a signal available only to the seller. In that case, we can define

$$v_i(x_1, x_2, \ldots, x_N) \equiv E[V_i \mid X_1 = x_1, X_2 = x_2, \ldots, X_N = x_N]$$

as the expected value to i conditional on all the information available to bidders. For operational purposes, this is the effective value that bidders can use in their calculations.

With either specification, we suppose that $v_i(0, 0, \ldots, 0) = 0$ and that $E[V_i] < \infty$. We continue to assume that bidders are risk neutral—each bidder maximizes the expectation of $V_i - p_i$, where p_i is the price paid.

Notice that this specification of the values includes, as an extreme case, the private values model of earlier chapters in which $v_i(\mathbf{X}) = X_i$. At the other end of the spectrum is the case of a pure *common value* in which all bidders assign the same value

$$V = v(X_1, X_2, \ldots, X_N)$$

to the object—the valuations of the bidders are identical. Bidders' information consists only of their own signals of course, so while the *ex post* value is common to all, it is unknown to any particular bidder. A special case that is of both analytic and practical interest entails first specifying a distribution for the common value V and then assuming that conditional on the event $V = v$, bidders' signals X_i are independently distributed. Typically, it is also assumed that each X_i is an unbiased estimator of V, so that $E[X_i \mid V = v] = v$. This particular specification has been used to model the information structure associated with auctions of oil-drilling leases and is sometimes called the "mineral rights" model.

The interdependence of values complicates the decision problem facing a bidder. In particular, since the exact value of the object is unknown and depends also on other bidders' signals, an *a priori* estimate of this value may need to be revised as a result of events that take place during, and even after, the auction. The reason is that these events may convey valuable information about the signals of other bidders. One such event is the announcement that the bidder has won the auction.

The Winner's Curse

Prior to the auction the only information available to a bidder, say 1, is that his own signal $X_1 = x$. Based on this information alone, his estimate of the value is $E[V \mid X_1 = x]$. Now suppose that the object is sold using a sealed-bid first-price auction and consider what happens when and if it is announced that bidder 1 is, in fact, the winner. If all bidders are symmetric and follow the same strategy β, then this fact reveals to bidder 1 that the highest of the other $N - 1$ signals is less than x. As a result, his estimate of the value upon learning that he is the winner is $E[V \mid X_1 = x, Y_1 < x]$, which is *less* than $E[V \mid X_1 = x]$. The announcement that he has won leads to a decrease in the estimated value; in this sense, winning brings "bad news." A failure to foresee this effect and take it fully into account when formulating bidding strategies will result in what has been called the *winner's curse*—the possibility that the winner pays more than the value.

The phenomenon is most apparent in a pure common value model in which each bidder's signal $X_i = V + \varepsilon_i$. Suppose that the different ε_i's are independently and identically distributed and satisfy $E[\varepsilon_i] = 0$. Then each bidder's signal is an unbiased estimator of the common value—that is, for all i, $E[X_i \mid V = v] = v$. But now notice that even though each individual signal is an unbiased estimator of the value, the largest of N such signals is not. In fact, since "max" is convex function, $E[\max X_i \mid V = v] > \max E[X_i \mid V = v] = v$, showing that the expectation of the highest signal, in fact, overestimates the value. A bidder who does not take this fully into account and bids an amount $\beta(X_i)$ which is close to X_i would, upon winning, pay more than the estimated worth of the object. Put another way, bidders may need to shade their bids well below their initial estimates in order to avoid the winner's curse. Note also that the magnitude of the winner's curse increases with the number of bidders in the auction. The news that a signal is the highest of, say, 20 bidders is worse than the news that it is the highest of 10 bidders.

We emphasize that the winner's curse arises only if bidders do not calculate the value of winning correctly and overbid as a result—it does not arise in equilibrium.

Nonequivalence of English and Second-Price Auctions

A second consequence of interdependent values is that it is no longer the case that the English (or open ascending) auction is strategically equivalent to the sealed-bid second-price auction. The difference in the two auction formats is that in an English auction active bidders get to know the prices at which the bidders who have dropped out have done so. This allows the active bidders to make inferences about the information that the inactive bidders had and in this way to update their estimates of the true value. A sealed-bid second-price auction, by its very nature, makes no such information available.

There are two cases in which this information is irrelevant. First, if there are only two bidders, then the English auction is always equivalent to a second-price auction; in this case, when one of the bidders drops out in an English auction, the auction is over. The second case arises if the bidders have private values; in this case, the information gleaned from others is irrelevant.

Affiliation

We also relax the assumption that bidders' information is independently distributed by allowing for the possibility that bidders' signals are correlated. Thus, the joint density of the bidders' signals, $f(\mathbf{X})$, need not be a product of densities of individual signals, $f_i(X_i)$. In fact, we will assume that the signals $X_1, X_2, \ldots, X_N$ are positively *affiliated*. Affiliation is a strong form of positive correlation and roughly means that if a subset of the X_i's are all large, then this makes it more likely that the remaining X_j's are also large. While a formal definition and a more detailed discussion may be found in Appendix D, for the purposes of this chapter, the following three implications of affiliation are sufficient.

First, define, as usual, the random variables $Y_1, Y_2, \ldots, Y_{N-1}$ to be the largest, second largest, $\ldots$, smallest from among $X_2, X_3, \ldots, X_N$. If the variables $X_1, X_2, \ldots, X_N$ are affiliated, then the variables $X_1, Y_1, \ldots, Y_{N-1}$ are also affiliated.

Second, let $G(\cdot \mid x)$ denote the distribution of Y_1 conditional on $X_1 = x$. Then the fact that X_1 and Y_1 are affiliated implies that if $x' > x$, then $G(\cdot \mid x')$ dominates $G(\cdot \mid x)$ in terms of the reverse hazard rate—that is, for all y,

$$\frac{g(y \mid x')}{G(y \mid x')} \geq \frac{g(y \mid x)}{G(y \mid x)} \tag{6.1}$$

Third, if γ is any increasing function, then $x' > x$ implies that

$$E\left[\gamma(Y_1) \mid X_1 = x'\right] \geq E\left[\gamma(Y_1) \mid X_1 = x\right] \tag{6.2}$$

6.1   The Symmetric Model

As in the case of independent private values, it is instructive to begin by considering symmetric situations. As before, we will first derive symmetric equilibrium strategies in the three auction formats: second-price, English, and first-price. We will then compare the expected revenues from these auctions.

In a model with independent private values, bidders are symmetric if their values are drawn from the same distribution. With interdependent values and affiliated signals, however, there are two aspects to symmetry. The first concerns the symmetry of the valuations v_i and the second concerns the symmetry of the distribution of signals.

It is assumed that all signals X_i are drawn from the same interval $[0, \omega]$ and that the valuations of the bidders are symmetric in the following sense.

For all i, we can write these in the form

$$v_i(\mathbf{X}) = u(X_i, \mathbf{X}_{-i})$$

and the function u, which is the same for all bidders, is symmetric in the last $N-1$ components. This means that from the perspective of a particular bidder, the signals of other bidders can be interchanged without affecting the value. For instance, when $N = 3$, the value to bidder 1 depends on his or her own signal and the signals of bidders 2 and 3, but if the signals of the other bidders were interchanged, then the value would not be affected. Thus, for all x, y, and z it is the case that $u(x, y, z) = u(x, z, y)$.

It is also assumed that the joint density function of the signals f, defined on $[0, \omega]^N$, is a symmetric function of its arguments and the signals are affiliated.

Define the function

$$v(x, y) = E[V_1 \mid X_1 = x, Y_1 = y] \tag{6.3}$$

to be the expectation of the value to bidder 1 when the signal he or she receives is x and the highest signal among the other bidders, Y_1, is y. Because of symmetry this function is the same for all bidders and from (6.2), v is a nondecreasing function of x and y. We will, in fact, assume that v is strictly increasing in x. Moreover, since $u(\mathbf{0}) = 0$, $v(0,0) = 0$. The function v plays an important role in what follows.

For the symmetric model with interdependent values, we proceed in a manner parallel to the development of Chapter 2 concerning the symmetric independent private values model. As in Chapter 2, we first derive symmetric equilibrium strategies in the three common formats: the second-price, English, and first-price auctions. We then compare the three formats by directly computing the expected revenues in each.

6.2   Second-Price Auctions

We begin by deriving a symmetric equilibrium in a second-price sealed-bid auction.

Proposition 6.1 *Symmetric equilibrium strategies in a second-price auction are given by:*

$$\beta^{\mathrm{II}}(x) = v(x, x)$$

Proof. Suppose all other bidders $j \neq 1$ follow the strategy $\beta \equiv \beta^{II}$. Bidder 1's expected payoff when his signal is x and he bids an amount b is

$$\Pi(b, x) = \int_0^{\beta^{-1}(b)} (v(x, y) - \beta(y)) g(y \mid x) \, dy$$

$$= \int_0^{\beta^{-1}(b)} (v(x, y) - v(y, y)) g(y \mid x) \, dy$$

where $g(\cdot \mid x)$ is the density of $Y_1 \equiv \max_{i \neq 1} X_i$ conditional on $X_1 = x$.

Since v is increasing in the first argument, for all $y < x$, $v(x, y) - v(y, y) > 0$ and for all $y > x$, $v(x, y) - v(y, y) < 0$. Thus, Π is maximized by choosing b so that $\beta^{-1}(b) = x$ or equivalently, by choosing $b = \beta(x)$. ∎

The nature of the bidding strategies in Proposition 6.1 can be understood as follows. A bidder, say 1, with signal x is asked to bid an amount $\beta^{II}(x)$ such that if he were to just win the auction with that bid—if the highest competing bid, and hence the price, were also $\beta^{II}(x)$—he would just "break even." This is because if the highest competing bid were $\beta^{II}(x)$, then bidder 1 would infer that $Y_1 = x$ and the expected value of the object conditional on this new piece of information would be $E[V_1 \mid X_1 = x, Y_1 = x] = v(x, x) = \beta^{II}(x)$.

Proposition 6.1 applies, of course, to the special case of private values (where $v(x, x) = x$) and in those circumstances the equilibrium strategy is weakly dominant. With general interdependent values, however, the strategy β^{II} identified above is not a dominant strategy.

The equilibrium identified above is unique in the class of symmetric equilibria with an increasing strategy. To see this, suppose that β is an increasing symmetric equilibrium strategy. Writing $\Pi(b, x)$ as in the proof of Proposition 6.1 and optimizing over b, the first-order condition immediately implies that $\beta(x)$ must equal $v(x, x)$. We will see in Chapter 8, however, that even symmetric second-price auctions may have other, asymmetric equilibria.

It is instructive to find the equilibrium bidding strategies explicitly in an example. In the example that follows, there is a common value and conditional on that value, bidders' signals are independently distributed. In other words, it is an instance of the "mineral rights" model.

Example 6.1 *Suppose that there are three bidders with a common value V for the object that is uniformly distributed on $[0, 1]$. Given $V = v$, bidders' signals X_i are uniformly and independently distributed on $[0, 2v]$.*

As usual, $\mathbf{X} = (X_1, X_2, X_3)$ and it is convenient to define the random variable $Z \equiv \max\{X_1, X_2, X_3\}$.

The density of X_i conditional on $V = v$ is $1/2v$ on the interval $[0, 2v]$, so the joint density of $(V, \mathbf{X})$ is $1/8v^3$ on the set $\{(V, \mathbf{X}) \mid \forall i, X_i \leq 2V\}$. Now

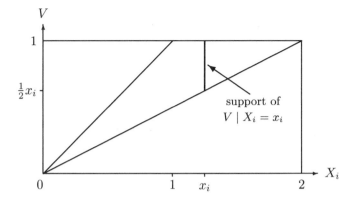

FIGURE 6.1. Support of $V \mid X_i = x_i$ in Example 6.1

notice that the only information about V that knowledge of X_1, X_2, X_3 provides is that $V \geq \frac{1}{2}Z$. (See Figure 6.1.) Thus, the joint density of $\mathbf{X}$ is

$$
\begin{aligned}
f(x_1, x_2, x_3) &= \int_{\frac{1}{2}z}^{1} \frac{1}{8v^3}\, dv \\
&= \frac{4 - z^2}{16z^2}
\end{aligned}
$$

where $z = \max\{x_1, x_2, x_3\}$. Thus, the density of V conditional on $\mathbf{X} = \mathbf{x}$ is the same as the density of V conditional on $Z = z$, so

$$
\begin{aligned}
f(v \mid \mathbf{X} = \mathbf{x}) &= f(v \mid Z = z) \\
&= \frac{1}{8v^3} \times \frac{16z^2}{4 - z^2}
\end{aligned}
$$

on the interval $\left[\frac{1}{2}z, 1\right]$. Thus,

$$
\begin{aligned}
E\left[V \mid \mathbf{X} = \mathbf{x}\right] &= E\left[V \mid Z = z\right] \\
&= \int_{\frac{1}{2}z}^{1} v f(v \mid \mathbf{X} = \mathbf{x})\, dv \\
&= \frac{2z}{2 + z}
\end{aligned}
$$

Notice that since $Y_1 = \max\{X_2, X_3\}$ and $Z = \max\{X_1, X_2, X_3\}$, $Z = \max\{X_1, Y_1\}$

$$
\begin{aligned}
v(x, y) &= E\left[V \mid X_1 = x, Y_1 = y\right] \\
&= E\left[V \mid Z = \max\{x, y\}\right] \\
&= \frac{2\max\{x, y\}}{2 + \max\{x, y\}}
\end{aligned}
$$

Thus, from Proposition 6.1 we obtain

$$\begin{aligned}\beta^{\text{II}}(x) &= v(x,x) \\ &= \frac{2x}{2+x}\end{aligned}$$

▲

6.3   English Auctions

In sealed-bid auctions, a bidder's strategy determines the amount of his bid as a function of his private information. In an English, or open ascending, auction, additional information—the identities of the bidders who drop out and the prices at which they do so—becomes available. In the symmetric model considered here, the exact identities of the bidders who drop out are not relevant, but the prices at which bidders dropped out are. Similarly, the identities of the bidders who are active are not relevant, but the number of active bidders is.

The term "English auction" encompasses a variety of open ascending price formats, which differ in their precise rules. In one format the price is raised by the bidders themselves as they outbid each other. We adopt a formulation of the rules that is particularly convenient for analytic purposes. An auctioneer sets the price at zero and gradually raises it. The current price is observed by all and bidders signal their willingness to buy by raising a hand, holding up a sign, or pushing a button that controls a light. The important aspect is that this action is witnessed by all, so at any time the set of active bidders—those who signal their willingness to buy at the current price—is commonly known. Bidders may drop out at any time, but once they do so cannot reenter the auction at a higher price. The auction ends when there is only one active bidder.

A symmetric equilibrium strategy in an English auction is thus a collection $\beta = (\beta^N, \beta^{N-1}, \ldots, \beta^2)$ of $N-1$ functions $\beta^k : [0,1] \times \mathbb{R}_+^{N-k} \to \mathbb{R}_+$, for $1 < k \leq N$, where $\beta^k(x, p_{k+1}, \ldots, p_N)$ is the price at which bidder 1 will drop out if the number of bidders who are still active is k, his own signal is x, and the prices at which the other $N-k$ bidders dropped out were $p_{k+1} \geq p_{k+2} \geq \ldots \geq p_N$.

Now consider the following strategies for the bidders. When all bidders are active, let

$$\beta^N(x) = u(x, x, \ldots, x) \tag{6.4}$$

and notice that $\beta^N(\cdot)$ is a continuous and increasing function.

Suppose that bidder N, say, is the first to drop out at some price p_N and let x_N be the unique signal such that $\beta^N(x_N) = p_N$ (since $\beta^N(\cdot)$ is continuous and increasing there exists a unique such x_N). When some bidder drops out at a price p_N, let the remaining $N-1$ bidders who are still active follow the strategy

$$\beta^{N-1}(x, p_N) = u(x, \ldots, x, x_N)$$

where $\beta^N(x_N) = p_N$. The function $\beta^{N-1}(\cdot, p_N)$ is also continuous and increasing.

Proceeding recursively in this way, for all k such that $2 \le k < N$ suppose that bidders $N, N-1, \ldots, k+1$ have dropped out of the auction at prices $p_N, p_{N-1}, \ldots, p_{k+1}$, respectively. Let the remaining k bidders who are still active follow the strategy

$$\beta^k(x, p_{k+1}, \ldots, p_N) = u(x, \ldots, x, x_{k+1}, \ldots, x_N) \tag{6.5}$$

where $\beta^{k+1}(x_{k+1}, p_{k+2}, \ldots, p_N) = p_{k+1}$.

We will argue that these strategies constitute an equilibrium of the English auction, but before doing so formally it is worthwhile to understand the nature of the bidding strategies. Suppose that bidders $k+1, k+2, \ldots, N$ have dropped out, so only k bidders are still active. Because the strategies are revealing, the signals $x_{k+1}, x_{k+2}, \ldots, x_N$ of the bidders who have dropped out become known to the other bidders. Consider a particular bidder, say 1, with signal x, and suppose the other bidders are following β^k. Bidder 1 evaluates whether or not he should drop out at the current price p and does the following "mental calculation." He asks what would happen if he were to win the good at the current price p. Now the only way this can happen is if *all* the other $k-1$ bidders drop out at p. In that case, bidder 1 would infer that each of their signals were equal to a y such that $\beta^k(y, p_{k+1}, \ldots, p_N) = p$. The value of the object would then be inferred to be $u(x, y, \ldots, y, x_{k+1}, x_{k+2}, \ldots, x_N)$. It is worth continuing in the auction if and only if the inferred value of the object exceeds the current price p. Thus, the strategy calls for bidder 1 to continue until the price is such that if he were to win the object at that price he would just break even.

Proposition 6.2 *Symmetric equilibrium strategies in an English auction are given by β defined in (6.4) and (6.5).*

Proof. Consider bidder 1 with signal $X_1 = x$ and suppose that all other bidders follow the strategy β. As usual, define $Y_1, Y_2, \ldots, Y_{N-1}$ to be the largest, second-largest, ... , smallest of $X_2, X_3, \ldots, X_N$, respectively.

Suppose that the realizations of $Y_1, \ldots, Y_N$, denoted by $y_1, \ldots, y_N$, respectively, are such that bidder 1 wins the object if he also follows the strategy β. Then it must be that $x > y_1$. The price that bidder 1 pays is the price at which the bidder with the second-highest signal, y_1, drops out, and from (6.5) this is just $u(y_1, y_1, y_2, \ldots, y_N)$. Since $x > y_1$, the payoff to bidder 1 upon winning is

$$u(x, y_1, y_2, \ldots, y_N) - u(y_1, y_1, y_2, \ldots, y_N) > 0$$

Bidder 1 cannot affect the price he pays and winning yields a positive payoff. Thus, he cannot do better than to follow β also.

Next, suppose that the realizations of $Y_1, \ldots, Y_N$ are such that bidder 1 does not win the object by also following β. Then it must be that $x < y_1$. If bidder 1 does not drop out and wins the auction, then again it must be at a price of $u(y_1, y_1, y_2, \ldots, y_N)$. But since $x < y_1$, the price now exceeds the *ex post* value of the object to 1. So bidder 1 cannot do better than to drop out as specified by β. ∎

The equilibrium strategy β defined in (6.4) and (6.5) is quite remarkable in that it depends only on the valuation functions u and not on the underlying distribution of signals f: For any given u satisfying the assumptions made here, if β is an equilibrium for some joint density function f, then the same β would be remain an equilibrium if the signals were distributed according to some other density function, say $g \neq f$. In other words, the strategies form an *ex post* equilibrium: For any realization of signals the play prescribed by β forms a Nash equilibrium of the complete information game that results if the signals were commonly known. (See Appendix F.). This also means that the equilibrium strategy β has an important "no regret" feature—that is, for any realization of the signals the bidders have no cause to regret the outcome even if, after the fact, all signals were to become publicly known. In sharp contrast, once there are three or more bidders, bidders playing the symmetric equilibrium of the second-price auction, identified in the previous sections, may suffer from regret after the fact. The equilibrium of the second-price auction is not an *ex post* equilibrium. Nor is the symmetric equilibrium of the first-price auction an *ex post* equilibrium.

The symmetric equilibrium of the English auction has the strong no regret property because, in fact, in the course of the auction the signals of all other bidders are revealed to the winner, so he does not regret winning. On the other hand, bidders who drop out do not regret losing because if they were to win, it would be at a price that is too high. In Chapter 9, we undertake a further exploration of the English auction in cases where the valuation functions need not be symmetric.

6.4   First-Price Auctions

We now derive the equilibrium bidding strategies in a first-price auction, beginning, as usual, with a heuristic derivation.

Suppose all other bidders $j \neq 1$ follow the increasing and differentiable strategy β. Clearly, it does not pay for bidder 1 to bid less than $\beta(0)$ or more than $\beta(\omega)$.

As defined earlier, let $G(\cdot \mid x)$ denote the distribution of $Y_1 \equiv \max_{i \neq 1} X_i$ conditional on $X_1 = x$ and let $g(\cdot \mid x)$ be the associated conditional density function. The expected payoff to bidder 1 when his signal is x and he bids an amount $\beta(z)$ is

$$
\begin{aligned}
\Pi(z, x) &= \int_0^z (v(x, y) - \beta(z)) \, g(y \mid x) \, dy \\
&= \int_0^z v(x, y) \, g(y \mid x) \, dy - \beta(z) G(z \mid x)
\end{aligned}
$$

The first-order condition is

$$
(v(x, z) - \beta(z)) \, g(z \mid x) - \beta'(z) \, G(z \mid x) = 0
$$

At a symmetric equilibrium, the optimal $z = x$, so setting $z = x$ in the first-order condition, we obtain the differential equation:

$$
\beta'(x) = (v(x, x) - \beta(x)) \frac{g(x \mid x)}{G(x \mid x)} \tag{6.6}
$$

The differential equation (6.6) is only a necessary condition. We must also have that for all x, $v(x, x) - \beta(x) \geq 0$, since otherwise a bid of 0 would be better. Since, by assumption, $v(0, 0) = 0$, it is the case that $\beta(0) = 0$. Thus, associated with (6.6) we have the boundary condition $\beta(0) = 0$.

The solution to the differential equation (6.6) together with the boundary condition $\beta(0) = 0$, as stated in the next proposition, constitutes a symmetric equilibrium.

Proposition 6.3 *Symmetric equilibrium strategies in a sealed-bid first-price auction are given by*

$$
\beta^{\mathrm{I}}(x) = \int_0^x v(y, y) \, dL(y \mid x)
$$

where

$$
L(y \mid x) = \exp\left(-\int_y^x \frac{g(t \mid t)}{G(t \mid t)} \, dt\right) \tag{6.7}
$$

Proof. First, note that $L(\cdot \mid x)$ can be thought of as a distribution function with support $[0, x]$. To see this recall that, because of affiliation (see Appendix D), for all $t > 0$,

$$
\frac{g(t \mid t)}{G(t \mid t)} \geq \frac{g(t \mid 0)}{G(t \mid 0)}
$$

and so

$$-\int_0^x \frac{g(t \mid t)}{G(t \mid t)} \, dt \; \leq \; -\int_0^x \frac{g(t \mid 0)}{G(t \mid 0)} \, dt$$

$$= \; -\int_0^x \frac{d}{dt} \left(\ln G(t \mid 0) \right) dt$$

$$= \; \ln G(0 \mid 0) - \ln G(x \mid 0)$$

$$= \; -\infty$$

Applying the exponential function to both sides implies that for all x, $L(0 \mid x) = 0$. Moreover, $L(x \mid x) = 1$ and $L(\cdot \mid x)$ is nondecreasing. Thus, $L(\cdot \mid x)$ is a distribution function.

Next, notice that if $x' > x$, then for all y, $L(y \mid x') \leq L(y \mid x)$. In other words, the distribution $L(\cdot \mid x')$ stochastically dominates the distribution $L(\cdot \mid x)$.

Since $v(y, y)$ is an increasing function of y, this means that $\beta \equiv \beta^{\mathrm{I}}$ is an increasing function of x.

Now consider a bidder who bids $\beta(z)$ when his signal is x. The expected profit from such a bid can be written as

$$\Pi(z, x) = \int_0^z \left(v(x, y) - \beta(z) \right) g(y \mid x) \, dy$$

since β is increasing.

Differentiating with respect to z yields

$$\frac{\partial \Pi}{\partial z} \; = \; \left(v(x, z) - \beta(z) \right) g(z \mid x) - \beta'(z) G(z \mid x)$$

$$= \; G(z \mid x) \left[\left(v(x, z) - \beta(z) \right) \frac{g(z \mid x)}{G(z \mid x)} - \beta'(z) \right]$$

If $z < x$, then since $v(x, z) > v(z, z)$ and because of affiliation,

$$\frac{g(z \mid x)}{G(z \mid x)} > \frac{g(z \mid z)}{G(z \mid z)}$$

we obtain that

$$\frac{\partial \Pi}{\partial z} > G(z \mid x) \left[\left(v(z, z) - \beta(z) \right) \frac{g(z \mid z)}{G(z \mid z)} - \beta'(z) \right] = 0$$

using (6.6). Similarly, if $z > x$, then $\frac{\partial \Pi}{\partial z} < 0$. Thus, $\Pi(z, x)$ is maximized by choosing $z = x$. ∎

Proposition 6.3 is, of course, a generalization of Proposition 2.2. When values are private, $v(y, y) = y$. Also, when signals are independent, $G(\cdot \mid x)$

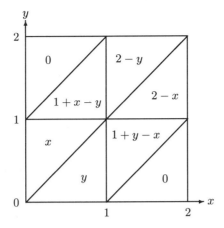

FIGURE 6.2. Joint Density of X_1 and Y_1 in Example 6.2

does not depend on x, so we can write $G(\cdot \mid x) \equiv G(\cdot)$. Thus,

$$
\begin{aligned}
L(y \mid x) &= \exp\left(-\int_y^x \frac{g(t)}{G(t)}\,dt\right) \\
&= \frac{1}{G(x)}G(y)
\end{aligned}
$$

so $\beta^{\mathrm{I}}(x)$ in the previous derivation reduces to $E\left[Y_1 \mid Y_1 < x\right]$, the equilibrium bid with private values.

Again, it is instructive to find the equilibrium bidding strategy explicitly in the context of a relatively simple example in which values are interdependent and signals are affiliated.

Example 6.2 *Suppose S_1, S_2, and T are uniformly and independently distributed on $[0, 1]$. There are two bidders. Bidder 1 receives the signal $X_1 = S_1 + T$, and bidder 2 receives the signal $X_2 = S_2 + T$. The object has a common value*

$$
V = \frac{1}{2}(X_1 + X_2)
$$

for both the bidders.

Even though S_1, S_2, and T are independently distributed, the random variables X_1 and X_2 are affiliated. Moreover, since there are only two bidders, $Y_1 = X_2$. The joint density of X_1 and Y_1 is given in Figure 6.2 and from this it may be calculated that for all $x \in [0, 2]$,

$$
\frac{g(x \mid x)}{G(x \mid x)} = \frac{2}{x}
$$

and for all $y \in [0, x]$,

$$L(y \mid x) = \frac{y^2}{x^2}$$

From Proposition 6.3 the equilibrium bidding strategy in a first-price auction is

$$
\begin{aligned}
\beta^{\mathrm{I}}(x) &= \int_0^x v(y, y) \, dL(y \mid x) \\
&= \frac{2}{3}x
\end{aligned}
$$

using the fact that $v(x, y) = \frac{1}{2}(x + y)$. ▲

6.5   Revenue Comparisons

We now examine the performance of the three auctions studied here by comparing the expected revenues resulting in symmetric equilibria of each. Our main finding will be that under the assumption that signals are affiliated, the English auction out-performs the second-price auction, which in turn, out-performs the first-price auction. The reasons underlying these results are explored in the next chapter.

6.5.1   English versus Second-Price Auctions

Proposition 6.4 *The expected revenue from an English auction is at least as great as the expected revenue from a second-price auction.*

Proof. Recall from Proposition 6.1 that symmetric equilibrium strategies in a second-price auction are given by $\beta^{\mathrm{II}}(x) = v(x, x)$, where $v(x, y)$ is defined in (6.3). Thus, we have that, if $x > y$,

$$
\begin{aligned}
v(y, y) &= E\left[u(X_1, Y_1, Y_2, \ldots, Y_{N-1}) \mid X_1 = y, Y_1 = y\right] \\
&= E\left[u(Y_1, Y_1, Y_2, \ldots, Y_{N-1}) \mid X_1 = y, Y_1 = y\right] \\
&\leq E\left[u(Y_1, Y_1, Y_2, \ldots, Y_{N-1}) \mid X_1 = x, Y_1 = y\right] \quad (6.8)
\end{aligned}
$$

where the last inequality follows from the fact that u is increasing in all its arguments and all signals are affiliated. The expected revenue in a second-price auction can be written as

$$
\begin{aligned}
E\left[R^{\mathrm{II}}\right] &= E\left[\beta^{\mathrm{II}}(Y_1) \mid X_1 > Y_1\right] \\
&= E\left[v(Y_1, Y_1) \mid X_1 > Y_1\right] \\
&\leq E\left[E\left[u(Y_1, Y_1, Y_2, \ldots, Y_{N-1}) \mid X_1 = x, Y_1 = y\right] \mid X_1 > Y_1\right] \\
&= E\left[u(Y_1, Y_1, Y_2, \ldots, Y_{N-1}) \mid X_1 > Y_1\right] \\
&= E\left[\beta^2(Y_1, Y_2, \ldots, Y_{N-1})\right] \\
&= E\left[R^{\mathrm{Eng}}\right]
\end{aligned}
$$

where we have used (6.8) and, as defined in Proposition 6.2, β^2 is the strategy used in an English auction when only two bidders remain. The price at which the second-to-last bidder drops out, $\beta^2(Y_1, Y_2, \ldots, Y_{N-1})$, is, of course, the price paid by the winning bidder. ∎

We postpone discussion of this result, and the reasons underlying it, until the next chapter. For the moment, notice that the English auction yields a strictly higher revenue than a second-price auction only if values are interdependent *and* signals are affiliated. With private values, the two are equivalent. The same is true if signals are independent.

6.5.2   Second-Price versus First-Price Auctions

Proposition 6.5 *The expected revenue from a second-price auction is at least as great as the expected revenue from a first-price auction.*

Proof. The payment of a bidder with signal x upon winning the object in a first-price auction is just his bid $\beta^{\mathrm{I}}(x)$, where β^{I} is defined in Proposition 6.3. The expected payment of a bidder with signal x upon winning the object in a second-price auction is $E[\beta^{\mathrm{II}}(Y_1) \mid X_1 = x, Y_1 < x]$, where β^{II} is defined in Proposition 6.1. We will show that the former is no greater than the latter. Since in both auctions the probability that a bidder with signal x will win the auction is the same—it is just the probability that x is the highest signal—this will establish the proposition.

From Proposition 6.1,

$$
\begin{aligned}
E\left[\beta^{\mathrm{II}}(Y_1) \mid X_1 = x, Y_1 < x\right] &= E\left[v(Y_1, Y_1) \mid X_1 = x, Y_1 < x\right] \\
&= \int_0^x v(y, y)\, dK(y \mid x)
\end{aligned}
$$

and where for all $y < x$,

$$
K(y \mid x) \equiv \frac{1}{G(x \mid x)} G(y \mid x) \tag{6.9}
$$

and notice that $K(\cdot \mid x)$ is a distribution function with support $[0, x]$.

Now recall from Proposition 6.3 that

$$\beta^{\mathrm{I}}(x) = \int_0^x v(y, y) \, dL(y \mid x)$$

where $L(\cdot \mid x)$, defined in (6.7), is also a distribution function with support $[0, x]$.

We will argue that for all $y < x$, $K(y \mid x) \leq L(y \mid x)$ or, in other words, that $K(\cdot \mid x)$ stochastically dominates $L(\cdot \mid x)$. Since v is an increasing function of its arguments, this will complete the proof of the proposition.

To verify the stochastic dominance, note that because of affiliation, for all $t < x$, $G(\cdot \mid x)$ dominates $G(\cdot \mid t)$ in terms of the reverse hazard rate (see (6.1)), so for all $t < x$,

$$\frac{g(t \mid t)}{G(t \mid t)} \leq \frac{g(t \mid x)}{G(t \mid x)}$$

and hence, for all $y < x$,

$$
\begin{aligned}
-\int_y^x \frac{g(t \mid t)}{G(t \mid t)} \, dt \quad &\geq \quad -\int_y^x \frac{g(t \mid x)}{G(t \mid x)} \, dt \\
&= \quad -\int_y^x \frac{d}{dt} \left(\ln G(t \mid x) \right) dt \\
&= \quad \ln G(y \mid x) - \ln G(x \mid x) \\
&= \quad \ln \left(\frac{G(y \mid x)}{G(x \mid x)} \right)
\end{aligned}
$$

Applying the exponential function to both sides, we obtain that for all $y < x$,

$$L(y \mid x) \geq K(y \mid x)$$

and this completes the proof. ∎

The next example illustrates the workings of Proposition 6.5 by explicitly calculating the expected revenues in the second- and first-price auctions in the setting of Example 6.2.

Example 6.3 *As in Example 6.2, suppose that S_1, S_2, and T are uniformly and independently distributed on $[0, 1]$. Bidder 1 receives the signal $X_1 = S_1 + T$, and bidder 2 receives the signal $X_2 = S_2 + T$. The object has a common value*

$$V = \frac{1}{2}(X_1 + X_2)$$

to both the bidders.

In this example, $v(x,y) = \frac{1}{2}(x+y)$, so in a second-price auction the equilibrium bidding strategy is

$$\beta^{\mathrm{II}}(x) = x$$

The expected revenue in a second-price auction is thus

$$
\begin{aligned}
E\left[R^{\mathrm{II}}\right] &= E\left[\min\{X_1, X_2\}\right] \\
&= E\left[\min\{S_1, S_2\}\right] + E\left[T\right] \\
&= \frac{5}{6}
\end{aligned}
$$

In a first-price auction, we know from Example 6.2 that the equilibrium bidding strategy is

$$\beta^{\mathrm{I}}(x) = \frac{2}{3}x$$

The expected revenue in a first-price auction is thus

$$
\begin{aligned}
E\left[R^{\mathrm{I}}\right] &= E\left[\max\left\{\frac{2}{3}X_1, \frac{2}{3}X_2\right\}\right] \\
&= \frac{2}{3}E\left[\max\{S_1, S_2\}\right] + \frac{2}{3}E\left[T\right] \\
&= \frac{7}{9}
\end{aligned}
$$

and so $E\left[R^{\mathrm{II}}\right] > E\left[R^{\mathrm{I}}\right]$. ▲

The conclusions of Propositions 6.4 and 6.5 are summarized as follows:

Proposition 6.6 *In the symmetric model with interdependent values and affiliated signals, the English, second-price, and first-price auctions can be ranked in terms of expected revenue as follows:*

$$E\left[R^{\mathrm{Eng}}\right] \geq E\left[R^{\mathrm{II}}\right] \geq E\left[R^{\mathrm{I}}\right]$$

Equilibrium Bidding and the Winner's Curse

At the beginning of the chapter we pointed out that a bidder in a first-price auction needs to shade his bid, relative to the estimated value based on his own signal alone, by a factor large enough to avoid the winner's curse. We now verify that the equilibrium bidding strategies in a first-price auction indeed have this feature. Observe that

$$
\begin{aligned}
\beta^{\mathrm{I}}(x) &= \int_0^x v(y,y)\, dL(y \mid x) \\
&\le \int_0^x v(y,y)\, dK(y \mid x) \\
&< \int_0^x v(x,y)\, dK(y \mid x) \\
&= E\left[V_1 \mid X_1 = x, Y_1 < x\right]
\end{aligned}
$$

where $L(\cdot \mid x)$ is defined in (6.7), $K(\cdot \mid x)$ is defined in (6.9). The proof of Proposition 6.5 shows that $K(\cdot \mid x)$ stochastically dominates $L(\cdot \mid x)$, and this implies the first inequality. The second inequality follows from the fact that $v(\cdot, y)$ is increasing. Thus, we have shown that the equilibrium bid in a first-price auction is less than the expected value conditional on winning—such behavior shields bidders from the winner's curse.

The same is true in a sealed-bid second-price auction. The expected selling price upon winning is

$$
\begin{aligned}
E\left[\beta^{\mathrm{II}}(Y_1) \mid X_1 = x, Y_1 < x\right] &= \int_0^x v(y,y)\, dK(y \mid x) \\
&< E\left[V_1 \mid X_1 = x, Y_1 < x\right]
\end{aligned}
$$

as noted earlier. Thus, equilibrium bidding strategies in a second-price auction are also immune to the winner's curse.

6.6   Efficiency

In the context of the symmetric model used in this chapter, all three of the auction forms considered here—second-price, English, and first-price—have symmetric and increasing equilibria. This means that the winning bidder is the one with the highest *signal*. An auction allocates efficiently if the bidder with the highest *value* is awarded the object and the bidder with the highest signal need not be the one with the highest value.

Example 6.4 *Symmetric equilibria may be inefficient.*

For instance, if the valuations in a two-bidder symmetric situation are

$$
\begin{aligned}
v_1(x_1, x_2) &= \tfrac{1}{3}x_1 + \tfrac{2}{3}x_2 \\
v_2(x_1, x_2) &= \tfrac{2}{3}x_1 + \tfrac{1}{3}x_2
\end{aligned}
$$

then $v_1 > v_2$ if and only if $x_2 > x_1$. Thus, in this example, the bidder with the higher signal is the one with the *lower* value, so all three auction forms, almost always, allocate the object inefficiently. The reason is that each bidder's signal has a greater influence on the other bidder's valuation than it does on his own valuation. ▲

We will say that the valuations satisfy the *single crossing condition* if for all i and $j \neq i$ and for all $\mathbf{x}$,

$$\frac{\partial v_i}{\partial x_i}(\mathbf{x}) \geq \frac{\partial v_j}{\partial x_i}(\mathbf{x}) \tag{6.10}$$

The single crossing condition—so named because it implies that, keeping all other signals fixed, i's valuation as a function of i's signal x_i is steeper than j's valuation, so the two cross at most once—will play a significant role in later chapters.

Recall that in the symmetric model with interdependent values, the value to i is written as

$$v_i(\mathbf{x}) = u(x_i, \mathbf{x}_{-i})$$

and it is assumed that the function u is symmetric in its last $N - 1$ arguments. Let u_1' denote the partial derivative of u with respect to its first argument and, in general, let u_j' denote the partial derivative of u with respect to its jth argument. In the symmetric case, the single crossing condition reduces to requiring that for all $j \neq 1$, $u_1' \geq u_j'$ and since u is symmetric in the last $N - 1$ arguments, it is enough to suppose that $u_1' > u_2'$.

The single crossing condition ensures that the *ex post* values of different bidders will be ordered in the same way as their signals. To see this, suppose that $x_i > x_j$, and define $\boldsymbol{\alpha}(t) = (1 - t)(x_j, x_i, \mathbf{x}_{-ij}) + t(x_i, x_j, \mathbf{x}_{-ij})$ to be the line joining the points $(x_j, x_i, \mathbf{x}_{-ij})$ and $(x_i, x_j, \mathbf{x}_{-ij})$. Using the fundamental theorem of calculus for line integrals, we can write

$$u(x_i, x_j, \mathbf{x}_{-ij}) = u(x_j, x_i, \mathbf{x}_{-ij}) + \int_0^1 \nabla u(\boldsymbol{\alpha}(t)) \cdot \boldsymbol{\alpha}'(t)\, dt$$

where

$$
\begin{aligned}
\nabla u(\boldsymbol{\alpha}(t)) \cdot \boldsymbol{\alpha}'(t) &= u_1'(\boldsymbol{\alpha}(t))(x_i - x_j) + u_2'(\boldsymbol{\alpha}(t))(x_j - x_i) \\
&\geq 0
\end{aligned}
$$

since $x_i > x_j$ and $u_1' \geq u_2'$. So, $x_i > x_j$ implies that bidder i's value, $u(x_i, x_j, \mathbf{x}_{-ij})$, is greater than or equal to bidder j's value, $u(x_j, x_i, \mathbf{x}_{-ij})$.

Thus, we obtain the following:

Proposition 6.7 *With symmetric, interdependent values and affiliated signals, suppose the single crossing condition is satisfied. Then the second-price, English, and first-price auctions all have symmetric equilibria that are efficient.*

Chapter Notes

Auctions for off-shore oil drilling leases led to the development of the pure common value model, specifically the so-called "mineral rights" model. Moving beyond Vickrey's private value setting, early work on characterizing an equilibrium of first-price auctions in this alternative informational setting was carried out by Wilson (1969) and extended by Ortega Reichert (1968) (Wilson's article was available as a working paper in 1966). Wilson (1977) obtained an explicit expression for the equilibrium bidding strategy in a first-price auction in the same model. The presence of the winner's curse as an empirical fact was pointed out by Capen *et al.* (1971) in the context of bidding for offshore oil drilling leases.

The symmetric equilibrium of a second-price auction in a common value setting was derived in a paper by Milgrom (1981).

The symmetric model with interdependent values and affiliated signals— encompassing both the common value and private values models—was introduced by Milgrom and Weber (1982). This paper, now a classic, generalized all known equilibrium characterizations to date for the first-price, second-price, and English auctions and derived the general revenue rankings among the three formats. The main results of this chapter are almost entirely based on this paper.

Avery (1998) has studied an alternative model of the English auction in which bidders can call out prices. The equilibrium described in Proposition 6.2 survives in such a model, but there are other equilibria that involve "jump bidding," in which bidders sometime raise the price by a discrete amount. Avery (1998) shows, however, that the revenue to the seller in such equilibria cannot exceed the revenue from the equilibrium derived in Proposition 6.2.

Example 6.1 belongs to a special class of situations, studied by Harstad and Levin (1985), in which the equilibrium strategy in a second-price auction can be obtained by means of iterative elimination of weakly dominated strategies.

7

The Revenue Ranking ("Linkage") Principle

In the previous chapter we compared the three common auction formats by directly computing the expected revenues in the respective symmetric equilibria. In particular, we showed that the revenue in a second-price auction exceeded that in its first-price counterpart. Just as the revenue equivalence principle isolates the reasons underlying the equality of revenues between the second- and first-price auctions, the main result of this chapter, the *linkage* principle, isolates the reasons underlying the revenue rankings of the previous chapter.

7.1 The Main Result

As in the derivation of the revenue equivalence principle, it is convenient to abstract away from the specific rules of a particular format and concentrate on its essential mechanics. Consider the symmetric setting of the previous chapter. Suppose A is a standard auction in which the highest bid wins the object and that it has a symmetric equilibrium, β^A. Consider bidder 1, say, and suppose that all other bidders follow the symmetric equilibrium strategy. Let $W^A(z, x)$ denote the expected price paid by bidder 1 if he is the *winning* bidder when he receives a signal x but bids as if his signal were z (that is, he bids $\beta^A(z)$).

In a first-price auction, the winning bidder pays exactly what he bid, so

$$W^{\mathrm{I}}(z, x) = \beta^{\mathrm{I}}(z)$$

where β^{I} is the symmetric equilibrium strategy in the auction. In a second-price sealed-bid auction, however, the winning bidder pays the second-highest bid. From his perspective, the amount he will have to pay is uncertain, so the expected payment upon winning is

$$W^{\mathrm{II}}(z, x) = E[\beta^{\mathrm{II}}(Y_1) \mid X_1 = x, Y_1 < z]$$

where β^{II} is the symmetric equilibrium strategy in the second-price auction.

Let $W_2^A(z, x)$ denote the partial derivative of the function $W^A(\cdot, \cdot)$ with respect to its second argument, evaluated at the point (z, x). The following result is called the revenue ranking or linkage principle.

Proposition 7.1 *Let A and B be two auctions in which the highest bidder wins and only he pays a positive amount. Suppose that each has a symmetric and increasing equilibrium such that (i) for all x, $W_2^A(x, x) \geq W_2^B(x, x)$; (ii) $W^A(0, 0) = 0 = W^B(0, 0)$. Then the expected revenue in A is at least as large as the expected revenue in B.*

Proof. Consider auction A and suppose that all bidders $j \neq 1$ follow the symmetric equilibrium strategy β^A. The probability that bidder 1 with signal x who bids $\beta^A(z)$ will win is just $G(z \mid x) \equiv \mathrm{Prob}[Y_1 < z \mid X_1 = x]$. Thus, each bidder in auction A maximizes

$$\int_0^z v(x, y) g(y \mid x) \, dy - G(z \mid x) W^A(z, x)$$

In equilibrium it is optimal to choose $z = x$, so the relevant first-order condition is

$$g(x \mid x) v(x, x) - g(x \mid x) W^A(x, x) - G(x \mid x) W_1^A(x, x) = 0$$

where W_1^A denotes the partial derivative of W^A with respect to its first argument. This can be rearranged so that

$$W_1^A(x, x) = \frac{g(x \mid x)}{G(x \mid x)} v(x, x) - \frac{g(x \mid x)}{G(x \mid x)} W^A(x, x)$$

Similarly,

$$W_1^B(x, x) = \frac{g(x \mid x)}{G(x \mid x)} v(x, x) - \frac{g(x \mid x)}{G(x \mid x)} W^B(x, x)$$

and hence

$$W_1^A(x, x) - W_1^B(x, x) = -\frac{g(x \mid x)}{G(x \mid x)} [W^A(x, x) - W^B(x, x)] \qquad (7.1)$$

Now define

$$\Delta(x) = W^A(x, x) - W^B(x, x)$$

so that

$$\Delta'(x) = [W_1^A(x,x) - W_1^B(x,x)] + [W_2^A(x,x) - W_2^B(x,x)] \qquad (7.2)$$

Using (7.1) in (7.2) yields

$$\Delta'(x) = -\frac{g(x \mid x)}{G(x \mid x)}\Delta(x) + [W_2^A(x,x) - W_2^B(x,x)] \qquad (7.3)$$

By hypothesis, the second term in (7.3) is nonnegative. Thus, if $\Delta(x) \leq 0$, then $\Delta'(x) \geq 0$. Furthermore, by assumption $\Delta(0) = 0$. Thus, we must have that for all x, $\Delta(x) \geq 0$. ∎

Proposition 7.1 leads to a ranking of alternative auction forms by comparing the statistical linkages between a bidder's own signal and the price he would pay upon winning. The greater the linkage between a bidder's own information and how he perceives others will bid, the greater the expected price paid upon winning.

As such, Proposition 7.1 does not make any assumptions regarding the distribution of bidders' signals—whether they are affiliated or not. It relies only on the some properties of the maximization problem that bidders face. In applying it, however, we will make use of the assumption that bidders' signals are affiliated.

First-Price versus Second-Price Auctions

The revenue ranking principle sheds useful light on why the second-price auction out-performs the first-price auction in terms of revenue (Proposition 6.4). This is because for the first-price auction,

$$W^{\mathrm{I}}(z,x) = \beta^{\mathrm{I}}(z)$$

where β^{I} is the symmetric equilibrium strategy, so $W_2^{\mathrm{I}}(x,x) = 0$ for all x.

For a second-price auction, on the other hand,

$$W^{\mathrm{II}}(z,x) = E[\beta^{\mathrm{II}}(Y_1) \mid X_1 = x, Y_1 < z]$$

where β^{II} is the symmetric equilibrium strategy in a second-price auction. Since β^{II} is increasing, affiliation now implies that for all x, $W_2^{\mathrm{II}}(x,x) \geq 0$. Thus, from Proposition 7.1 we conclude that the revenue from the latter is no less than that from the former.

If signals are independently distributed, then in any auction A satisfying the preceding hypotheses, $W^A(z,x)$ does not depend on x. So $W_2^A(z,x) = 0 = W_2^B(z,x)$ for any two auctions A and B. In that case, $W^A(x,x) = W^B(x,x)$, so the revenues in the two auctions are the same.

Proposition 7.1 thus implies the revenue equivalence principle in Proposition 3.1. This argument also highlights the fact that the assumption of private values is unimportant for revenue equivalence—as long as the bidders' signals are independently distributed, revenue equivalence obtains even with interdependent values.

7.2   Public Information

In many instances the seller may have information that is potentially useful to the bidders. What should the seller do with this information? Should the seller keep it hidden or should she reveal it publicly? Should she be strategic, revealing the information only when it is favorable?

To address these and related questions, the symmetric model considered in Chapter 6 needs to be slightly amended. Specifically, let S be a random variable that denotes the information available to the seller. This information, if known, would affect the valuations of the bidders, so we now write these as a function of the $N + 1$ signals

$$V_i = v_i (S, X_1, X_2, \ldots, X_N)$$

and we assume, as before, that $v_i (\mathbf{0}) = 0$. In the symmetric case, which is our focus here, we write

$$v_i (S, \mathbf{X}) = u (S, X_i, \mathbf{X}_{-i})$$

where u is, as before, a symmetric function of its last $N - 1$ arguments. The variables $S, X_1, X_2, \ldots, X_N$ are assumed to be affiliated and distributed according to a joint density function f, which is a symmetric function of its last N arguments, the bidders' signals.

When public information is *not* available, the bidders do not know the realization of S before bidding, so we can, as before, define

$$v (x, y) = E [V_1 \mid X_1 = x, Y_1 = y] \tag{7.4}$$

where now the unknown public information S has also been integrated out.

Now suppose that the seller reveals the information in a nonstrategic manner—it is made public in all circumstances. As a result, the bidders know the realization of S before bidding and we define in an analogous manner

$$\widehat{v} (s, x, y) = E [V_1 \mid S = s, X_1 = x, Y_1 = y] \tag{7.5}$$

to be the expectation of the value to bidder 1 when the public signal is s, the signal the bidder receives is x and the highest signal among the other bidders is y. Because of symmetry, this function is the same for all bidders, and because of affiliation, $\hat{v}$ is an increasing function of its arguments. Moreover, $\hat{v}(0,0,0) = 0$. With publicly available information, the function $\hat{v}$ will play the same role as that played by v in the previous chapter. Clearly,

$$v(x, y) = E\left[\hat{v}(S, X_1, Y_1) \mid X_1 = x, Y_1 = y\right] \tag{7.6}$$

What effect does a policy of revealing information in all circumstances have on the seller's expected revenue? We begin by looking at first-price auctions.

Public Information in a First-Price Auction

To derive the effects of public information it is useful to think of the two situations—with and without the information—as two different "auctions." Then we can use the machinery of Proposition 7.1 to compare the two.

When public information is available, a bidder's strategy is a function of both the public information S and his own signal X_i. Temporarily, suppose that there exists a symmetric equilibrium strategy of the form $\hat{\beta}(S, X_i)$, which is increasing in both variables. The expected payment of a winning bidder when he receives a signal x but bids as if his signal were z (that is, for all $S = s$, he bids $\hat{\beta}(s,z)$) is

$$\widehat{W}^{\mathrm{I}}(z, x) = E\left[\hat{\beta}(S, z) \mid X_1 = x\right]$$

so that $\widehat{W}_2^{\mathrm{I}}(z, x) \geq 0$, because S and X_1 are affiliated.

When public information is not available, then, as before, we have that if $\beta \equiv \beta^{\mathrm{I}}$ is the equilibrium strategy in a first-price auction,

$$W^{\mathrm{I}}(z, x) = \beta(z)$$

so that $W_2^{\mathrm{I}}(z, x) = 0$.

Thus,

$$\widehat{W}_2^{\mathrm{I}}(z, x) \geq W_2^{\mathrm{I}}(z, x)$$

We can now apply the linkage principle: Proposition 7.1 implies that the expected revenue in a first-price auction is *higher* when public information is made available than when it is not.

In arguing that publicly available information enhances the revenue from a first-price auction, we temporarily supposed that there exists a symmetric and increasing equilibrium in the case when public information is made available. This may be verified in a manner analogous to Proposition 6.3. By mimicking the arguments there, it can be shown that the strategy

$$\hat{\beta}^{\mathrm{I}}(s, x) = \int_0^x \hat{v}(s, y, y) \, d\hat{L}(y \mid s, x)$$

where

$$\widehat{L}\left(y \mid s, x\right) = \exp\left(-\int_{y}^{x} \frac{g\left(t \mid s, t\right)}{G\left(t \mid s, t\right)}\, dt\right)$$

constitutes an equilibrium of the first-price auction with publicly available information.

Public Information in Second-Price and English Auctions

The release of public information also raises revenues in both second-price and English auctions. The arguments are almost the same as in Proposition 6.4, so are omitted.

7.3   An Alternative Linkage Principle

Proposition 7.1 applies to auctions in which only the winner pays a positive amount; it does not apply, for instance, to all-pay auctions. A similar result that does apply to such situations is available.

Let $M^{A}\left(z, x\right)$ be the expected payment by a bidder with signal x who bids as if his or her signal were z in an auction mechanism A. The advantage of this specification is that we do not assume that only the winner pays a positive amount.

For instance, for an all-pay auction, $M^{\mathrm{AP}}\left(z, x\right) = \beta^{\mathrm{AP}}\left(z\right)$, where β^{AP} is a symmetric and increasing equilibrium strategy if one exists. For auctions in which only the winner pays, $M^{A}\left(z, x\right) = F_{Y_{1}}\left(z \mid x\right) W^{A}\left(z, x\right)$. So in a first-price auction, $M^{\mathrm{I}}\left(z, x\right) = F_{Y_{1}}\left(z \mid x\right) \beta^{\mathrm{I}}\left(z\right)$.

The following is an alternative version of the linkage principle. While it reaches the same conclusion as does Proposition 7.1, its hypotheses concern the relative responsiveness of the unconditional expected payment, $M^{A}\left(z, x\right)$, to a change in a bidder's own signal rather than the relative responsiveness of the expected payment conditional on winning, $W^{A}\left(z, x\right)$, to the same change.

Proposition 7.2 *Let A and B be two auctions in which the highest bidder wins. Suppose that each has a symmetric and increasing equilibrium such that (i) for all x, $M_{2}^{A}(x, x) \geq M_{2}^{B}(x, x)$; (ii) $M^{A}(0, 0) = 0 = M^{B}(0, 0)$. Then the expected revenue in A is at least as large as the expected revenue in B.*

Proof. The expected payoff of a bidder with signal x who bids $\beta^{A}(z)$ is

$$\int_{-\infty}^{z} v\left(x, y\right) g\left(y \mid x\right) dy - M^{A}\left(z, x\right)$$

In equilibrium, it is optimal to choose $z = x$ and the resulting first-order conditions imply that

$$M_1^A(x, x) = v(x, x) g(x \mid x) \tag{7.7}$$

Now writing $\Delta(x) = M^A(x, x) - M^B(x, x)$ and using (7.7) we deduce that

$$\Delta'(x) = M_2^A(x, x) - M_2^B(x, x) \geq 0$$

by assumption. Since $\Delta(0) = 0$, for all x, $\Delta(x) \geq 0$. ∎

Ranking All-Pay Auctions

To see how Proposition 7.2 can be used to rank other auction forms, consider an all-pay auction in an environment with interdependent values and affiliated signals.

First, as noted earlier, in a first-price auction,

$$M^I(z, x) = G(z \mid x) \beta^I(z)$$

so

$$M_2^I(z, x) = \frac{\partial}{\partial x} \left[G(z \mid x) \beta^I(z) \right] < 0$$

since affiliation implies that $G(z \mid \cdot)$ is decreasing.

Suppose that there is a symmetric, increasing equilibrium in the all-pay auction, say β^{AP}. Then, by definition,

$$M^{AP}(z, x) = \beta^{AP}(z)$$

so that

$$M_2^{AP}(z, x) = \frac{\partial}{\partial x} \beta^{AP}(z) = 0$$

Since, $M_2^{AP}(x, x) > M_2^I(x, x)$, an application of Proposition 7.2 implies that the expected revenue from an all-pay auction, provided it has an increasing equilibrium, is greater than that from a first-price auction.

It can be argued that, provided that the function $v(\cdot, y)g(y \mid \cdot)$ is increasing, the following is a symmetric increasing equilibrium of the all-pay auction:

$$\beta^{AP}(x) = \int_0^x v(y, y) g(y \mid y) \, dy$$

Chapter Notes

The revenue ranking (or linkage) principle, Proposition 7.1, was first set forth and used by Milgrom and Weber (1982). The results on public information are also from this paper.

The alternative form of the linkage principle, Proposition 7.2, and its application to ranking the all-pay auction relative to the first-price auction is due to Krishna and Morgan (1997). This paper also derives some sufficient conditions for the existence of a symmetric, increasing equilibrium in the all-pay auction. Amann and Leininger (1995) also compare the revenues from all-pay auctions to those from a first-price auction.

Biologists have studied the *war of attrition*, in which two players engage in a struggle during which both expend resources. The game ends when one of the players gives up so that the winning player expends the same amount as the losing player. This is essentially a *second-price all-pay auction*, and it can be shown that if it has a symmetric, increasing equilibrium, then it is revenue superior to the ordinary second-price auction (see Krishna and Morgan, 1997).

8
Asymmetries and Other Complications

The symmetric model with interdependent values and affiliated signals provides many important insights into the functioning of different auction institutions. First, the three common formats—the first-price, second-price, and English auctions—can be unambiguously ranked in terms of revenue. Second, the release of public information in any of the three formats erodes the exclusivity of bidders' information, dissipating informational rents and leading to higher revenues. When bidders are *ex ante* symmetric, both categories of results hold regardless of the specific valuation function that bidders have and the specific distribution of their signals. The theory is both powerful and elegant.

This chapter strikes a discordant note. Much of the theory developed in the symmetric case is fragile and does not extend to situations in which bidders are asymmetric.

8.1 Failures of the Linkage Principle

Revenue Rankings Do Not Extend

We have already seen that the fact that in a symmetric model the second-price auction out-performs the first-price auction in terms of revenue does not extend to the case of asymmetric bidders. In Example 4.3, the expected revenue in a first-price auction exceeded that in a second-price auction. We now demonstrate, by means of another example, that the other revenue ranking result from the symmetric model—showing that the English auction out-performs the second-price auction—also does not extend to the case of asymmetric bidders. Since the two auctions are strategically equivalent when there are only two bidders, such an example must involve at least three bidders.

Example 8.1 *With asymmetric bidders, the expected revenue in a second-price auction may exceed that in an English auction.*

Suppose that there are three bidders. Bidders 1 and 2 attach a common value to the object, whereas bidder 3 has private values. Specifically,

$$v_1(x_1, x_2, x_3) = \tfrac{1}{2}x_1 + \tfrac{1}{2}x_2$$
$$v_2(x_1, x_2, x_3) = \tfrac{1}{2}x_1 + \tfrac{1}{2}x_2$$
$$v_3(x_1, x_2, x_3) = x_3$$

Further, suppose that X_1, X_2, and X_3 are independently and uniformly distributed on $[0, 1]$.

Equilibrium and Revenues in a Second-Price Auction

Since she has private values, it is a weakly dominant strategy for bidder 3 to bid her value. Let β denote the bidding strategy for bidders 1 and 2 (by symmetry we can suppose that they use the same strategy) and suppose that β is increasing and continuous. Armed with some foreknowledge, let us suppose that for $i = 1, 2$, $\beta(x_i) = kx_i$ where $k > 0$ is a constant. Given that bidder 2 bids according to $\beta(x_2) = kx_2$ and bidder 3 bids her value x_3, the price that bidder 1 pays upon winning is $\max\{kX_2, X_3\}$. The expected payoff of bidder 1 when his signal is x_1 and he bids b is

$$\Pi_1(b, x_1) = \int_0^{b/k}\left[\int_0^{kx_2}\left(\frac{x_1 + x_2}{2} - kx_2\right)dx_3\right.$$
$$\left. + \int_{kx_2}^b\left(\frac{x_1 + x_2}{2} - x_3\right)dx_3\right]dx_2$$

where the first integral in the square brackets comes from the event $\beta(X_2) > X_3$ and the second from the event $\beta(X_2) < X_3$. It may be verified that

$$\Pi_1(b, x_1) = \frac{1}{12k^2}\left(6x_1 b^2 k + 3b^3 - 8b^3 k\right)$$

Maximizing this with respect to b shows that if bidder 2 follows the strategy $\beta(x_2) = kx_2$, it is also optimal for bidder 1 to follow a linear strategy. Since bidders 1 and 2 follow the same strategy, setting $b = kx_1$ at the optimum yields the solution that $k = 7/8$.

Thus, it is an equilibrium for both bidders 1 and 2 to bid k times their values and for bidder 3 to bid her value. The price is then the second highest of kX_1, kX_2, X_3, and its distribution is easily computed to be as follows: for any $p \leq k$,

$$L^{II}(p) \equiv \text{Prob}\left[R^{II} \leq p\right] = \frac{p^2 + 2kp^2 - 2p^3}{k^2}$$

Thus,

$$E\left[R^{II}\right] = \int_0^k p \, dL^{II}(p) = \frac{175}{384}$$

Equilibrium and Revenues in an English Auction

Once again, since she has private values, it is a weakly dominant strategy for bidder 3 to drop out at her value regardless of the history and who else is active. Moreover, bidder 3's signal affects neither bidder 1's value nor bidder 2's value. The following strategies constitute an *ex post* equilibrium:

	$\{1,2,3\}$	$\{1,2\}$	$\{1,3\}$	$\{2,3\}$
1	x_1	x_1	$\frac{1}{2}x_1 + \frac{1}{2}x_2$	-
2	x_2	x_2	-	$\frac{1}{2}x_1 + \frac{1}{2}x_2$
3	x_3	-	x_3	x_3

The table indicates the price at which each bidder should drop out given the set of active bidders and the previous history of exits. Thus, for instance, bidder 1 should drop out at a price $p = x_1$ if the set of active bidders is $\{1,2,3\}$; at $p = x_1$ if the set of active bidders is $\{1,2\}$; and at $p = \frac{1}{2}x_1 + \frac{1}{2}x_2$ if the set of active bidders is $\{1,3\}$ and bidder 2 dropped out at a price $p_2 = x_2$, so that his equilibrium strategy revealed his signal to bidders 1 and 3. This equilibrium is also completely analogous to the equilibrium of the English auction in the symmetric setting of the previous chapter. It is an *ex post* equilibrium and, given any history, each bidder stays in until the break-even price p such that if all other active bidders were to drop out at p, the value of the object to i would be exactly p.

Figure 8.1 depicts the resulting equilibrium outcomes. Bidder 3's signal is held fixed at some $X_3 = x_3 < \frac{1}{2}$ and in the different regions of (x_1, x_2) space, both the winner's identity—the circled numbers—and the price he or she pays is indicated. Thus, for instance, in the right-hand quadrilateral region, bidder 1 is a winner. When $x_2 > x_3$—above the dotted line—the price is x_2 and when $x_2 < x_3$—below the dotted line—the price is x_3. A similar figure can be drawn for the case where $X_3 = x_3 \geq \frac{1}{2}$.

To compute the expected revenue in the English auction, it is convenient to derive the expected payments of each bidder separately and then find the expected revenue as the sum of these payments. Bidder 1's expected payment is computed as follows. Bidder 1 wins if and only if (i) he is not the

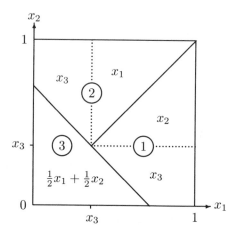

FIGURE 8.1. Equilibrium Outcomes for the English Auction in Example 8.1

first to drop out when all the bidders are active—that is, $x_1 > \min\{x_2, x_3\}$ and (ii) if $x_2 > x_3$, so that bidder 3 drops out first, then $x_1 > x_2$ and the price is x_2; if $x_2 < x_3$, so that bidder 2 drops out first, then $\frac{1}{2}x_1 + \frac{1}{2}x_2 > x_3$ and the price is x_3. Bidder 1's expected payment is (see Figure 8.1)

$$m_1 = \int_0^1 \int_0^{x_1} \left[\int_0^{x_2} x_2 \, dx_3 + \int_{x_2}^{\frac{1}{2}x_1 + \frac{1}{2}x_2} x_3 \, dx_3 \right] dx_2 \, dx_1 = \frac{11}{96}$$

By symmetry, bidder 2's expected payment is the same. Bidder 3's expected payment can be computed in a similar fashion. Bidder 3 wins if and only if $x_3 > \frac{1}{2}x_1 + \frac{1}{2}x_2$, and in that case the price is $\frac{1}{2}x_1 + \frac{1}{2}x_2$. Calculations similar to those above result in

$$\begin{aligned}
m_3 &= 2 \int_0^1 \left[\int_0^{x_3} \int_0^{x_1} \left(\frac{1}{2}x_1 + \frac{1}{2}x_2 \right) dx_2 \, dx_1 \right. \\
&\quad \left. + \int_{x_3}^{\min\{2x_3, 1\}} \int_0^{2x_3 - x_1} \left(\frac{1}{2}x_1 + \frac{1}{2}x_2 \right) dx_2 \, dx_1 \right] dx_3 \\
&= \frac{5}{24}
\end{aligned}$$

The total revenue in an English auction is, therefore,

$$E\left[R^{\text{Eng}} \right] = 2m_1 + m_3 = \frac{7}{16}$$

It may be verified that

$$E\left[R^{\text{Eng}} \right] = \frac{7}{16} < \frac{175}{384} = E\left[R^{\text{II}} \right]$$

and so the expected revenue in a second-price auction is greater than that in an English auction. ▲

Public Information May Decrease Revenue

We saw in the previous chapter that in the symmetric model the release of public information raised the expected revenue of the seller. This is no longer the case once bidders' valuations are asymmetric. Consider the following simple example.

Example 8.2 *With asymmetric bidders, the release of public information in a second-price auction may cause revenues to decrease.*

Suppose there are two bidders who receive private signals X_1 and X_2, respectively. The value of the object to them depends on these signals and also a public signal S. The signals X_1, X_2, and S are uniformly and independently distributed on $[0, 1]$. The valuations are as follows:

$$
\begin{aligned}
v_1(x_1, x_2, s) &= x_1 + \alpha(x_2 + s) \\
v_2(x_1, x_2, s) &= x_2
\end{aligned}
$$

where $0 < \alpha < \frac{2}{3}$.

Suppose that the object is sold using a *second-price* auction. When S is not disclosed, it is an equilibrium for the two bidders to follow the strategies:

$$
\begin{aligned}
\beta_1(x_1) &= \min\left\{\frac{1}{1-\alpha}x_1 + \frac{\alpha}{1-\alpha}E[S], 1\right\} \\
\beta_2(x_2) &= x_2
\end{aligned}
$$

To verify that these constitute an equilibrium, note that $\beta_1(x_1) > \beta_2(x_2)$ if and only if $E[v_1(x_1, x_2, S)] > \beta_2(x_2)$. This implies that regardless of whether he wins or loses, bidder 1 does not regret his bid *ex post*. Likewise, $\beta_2(x_2) > \beta_1(x_1)$ if and only if $E[v_2(x_1, x_2, S)] > \beta_1(x_1)$, so regardless of whether she wins or loses, bidder 2 does not regret her bid *ex post*. The equilibrium price is

$$
R^{\mathrm{II}} = \min\left\{\frac{1}{1-\alpha}X_1 + \frac{\alpha}{1-\alpha}E[S], X_2\right\}
$$

When S is publicly disclosed, both bidders can condition their bids on this information, and now it is an equilibrium for the two bidders to follow the strategies:

$$
\begin{aligned}
\widehat{\beta}_1(x_1, s) &= \min\left\{\frac{1}{1-\alpha}x_1 + \frac{\alpha}{1-\alpha}s, 1\right\} \\
\widehat{\beta}_2(x_2, s) &= x_2
\end{aligned}
$$

It may be verified that these also constitute an equilibrium, much along the same lines as noted earlier. The equilibrium price when S is publicly disclosed is

$$\widehat{R}^{\mathrm{II}} = \min\left\{\frac{1}{1-\alpha}X_1 + \frac{\alpha}{1-\alpha}S, X_2\right\}$$

Now notice that

$$
\begin{aligned}
E\left[\widehat{R}^{\mathrm{II}} \mid X_1 = x_1, X_2 = x_2\right] &= E\left[\min\left\{\frac{1}{1-\alpha}x_1 + \frac{\alpha}{1-\alpha}S, x_2\right\}\right] \\
&< \min\left\{\frac{1}{1-\alpha}x_1 + \frac{\alpha}{1-\alpha}E\left[S\right], x_2\right\} \\
&= E\left[R^{\mathrm{II}} \mid X_1 = x_1, X_2 = x_2\right]
\end{aligned}
$$

since $\min\{\cdot, \cdot\}$ is a concave function. Thus, the expected revenue when information is publicly released is lower than when it is not. ▲

8.2   Asymmetric Equilibria in Symmetric Second-Price Auctions

With private values, it is a weakly dominant strategy to bid one's value in a second-price auction (in an English auction, it is a dominant strategy to drop out when the price reaches the value). With interdependent values, however, bidders typically do not have dominant strategies in either auction format. In the previous chapter, we derived symmetric equilibria of both auctions and compared the resulting revenues. But even with symmetric bidders, the second-price and English auctions may have other, asymmetric, equilibria. Some of these are not without interest.

Consider a situation with only two bidders; in that case, the second-price and English auctions are, of course, equivalent. For the purposes of the examples, it is convenient to denote the signals of the two bidders by X and Y, respectively. It is also convenient to denote by $v_1(x, y)$ the value of the object to bidder 1 and by $v_2(x, y)$ the value to bidder 2. In the symmetric model, for any two possible signals z' and z'', it is the case that $v_1(z', z'') = v_2(z'', z')$. How the signals are distributed does not affect any of what follows.

The situation is symmetric, and in a second-price auction the symmetric equilibrium, as derived in the previous chapter, is $\beta^{\mathrm{II}}(x) = v(x, x) \equiv v_1(x, x)$.

The simplest kind of asymmetric equilibrium is one in which, regardless of his signal, bidder 1, say, never drops out and confronted with this, the other bidder can do no better than to drop out immediately. Specifically, suppose that bidder 1 follows the strategy $\beta_1(x) = 1$, for all x, and bidder 2 follows the strategy $\beta_2(y) = 0$, for all y. This equilibrium, however, involves the use of dominated strategies. In particular, any strategy that calls on bidder 1 with signal $x < 1$ to drop out at a price higher than $v_1(x, 1)$ is dominated.

Example 8.3 *With symmetric pure common values, the second-price auction has asymmetric equilibria that are undominated.*

The situation is one of pure common values if for all possible realizations of the signals X and Y, the value of the object to the two bidders is the same—that is, $v_1(x, y) = v_2(x, y) \equiv u(x, y)$, say. One variety of asymmetric equilibria may be constructed as follows.

Let $\varphi : [0, \omega] \to [0, \omega]$ be an increasing function that is onto. Consider the strategies

$$\begin{aligned}
\beta_1(x) &= u(x, \varphi(x)) \\
\beta_2(y) &= u(\varphi^{-1}(y), y)
\end{aligned}$$

We claim that (β_1, β_2) constitutes an equilibrium of the second-price auction. In fact, it is an *ex post* equilibrium. To see this, consider a particular realization of the signals (x, y) such that $\beta_1(x) > \beta_2(y)$ so that bidder 1 wins the auction and pays a price $p_2 = \beta_2(y)$. Now notice that $\beta_1(\varphi^{-1}(y)) = \beta_2(y)$, and since bidder 1 wins the auction, $\beta_1(x) > \beta_2(y) = \beta_1(\varphi^{-1}(y))$. The equilibrium strategy β_1 is increasing, so $x > \varphi^{-1}(y)$. The *ex post* value of the object is $u(x, y) > u(\varphi^{-1}(y), y) = \beta_2(y)$, the price paid by bidder 1. Thus, bidder 1 makes a positive surplus by winning, and since he cannot affect the price he pays, he cannot do better. A similar argument shows that bidder 2 cannot do better by winning since in order to do so he would have to out-bid bidder 1. The price he would have to pay, $\beta_1(x)$, is such that $\beta_1(x) > u(x, y)$, so bidder 2 does not regret losing. Since neither bidder can gain by deviating, we have argued that (β_1, β_2) constitutes an *ex post* equilibrium.

Since φ was arbitrary, there is a continuum of such equilibria.

Finally, note that for all x, $u(x, 0) < \beta_1(x) < u(x, 1)$ and for all y, $u(0, y) < \beta_2(y) < u(1, y)$. It can be verified that any strategies β_1 and β_2 that are so bounded are undominated. Thus, none of the equilibria constructed here involve the use of dominated strategies. ▲

Example 8.4 *The second-price auction has asymmetric equilibria that are undominated but are discontinuous and inefficient.*

Consider a symmetric situation with two bidders whose signals are X and Y, respectively, and whose values are $v_1(x, y)$ and $v_2(x, y) = v_1(y, x)$. An equilibrium of the second-price auction in which the bidding strategies are discontinuous may be constructed as follows.

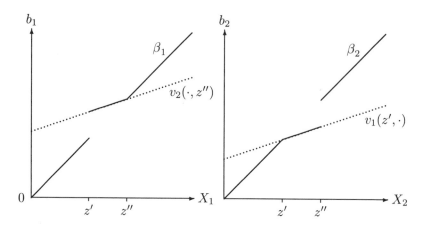

FIGURE 8.2. A Discontinuous Equilibrium in the Second-Price Auction

First, choose two points z' and z'' such that $0 < z' < z'' < 1$. Next consider the following strategies for the two bidders:

$$\beta_1(x) = \begin{cases} v_2(x, z'') & \text{if } x \in [z', z''] \\ \beta^{\text{II}}(x) & \text{otherwise} \end{cases}$$

$$\beta_2(y) = \begin{cases} v_1(z', y) & \text{if } y \in [z', z''] \\ \beta^{\text{II}}(y) & \text{otherwise} \end{cases}$$

where $\beta^{\text{II}}(x) = v_1(x, x)$ is the symmetric equilibrium strategy from the previous chapter. The strategies β_1 and β_2 are discontinuous and differ from β^{II} only in the interval $[z', z'']$. Figure 8.2 depicts the strategies for an example in which

$$v_1(x, y) = \tfrac{2}{3}x + \tfrac{1}{3}y$$
$$v_2(x, y) = \tfrac{1}{3}x + \tfrac{2}{3}y$$

Notice that since $z' < z''$, $\beta_2(z'') = v_1(z', z'') < v_2(z', z'') = \beta_1(z')$. Thus, if both $x, y \in [z', z'']$, then bidder 1 wins the auction.

To see that these strategies form an equilibrium, first suppose that neither x nor y lies in $[z', z'']$. In that case, the bids are the same as in the symmetric equilibrium $\beta^{\text{II}}(x)$, so neither bidder suffers from any *ex post* regret. Second, suppose that both x and y are in $[z', z'']$. In that case, bidder 1 wins the auction and pays $\beta_2(y) = v_1(z', y) \leq v_1(x, y)$, the *ex post* value to bidder 1, so he does not regret winning. Moreover, in order to win, bidder 2 would have to pay $\beta_1(x) = v_2(x, z'') \geq v_2(x, y)$, the *ex post* value to bidder 2, so bidder 2 does not regret losing. Third, suppose that

$x \in [z', z'']$ and $y < z'$. In that case, bidder 1 wins the auction and pays $\beta^{\mathrm{II}}(y) < v_1(z', y) \le v_1(x, y)$, so that he does not regret winning. To win, bidder 2 would have to pay $\beta_1(x) = v_2(x, z'') > v_2(x, y)$, so that he does not regret losing, either. The remaining cases are similar and this shows that the strategies constitute an *ex post* equilibrium.

The asymmetric equilibrium is not efficient, however. If both $x, y \in [z', z'']$, then bidder 1 wins the auction when $x < y$, even though in that case, it is efficient for bidder 2 to win.

Note that by choosing z' and z'' close enough to each other, we can ensure that $v_1(x, 0) < \beta_1(x) < v_1(x, 1)$ and $v_2(0, y) < \beta_2(y) < v_2(1, y)$. This ensures that the equilibrium strategies are not dominated.

Since z' and z'' were arbitrary, we have argued that the second-price auction has a continuum of undominated *ex post* equilibria. ▲

8.3 Asymmetrically Informed Bidders

In this section we consider a different kind of asymmetry among the bidders in the context of interdependent values. Specifically, we consider a situation in which the bidders are asymmetrically informed.

As an extreme case, suppose that bidder 1 is perfectly *informed* of the common value of the object and bidder 2 is completely *uninformed*. In terms of the formulation of the previous chapter, the value of the object to both bidders is the same: $v_1(X_1, X_2) = X_1 = v_2(X_1, X_2)$.

Suppose further that X_1 and X_2 are independently distributed. Thus, bidder 2's signal, X_2, cannot provide any information about the value.

In what follows, let F denote the (marginal) distribution of X_1 with associated density f. We examine equilibrium bidding behavior in first-price sealed-bid auctions.

Notice that in equilibrium it cannot be the case that the uninformed bidder, bidder 2, employs a pure-strategy and always bids a certain amount b, say. If that were the case, then the informed bidder, bidder 1, would bid just over b whenever $X_1 > b$ and bid below b whenever $X_1 < b$. In that case, bidder 2 would win only if $X_1 < b$ and as a result always make a loss. Thus, in equilibrium, bidder 2 must play a mixed or randomized strategy.

Proposition 8.1 *Equilibrium strategies in a first-price sealed-bid auction when bidder 1 is perfectly informed and bidder 2 is completely uninformed are as follows. Bidder 1 bids according to the strategy*

$$\beta(x) = E[X_1 \mid X_1 \le x] \tag{8.1}$$

Bidder 2 chooses a bid at random from the interval $[0, E[X_1]]$ according to the distribution H defined by

$$H(b) = \mathrm{Prob}[\beta(X_1) \le b] \tag{8.2}$$

Proof. Suppose bidder 2 uses the randomized strategy H. Clearly, bidder 1 will never choose a bid that exceeds $E[X_1]$. If bidder 1 with signal x bids an amount $\beta(z) \le E[X_1]$, the probability that bidder 1 will win the auction is just $H(\beta(z))$ and his expected profit is:

$$\begin{aligned} \Pi_1(z, x) &= H(\beta(z)) \times (x - \beta(z)) \\ &= \text{Prob}[X_1 \le z] \times (x - \beta(z)) \\ &= F(z)(x - \beta(z)) \end{aligned}$$

Differentiating this with respect to z yields

$$\begin{aligned} \frac{\partial \Pi_1}{\partial z} &= f(z)(x - \beta(z)) - F(z)\beta(z) \\ &= f(z)x - \frac{d}{dz}(F(z)\beta(z)) \end{aligned} \tag{8.3}$$

Now notice that from (8.1), for all $z \in [0, E[X_1]]$,

$$F(z)\beta(z) = \int_0^z t f(t)\, dt$$

and thus,

$$\frac{d}{dz}(F(z)\beta(z)) = z f(z)$$

Substituting into (8.3) results in

$$\frac{\partial \Pi_1}{\partial z} = f(z)(x - z)$$

so that $\frac{\partial \Pi_1}{\partial z} > 0$ for all $z < x$ and $\frac{\partial \Pi_1}{\partial z} < 0$ for all $z > x$. Thus, it is optimal for bidder 1 to choose $z = x$ or, in other words, to bid $\beta(x)$.

Now consider bidder 2 and suppose that bidder 1 follows the strategy β. Again, clearly bidder 2 will never choose $b > E[X_1]$. If bidder 2 bids b and *wins*, her expected profit is

$$\begin{aligned} E[X_1 \mid \beta(X_1) < b] - b &= E[X_1 \mid X_1 < \beta^{-1}(b)] - b \\ &= \beta(\beta^{-1}(b)) - b \\ &= 0 \end{aligned}$$

The profit if bidder 2 loses is, of course, 0 and thus bidder 2's expected profit from bidding *any* $b \le E[X_1]$ is exactly 0. Thus, we have shown that bidder 2 is indifferent on the support of her mixed strategy. This establishes that bidder 2's strategy is also a best response.

Thus, we have shown that if bidder 1 follows β and bidder 2 randomizes using the distribution H, then this constitutes an equilibrium. ∎

Some features of the equilibrium are worth noting. First, the equilibrium bidding strategy of the informed bidder, β, is the *same* as the equilibrium strategy in a symmetric two-bidder first-price auction with private values independently distributed according to F (as in Proposition 2.2). Although bidder 2 has no information regarding the value, his randomized strategy, H, is such that the distribution of competing bids that bidder 1 faces is the same as if she were confronting a bidder with private values that are independently distributed, also according to F. Now bidder 1 has "private" values since $v_1(X_1, X_2) = X_1$, and because bidder 2's behavior is "as if" he were also in a private value auction, it is a best response for bidder 1 to use β. Second, the expected profits of the uninformed bidder are exactly zero.

8.4   Reserve Prices and Entry Fees

Reserve prices and entry fees serve to exclude buyers with low estimated values. With symmetrically distributed independent private values, we saw that it was always advantageous for the seller to set a positive reserve price, a result called the *exclusion principle* (see Section 2.5 in Chapter 2). We now show that the exclusion principle is no longer valid once values are interdependent and bidders' signals are affiliated. Indeed as the next example demonstrates, the failure of the exclusion principle results neither from the interdependence of values nor from any asymmetry among bidders, but rather from the fact that bidders' information is no longer statistically independent. In the example, bidders have affiliated private values, which are symmetrically distributed.

Example 8.5 *The exclusion principle does not hold if bidders' signals are affiliated.*

Suppose that there are two bidders with private values X_1 and X_2, which are jointly distributed on $[0, 1]^2$ according to the density function

$$f(x_1, x_2) = \begin{cases} \frac{4}{3}x_1 x_2 \left(x_1^{-3} - 1\right) & \text{if } x_1 \geq x_2 \\ \frac{4}{3}x_1 x_2 \left(x_2^{-3} - 1\right) & \text{if } x_1 < x_2 \end{cases}$$

It may be verified that X_1 and X_2 are affiliated. The marginal density of X_1 (or X_2) is

$$f(x) = 2(1 - x)$$

Since there are only two bidders, $Y_1 = X_2$ and the distribution of Y_1 conditional on $X_1 = x$ is

$$G(y \mid x) = \begin{cases} \frac{y^2 \left(x^2 + x + 1\right)}{3x^2} & \text{if } x \geq y \\ \frac{3y - y^3 x - 2x}{3y(1 - x)} & \text{if } x < y \end{cases}$$

Suppose that the object is sold using a second-price auction by a seller who attaches a value of zero to the object. Further, suppose that the seller sets a reserve price of $r \geq 0$. Since values are private, it is a dominant strategy for the bidders to bid their values. The expected payment of bidder 1 with a value $x \geq r$ is then

$$
\begin{aligned}
m^{\mathrm{II}}(x, r) &= rG(r \mid x) + \int_r^x yg(y \mid x)\, dy \\
&= (x^2 + x + 1)\left(\frac{r^3 + 2x^3}{9x^2}\right)
\end{aligned}
$$

The first term in the preceding expression comes from the event that $Y_1 < r$ so that bidder 1 wins and pays the reserve price r. The second term comes from the event that $Y_1 > r$ so that the reserve price does not bind. The *ex ante* expected payment of a bidder when the reserve price is set at r is

$$
\begin{aligned}
E\left[m^{\mathrm{II}}(X_1, r)\right] &= \int_r^1 m(x, r) f(x)\, dx \\
&= \frac{2}{15} - \frac{1}{3}r^3 + \frac{1}{5}r^5
\end{aligned}
$$

and since for all $r > 0$,

$$
\frac{d}{dr}E\left[m^{\mathrm{II}}(X_1, r)\right] < 0
$$

it is optimal to set a reserve price $r^* = 0$. ▲

Why does the exclusion principle fail when values are positively affiliated? The underlying reasons are best seen in the context of a second-price auction. A reserve price r affects revenue in two ways. If the highest value $Y_1^{(N)} < r$, then no sale takes place and this leads to a loss of revenue. On the other hand, if highest value $Y_1^{(N)} > r$ but the second-highest value $Y_2^{(N)} < r$, then there is a gain in revenue since the selling price is now r instead of $Y_2^{(N)}$. Thus, the benefits arise from the event $Y_2^{(N)} < r < Y_1^{(N)}$ and with independent private values, these benefits outweigh the losses from events in which no sale occurs. With affiliated values, the event $Y_2^{(N)} < r < Y_1^{(N)}$ is rarer than if values were independent. This means that with sufficiently strong affiliation, as in Example 8.5, the benefits of a reserve price no longer outweigh the potential losses from not making a sale.

An entry fee excludes buyers as well, so a similar conclusion holds. But entry fees also cause additional complications which are, from the theoretical perspective, more serious. Say that an equilibrium of a symmetric

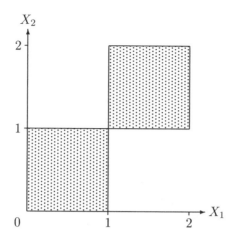

FIGURE 8.3. Support of Joint Distribution of Values in Example 8.6

auction is *monotonic* if (i) there is a threshold x^* such that all buyers with signals $x > x^*$ enter the auction, and (ii) every bidder uses an increasing bidding strategy β upon entering. With independent private values, monotone equilibria exist in all the common auction forms if a positive entry fee is imposed. If signals are affiliated, however, this is no longer the case. It may be that a buyer with signal x' decides to enter the auction, but a buyer with signal $x'' > x'$ decides to stay out. Once again, this is most simply illustrated in an example with affiliated private values.

Example 8.6 *When signals are affiliated, there may not exist a monotonic equilibrium if a positive entry fee is imposed.*

Suppose there are two bidders with private values X_1 and X_2. Suppose that the joint distribution of values f is uniform with support $[0, 1]^2 \cup [1, 2]^2$ (the shaded area in Figure 8.3). It is easy to verify that X_1 and X_2 are affiliated. In particular, if bidder 1 has a value $x_1 \in [0, 1]$, then he knows that $x_2 \in [0, 1]$ also. Similarly, if $x_1 \in [1, 2]$, then $x_2 \in [1, 2]$ also.

Consider a second-price auction in which the bidders are asked to pay a small entry fee e. Once a buyer enters the auction, it is a dominant strategy for him to bid his value. But consider buyer 1 with value $x_1' = 1 - \varepsilon$, where $\varepsilon > 0$ is small. He knows that buyer 2's value $x_2 \in [0, 1]$, so buyer 1 is almost assured of winning. His expected payoff is positive—it is close to 0.5—and if e is small such a buyer will find it worthwhile to enter. Next consider a buyer with value $x_1'' = 1 + \varepsilon$, who then knows that $x_2 \in [1, 2]$ and thus that he will almost surely lose. When ε is small, his expected payoff is close to zero, so he will not be willing to pay the entry fee in order to participate. Thus, a monotonic equilibrium does not exist. ▲

We have seen that great caution is needed in drawing any general conclusions regarding asymmetric auctions. The examples presented in this chapter demonstrate that none of the results along the *revenue* dimension generalize from the symmetric to the asymmetric case. The same is not true of results along the *efficiency* dimension. Some of these do generalize, and in the next chapter we turn in this direction.

Chapter Notes

Example 8.2 which shows that the public release of information may decrease revenues is an adaptation of a multi-object example due to Perry and Reny (1999). Milgrom (1981) pointed out the great multiplicity of equilibria in second-price and English auctions with common values. The construction in Example 8.3 originates there. Bikhchandani and Riley (1991) have also pointed out the great multiplicity of equilibria in second-price and English auctions. The example of a discontinuous *ex post* equilibrium, Example 8.4, is due to Birulin (2001).

In a model introduced by Wilson (1967), Ortega Reichert (1968) studied a common value model with two bidders, one of whom was informed about the value while the other received only a noisy signal. He identified an equilibrium of the resulting game as the implicit solution to a system of differential equations. The treatment of asymmetrically informed bidders in this chapter closely follows that of Engelbrecht-Wiggans *et al.* (1983). Proposition 8.1 is from this paper.

The fact that the exclusion principle fails once values are affiliated was pointed out by Levin and Smith (1996). Example 8.5 is adapted from their paper. Levin and Smith (1996) go on to study how an increase in the number of bidders affects the optimal reservation price in the general symmetric model with interdependent values and affiliated signals, finding that an increase in numbers will typically lead to a decrease in the reservation price.

Milgrom and Weber (1982) recognized that entry fees may lead to problems with the existence of monotonic equilibria and Example 8.6 occurs in their paper. The underlying issues are explored in more detail by Landsberger and Tsirelson (2000), who show that with entry fees or other participation costs, monotonic equilibria become increasingly unlikely once the number of bidders is large.

9

Efficiency and the English Auction

The English auction is perhaps the most widely used auction format, and indeed, it has many attractive features. First, from the perspective of the bidders it is strategically simple—given the current price in the auction, each bidder need only decide whether or not to drop out at that instant—and this is important from a practical standpoint. The fact that the current price can be observed means that bidders should stay in until the price is the same as their estimate of the value, conditional on all available information. Second, from the perspective of the seller, we saw in Chapter 6 that in the symmetric model with interdependent values and affiliated signals, the English auction out-performs both the first- and second-price auctions in terms of revenue. Like other revenue results, however, this conclusion does not extend to situations where bidders are asymmetric.

In this chapter we direct our attention away from the revenue question and focus instead on efficiency properties of the English auction in situations where bidders may be asymmetric. With private values, of course, the English auction—and, in that setting, the second-price auction as well—always allocates efficiently. If every bidder adopts the equilibrium strategy calling for him to drop out when the price reaches his privately known value, the bidder with the highest value will win the object. With interdependent values, however, the question of efficiency is more delicate. In this setting, bidders cannot behave in the same manner as noted earlier—dropping out when the price reaches the value—since they have only partial information about their own values. At best, they can drop out when the price reaches the *estimated* value. Efficiency requires that the person with the highest *actual* (realized) value obtain the object; and when each bidder is only partly informed, this is a strong requirement.

We examine circumstances under which in the general model with interdependent and possibly asymmetric values, the English auction, nevertheless, allocates efficiently. We retain all the assumptions made in Chapter 6. In particular, it is assumed that the valuations $v_i(\mathbf{x})$ are continuously differentiable functions of all the signals and that $v_i(\mathbf{0}) = 0$. Furthermore, we have assumed that for all i and j,

$$\frac{\partial v_i}{\partial x_j} \geq 0$$

with a strict inequality when $i = j$. In this chapter, the joint distribution of bidders' signals, f, will play no further role since we will be concerned with *ex post* equilibria and these depend only on the valuation functions v_i. Recall that in Chapter 6 the symmetric equilibrium of the English auction was in fact an *ex post* equilibrium.

We should alert the reader that the proofs in this chapter are somewhat involved, perhaps more so than elsewhere in the book. This is not surprising given the nature of the problem—we are looking at situations that simultaneously involve both asymmetries and the interdependence of values. For this reason, the technicalities have been collected in a separate section. The reader would do well to understand the statement and content of the main result before delving into its proof.

In Chapter 6 we also saw that even when bidders were symmetric, symmetric equilibria of the common auction forms, including the English auction, need not be efficient (Example 6.4 on page 100). They were efficient, however, if the valuations satisfied a single crossing condition (Proposition 6.7 on page 101). The same condition, stated in a slightly more general form, plays a key role in the asymmetric case.

9.1   The Single Crossing Condition

The single crossing condition embodies the notion that a bidder's own information has a greater influence on his own value than it does on some other bidder's value.

The valuations **v** satisfy the pairwise *single crossing condition* if for all j and $i \neq j$,

$$\frac{\partial v_j}{\partial x_j}(\mathbf{x}) > \frac{\partial v_i}{\partial x_j}(\mathbf{x}) \tag{9.1}$$

at every **x** such that $v_i(\mathbf{x}) = v_j(\mathbf{x}) = \max_{k \in \mathcal{N}} v_k(\mathbf{x})$, so that the values of i and j are equal and maximal.

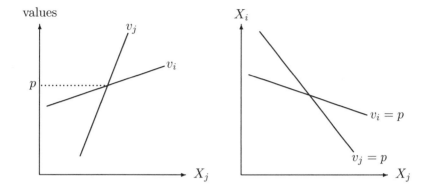

FIGURE 9.1. Single Crossing Condition

This is weaker than the condition introduced in Chapter 6 since the inequality in (9.1) is required to hold only at points $\mathbf{x}$ where the values v_i and v_j are the same and maximal. The single crossing condition is depicted in Figure 9.1. In the left-hand panel, the slope of v_j with respect to x_j is greater than that of v_i whenever they have the same value. The right-hand panel depicts the iso-value or "indifference" curves of the two bidders, both at the same level, p. Whenever they intersect, bidder j's indifference curve is steeper, so they can cross at most once.

It will be convenient to denote the partial derivative of bidder i's valuation with respect to bidder j's signal by v'_{ij}, that is,

$$v'_{ij}(\mathbf{x}) \equiv \frac{\partial v_i}{\partial x_j}(\mathbf{x}) \tag{9.2}$$

In this notation, the inequality in (9.1) can be written as $v'_{jj}(\mathbf{x}) > v'_{ij}(\mathbf{x})$.

9.2 Two-Bidder Auctions

When there are only two bidders, the single crossing condition is sufficient to guarantee the existence of an efficient equilibrium in an English auction.

Proposition 9.1 *Suppose that the valuations* $\mathbf{v}$ *satisfy the single crossing condition. Then there exists an* ex post *equilibrium of the two-bidder English auction that is efficient.*

First, suppose that there exist continuous and increasing functions ϕ_1 and ϕ_2 such that for all $p \leq \min_i \phi_i(\omega_i)$, these solve the following pair of equations

$$v_1\left(\phi_1\left(p\right),\phi_2\left(p\right)\right) = p$$
$$v_2\left(\phi_1\left(p\right),\phi_2\left(p\right)\right) = p \tag{9.3}$$

The inverses of ϕ_1 and ϕ_2 constitute an equilibrium of the two-bidder English auction. In other words, if we define $\beta_i : [0,\omega_i] \to \mathbb{R}_+$ by $\beta_i = \phi_i^{-1}$, then these form an equilibrium.

Indeed, suppose that there exists such a solution and, without loss of generality, suppose that $\beta_1(x_1) = p_1 > p_2 = \beta_2(x_2)$. Then from (9.3)

$$v_1\left(\phi_1\left(p_2\right),\phi_2\left(p_2\right)\right) = p_2$$

and since $x_1 = \phi_1(p_1) > \phi_1(p_2)$ and $\phi_2(p_2) = x_2$,

$$v_1\left(x_1, x_2\right) > p_2$$

because, by assumption, $v_{11}' > 0$. This implies that the winning bidder makes an *ex post* profit when he wins and since he cannot affect the price he pays, he cannot do better.

It is also the case that

$$v_2\left(\phi_1\left(p_1\right),\phi_2\left(p_1\right)\right) = p_1$$

and since $\phi_2(p_1) > \phi_2(p_2) = x_2$ and $\phi_1(p_1) = x_1$,

$$v_2\left(x_1, x_2\right) < p_1$$

because $v_{22}' > 0$. This implies that the losing bidder has no incentive to raise his bid since if he were to do so and win the auction, it would be at a price that is too high. Thus, if there is an increasing solution to (9.3), there exists an *ex post* equilibrium.

The equilibrium constructed here is efficient because from (9.3)

$$v_1\left(\phi_1\left(p_2\right),\phi_2\left(p_2\right)\right) = v_2\left(\phi_1\left(p_2\right),\phi_2\left(p_2\right)\right)$$

and again since $x_1 = \phi_1(p_1) > \phi_1(p_2)$ and $\phi_2(p_2) = x_2$,

$$v_1\left(x_1, x_2\right) > v_2\left(x_1, x_2\right)$$

because $v_{11}' > v_{21}'$ by the single crossing condition.

Note that (9.3) asks a bidder, say 1, to stay in until a price $\beta_1(x_1)$ such that if bidder 2 were to drop out at $\beta_1(x_1)$, and his signal $x_2 = \phi_2(\beta_1(x_1))$ were inferred, bidder 1 would just break even since

$$v_1\left(x_1, \phi_2\left(\beta_1\left(x_1\right)\right)\right) = \beta_1\left(x_1\right)$$

The equations (9.3) will thus be referred to as the *break-even* conditions.

In two-bidder auctions the single crossing condition guarantees that there is a pair of continuous and increasing functions (ϕ_1, ϕ_2) satisfying the break-even conditions (9.3) and, as argued above, in that case, $(\beta_1, \beta_2) = \left(\phi_1^{-1}, \phi_2^{-1}\right)$ constitutes an efficient equilibrium. We omit a proof of the existence of such functions for the moment as this is implied by a more general result to follow (Proposition 9.2).

Note that when there are only two bidders, the English auction is strategically equivalent to the sealed-bid second-price auction. This is because the only information available in the open format—that the other bidder dropped out—comes too late to be of any use since it signals only that the auction is over. The fact that the two auctions are equivalent means that Proposition 9.1 applies to the second-price auction as well. This equivalence does not hold, of course, once there are three or more bidders. Now information that one of the bidders has dropped out can be used by the remaining bidders to update their behavior in the remaining auction. But is the English auction still efficient? The answer is no, as the following example demonstrates: When there are three or more bidders, the single crossing condition by itself is not sufficient to guarantee that the English auction is efficient.

Example 9.1 *With three or more bidders, there may not exist an efficient equilibrium of the English auction even if the single crossing condition is satisfied.*

Suppose that there are three bidders whose signals $x_i \in [0, 1]$ and whose valuations are

$$
\begin{aligned}
v_1(x_1, x_2, x_3) &= x_1 + 2x_2 x_3 + \alpha(x_2 + x_3) \\
v_2(x_1, x_2, x_3) &= \tfrac{1}{2}x_1 + x_2 \\
v_3(x_1, x_2, x_3) &= x_3
\end{aligned}
$$

where $\alpha < \frac{1}{18}$ is a parameter.

Let us verify that the single crossing condition is satisfied. First, consider changes in x_2. Now $v_1 = v_2$ implies that $(v'_{22} - v'_{12}) x_2 = (1 - 2x_3 - \alpha) x_2 = \frac{1}{2}x_1 + \alpha x_3$. If either $x_1 > 0$ or $x_3 > 0$, then $v'_{22} > v'_{12}$. On the other hand, if both $x_1 = 0$ and $x_3 = 0$, then again $v'_{22} = 1 > \alpha = v'_{12}$. Thus, whenever $v_1 = v_2$, we have $v'_{22} > v'_{12}$. Likewise, whenever $v_1 = v_3$, $v'_{33} > v'_{13}$. All other comparisons are straightforward.

Suppose, by way of contradiction, that there is an efficient equilibrium in the English auction and let β denote the strategies when all bidders are active. If x_2 and x_3 are both greater than $\frac{1}{2}$, then for all x_1, v_1 is greater than both v_2 and v_3. Efficiency requires, therefore, that when all bidders are active, bidder 1 is *never* the first to drop out.

But now consider signals x_1, x_2 and x_3 such that bidders 2 and 3 have the same value and bidder 1 has a lower value (for example, let $x_1 = \frac{1}{8}$, $x_2 = \frac{1}{4}$, and $x_3 = \frac{5}{16}$). Clearly, $\beta_2(x_2) = \beta_3(x_3)$ is impossible since then bidder 1 would win the object and that is inefficient. Suppose that $\beta_2(x_2) < \beta_3(x_3)$, so that bidder 2 drops out first. For small $\varepsilon > 0$, if bidder 1's signal is $x_1 + \varepsilon$, bidder 2 has the highest value and it is inefficient for her to drop out. On the other hand, suppose $\beta_2(x_2) > \beta_3(x_3)$, so that bidder 3 drops out first. Now if bidder 1's signal is $x_1 - \varepsilon$, bidder 3 has the highest value and it is inefficient for him to drop out. This is a contradiction, so there cannot be an efficient equilibrium. ▲

The single crossing condition is a *bilateral* condition—it is separately applied to pairs of bidders—and, as we have seen, is not sufficient to guarantee that the English auction has an efficient equilibrium once there are three or more bidders. We now introduce a *multilateral* extension of the single crossing condition, called the *average crossing condition*, that links the valuations of all the bidders more closely and guarantees the existence of an efficient equilibrium in the English auction for any number of bidders.

9.3   The Average Crossing Condition

For any subset of bidders $\mathcal{A} \subseteq \mathcal{N}$, define

$$\overline{v}_\mathcal{A}(\mathbf{x}) = \frac{1}{\#\mathcal{A}} \sum_{i \in \mathcal{A}} v_i(\mathbf{x})$$

to be the *average* of the values of the bidders in $\mathcal{A}$ when the signals are $\mathbf{x}$. The average crossing condition is just a single crossing condition between a bidder's value v_i and the average value $\overline{v}_\mathcal{A}$ with respect to signals x_j of other bidders $j \in \mathcal{A}$.

The valuations $\mathbf{v}$ are said to satisfy the *average crossing* condition if for all $\mathcal{A} \subseteq \mathcal{N}$, for all $i, j \in \mathcal{A}$, $i \neq j$,

$$\frac{\partial \overline{v}_\mathcal{A}}{\partial x_j}(\mathbf{x}) > \frac{\partial v_i}{\partial x_j}(\mathbf{x}) \tag{9.4}$$

at every $\mathbf{x}$ such that for all $l \in \mathcal{A}$, $v_l(\mathbf{x}) = \max_{k \in \mathcal{N}} v_k(\mathbf{x})$, so that the values of the bidders in $\mathcal{A}$ are maximal.

The average crossing condition requires that the influence of any bidder's signal on some other bidder's value is smaller than its influence on the average of all the bidders' values (or equivalently, on the average of the influences on other bidder's values). Since all influences cannot be below average, it must be that for all $i, j \in \mathcal{A}$, $i \neq j$,

$$\frac{\partial v_j}{\partial x_j}(\mathbf{x}) > \frac{\partial \overline{v}_\mathcal{A}}{\partial x_j}(\mathbf{x}) > \frac{\partial v_i}{\partial x_j}(\mathbf{x}) \tag{9.5}$$

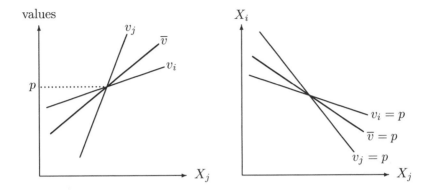

FIGURE 9.2. Average Crossing Condition

at every $\mathbf{x}$ such that for all $l \in \mathcal{A}$, $v_l(\mathbf{x}) = \max_{k \in \mathcal{N}} v_k(\mathbf{x})$. Thus, the average crossing condition implies the single crossing condition and is equivalent to it when there are only two bidders.

The average crossing condition is depicted in Figure 9.2 in much the same manner as the single crossing condition was depicted in Figure 9.1. The figure represents the different values at a point $\mathbf{x}$ such that all the values are equal to p. In that case, the average value is also p and the left-hand panel depicts the inequalities in (9.5) directly. As in Figure 9.1, the right-hand panel of Figure 9.2 shows the three iso-value curves and their relative slopes in (x_j, x_i) space.

9.4   Three or More Bidders

The main result of this chapter is as follows:

Proposition 9.2 *Suppose that the valuations* $\mathbf{v}$ *satisfy the average crossing condition. Then there exists an* ex post *equilibrium of the English auction that is efficient.*

Before proceeding with the proof of Proposition 9.2, it is worthwhile to understand the nature of the average crossing condition.

First, as noted earlier, when there are only two bidders, the average crossing condition is equivalent to the single crossing condition. How strong is the average crossing condition relative to the single crossing condition when there are three or more bidders? With three bidders, the two conditions can be conveniently represented as in Figure 9.3. For $j = 1, 2, 3$, define $\mathbf{v}'_j = (v'_{1j}, v'_{2j}, v'_{3j})$ to be the vector of influences of bidder j's signal x_j

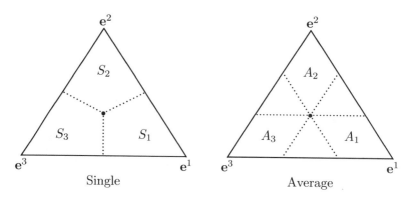

FIGURE 9.3. A Comparison of the Crossing Conditions

on all three bidders. Suppose further that these are rescaled so that they lie in the unit simplex Δ (the labels on the vertices, $\mathbf{e}^1, \mathbf{e}^2$ and $\mathbf{e}^3$, denote the three unit vectors). The single crossing condition requires that each $\mathbf{v}'_j \in S_j = \{\mathbf{t} \in \Delta : \forall i \neq j, \, t_i < t_j, \}$. Because of the rescaling, the average of the elements of $\mathbf{v}'_j$ is just $\frac{1}{3}$ and the average crossing condition requires that each $\mathbf{v}'_j \in A_j = \{\mathbf{t} \in \Delta : \forall i \neq j, \, t_i < \frac{1}{3}\}$.

Second, the average crossing condition is flexible enough to accommodate both pure *private* values—that is, for all i, $v_i(\mathbf{x}) = u_i(x_i)$—and, as a limiting case, pure *common* values—that is, for all i, $v_i(\mathbf{x}) = w(\mathbf{x})$.[1] (In Figure 9.3, these correspond to the vertices and the center of the simplex, respectively.) More generally, if the valuations are additively *separable* into a private value and a common value component—that is, for all i, $v_i(\mathbf{x}) = u_i(x_i) + w(\mathbf{x})$, where $u'_i > 0$, then the average crossing conditions is satisfied. To see this, note first that with separability, for all $i, j \in \mathcal{A}$ and $i \neq j$,

$$
\begin{aligned}
\frac{\partial \overline{v}_{\mathcal{A}}}{\partial x_j}(\mathbf{x}) &= \frac{1}{\#\mathcal{A}} u'_j(x_j) + \frac{\partial w}{\partial x_j}(\mathbf{x}) \\
&> \frac{\partial w}{\partial x_j}(\mathbf{x}) \\
&= \frac{\partial v_i}{\partial x_j}(\mathbf{x})
\end{aligned}
$$

The additively separable specification is commonly employed in empirical work.

---

[1] Because of the strict inequality in its definition, the single crossing condition, and *a fortiori* the average crossing condition, rules out the case of pure common values.

9.5   Proof of Proposition 9.2

In an English auction, a strategy for bidder i determines the price at which he would drop out given his private information and given the history of who dropped out at what price. When there are only two bidders, this strategy is simple since the dropping out of either bidder ends the auction. In this case, a strategy of a bidder can depend only on his own signal—and that is why with only two bidders, the English and sealed-bid second-price auctions are equivalent.

If there are more than two bidders, however, the strategy of a bidder in an English auction is more complicated. We saw in Chapter 6 that when bidders are symmetric, the number of active bidders and the prices at which the bidders who dropped out did so were important but their identities were not. With asymmetric bidders, the identities of the bidders are also important since the inference that bidder 1, say, would draw if bidder 2 dropped out at a price p may be very different from the inference he would draw if instead, bidder 3 were to drop out at the same price p.

Formally, a bidding strategy for bidder i is a collection of functions

$$\beta_i^{\mathcal{A}} : [0, \omega_i] \times \mathbb{R}_+^{\mathcal{N} \setminus \mathcal{A}} \to \mathbb{R}_+$$

where $i \in \mathcal{A} \subseteq \mathcal{N}$ and $\#\mathcal{A} > 1$. The function $\beta_i^{\mathcal{A}}$ determines the price $\beta_i^{\mathcal{A}}(x_i, \mathbf{p}_{\mathcal{N} \setminus \mathcal{A}})$ at which i will drop out when the set of *active* bidders, including i, is $\mathcal{A}$; his own signal is x_i; and the bidders in $\mathcal{N} \setminus \mathcal{A}$ have dropped out at prices $\mathbf{p}_{\mathcal{N} \setminus \mathcal{A}} = (p_j)_{j \in \mathcal{N} \setminus \mathcal{A}}$. We will require that

$$\beta_i^{\mathcal{A}}(x_i, \mathbf{p}_{\mathcal{N} \setminus \mathcal{A}}) > \max \{p_j : j \in \mathcal{N} \setminus \mathcal{A}\}$$

Let $\boldsymbol{\beta} = ((\beta_i^{\mathcal{A}})_{i \in \mathcal{A}})_{\mathcal{A} \subseteq \mathcal{N}}$ be the collection of all bidders' strategies. If there is an equilibrium $\boldsymbol{\beta}$ such that the functions $\beta_i^{\mathcal{A}}$ are increasing in x_i and bidder i drops out at some price $p_i = \beta_i^{\mathcal{A}}(x_i, \mathbf{p}_{\mathcal{N} \setminus \mathcal{A}})$, then all remaining bidders $j \neq i$ would deduce that $X_i = x_i$. In that case, with a slight abuse of notation, we will write

$$\beta_i^{\mathcal{A}}(x_i, \mathbf{x}_{\mathcal{N} \setminus \mathcal{A}}) \equiv \beta_i^{\mathcal{A}}(x_i, \mathbf{p}_{\mathcal{N} \setminus \mathcal{A}})$$

Finally, let $\Gamma(\mathcal{A}, \mathbf{x}_{\mathcal{N} \setminus \mathcal{A}})$ denote the *subauction* in which the set of active bidders is $\mathcal{A} \subset \mathcal{N}$ and the signals of the bidders in the set $\mathcal{N} \setminus \mathcal{A}$, who have dropped out, are $\mathbf{x}_{\mathcal{N} \setminus \mathcal{A}}$.

Proposition 9.2 is the consequence of the following three lemmas.

Lemma 9.1 *Suppose that for all $\mathcal{A} \subseteq \mathcal{N}$ and for all $\mathbf{x}_{\mathcal{N} \setminus \mathcal{A}}$, there exist a unique set of continuous and increasing functions $\phi_i : \mathbb{R}_+ \to [0, \omega_i]$, $i \in \mathcal{A}$ such that for all $p \leq \min_{i \in \mathcal{A}} \phi_i^{-1}(\omega_i)$, for all $j \in \mathcal{A}$,*

$$v_j(\boldsymbol{\phi}_{\mathcal{A}}(p), \mathbf{x}_{\mathcal{N} \setminus \mathcal{A}}) = p \tag{9.6}$$

Define $\beta_i^{\mathcal{A}} : [0, \omega_i] \times \prod_{j \in \mathcal{N} \backslash \mathcal{A}} [0, \omega_j] \rightarrow \mathbb{R}_+$ by

$$\beta_i^{\mathcal{A}} (x_i, \mathbf{x}_{\mathcal{N} \backslash \mathcal{A}}) = \phi_i^{-1} (x_i)$$

Then $\boldsymbol{\beta}$ is an ex post *equilibrium of the English auction.*[2]

Proof. Consider bidder 1, say, and suppose that all other bidders $i \neq 1$ are following the strategies $\beta_i^{\mathcal{A}}$ as specified above. Suppose that bidder 1 gets the signal x_1 but deviates and decides to drop out at some price other than $\beta_1^{\mathcal{A}} (x_1)$. It will be argued that no such deviation is profitable.

For purposes of exposition, the arguments that follow assume that it is never the case that two bidders drop out simultaneously at the same price. The arguments can be easily extended to account for simultaneous exits.

First, suppose that bidder 1 gets the signal x_1 and wins the object by following the strategy β_1 as prescribed above. Bidder 1 cannot affect the price he pays for the object. So the only way that a deviation could be profitable is if winning leads to a loss for bidder 1 and the deviation causes him to drop out. Suppose that he wins the object when the set of active bidders is $\mathcal{A} = \{1, 2\}$ and bidder 2 drops out at price

$$p^* = \beta_2^{\mathcal{A}} (x_2)$$

Since the equilibrium strategies in every subauction are increasing, the signals of the inactive bidders can be perfectly inferred from the prices at which they dropped out. The break-even conditions (9.6) imply that

$$v_1 \left(\phi_1 (p^*), \phi_2 (p^*), \mathbf{x}_{\mathcal{N} \backslash \mathcal{A}} \right) = p^*$$

By definition, $\phi_2 (p^*) = x_2$ and since $\beta_1^{\mathcal{A}} (x_1) > p^*$, $x_1 > \phi_1 (p^*)$. Now since $v_{11}' > 0$, this implies that

$$v_1 (x_1, \mathbf{x}_{-1}) > p^*$$

showing that in equilibrium bidder 1 makes an *ex post* profit whenever he wins with a bid of $\beta_1^{\mathcal{A}} (x_1)$. Thus, any deviation that causes him to drop out is not profitable.

Second, suppose that the strategy β_1 calls on bidder 1 to drop out at some price p_1^* but bidder 1 deviates and remains active longer than $\beta_1^{\mathcal{A}} (x_1) = p_1^*$ in some subauction $\Gamma(\mathcal{A}, \mathbf{x}_{\mathcal{N} \backslash \mathcal{A}})$. This makes a difference only if he stays active until all other bidders have dropped out and he actually wins the object. So suppose this is the case and suppose, without loss of generality, that the bidders in $\mathcal{A} = \{1, 2, \ldots, A\}$ drop out in the order $A, (A - 1), \ldots, 2$

---

[2]To ease the notational burden, the dependence of ϕ_i on the set of active bidders, $\mathcal{A}$, and the signals of the bidders who have already dropped out, $\mathbf{x}_{\mathcal{N} \backslash \mathcal{A}}$, has been suppressed.

at prices $p_A \leq p_{A-1} \leq \ldots \leq p_2$, respectively, so that bidder 1 wins the object at a price of p_2. We will argue that such a deviation cannot be profitable for him.

When bidder $j + 1 \in \mathcal{A}$ drops out at price p_{j+1}, (9.6) implies that

$$v_1 \left(\phi_1^{j+1}(p_{j+1}), \phi_2^{j+1}(p_{j+1}), \ldots, \phi_{j+1}^{j+1}(p_{j+1}), x_{j+2}, \ldots, x_N \right) = p_{j+1} \quad (9.7)$$

where ϕ_i^{j+1} are the inverse bidding strategies being played when the set of active bidders is $\{1, 2, \ldots, j + 1\}$, and since bidder $j + 1$ drops out at p_{j+1}, $\phi_{j+1}^{j+1}(p_{j+1}) = x_{j+1}$. But the break-even conditions when the set of active bidders is $\{1, 2, \ldots, j\}$ imply that

$$v_1 \left(\phi_1^{j}(p_{j+1}), \phi_2^{j}(p_{j+1}), \ldots, \phi_j^{j}(p_{j+1}), x_{j+1}, x_{j+2}, \ldots, x_N \right) = p_{j+1}$$

Thus, for all $j < A$ and $i = 1, 2, \ldots, j$,

$$\phi_i^{j}(p_{j+1}) = \phi_i^{j+1}(p_{j+1})$$

and since $p_j \geq p_{j+1}$ this implies that for all $j < A$ and $i = 1, 2, \ldots, j$,

$$\phi_i^{j}(p_j) \geq \phi_i^{j+1}(p_{j+1}) \quad (9.8)$$

Similarly, at the last stage, when bidder 2 drops out it must be that

$$v_1 \left(\phi_1^2(p_2), x_2, x_3, \ldots, x_N \right) = p_2$$

and now applying (9.8) repeatedly when $i = 1$ results in

$$\phi_1^2(p_2) \geq \phi_1^3(p_3) \geq \ldots \geq \phi_1^A(p_A)$$

But $p_A > p_1^*$, so $\phi_1^A(p_A) > \phi_1^A(p_1^*) = x_1$. Thus, $\phi_1^2(p_2) > x_1$ and since $v_{11}' > 0$,

$$v_1(x_1, x_2, \ldots, x_N) < p_2$$

and by staying in and winning the object at a price p_2, bidder 1 makes a loss. Thus, bidder 1 cannot benefit by remaining active longer than $\beta_1^A(x_1)$.

Finally notice that none of these arguments would be affected if the signals $\mathbf{x}$ were common knowledge. Thus, we have shown that $\boldsymbol{\beta}$ is an *ex post* equilibrium. ∎

Lemma 9.2 *Suppose that the valuations $\mathbf{v}$ satisfy the average crossing condition. Then for all $\mathcal{A} \subseteq \mathcal{N}$, for all $x_{\mathcal{N} \setminus \mathcal{A}}$, there exists a unique set of differentiable and increasing functions $\phi_i : \mathbb{R}_+ \to [0, \omega_i]$, $i \in \mathcal{A}$ such that for all $p \leq \min \phi_i^{-1}(\omega_i)$, for all $j \in \mathcal{A}$,*

$$v_j \left(\boldsymbol{\phi}_{\mathcal{A}}(p), \mathbf{x}_{\mathcal{N} \setminus \mathcal{A}} \right) = p \quad (9.9)$$

Proof. First, consider $\mathcal{A} = \mathcal{N}$. Then the break-even conditions (9.9) may be compactly written as

$$\mathbf{v}\left(\boldsymbol{\phi}\left(p\right)\right) = p\mathbf{e} \qquad (9.10)$$

where $\mathbf{e} \in \mathbb{R}^N$ is a vector of 1's. Recall that $\mathbf{v}\left(\mathbf{0}\right) = \mathbf{0}$, so when $p = 0$, it is possible to set $\boldsymbol{\phi}\left(0\right) = \mathbf{0}$.

Differentiating (9.10) with respect to p results in

$$\mathbf{Dv}\left(\boldsymbol{\phi}\left(p\right)\right)\boldsymbol{\phi}'\left(p\right) = \mathbf{e}$$

where $\mathbf{Dv} \equiv \left[v'_{ij}\right]$ is the $N \times N$ matrix of partial derivatives of $\mathbf{v}$ and

$$\boldsymbol{\phi}'\left(p\right) \equiv \left(\phi'_i\left(p\right)\right)_{i=1}^N$$

A differentiable and increasing solution $\boldsymbol{\phi}$ to (9.10) exists if and only if there is an increasing solution to the system of differential equations

$$\begin{aligned} \mathbf{Dv}\left(\boldsymbol{\phi}\right)\boldsymbol{\phi}' &= \mathbf{e} \\ \boldsymbol{\phi}(0) &= \mathbf{0} \end{aligned}$$

The fundamental theorem of differential equations guarantees that there exists a unique solution $\boldsymbol{\phi}$ to this system for all $p \leq \min_{i \in \mathcal{N}} \phi_i^{-1}\left(w_i\right)$ and Lemma E.1 in Appendix E ensures that $\boldsymbol{\phi}'\left(p\right) \gg \mathbf{0}$.

The same argument can be applied in a subauction $\Gamma(\mathcal{A}, \mathbf{x}_{\mathcal{N}\backslash\mathcal{A}})$ once the initial conditions are chosen with some care. As an example, consider the subauction where one of the bidders, say N, with signal x_N has dropped out. Let $\mathcal{A} = \mathcal{N} \setminus \{N\}$ and consider the subauction $\Gamma(\mathcal{A}, x_N)$. From the solution to the game $\Gamma\left(\mathcal{N}\right)$ as above, this must have been at a price p_N such that $\phi_N^{\mathcal{N}}\left(p_N\right) = x_N$. For all $i \in \mathcal{A}$, let $x_i = \phi_i^{\mathcal{N}}\left(p_N\right)$, where $\phi_i^{\mathcal{N}}$ are the inverse bidding strategies in $\Gamma(\mathcal{N})$. Then in the subauction $\Gamma(\mathcal{A}, x_N)$, a solution the system

$$\begin{aligned} \mathbf{Dv}_{\mathcal{A}}\left(\boldsymbol{\phi}_{\mathcal{A}}\right)\boldsymbol{\phi}'_{\mathcal{A}} &= \mathbf{e} \\ \boldsymbol{\phi}_{\mathcal{A}}(p_N) &= \mathbf{x}_{\mathcal{A}} \end{aligned}$$

determines the inverse bidding strategies. This has a solution and the average crossing condition guarantees that the matrix $\mathbf{Dv}_{\mathcal{A}}\left(\boldsymbol{\phi}_{\mathcal{A}}\right)$ satisfies the conditions of Lemma E.1 in Appendix E, so $\boldsymbol{\phi}'_{\mathcal{A}} \gg \mathbf{0}$.

Proceeding recursively in this way results in strategies satisfying (9.10) in all subauctions. ∎

Lemmas 9.1 and 9.2 together imply that under the average crossing condition there exists an *ex post* equilibrium satisfying the break-even conditions (9.6). To complete the proof of Proposition 9.2, we now show that the equilibrium is efficient.

Lemma 9.3 *Suppose that the valuations* **v** *satisfy the average crossing condition and* β *is an equilibrium of the English auction such that* β_i^A *are continuous and increasing functions whose inverses satisfy the break-even conditions (9.6). Then* β *is efficient.*

Proof. Consider the case when all bidders are active. To economize on notation, let $\beta_i^N \equiv \beta_i$ and $\phi_i = \beta_i^{-1}$. Suppose that the signals are $x_1, x_2, \ldots, x_N$ and that $\beta_i(x_i) = p_i$. Without loss of generality, suppose that $p_1 \geq p_2 \geq \ldots \geq p_{N-1} > p_N$ so that bidder N is the first to drop out.[3] Now (9.6) implies that for all i,

$$v_i(\phi_1(p_N), \phi_2(p_N), \ldots, \phi_N(p_N)) = p_N$$

that is, all the values at $\phi(p_N)$ are the same. Thus, they all equal the average value, so, in particular,

$$v_N(\phi_1(p_N), \phi_2(p_N), \ldots, \phi_N(p_N)) = \overline{v}(\phi_1(p_N), \phi_2(p_N), \ldots, \phi_N(p_N))$$

Since $\phi_N(p_N) = x_N$ and for all $i \neq N$, $\phi_i(p_i) > \phi_i(p_N)$, the average crossing condition implies that

$$v_N(x_1, x_2, \ldots, x_N) < \overline{v}(x_1, x_2, \ldots, x_N)$$

Since the *ex post* value of bidder N is less than the average *ex post* value of all the bidders, it must be that

$$v_N(x_1, x_2, \ldots, x_N) < \max_i v_i(x_1, x_2, \ldots, x_N)$$

Thus, the person who is the first to drop out does not have the highest value.

The same argument can be made in every subauction $\Gamma(\mathcal{A}, \mathbf{x}_{\mathcal{N} \setminus \mathcal{A}})$, so that at no stage does the bidder with the highest value drop out. Thus, the equilibrium is efficient. ∎

9.6   Miscellany

An equilibrium of the English auction is efficient if and only if at every stage, the bidder who drops out is not the bidder with the highest value. In a completely symmetric model, however, a stronger property holds: At every stage, the bidder who drops out is the bidder with the *lowest* value among those remaining. In other words, in a symmetric model, the bidder

---

[3]Again, in the interest of simplicity, it is assumed that multiple bidders do not drop out at the same price.

with the lowest value drops out first, followed by the bidder with second lowest value, and so on. The same is true when values are separable into private and common components. Bidders need not drop out according to increasing values, however, when bidders are asymmetric and values are interdependent. The English auction is remarkable in that it allocates efficiently even when the bidders do not drop out in order. The average crossing condition permits such interesting behavior to emerge in equilibrium.

Example 9.2 *In an efficient equilibrium of the English auction, bidders need not drop out in order of their ex post values.*

Suppose that there are three bidders with valuations

$$
\begin{aligned}
v_1(x_1, x_2, x_3) &= x_1 + \tfrac{1}{3}x_3 \\
v_2(x_1, x_2, x_3) &= \tfrac{1}{3}x_1 + x_2 \\
v_3(x_1, x_2, x_3) &= \tfrac{1}{3}x_2 + x_3
\end{aligned}
$$

and all signals lie in $[0, 1]$.

The average crossing condition is satisfied, so there exists an efficient equilibrium satisfying the break-even conditions. When all bidders are active, the equilibrium prescribes that bidders follow the strategy $\beta_i^N(x_i) = \tfrac{4}{3}x_i$.

Suppose that $(x_1, x_2, x_3) = \left(\varepsilon^2, \varepsilon, 1 - \varepsilon\right)$ where $\varepsilon < \tfrac{1}{2}$. Then bidder 1 is the first to drop out. But for small enough ε, $v_2 < v_1 < v_3$. Thus, while the equilibrium is efficient, bidders do not necessarily drop out in order of increasing values. ▲

The average crossing condition guarantees that there is an equilibrium satisfying the break-even conditions and this is efficient. Are there efficient equilibria that do not satisfy the break-even conditions (9.6)? The answer is yes, as the following example shows.

Example 9.3 *There may be an efficient equilibrium of the English auction that does not satisfy the break-even conditions.*

Suppose that there are three bidders with valuations

$$
\begin{aligned}
v_1(x_1, x_2, x_3) &= x_1 + \tfrac{2}{3}x_2 + \tfrac{2}{3}x_3 \\
v_2(x_1, x_2, x_3) &= x_2 \\
v_3(x_1, x_2, x_3) &= x_3
\end{aligned}
$$

and all signals lie in $[0, 1]$.

In this case, the average crossing condition is not satisfied. In fact, there is no increasing solution (ϕ_1, ϕ_2, ϕ_3) to the break-even conditions. But the following constitutes an efficient equilibrium. Bidders 2 and 3 have private values and drop out when the price reaches their values regardless of the set of active bidders. Bidder 1 adopts a "wait-and-see" strategy; if all bidders are active, bidder 1 remains active no matter what his signal. Formally, his strategy is: for all x_1, $\beta_1^N(x_1) = 1$; and if bidder 3, say, drops out at a price p_3 and $\mathcal{A} = \{1, 2\}$, then $\beta_1^{\mathcal{A}}(x_1, p_3) = \min\{3x_1 + 2p_3, 1\}$. If bidder 2 drops out, then an analogous strategy is followed.

This is an efficient equilibrium because if all bidders are active, then between bidders 2 and 3, the one who drops out first has the lower value. Once bidder 3, say, has dropped out, the winning bidder has the higher value. ▲

Finally, we end with an example in which the second-price auction does not have an efficient equilibrium, whereas the English auction does.

Example 9.4 *With three or more bidders, the second-price auction may not have an efficient equilibrium.*

The valuations are the same as in Example 9.2, that is,

$$
\begin{aligned}
v_1(x_1, x_2, x_3) &= x_1 + \tfrac{1}{3}x_3 \\
v_2(x_1, x_2, x_3) &= \tfrac{1}{3}x_1 + x_2 \\
v_3(x_1, x_2, x_3) &= \tfrac{1}{3}x_2 + x_3
\end{aligned}
$$

and we make no specific assumptions regarding the distribution of signals. Notice that the example does not satisfy the assumptions of the symmetric model—bidder 2's signal and bidder 3's signal do not affect bidder 1's value in the same way.

Suppose, by way of contradiction, that the second-price auction has an efficient equilibrium. Let $x_1 = \frac{1}{2}$, $x_2 = \frac{5}{12}$, and $x_3 = \frac{1}{4}$. Then $v_1 = v_2 > v_3$. Fix x_1 and x_2. For small $\varepsilon > 0$, when $x_3 = \frac{1}{4} + \varepsilon$, $v_1 > v_2 > v_3$ and bidder 1 should win. On the other hand, when $x_3 = \frac{1}{4} - \varepsilon$, $v_2 > v_1 > v_3$ and bidder 2 should win. But since 1 and 2's signals are unchanged, in a second-price auction, the same bidder wins in both cases. This is a contradiction.

This example satisfies the average crossing condition, so the English auction does have an efficient equilibrium. ▲

It should be noted that the results of this chapter are all of an *ex post* nature—the equilibrium strategies depend only on the valuations v_i and not on the distribution of signals.[4]

---

[4]Of course, the functions v_i may have been derived from a more primitive model as in Chapter 6 and so may actually be expected values conditional on bidders' signals. In that case, the distribution matters only via its effect on the valuations.

Chapter Notes

The efficiency properties of the English auction were first pointed out by Maskin (1992). He showed that the single crossing condition was sufficient to guarantee that with two bidders, the English auction had an efficient equilibrium (Proposition 9.1). The weak form of the single crossing condition was introduced by Dasgupta and Maskin (2000).

Wilson (1998) derived efficient equilibria of asymmetric English auctions in the case where each bidder's valuation was separable into a purely private and purely common component and all signals were log-normally distributed. This specification is particularly useful for empirical work.

The general case of three or more bidders was considered by Krishna (2000). The average crossing condition and Proposition 9.2 originate there. This paper also introduces an alternative condition, called cyclical crossing, that is also sufficient for the English auction to have an efficient equilibrium. The cyclical crossing condition requires that the influences of a particular bidder's signal on others' values be cyclically ordered.

In an interesting paper, Izmalkov (2001) shows that the failure of the English auction to achieve efficiency—for instance, in Example 9.1—stems largely from the fact that in the standard model once a bidder drops out he cannot reenter at a higher price. Izmalkov (2001) goes on to study an alternative model of the English auction in which bidders can exit and enter the auction at will and identifies conditions under which the English auction with reentry has an efficient equilibrium. These conditions are quite weak; in particular, they are weaker than the average crossing condition. Moreover, whenever the standard model of an English auction (in which dropping out is irrevocable) has an efficient equilibrium, so does the English auction with reentry.

10
Mechanism Design with Interdependent Values

In the preceding chapters we considered the relative performance of three common formats—the first-price, second-price, and English auctions—in a setting with interdependent values and affiliated signals. Here, as in Chapter 5, we study abstract selling mechanisms with a view to comparing the performance of the common auction forms to that of the "ideal" method of selling a single object. Again our search is for both optimal and efficient mechanisms, but in a more general informational setting. In this setting, it is convenient to tackle the efficiency question first, so we begin by ascertaining circumstances under which an efficient mechanism exists. We then look for optimal, or revenue maximizing, mechanisms.

As a preliminary observation, note that the revelation principle from Chapter 5 applies equally well to the setting of interdependent values and affiliated signals. Proposition 5.1 continues to hold in this general setting without amendment: Given a mechanism and an equilibrium for that mechanism, there exists a direct mechanism in which (i) it is an equilibrium for each buyer to report his signal truthfully, and (ii) the outcomes are the same as in the original mechanism. A direct mechanism asks buyers to report their private information—in this case, their signals—and replicates the equilibrium outcomes of the original mechanism.

As before, denote by $\mathcal{X}_i$ the set of signals that buyer i can receive and let $\mathcal{X} = \times_j \mathcal{X}_j$. Let $\boldsymbol{\Delta}$ denote the set of probability distributions over the set of buyers $\mathcal{N}$. The revelation principle allows us to restrict attention to mechanisms of the form $(\mathbf{Q}, \mathbf{M})$ consisting of a pair of functions $\mathbf{Q} : \mathcal{X} \to \boldsymbol{\Delta}$

and $\mathbf{M} : \mathcal{X} \to \mathbb{R}^N$, where $Q_i(\mathbf{x})$ is the probability that i will get the object and $M_i(\mathbf{x})$ is the payment that i is asked to make.

10.1 Efficient Mechanisms

With private values, the second-price auction allocates efficiently but as we have seen, the question is more delicate once values are interdependent. In particular, with interdependent values none of the common auction forms is efficient in general. The previous chapter was devoted to deriving a sufficient condition for the English auction to have an efficient equilibrium—the average crossing condition—but question of whether there exists a mechanism that allocates efficiently even when this condition does not hold remains to be explored.

Recall from the Chapter 9 that the valuations $\mathbf{v}$ are said to satisfy the *single crossing condition* if for all j and $i \neq j$,

$$\frac{\partial v_j}{\partial x_j}(\mathbf{x}) > \frac{\partial v_i}{\partial x_j}(\mathbf{x})$$

at every $\mathbf{x}$ such that $v_i(\mathbf{x})$ and $v_j(\mathbf{x})$ are equal and maximal over all buyers.

We have already seen that the English auction need not allocate efficiently if the single crossing condition is not satisfied. A simple example illustrates that the single crossing condition cannot be dispensed with even if we consider general, abstract mechanisms.

Example 10.1 *If the single crossing condition does not hold, then there may be no mechanism that allocates the object efficiently. Suppose*

$$\begin{aligned} v_1(x_1, x_2) &= x_1 \\ v_2(x_1, x_2) &= (x_1)^2 \end{aligned}$$

Suppose that buyer 1's signal X_1 lies in $[0, 2]$. Notice that buyer 2's signal does not affect the value of either buyer, so there is no loss in supposing that it is a constant. The valuations do not satisfy the single crossing condition since $v_1(1, x_2) = v_2(1, x_2)$ but

$$\frac{\partial v_1}{\partial x_1}(1, x_2) < \frac{\partial v_2}{\partial x_1}(1, x_2)$$

Clearly, $v_1(x_1, x_2) > v_2(x_1, x_2)$ if and only if $x_1 < 1$, so it is efficient to allocate the object to buyer 1 when his signal is low and to buyer 2 when it is high.

Suppose there is a mechanism that is efficient and has the payment rule $M_1 : [0, 2] \to \mathbb{R}$ for buyer 1. Since buyer 2 has no private information that is relevant, her signal is assumed to be a constant, so buyer 1's payment can only depend on his own reported signal.

Now if $y_1 < 1 < z_1$, then efficiency and incentive compatibility together require that when his true signal is z_1,

$$0 - M_1(z_1) \geq z_1 - M_1(y_1)$$

and likewise, when his true signal is y_1,

$$y_1 - M_1(y_1) \geq 0 - M_1(z_1)$$

Together these imply that $y_1 \geq z_1$, which is a contradiction. ▲

In general, suppose that there exists an efficient mechanism with an *ex post* equilibrium. Then by a version of the revelation principle there exists an efficient direct mechanism in which truth-telling is an *ex post* equilibrium. We will now argue that the valuation functions must satisfy the single crossing condition. Consider the signals of all buyers other than i, $\mathbf{x}_{-i}$. If regardless of his signal x_i, buyer i either always wins or always loses, then the single crossing condition holds vacuously for x_i. Otherwise, we will say that buyer i is *pivotal* at $\mathbf{x}_{-i}$ if there exist signals y_i and z_i such that $v_i(y_i, \mathbf{x}_{-i}) > \max_{j \neq i} v_j(y_i, \mathbf{x}_{-i})$ and $v_i(z_i, \mathbf{x}_{-i}) < \max_{j \neq i} v_j(z_i, \mathbf{x}_{-i})$. In other words, when the others' signals are $\mathbf{x}_{-i}$, i's signal is crucial in determining whether or not it is efficient for him to get the object. Incentive compatibility requires that when his signal is y_i, it is optimal for i to report y_i rather than z_i, so that

$$v_i(y_i, \mathbf{x}_{-i}) - M_i(y_i, \mathbf{x}_{-i}) \geq -M_i(z_i, \mathbf{x}_{-i})$$

Likewise, when his signal is z_i, it is optimal to report z_i rather than y_i, so that

$$-M_i(z_i, \mathbf{x}_{-i}) \geq v_i(z_i, \mathbf{x}_{-i}) - M_i(y_i, \mathbf{x}_{-i})$$

Combining the two conditions results in

$$v_i(y_i, \mathbf{x}_{-i}) \geq M_i(y_i, \mathbf{x}_{-i}) - M_i(z_i, \mathbf{x}_{-i}) \geq v_i(z_i, \mathbf{x}_{-i})$$

so a necessary condition for incentive compatibility is

$$v_i(y_i, \mathbf{x}_{-i}) \geq v_i(z_i, \mathbf{x}_{-i}) \tag{10.1}$$

that is, buyer i's value when he wins the object must be at least as high as when he does not. Put another way, keeping others' signals fixed, an increase in buyer i's value that results from a change in his own signal cannot cause him to lose if he were winning earlier. Thus, *ex post* incentive compatibility implies that the mechanism must be *monotonic* in values. But by assumption buyer i's value is an increasing function of his own signal, so we conclude that an increase in buyer i's signal cannot cause him to lose if he were winning earlier.

Efficiency now this requires that if i has the highest value, and he wins the object, he should still have the highest value, and win the object, if his signal increases. This in turn requires that at any x_i such that $v_i(x_i, \mathbf{x}_{-i}) = v_j(x_i, \mathbf{x}_{-i})$, we must have

$$\frac{\partial v_i}{\partial x_i}(x_i, \mathbf{x}_{-i}) > \frac{\partial v_j}{\partial x_i}(x_i, \mathbf{x}_{-i})$$

Thus, the single crossing condition is necessary for efficiency.

We now show that the single crossing condition is also sufficient to guarantee efficiency. If it is satisfied, then a generalization of the Vickrey-Clarke-Groves (VCG) mechanism, introduced in Chapter 5, to the interdependent values environment accomplishes the task.

The Generalized VCG Mechanism

Consider the following direct mechanism. Each buyer is asked to report his or her signal. The object is then awarded efficiently relative to these reports—it is awarded to the buyer whose value is the highest when evaluated at the reported signals. Formally,

$$Q_i^*(\mathbf{x}) = \begin{cases} 1 & \text{if } v_i(\mathbf{x}) > \max_{j \neq i} v_j(\mathbf{x}) \\ 0 & \text{if } v_i(\mathbf{x}) < \max_{j \neq i} v_j(\mathbf{x}) \end{cases} \tag{10.2}$$

and if more than one buyer has the highest value, the object is awarded to each of these buyers with equal probability. The buyer who gets the object pays an amount

$$M_i^*(\mathbf{x}) = v_i(y_i(\mathbf{x}_{-i}), \mathbf{x}_{-i}) \tag{10.3}$$

where

$$y_i(\mathbf{x}_{-i}) = \inf\left\{ z_i : v_i(z_i, \mathbf{x}_{-i}) \geq \max_{j \neq i} v_j(z_i, \mathbf{x}_{-i}) \right\}$$

is the smallest signal such that given the reports $\mathbf{x}_{-i}$ of the other buyers, it would still be efficient for buyer i to get the object. A buyer who does not obtain the object does not pay anything. The workings of the mechanism are illustrated in Figure 10.1, which depicts the values of buyers i and j as functions of i's signal (the reported signals of the others, $\mathbf{x}_{-i}$, are held fixed). At the signal x_i, buyer i has the highest value. In particular, it exceeds that of buyer j. The signal $y_i(\mathbf{x}_{-i}) < x_i$ is the smallest signal such that his value is at least as large as that of another buyer, in this case, buyer j and buyer i is asked to pay an amount $p = v_i(y_i(\mathbf{x}_{-i}), \mathbf{x}_{-i})$.

The generalized VCG mechanism adapts the workings of a second-price auction with private values to the interdependent values setting. Notice that if the buyer, say i, who obtains the object were asked to pay the

values

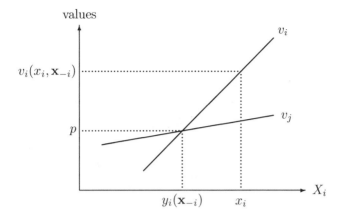

FIGURE 10.1. The Generalized VCG Mechanism

second-highest value at the reported signals, say $v_j(x_i, \mathbf{x}_{-i})$, then he would have the incentive to report a lower signal in order to lower the price paid. The generalized VCG mechanism restores the incentive to tell the truth by asking the winning buyer to pay $v_j(y_i(\mathbf{x}_{-i}), \mathbf{x}_{-i})$ instead of $v_j(x_i, \mathbf{x}_{-i})$. The key point is that, as in a second-price auction with private values, the reports of a buyer influence whether or not he obtains the object but do not influence the price paid if indeed he does so.

Proposition 10.1 *Suppose that the valuations* $\mathbf{v}$ *satisfy the single cross-ing condition. Then truth-telling is an efficient* ex post *equilibrium of the generalized VCG mechanism* $(\mathbf{Q}^*, \mathbf{M}^*)$.

Proof. Suppose that when all buyers report their signals truthfully, it is efficient for buyer i to be awarded the object with positive probability. In other words, buyer i's value is the highest when evaluated at the reported signals so that

$$v_i(x_i, \mathbf{x}_{-i}) \geq \max_{j \neq i} v_j(x_i, \mathbf{x}_{-i})$$

Buyer i pays an amount $v_i(y_i(\mathbf{x}_{-i}), \mathbf{x}_{-i})$, which is no greater than the true value of the object, so he makes a nonnegative surplus. If buyer i reports a z_i such that $z_i > y_i(\mathbf{x}_{-i})$, then by the single crossing condition, $v_i(z_i, \mathbf{x}_{-i}) > \max_{j \neq i} v_j(z_i, \mathbf{x}_{-i})$, so he would still obtain the object and pay the same amount as if he had reported x_i. Thus, reporting a $z_i > y_i(\mathbf{x}_{-i})$ makes no difference to the outcome. On the other hand, if he reports a $z_i \leq y_i(\mathbf{x}_{-i})$, then again by the single crossing condition his surplus is zero. Thus, no $z_i \neq x_i$ can be a profitable deviation in the circumstances that it is efficient for i to win the object.

Now suppose that when all buyers report their signals truthfully, it is efficient for a buyer other than i to win the object; that is

$$v_i(x_i, \mathbf{x}_{-i}) < \max_{j \neq i} v_j(x_i, \mathbf{x}_{-i})$$

and so buyer i's payoff is zero. This means that $x_i < y_i(\mathbf{x}_{-i})$ and for him to win, the single crossing condition ensures that buyer i would have to report a $z_i \geq y_i(\mathbf{x}_{-i}) > x_i$. In that case, he would pay an amount

$$M_i^*(z_i, \mathbf{x}_{-i}) = v_i(y_i(\mathbf{x}_{-i}), \mathbf{x}_{-i}) > v_i(\mathbf{x})$$

and so this would not be profitable either. ∎

In the case of private values, the generalized VCG mechanism reduces to the ordinary second-price auction and in that case, of course, truth-telling is a dominant strategy. Also, when there are only *two* buyers the generalized VCG mechanism is the direct mechanism that corresponds to the efficient equilibrium of the English auction identified in Proposition 9.1: The allocations and payments in the two are the same.

Finally, note that when values are interdependent, the generalized VCG mechanism is *not* "detail free" in the sense discussed in Chapter 5—it is not an auction. The mechanism designer is assumed to have knowledge of the valuation functions v_i and the mechanism is then able to elicit information regarding the signals x_i that is privately held by the buyers. Moreover, buyers with different valuation functions are treated differently so that the mechanism is not anonymous.

10.2 Optimal Mechanisms

In the independent private values model considered in Chapter 5 we saw that even in the optimal mechanism each buyer was able to appropriate positive informational rents. Put another way, the incomplete nature of the information available to the seller—his knowledge consisted only of the underlying distributions and not the actual realized values—meant that he was unable to extract all the surplus from the buyers. Actually, as we will see in this section, the key feature is not that the values are private but rather that they are independently distributed. This means that each buyer has private information that is exclusive in a strong sense. Not only does no one else know his value, but no one else knows anything that could provide even statistical information about it. The informational rents accruing to the buyers come solely from this strong exclusivity of information.

In this section we argue that if buyers' information is correlated—and so, statistically dependent—they are unable to garner any informational rents whatsoever. The surprising conclusion is that the slightest degree of correlation in information among the buyers allows the seller extract *all* the surplus.

This quite remarkable result is easiest to derive in a context in which each buyer's signal is a *discrete* random variable. This constitutes a departure from the informational structure used until now—each buyer's information was in the form of a continuous random variable distributed over some interval $[0, \omega_i]$—but simplifies the analysis greatly and makes the point most clearly. Specifically, in this section we assume that each buyer's signal X_i is drawn at random from a finite set

$$\mathcal{X}_i = \{0, \Delta, 2\Delta, \ldots, (t_i - 1)\Delta\}$$

with t_i possible signals. All other features of the model remain unaltered, in essence. Specifically, buyers' values are determined by the joint signal via the valuation functions $v_i : \mathcal{X} \to \mathbb{R}_+$ satisfying $v_i(\mathbf{0}) = 0$. Other assumptions regarding the valuation functions are translated in a natural manner into their discrete counterparts. We suppose that the v_i are nondecreasing: $v_i(x_j + \Delta, \mathbf{x}_{-j}) \geq v_i(x_j, \mathbf{x}_{-j})$ with a strict inequality if $i = j$. The discrete version of the *single crossing condition* is as follows: for all i and $j \neq i$,

$$v_i(x_i, \mathbf{x}_{-i}) \geq v_j(x_i, \mathbf{x}_{-i}) \Rightarrow v_i(x_i + \Delta, \mathbf{x}_{-i}) \geq v_j(x_i + \Delta, \mathbf{x}_{-i}) \quad (10.4)$$

and if the former is a strict inequality, then so is the latter.

Full Surplus Extraction

In the preceding section we saw that, provided that the single crossing condition was satisfied, truth-telling was an efficient *ex post* equilibrium of the generalized VCG mechanism. Although we derived this result in a context where signals were continuously distributed, the same is true when they are discrete variables. Thus, as long as the (discrete) single crossing condition (10.4) is satisfied, the generalized VCG mechanism is efficient in the current context as well. Recall also that the efficiency properties of the generalized VCG mechanism did not depend on the distribution of signals but only on the valuation functions v_i. The optimal, revenue maximizing, mechanism when values are interdependent and buyers' information—their signals—are statistically related is a modification of the generalized VCG mechanism. It shares many important features with the generalized VCG mechanism—it also allocates efficiently and truth-telling is an *ex post* equilibrium. Unlike the generalized VCG mechanism, however, the optimal mechanism depends critically on the distribution of signals. This last feature allows it to extract *all* the surplus from buyers so that their expected payoffs are exactly zero. From the perspective of the seller, this is clearly the best possible outcome as he is able to, in effect, act as a perfectly price-discriminating monopolist.

Let Π denote the joint probability distribution of buyers' signals: $\Pi(\mathbf{x})$ is the probability that $\mathbf{X} = \mathbf{x}$. (This is just the discrete analog of the joint density function, f, in the case of continuously distributed signals.)

Let Π_i be a matrix with t_i rows and $\times_{j \neq i} t_j$ columns whose elements are the conditional probabilities $\pi(\mathbf{x}_{-i} \mid x_i)$. Each row of Π_i corresponds to a signal x_i of buyer i, whereas each column corresponds to a vector of signals $\mathbf{x}_{-i}$ of the other buyers. The entry $\pi(\mathbf{x}_{-i} \mid x_i)$ then represents the *beliefs* of buyer i regarding the signals of the other buyers conditional on his own information. Hence, we will refer to Π_i as the matrix of beliefs of buyer i. If the signals are independent, buyer i's own signal provides no information about the signals of the other buyers. As a result, with independent signals the rows of Π_i are identical and hence Π_i is of rank one. When signals are correlated, i's signal provides information about the signals of the others and the rows of Π_i are typically different.

The main result of this section is as follows:

Proposition 10.2 *Suppose that signals are discrete and the valuations* $\mathbf{v}$ *satisfy the single crossing condition. If for every i, the matrix of beliefs Π_i is of full rank, then there exists a mechanism in which truth-telling is an efficient ex post equilibrium in which the expected payoff of every buyer is exactly zero.*

Proof. First, consider the generalized VCG mechanism $(\mathbf{Q}^*, \mathbf{M}^*)$ defined in (10.2) and (10.3). Define

$$U_i^*(x_i) = \sum_{\mathbf{x}_{-i}} \pi(\mathbf{x}_{-i} \mid x_i) [Q_i^*(\mathbf{x}) v_i(\mathbf{x}) - M_i^*(\mathbf{x})]$$

to be the expected payoff of buyer i with signal x_i in the truth-telling equilibrium of the generalized VCG mechanism. Let $\mathbf{u}_i^*$ denote the t_i sized column vector $(U_i^*(x_i))_{x_i \in \mathcal{X}_i}$.

Since the matrix Π_i is of full row rank t_i, there exists a column vector $\mathbf{c}_i = (c_i(\mathbf{x}_{-i}))_{\mathbf{x}_{-i} \in \mathcal{X}_{-i}}$ of size $\times_{j \neq i} t_j$ such that

$$\Pi_i \mathbf{c}_i = \mathbf{u}_i^*$$

Equivalently, for all x_i,

$$\sum_{\mathbf{x}_{-i}} \pi(\mathbf{x}_{-i} \mid x_i) c_i(\mathbf{x}_{-i}) = U_i^*(x_i)$$

Consider the Crémer-McLean (CM) mechanism $(\mathbf{Q}^*, \mathbf{M}^C)$ defined by

$$M_i^C(\mathbf{x}) = M_i^*(\mathbf{x}) + c_i(\mathbf{x}_{-i})$$

Now observe that truth-telling is also an *ex post* equilibrium of the CM mechanism. This is because the allocation rule $\mathbf{Q}^*$ is the same as in the generalized VCG mechanism and the payment rule M_i^C for buyer i differs from M_i^* by an amount that does not depend on his own report. In this equilibrium, the expected payoff of buyer i with signal x_i is

$$U_i^C(x_i) = \sum_{\mathbf{x}_{-i}} \pi(\mathbf{x}_{-i} \mid x_i) \left[Q_i^*(\mathbf{x}) v_i(\mathbf{x}) - M_i^C(\mathbf{x}) \right] = 0$$

by construction. ∎

The previous result is quite remarkable in that it shows that with the slightest degree of correlation among the signals, the seller can prevent the buyers from sharing any of the surplus resulting from the sale. Some remarks are in order.

First, if there are private values but these are correlated, then the payment in an optimal mechanism is a just the payment in a second-price auction plus the terms $c_i(\mathbf{x}_{-i})$. In that case, truth-telling is a dominant strategy in the optimal auction as well.

Second, the optimal mechanism $(\mathbf{Q}^*, \mathbf{M}^C)$ has two separate components: the generalized VCG mechanism and the additional payments determined by the function c_i. The latter constitute a "lottery" $c_i(\mathbf{X}_{-i})$ that buyer i faces and the outcomes of this lottery—the amounts he is asked to pay—are determined by the reports of the other buyers. How buyer i evaluates this lottery depends on his own signal since, given the statistical dependence among signals, for different realizations of X_i the expected payment implicit in the lottery is different. The lottery is, as it were, an entry fee that allows buyer i to participate in the workings of the generalized VCG mechanism and in expectation the buyer is just indifferent between entering and not.

Third, for some realizations of all the signals, a buyer's payoffs may be negative—he may end up paying something to the seller even if he does not get the object—and so, unlike the common auction formats, the mechanism is not *ex post* individually rational. Of course, by construction, the mechanism is *interim* individually rational: For every realization of his own signal, a buyer's expected payoff is exactly zero.

Fourth, while the conditions of the result require only that the matrix of beliefs be of full rank, when buyers' signals are "almost independent," the lottery $c_i(\mathbf{X}_{-i})$ may involve, with small probabilities, very large payments. In this case, it becomes increasingly untenable to maintain the assumption that buyers remain risk-neutral over the range of payoffs they may encounter while participating in a mechanism.

Finally, we draw attention to the fact that while the results of the preceding section regarding efficient mechanisms did not depend on the distribution of signals—all the complications there arose solely from the interdependence of values—the results of this section depend only on the correlation between the signals of the buyers—they are unaffected by the interdependence of the values.

Chapter Notes

The possibility that the seller may be able to extract all the surplus when signals are correlated was raised by Myerson (1981) in the context of an example. The developments of this chapter are based, in large part, on the subsequent work of Crémer and McLean (1985, 1988). The generalized VCG mechanism and the single crossing condition were introduced there. The second paper also provides a slightly weaker condition on the matrix of beliefs Π_i that ensures full surplus extraction. More recent work on the generalized VCG mechanism is contained in Ausubel (2001).

In the context of a pure common value auction, McAfee *et al.* (1989) relax the assumption that buyers' signals are discrete. With continuously distributed signals, almost all the surplus can be extracted: For any $\varepsilon > 0$, there exists a mechanism such that no buyer's surplus exceeds ε. They also show that this is the best possible result in general—in an example, no mechanism can leave the buyers with a surplus of exactly zero. McAfee and Reny (1992) extend this result to other mechanism design settings. In particular, they show that with correlated signals and interdependent values, efficient trade between a privately informed seller and a privately informed buyer is possible. Thus, the impossibility of efficient bilateral trade, derived in Chapter 5, does not hold once signals are correlated.

11
Bidding Rings

We have looked at an assortment of models with varying features: the auction format, the valuation structure, the informational structure, and so on. The one common feature across all these models has been the assumption that bidders make their decisions independently—that they do not act in a concerted way. In other words, the bidders were assumed to be engaged in a noncooperative game. This chapter explores some issues that arise when a subset, or possibly all, of the bidders act collusively and engage in bid rigging with a view to obtaining lower prices. The resulting arrangement—a *bidding ring*—resembles an industrial cartel and many of the issues surrounding cartels resurface in this context. How can the cartel enforce the agreed upon mode of behavior? How are the gains from collusion to be shared? How should economic agents on the other side of the market—in this case, the seller—respond to the operation of the cartel?

While bidding rings are illegal, they appear to be widely prevalent. Investigations of collusion in auctions constitute a significant component of antitrust activity: over three-quarters of the criminal cases filed in the 1980s under Section 1 of the Sherman Act—the section pertaining to trusts and the illegal restraint of trade—concerned auction markets.

Theoretical models of collusion among bidders involve a mix of cooperative and noncooperative game theory. Difficulties of both a conceptual and technical nature arise, and in order to illustrate the underlying issues in the simplest context, we return to the independent private values model.

Our setup is the same as in Chapter 5—specifically, we assume that bidders' values are private and independently distributed but allow bidders to be asymmetric. Specifically, suppose that each bidder's value is a random variable X_i which is distributed according to the cumulative distribution function F_i over some common interval $[0, \omega]$. The assumption of a common interval is made only for notational convenience and is easily relaxed.

Even if bidders were *ex ante* symmetric, the presence of a ring would naturally introduce asymmetries between bidders who are members of the ring and those who are not. As we have seen, equilibrium behavior in asymmetric first-price auctions does not lend itself to ready analysis. The equilibrium behavior of bidders in asymmetric second-price auctions, with or without a ring, is, however, quite transparent and allows us to focus our attention on a new set of issues surrounding collusion among bidders.

11.1   Collusion in Second-Price Auctions

Let $\mathcal{I} \subseteq \mathcal{N}$ be the set of bidders in the *bidding ring* or *cartel*. Without loss of generality, we will suppose that $\mathcal{I} = \{1, 2, \ldots, I\}$ and denote by $\mathcal{N} \setminus \mathcal{I} = \{I + 1, I + 2, \ldots, N\}$ the set of bidders outside the ring.

For any set of bidders $\mathcal{S} \subseteq \mathcal{N}$, let the random variable $Y_1^{\mathcal{S}}$ denote the highest of the values of the bidders in $\mathcal{S}$.

It is in the interests of the bidding ring to make sure that the object goes in the hands of the ring member who values it the most, provided, of course, that it manages to win the object. In other words, in order to maximize profits the bidding ring must allocate the object efficiently among its members. But information regarding their values is privately held by the members and in order to function effectively, a bidding ring needs to gather this information and then to divide the gains from collusion amongst its members. How, and whether, both tasks can be accomplished is a key question. In what follows, however, we temporarily put aside the question of the internal functioning of a ring—returning to it later—and, assuming that it functions effectively, seek to identify the resulting gains and losses to the various parties.

The Gains and Losses from Collusion

The presence of a ring in a second-price auction does not affect the behavior of bidders who are not members of the ring. It is still a weakly dominant strategy for a bidder $j \notin \mathcal{I}$ to bid his or her value X_j. It is also weakly dominant for the ring to submit a bid equal to the highest value among its members—that is, $Y_1^{\mathcal{I}}$. Equivalently, we may think of the ring as being represented at the auction by the member with the highest value in the ring. The other members submit bids of 0, or if there is a reserve price, they bid at or below this price.

A bidding ring generates profits for its members, of course, by suppressing competition. Specifically, instead of N effective bids, only $N-I+1$ effective bids are submitted since only one member of the cartel—the one with the highest value in the ring—submits a serious bid by bidding according to his or her value. The rest submit nonserious bids by bidding at or below the reserve price. The ring's profits come from the fact that, in certain circumstances, the price paid by a winning bidder from the ring is lower than it would be if there were no ring. Specifically, suppose that one of the ring members $i \in \mathcal{I}$ has a value X_i that is the highest of all bidders in the ring or otherwise—that is, $X_i = Y_1^{\mathcal{N}}$. Assuming that $X_i > r$, in the absence of a ring, this bidder would pay an amount equal to $P_i = \max\{Y_1^{\mathcal{N}\backslash i}, r\}$ for the object. But if he were part of a functioning ring, then his fellow members in $\mathcal{I}$ would bid at most r, so he would pay only

$$\widehat{P}_{\mathcal{I}} \equiv \max\{Y_1^{\mathcal{N}\backslash\mathcal{I}}, r\}$$

Thus, the expected payments of ring members are lower than they would be if the ring did not exist.

For a fixed reserve price r, let $m_i(x_i)$ denote the expected payment of bidder i with value x_i when there is no ring operating and all bidders behave noncooperatively. Likewise, let $\widehat{m}_i(x_i)$ denote i's expected payment when there is a ring. As we have argued, for all ring members $i \in \mathcal{I}$, and for all $x_i > r$, $\widehat{m}_i(x_i) < m_i(x_i)$. Then

$$t_i(x_i) \equiv m_i(x_i) - \widehat{m}_i(x_i) \tag{11.1}$$

represents the contribution of bidder i to the ring's expected profits when his value is x_i. The total *ex ante* expected profits of the ring—the spoils of collusion, as it were—amount to

$$t_{\mathcal{I}} \equiv \sum_{i \in \mathcal{I}} E\left[t_i(X_i)\right]$$

What about bidders who are not members of the ring? In market contexts, the presence of a cartel usually exerts a positive externality on firms who are not part of the cartel. Cartels result in higher prices and these benefit all sellers. In the present context, however, the bidding ring exerts no externality whatsoever on bidders who are not part of the ring. First, the probability that a bidder who is not a member of the ring will win the object is the same whether or not the ring is functioning; in both cases it is just the probability that she has the highest value among all bidders. Furthermore, the price that a bidder $j \notin \mathcal{I}$ would pay in the event that she wins is

$$\max\{Y_1^{\mathcal{I}}, Y_1^{\mathcal{N}\backslash\mathcal{I}\backslash j}, r\} = \max\{Y_1^{\mathcal{N}\backslash j}, r\}$$

the same as the price she would pay if there were no ring. Since for all bidders who are not part of the ring, neither the probability of winning nor the price upon winning is affected, the expected payments in the two situations are the *same*—that is, for all $j \notin \mathcal{I}$ and x_j,

$$\widehat{m}_j(x_j) = m_j(x_j)$$

For the same reasons, the profits of these bidders are also unaffected. Since the profits of bidders outside the cartel are unaffected by its presence, the gains accruing to the cartel as a whole are equal to the loss suffered by the seller.

This reasoning also leads to the conclusion that the gains from collusion increase as the size of the ring increases. Specifically, consider the addition of another member to the ring $\mathcal{I}$ and, without loss of generality, suppose that the new ring consists of bidders in $\mathcal{J} = \{1, 2, \ldots, I, I+1\}$. To see that this increases ring profits, first consider a bidder $i \in \mathcal{I}$ who is a member of the "original" ring and has a value $X_i > r$ that is the highest of all bidders. With the larger ring, his fellow members in $\mathcal{J}$ would bid at most r and since

$$\widehat{P}_{\mathcal{J}} = \max\{Y_1^{\mathcal{N} \setminus \mathcal{J}}, r\} \leq \max\{Y_1^{\mathcal{N} \setminus \mathcal{I}}, r\} = \widehat{P}_{\mathcal{I}}$$

the price he would pay would be lower than the price paid when the ring consisted only of bidders in $\mathcal{I}$. Thus, the price paid by any member of the original ring $i \in \mathcal{I}$ is lower when a bidder is added to the ring (with positive probability, the price is strictly lower). For bidder $I + 1$, certainly, joining the ring also means that the price she would pay upon winning is lower than otherwise. Thus, the profits of the ring increase as the membership increases. Once again, this increase comes solely at the expense of the seller.

For future reference it is useful to summarize the main conclusions reached so far. These are

- The operation of a bidding ring does not affect the payments or profits of bidders outside the ring.

- An increase in the membership of the ring increases ring profits, so the most effective ring is one that includes all bidders.

11.1.1 *Efficient Collusion*

The arguments made thus far have all assumed that the bidding ring submitted only one serious bid, and this was the highest of the values of its members. To do this, however, the ring has to induce its members to truthfully reveal private information regarding their values. In addition, cartel profits have to be shared among the members—the spoils have to be divided—in a way that the members would wish to participate in its workings. In other words, the bidding ring faces a mechanism design problem akin to those considered in Chapter 5. Indeed, the mechanism design perspective offers many insights into the workings of bidding rings.

Consider a bidding ring $\mathcal{I}$ and a *ring center*, which coordinates the activities of the ring. The mechanism designer—in this case, the center—must choose an internal mechanism that allocates the right to represent the cartel in the auction to the member with the highest value and determines the payment that each $i \in \mathcal{I}$ is asked to make to the center. These payments may be negative since it may be necessary for the center to make transfers to members of the ring other than the winner. It is in the interests of the center, acting on behalf of the ring, to allocate the representation right efficiently. Temporarily, suppose that the internal mechanism is incentive compatible so that the ring member with the highest value wins the right to represent the cartel in the auction. It is natural to call this *efficient collusion.*

For any bidder $i \in \mathcal{N}$, let $Q_i^r(\mathbf{x})$ denote the probability that bidder $i \in \mathcal{N}$ will get the object in a second-price auction with a reserve price of r if the vector of values of all the bidders is $\mathbf{x}$. Since the cartel is represented by the ring member with the highest value, this is just the probability that $X_i > \max\{Y_1^{\mathcal{N}\setminus i}, r\}$, neglecting any ties. But this probability is the same as it would be if there were *no* bidding ring and all bidders behaved noncooperatively. Put another way, if we think of the auction in which a bidding ring operates efficiently as just another mechanism, say $(\mathbf{Q}^r, \widehat{\mathbf{M}})$, then the resulting allocation rule is the *same* as in an auction without any collusion—that is, $(\mathbf{Q}^r, \mathbf{M})$. But since the two mechanisms have the same allocation rule, the revenue equivalence principle (Proposition 5.2 on page 66) applies. This means that the expected payments of any bidder in the two mechanisms—with the operation of the ring and without—differ by at most a constant. Formally, the revenue equivalence principle implies that for all $i \in \mathcal{N}$ there exist constants t_i such that for all x_i,

$$m_i(x_i) - \widehat{m}_i(x_i) = t_i \tag{11.2}$$

The difference in the two expected payments t_i then represents the *gains* from collusion accruing to members of the ring.

We have already argued that bidders who are not members of the ring are unaffected by its operation, so for all $j \notin \mathcal{I}$ and x_j,

$$m_j(x_j) - \widehat{m}_j(x_j) = 0$$

and that for all ring members $i \in \mathcal{I}$ and x_i,

$$m_i(x_i) - \widehat{m}_i(x_i) = t_i \geq 0$$

This leads to the following:

Proposition 11.1 *In a second-price auction with a reserve price, the expected gains from efficient collusion obtained by a ring member depend on the ring member's identity but not on his or her value. Furthermore, the operation of the ring does not affect any bidder outside the ring.*

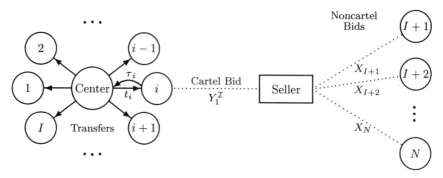

FIGURE 11.1. A Bidding Ring

In a second-price auction the cartel agreement—only the member with the highest value submits a serious bid; all others bid at or below the reserve price—is self-enforcing in the following sense. A member of the cartel who does not have the highest value has no incentive to cheat on the agreement and bid higher since doing this cannot possibly be profitable. If such a member were to win the object, it would be at a price that exceeds his own value. This is because there is going to be at least one bid in the auction that exceeds his value: that of the cartel representative.

Preauction Knockouts

One method of ensuring efficient collusion is for the ring center itself to conduct, prior to the actual sale, an auction among members of the ring. The winner of this auction, called a preauction knockout (PAKT), wins the right to represent the bidding ring at the main auction. A preauction knockout is akin to a party primary in the context of a political election; it selects the ring's "nominee" for the main auction.

The PAKT is also conducted under second-price rules, and its workings are as follows. First, each member of the ring is asked to reveal his or her private value to the center. The member reporting the highest value then represents the ring at the main auction and, if he wins the auction, pays the center an amount

$$\tau_i = P_i - \widehat{P}_\mathcal{I}$$

which is the difference in the price he would have paid if there were no ring and the price actually paid. This amount is easily determined if all ring members report their values truthfully. Figure 11.1 is a schematic representation of a bidding ring using a PAKT.

The center makes a lump-sum transfer to each ring member i of t_i (as defined in (11.2)). By definition, the center's budget is balanced in expected terms. In particular realizations, however, the sum of the transfers made by the center may exceed or fall short of what it receives. Certainly, there are circumstances in which the ring is unable to obtain the object, so there are no receipts while the lump-sum payments to the ring members have still to be made. Thus, the workings of a PAKT require that the ring center act as a banker who can finance the deficits and claim the surpluses.

The PAKT is incentive compatible—no ring member can do better than to report his true value to the center. Indeed, it is a weakly dominant strategy for every ring member to report truthfully. This is because the second-price PAKT requires the winning member, if and when he obtains the object, to pay the second-highest of *all* N values. So from each ring member's perspective, the situation is the same as in an ordinary second-price auction.

It is also individually rational—no member of the ring can do better by not participating since, no matter what the bidder's value, the gains from participating are positive. Its major weakness is that it needs an outside agency to finance its workings. It is not an *ex post* balanced budget mechanism.

A Balanced Budget Mechanism

Is efficient collusion feasible without the need for outside financing? To address this question it is useful to think of the bidding ring as facing an allocation problem: Who should be awarded the "right to represent" the cartel at the main auction? We will refer to this right as the *ticket*, thereby avoiding confusion with the object being offered for sale at the main auction. The ticket has a positive imputed value for each ring member—the expected gain from participating in the main auction. As a starting point, suppose that the center sells the ticket by means of a genuine second-price auction in which the winning member actually pays the center the second-highest imputed value for the ticket. In this case, the ring center would end up with a surplus for sure. But the second-price auction is the same as a Vickrey-Clarke-Groves (VCG) mechanism, introduced in Chapter 5, specialized to an auction context. Thus, if the ticket is allocated using the VCG mechanism, the center would run a surplus. Now Proposition 5.6 (see page 78) can be directly applied—if the VCG mechanism runs a surplus, there exists an efficient, incentive compatible, individually rational mechanism that also balances the budget in an *ex post* sense. The proof of Proposition 5.6, in fact, provides an explicit construction of such a mechanism.

The balanced budget mechanism from Proposition 5.6 is incentive compatible, but truth-telling is not a dominant strategy. In contrast, a PAKT balances the budget only in expected terms but has the property that truth-telling is a dominant strategy. In designing a mechanism to facilitate efficient collusion, the ring center thus faces a trade-off.

11.1.2   Reserve Prices in the Face of Collusion

Collusion among a subset of bidders reduces the profits of the seller, so it is natural to ask how she might respond to the presence of a bidding ring. But what recourse does the seller have? Assuming that the collusion cannot be detected by the antitrust authorities and that the seller cannot make a credible case for the presence of a bidding ring, the only instrument left in her hands with which to counter the actions of the bidding ring is to set a reserve price. Here we explore the issue of the optimal reserve price when the seller is aware that a bidding ring consisting of members in the set $\mathcal{I}$ is in operation and likely to act in concert in an upcoming auction.

From the seller's perspective, the presence of a ring that operates efficiently is equivalent to a situation with $N - I + 1$ bidders with values $Y_1^{\mathcal{I}}, X_{I+1}, X_{I+2}, \ldots, X_N$. This is because with efficient collusion, the members of the bidding ring submit only one serious bid of $Y_1^{\mathcal{I}}$, the highest value among its members; the rest of the $N - I$ bidders bid their values. The object is sold if and only if the highest of these, which is the same as $Y_1^{\mathcal{N}}$, is greater than the reserve price r. If, in addition,

$$Z^{\mathcal{I}} \equiv \text{2nd highest of } \{Y_1^{\mathcal{I}}, X_{I+1}, X_{I+2}, \ldots, X_N\} \tag{11.3}$$

is also greater than r, then the object is sold for $Z^{\mathcal{I}}$; otherwise, it is sold at the reserve price. Thus, if $Y_1^{\mathcal{N}} \geq r$, and the object is sold, the price obtained by the seller is

$$\widehat{P} = \max\{Z^{\mathcal{I}}, r\}$$

Let $H^{\mathcal{I}}$ denote the distribution function of $Z^{\mathcal{I}}$ with the density $h^{\mathcal{I}}$. It is also convenient to define G to be the distribution of $Y_1^{\mathcal{N}}$, so that

$$G(y) = \prod_{j \in \mathcal{N}} F_j(y)$$

and g to be the corresponding density.

Now the expected selling price that the seller receives can be written as

$$r\left(H^{\mathcal{I}}(r) - G(r)\right) + \int_r^{\omega} z h^{\mathcal{I}}(z)\, dz$$

The first term in the expression above comes from the event that the object is sold at the reserve price. This happens when the highest value from $\{Y_1^{\mathcal{I}}, X_{I+1}, X_{I+2}, \ldots, X_N\}$, which is just $Y_1^{\mathcal{N}}$, exceeds r but the second-highest value, $Z^{\mathcal{I}}$, does not. The second term comes from the event that the second-highest value, $Z^{\mathcal{I}}$, itself exceeds r, so the object is sold at a price equal to $Z^{\mathcal{I}}$.

Assuming that there is an interior maximum, the optimal reserve price $r^* > 0$ must satisfy the following first-order condition:

$$H^{\mathcal{I}}(r^*) - G(r^*) - r^* g(r^*) = 0 \tag{11.4}$$

The optimal reserve price is thus determined implicitly by (11.4). It may be verified that when there is no cartel and bidders are symmetric, the optimal reserve price is the same as that determined in Chapter 2.

Now suppose that the cartel is enlarged with the addition of another bidder so that it grows in size from $\mathcal{I}$ to $\mathcal{J} = \mathcal{I} \cup \{I + 1\}$. For the same reasons as noted earlier, the operation of this larger ring is equivalent in the eyes of the seller, to a second-price auction with $N - I$ bidders whose values are $Y_1^{\mathcal{J}}, X_{I+2}, X_{I+3}, \ldots, X_N$, respectively. Analogous to (11.3), let

$$Z^{\mathcal{J}} \equiv \text{2nd highest of } \{Y_1^{\mathcal{J}}, X_{I+2}, X_{I+3}, \ldots, X_N\} \qquad (11.5)$$

and let $H^{\mathcal{J}}$ be the distribution of $Z^{\mathcal{J}}$ with density $h^{\mathcal{J}}$. The expected selling price when the reserve price is set at r is now

$$r \left(H^{\mathcal{J}}(r) - G(r) \right) + \int_r^\omega z h^{\mathcal{J}}(z) \, dz$$

Comparing $Z^{\mathcal{J}}$ to $Z^{\mathcal{I}}$, we see that the only circumstances in which the two are different are when either

$$\begin{aligned}
(i) \ Z^{\mathcal{I}} &= X_{I+1} > Y_1^{\mathcal{N} \setminus \mathcal{J}}; \text{ or} \\
(ii) \ Z^{\mathcal{I}} &= Y_1^{\mathcal{I}} < X_{I+1}
\end{aligned}$$

In the first case, bidder $I + 1$ had the second-highest value, but once he joins the cartel the second-highest value becomes

$$Z^{\mathcal{J}} = Y_1^{\mathcal{N} \setminus \mathcal{J}} < X_{I+1} = Z^{\mathcal{I}}$$

In the second case, the "value" of the cartel $Y_1^{\mathcal{I}}$ was the second-highest value while bidder $I + 1$ won; once bidder $I + 1$ joins it, the cartel wins and the new price, the second-highest value, becomes

$$Z^{\mathcal{J}} = Y_1^{\mathcal{N} \setminus \mathcal{J}} < Y_1^{\mathcal{I}} = Z^{\mathcal{I}}$$

In all other circumstances, $Z^{\mathcal{J}} = Z^{\mathcal{I}}$.

The fact that $Z^{\mathcal{J}} \leq Z^{\mathcal{I}}$ implies, of course, that the distribution $H^{\mathcal{I}}$ stochastically dominates $H^{\mathcal{J}}$. The derivative of the expected selling price with the larger cartel $\mathcal{J}$, evaluated at the reserve price that is optimal for the smaller cartel $\mathcal{I}$, is

$$H^{\mathcal{J}}(r^*) - G(r^*) - r^* g(r^*) \leq 0$$

using (11.4) and the fact that $H^{\mathcal{I}}(r^*) \leq H^{\mathcal{J}}(r^*)$. Thus, the optimal reserve price r^{**} when the seller faces a larger cartel $\mathcal{J}$ must be at least as large as r^*. We state this finding formally as follows:

Proposition 11.2 *The addition of a bidder to a bidding ring causes the optimal reserve price for the seller to increase. In particular, the optimal reserve price with a bidding ring is always greater than the optimal reserve price with no ring.*

The increase in the optimal reserve price resulting from a cartel is illustrated in the following simple example.

Example 11.1 *Suppose that there are two bidders with values that are uniformly and independently distributed on* $[0, 1]$.

We saw in Chapter 2 that without a cartel the optimal reserve price was $r^* = \frac{1}{2}$.

Now suppose that both bidders are members of a cartel and suppose that the seller sets a reserve price of r. The cartel would bid $\max\{X_1, X_2\}$ and would purchase the good for r if this bid exceeds r. The seller's expected profit is

$$r \times \text{Prob}\left[\max\{X_1, X_2\} > r\right] = r\left(1 - r^2\right)$$

which is maximized by setting $r^{**} = \frac{1}{\sqrt{3}} > \frac{1}{2} = r^*$. ▲

11.2 Collusion in First-Price Auctions

The operation of bidding rings in first-price auctions introduces some new elements. First, unlike in a second-price auction, the cartel agreement in a first-price auction is *not* self-enforcing and, hence, is somewhat fragile. To see this simply, consider an all-inclusive cartel. Assuming that the highest value exceeds the reserve price set by the seller, such a cartel will try to obtain the object at the reserve price by submitting only one bid at this level and ensuring that no other bid exceeds this amount. But now consider a bidder whose value is greater than the reserve price but is not the highest. Such a bidder has the incentive to cheat on the cartel agreement and, by submitting a bid that just exceeds the reserve price, win the object. This suggests that second-price auctions are more susceptible to collusive practices—they have a built-in enforcement mechanism—than are first-price auctions. The analysis of cartels in the context of first-price auctions must postulate some enforcement mechanism that operates outside the model. Apart from physical coercion—always a possibility, especially given the criminal nature of the activity—the agreement may be enforced by repeated play. The same cartel may be involved in many auctions and cheating in one may be deterred by the threat of expulsion and the consequent loss of a share of the cartel's future profits.

Second, even if the bidders are *ex ante* symmetric, the operation of a cartel naturally introduces asymmetries among bidders. While this did not affect bidding behavior in second-price auctions—it was still a dominant strategy to bid one's value—it does affect behavior in first-price auctions. In particular, bidders not in the cartel face a different decision problem if there is a cartel in operation than if there is not. We have already seen that the analysis of bidding behavior in asymmetric first-price auctions is more problematic; as a result, our understanding of bidding rings in this context is more limited.

In what follows, we suppose that bidders are *ex ante* symmetric—that is, their values are drawn independently from the same distribution F. We also suppose that the cartel is all-inclusive. These two assumptions together ensure symmetry among bidders.

The behavior of an all-inclusive cartel is clear. It should submit only one serious bid—at the reserve price. But in order to operate efficiently, it still needs to determine what the highest valuation is. One option is to employ a first-price preauction knockout.

A First-Price PAKT

In a first-price PAKT, a bid is an offer to pay *all* other members of the bidding ring that amount. The winner of the PAKT then represents the cartel at the main auction, obtaining the good at the reserve price. What does a symmetric equilibrium of the first-price PAKT look like? The derivation is somewhat simpler if we suppose that the reserve price $r = 0$ and can be easily extended to the general case.

Proposition 11.3 *Symmetric equilibrium strategies in a first-price sealed-bid PAKT among all the bidders are given by*

$$\beta(x) = \frac{1}{N} E \left[Y_1^{(N)} \mid Y_1^{(N)} < x \right]$$

Proof. Suppose all other bidders follow the strategy β and suppose that bidder 1 with value x reports z. The expected profits from doing this are

$$\Pi(z, x) = \underbrace{G(z) \left[x - (N - 1) \beta(z) \right]}_{\text{Gain from winning PAKT}} + \underbrace{\int_z^1 \beta(y) g(y) \, dy}_{\text{Gain from losing PAKT}}$$

Differentiating with respect to z

$$
\begin{aligned}
\frac{\partial \Pi}{\partial z} &= g(z) \left[x - N\beta(z) \right] - (N - 1) G(z)\beta'(z) \\
&= (N - 1) F(z)^{N-2} \left[f(z)x - Nf(z)\beta(z) - F(z)\beta'(z) \right]
\end{aligned}
$$

But

$$\beta(z) = \frac{1}{F(z)^N} \int_0^z y F(y)^{N-1} f(y) \, dy$$

and differentiating this results in

$$\beta'(z) = \frac{f(z)}{F(z)}z - N\frac{f(z)}{F(z)}\beta(z)$$

which can be rearranged as

$$\beta'(z)F(z) + N\beta(z)f(z) = f(z)z$$

This implies that

$$
\begin{aligned}
\frac{\partial \Pi}{\partial z} &= (N-1)F(z)^{N-2}\left[f(z)x - Nf(z)\beta(z) - F(z)\beta'(z)\right] \\
&= (N-1)F(z)^{N-2}f(z)(x - z)
\end{aligned}
$$

and thus it is optimal to choose $z = x$. ∎

In the special case of an all-inclusive cartel, the first-price PAKT is an effective mechanism for eliciting private information while ensuring that the budget is always balanced.

Chapter Notes

The analysis of collusion in second-price auctions was initiated by Graham and Marshall (1987) in a symmetric independent private values model. Their model and results were later extended to accommodate asymmetric bidders by Mailath and Zemsky (1991). Most of the material in this chapter is based on these two papers.

Collusion in first-price auctions and the first-price PAKT were analyzed by McAfee and McMillan (1992). Robinson (1985) discusses the relative susceptibility of the different auction formats—second-price, first-price, and English—to collusion.

A general survey of the area, emphasizing many open questions, has been written by Hendricks and Porter (1989). The statistics on the level of antitrust activity that relates to bid rigging reported on page 151 are taken from a U.S. Department of Justice study that is quoted by Hendricks and Porter (1989).

Part II

Multiple Object Auctions

12

An Introduction to Multiple Object Auctions

In this part of the book we turn to the study of situations in which multiple, related objects are to be sold. The objects may be physically identical, say multiple cases of the same wine or treasury bills of the same denomination, or they may be physically distinct but still be good substitutes, say different apartments in the same building or different paintings by the same artist, so that the marginal value of acquiring a second item, say, is lower than the value of the first. Alternatively, the objects may be complements—that is, the value derived from a particular object may be greater if another has already been obtained. For instance, a philatelist may value a collection of stamps more than the sum of the values of the individual stamps. Similarly, how much an airline values an airport landing slot may increase with the number of slots it has already acquired.

Not surprisingly, when multiple objects are to be sold, many options are open to the seller. First, the seller must decide whether to sell the objects separately in *multiple auctions* or jointly in a *single auction*. In the former case, the objects are sold one at a time in separate auctions—conducted sequentially, say—in a way that the bids in the auction for one of the objects do not directly influence the outcome of the auction for another. In the latter case, the objects are sold at one go in a single auction, but not necessarily all to the same bidder, and the bids on the various objects collectively influence the overall allocation.

Second, the seller must choose among a variety of auction formats, and there is a wide range of possibilities to choose from. For instance, if the seller decides to sell the objects one at a time in a sequence of single-object

bids

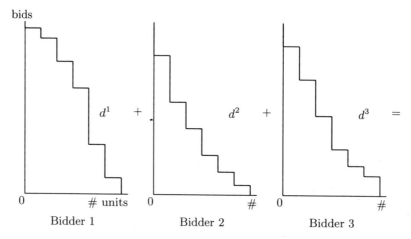

FIGURE 12.1. Individual Demand Functions

auctions, there is still the question of the particular auction form—first-price, second-price, or some other format—to adopt. If the seller decides to sell the objects at one go in a single auction, there are also many possibilities. We begin by outlining the workings of a few auction forms for the sale of multiple units of the same good at one go, returning to study multiple one at a time, sequential, or simultaneous auctions later.

12.1   Sealed-Bid Auctions for Selling Identical Units

Three sealed-bid auction formats for the sale of K identical objects are of particular interest. The first two are important on practical grounds—they are widely used in real-world auctions—and the last, although not widely used, is of special interest for theoretical reasons. All three are intended to be used in situations in which the marginal values are declining—that is, the value of an additional unit decreases with the number of units already obtained.

D. The *discriminatory* (or "pay-your-bid") auction.

U. The *uniform-price* auction.

V. The *Vickrey* auction.

In each of these auctions, a bidder is asked to submit K bids b_k^i, satisfying $b_1^i \geq b_2^i \geq \ldots \geq b_K^i$, to indicate how much he is willing to pay for each additional unit. Thus, b_1^i is the amount i is willing to pay for one unit, $b_1^i + b_2^i$ is the amount he is willing to pay for two units, $b_1^i + b_2^i + b_3^i$ is

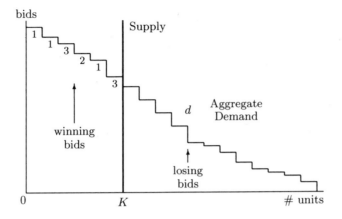

FIGURE 12.2. Aggregate Demand and Supply

the amount he is willing to pay for three units, and so on. We will refer to
$\mathbf{b}^i = \left(b_1^i, b_2^i, \ldots, b_K^i\right)$ as a *bid vector*. [1]

A bid vector $\mathbf{b}^i$ can be usefully thought of as an "inverse demand function" and can be inverted to obtain i's *demand function* $d^i : \mathbb{R}_+ \rightarrow \{1, 2, \ldots, K\}$:

$$d^i(p) \equiv \max\{k : p \le b_k^i\} \tag{12.1}$$

In particular, if $b_k^i > b_{k+1}^i$, then at any price p lying between b_k^i and b_{k+1}^i, bidder i is willing to buy exactly k units. A bidder's demand is clearly nonincreasing in the price. Since the demand function is just the "inverse" of the bid vector, and vice versa, submitting the bid vector $\mathbf{b}^i$ is equivalent to submitting the demand function d^i. We will thus use these interchangeably.

In all three of the auction formats considered here, a total of $N \times K$ bids $\{b_k^i : i = 1, 2, \ldots N; k = 1, 2, \ldots, K\}$ are collected and the K units are awarded to the K highest of these bids—that is, if bidder i has $k \le K$ of the K highest bids, then i is awarded k units.

As an example, consider a situation in which there are six units $(K = 6)$ to be sold to three bidders and the submitted bid vectors are

$$\begin{aligned} \mathbf{b}^1 &= (50, 47, 40, 32, 15, 5) \\ \mathbf{b}^2 &= (42, 28, 20, 12, 7, 3) \\ \mathbf{b}^3 &= (45, 35, 24, 14, 9, 6) \end{aligned}$$

The three bid vectors—equivalently, the three demand functions—are depicted in Figure 12.1. In this case, the six highest bids are

$$\left(b_1^1, b_2^1, b_1^3, b_1^2, b_3^1, b_2^3\right) = (50, 47, 45, 42, 40, 35)$$

---

[1]In this part of the book, superscripts identify bidders and subscripts identify units.

so that bidder 1 is awarded three units, bidder 2 is awarded one unit, and bidder 3 is awarded two units.

The allocation rule implicit in all three auctions may be framed in conventional supply and demand terms. First, an *aggregate demand* function d is obtained by "horizontally adding" the N individual demand functions, as depicted. For example, the demand function depicted in Figure 12.2 is the aggregate of the three individual demand functions in Figure 12.1. As usual, the aggregate demand function determines how many units are demanded *in toto* at different prices, so that for any p, $d(p) = \sum_i d^i(p)$. Since the number of units to be sold is fixed, the supply function is just a vertical line. All bids to the left of the intersection of the aggregate demand and supply functions—the K highest bids—are deemed "winning bids" and the number of units awarded to a bidder is equal to the number of winning bids submitted by him. All other bids are deemed "losing bids." In the figure each winning bid is labeled with the identity of the bidder who submitted the bid.

We will refer to an auction in which the K highest bids are deemed winning and awarded objects as a *standard auction*. The three auctions introduced next are all standard but differ in terms of their pricing rules— how much each bidder is asked to pay for the units he is awarded.

12.1.1 Discriminatory Auctions

In a discriminatory auction, each bidder pays an amount equal to the sum of his bids that are deemed to be winning—that is, the sum of his bids that are among the K highest of the $N \times K$ bids submitted in all. Formally, if exactly k^i of the ith bidder's K bids b_k^i are among the K highest of all bids received, then i pays

$$\sum_{k=1}^{k^i} b_k^i$$

This amounts to perfect price discrimination relative to the submitted demand functions; hence the name of the auction.

The discriminatory pricing rule can also be framed in terms of the *residual supply* function facing each bidder. At any price p the residual supply facing bidder i, denoted by $s^{-i}(p)$, is equal to the total supply K less the sum of the amounts demanded by other bidders, provided that this is nonnegative. Formally,

$$s^{-i}(p) \equiv \max \left\{ K - \sum_{j \neq i} d^j(p),\ 0 \right\} \tag{12.2}$$

and this is clearly a nondecreasing function of the price. The discriminatory auction asks each bidder to pay an amount equal to the area under his own

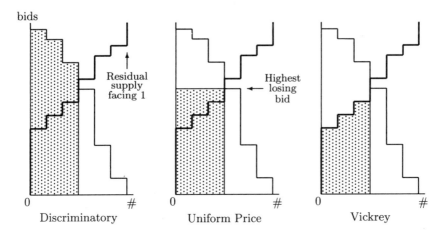

FIGURE 12.3. Bidder 1's Payments under Different Pricing Rules

demand function up to the point where it intersects the residual supply curve.

Figure 12.3 depicts the residual supply function facing bidder 1 in the example described above. The shaded area in the first panel of the figure is the total amount paid by bidder 1 in a discriminatory auction. In the example bidder 1 wins three units, so the total amount he pays for these is $b_1^1 + b_2^1 + b_3^1 = 50 + 47 + 40 = 137$.

At the risk of stating the obvious, we caution the reader not to infer from Figure 12.3 that the discriminatory auction raises more revenue than do the others. The reason is that so far nothing has been said about equilibrium bidding behavior in the three formats—this is the subject of the next chapter—and the figure illustrates only what would happen if the *same* set of bids were submitted in all three auctions. As we will see, bidding behavior in the three auctions differs substantially and reaching any conclusions regarding revenue is a delicate matter.

The discriminatory auction is the natural multiunit extension of the first-price sealed-bid auction. In particular, if there is only a single unit for sale ($K = 1$), then the discriminatory auction reduces to a first-price auction.

12.1.2   Uniform-Price Auctions

In a uniform-price auction all K units are sold at a "market-clearing" price such that the total amount demanded is equal to the total amount supplied. In the discrete model studied here, there is some leeway in defining the price that clears the market—any price lying between the highest losing bid and the lowest winning bid equates demand and supply. We adopt the rule that the *market-clearing price* is the same as the highest losing bid.

Denote by $\mathbf{c}^{-i}$ the K-vector of *competing bids* facing bidder i. This is obtained by rearranging the $(N-1)K$ bids b_k^j of bidders $j \neq i$ in decreasing order and selecting the first K of these. Thus, c_1^{-i} is the highest of the other bids, c_2^{-i} is the second-highest, and so on. The number of units that bidder i wins is just the number of competing bids he defeats. For instance, in order for i to win exactly one unit it must be the case that $b_1^i > c_K^{-i}$ and $b_2^i < c_{K-1}^{-i}$; that is, he must defeat the lowest competing bid but not the second lowest. Similarly, in order to win exactly two units, bidder i must defeat the two lowest competing bids but not the third lowest. More generally, bidder i wins exactly $k^i > 0$ units if and only if

$$b_{k^i}^i > c_{K-k^i+1}^{-i} \text{ and } b_{k^i+1}^i < c_{K-k^i}^{-i}$$

Observe that the residual supply function s^{-i} facing bidder i, defined in (12.2), can also be obtained from the vector of competing bids $\mathbf{c}^{-i}$ since

$$s^{-i}(p) = K - \max\left\{k : c_k^{-i} \geq p\right\} \tag{12.3}$$

The highest losing bid—the market-clearing price—is then just

$$p = \max\{b_{k^i+1}^i, c_{K-k^i+1}^{-i}\}$$

and in a uniform-price auction, if bidder i wins k^i units, then he pays k^i times p. The market-clearing price can also be written as

$$p = \max_i \left\{b_{k^i+1}^i\right\}$$

In the example considered above the vector of competing bids facing bidder 1 is

$$\mathbf{c}^{-1} = (45, 42, 35, 28, 24, 20)$$

whereas his own bid vector is

$$\mathbf{b}^1 = (50, 47, 40, 32, 15, 5)$$

and since $b_3^1 > c_4^{-1}$ but $b_4^1 < c_3^{-1}$, bidder 1 wins three units. The market-clearing price in this case is $\max\left\{b_4^1, c_4^{-1}\right\} = b_4^1 = 40$, so bidder 1 pays a total of 120. The shaded area in the second panel of Figure 12.3 depicts the total amount bidder 1 pays in a uniform-price auction.

The uniform-price auction reduces to a second-price sealed-bid auction when there is only a single unit for sale ($K = 1$).[2] It thus seems that it is a natural extension of the second-price auction to the multiunit case. As we will see, however, it does not share many important properties with the second-price auction, so the analogy is imperfect.

---

[2]Recall that the market-clearing price was defined as the highest losing bid.

12.1.3   Vickrey Auctions

In a Vickrey auction, a bidder who wins k^i units pays the k^i highest losing bids of the *other* bidders—that is, the k^i highest losing bids not including his own. As before, denote by $\mathbf{c}^{-i}$ the K-vector of competing bids facing bidder i, so that c_1^{-i} is the highest of the other bids, c_2^{-i} is the second-highest, and so on.

To win one unit, bidder i's highest bid must defeat the lowest competing bid—that is, $b_1^i > c_K^{-i}$. To win a second unit, i's second highest bid must defeat the second lowest competing bid—that is, $b_2^i > c_{K-1}^{-i}$. To win the kth unit, i's kth highest bid must defeat the kth lowest competing bid. The Vickrey pricing rule is the following. Bidder i is asked to pay c_K^{-i} for the first unit he wins, c_{K-1}^{-i} for the second unit, c_{K-2}^{-i} for the third unit, and so on. Thus, if bidder i wins k^i units, then the amount he pays is

$$\sum_{k=1}^{k^i} c_{K-k^i+k}^{-i}$$

Continuing with the example, bidder 1's payment is

$$c_6^{-1} + c_5^{-1} + c_4^{-1} = b_3^2 + b_3^3 + b_2^2$$

The Vickrey pricing rule is illustrated in the last panel of Figure 12.3. The shaded area is the total amount, $b_3^2 + b_3^3 + b_2^2 = 20 + 24 + 28 = 72$, paid by bidder 1; as depicted, this is the area lying under the residual supply function facing bidder 1.

The basic principle underlying the Vickrey auction is the same as the one underlying the Vickrey-Clarke-Groves mechanism discussed in Chapter 5: Each bidder is asked to pay an amount equal to the externality he exerts on other competing bidders. In the example, had bidder 1 been absent, the three units allocated to him would have gone to the other bidders: two to bidder 2 and one to bidder 3. According to the demand function submitted by him, bidder 2 is willing to pay b_2^2 and b_3^2, respectively, for two additional units. Similarly, bidder 3 is willing to pay b_3^3 for one additional unit. Bidder 1 is asked to pay the sum of these amounts. The amounts that bidders 2 and 3 are asked to pay are determined in similar fashion.

Like the uniform-price auction, the Vickrey auction also reduces to a second-price sealed-bid auction when there is only a single unit for sale ($K = 1$). Unlike the uniform-price auction, however, it shares many important properties with the second-price auction and is, as we will argue, the appropriate extension of the second-price auction to the case of multiple units.

Other possible pricing rules exist; the range of available options is virtually unlimited. For example, in one variant of the uniform pricing rule, all units are sold at a price equal to the average of all the winning bids.

12.2   Some Open Auctions

Each of the three sealed-bid auction formats introduced here has a corresponding open format.

12.2.1   Dutch Auctions

In the *multiunit Dutch* (or open descending price) auction, as in its single unit counterpart, the auctioneer begins by calling out a price high enough so that no bidder is willing to buy any units at that price. The price is then gradually lowered until a bidder indicates that he is willing to buy a unit at the current price. This bidder is then sold an object at that price and the auction continues—the price is lowered further until another unit is sold, and so on. This continues until all K units have been sold.

The multiunit Dutch auction is *outcome equivalent* to the discriminatory auction in the sense that if each bidder behaves according to a bid vector $\mathbf{b}^i$, indicating his interest in purchasing one unit when the price reaches b_1^i, another when the price reaches b_2^i, and so on, then the outcome is the same as when each bidder submits the bid vector $\mathbf{b}^i$ in a discriminatory auction. Recall from Chapter 1 that when a single object was for sale, the Dutch descending price auction was also equivalent to a first-price sealed-bid auction in a stronger sense—it was strategically equivalent and this equivalence held regardless of the informational environment. The multiunit extension of the Dutch auction, however, is not strategically equivalent to the multiunit extension of the first-price auction, the discriminatory auction. The reason is that if bidders' values are interdependent—the information available to one bidder may affect the valuation of objects by other bidders—then in the multiunit Dutch auction, once a bidder indicates a willingness to buy an object, this fact can be used by other bidders to update their own valuations. In a sealed-bid discriminatory auction, no such information is available. The two auctions are, however, weakly equivalent in the sense of Chapter 1—with private values the information acquired from the fact that one bidder is willing to buy at some price, while available, is irrelevant.

12.2.2   English Auctions

In the *multiunit English* (or open ascending-price) auction, the auctioneer begins by calling out a low price and then gradually raises it. Each bidder indicates—by using hand signals, by holding up numbered cards, or electronically—how many units he is willing to buy at that price—in other words, his demand at that price. As the price rises, bidders naturally reduce the number of units they are willing to buy. The auction ends when the total number of units demanded is exactly K and all units are sold at the price where the total demand changes from $K + 1$ to K.

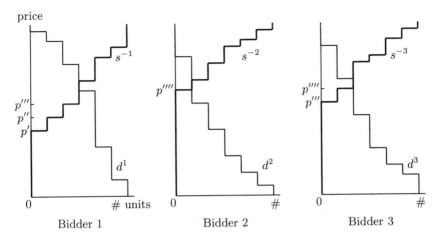

FIGURE 12.4. Prices in the Vickrey and Ausubel Auctions

The multiunit English auction bears the same relation to the uniform-price auction as the ordinary English auction does to the second-price sealed-bid auction—the two are outcome equivalent. The equivalence between the two multiunit auctions is weak for the same reason that the equivalence between the single unit auctions was weak—potentially useful information is available in the open auctions that is not available in the sealed-bid formats. Once again, with private values, this information is irrelevant.

12.2.3 Ausubel Auctions

The *Ausubel* auction is an alternative ascending-price format that is outcome equivalent to the Vickrey auction. As in the English auction, the auctioneer begins by calling out a low price and then raises it. Each bidder indicates his demand $d^i(p)$ at the current price p and the quantity demanded is reduced as the price rises. The goods are sold according to the following procedure.

At every price, the residual supply facing every bidder i, $s^{-i}(p)$ is computed according to (12.2). Of course, when the price is very low, then for all i, $s^{-i}(p) = 0$, whereas $d^i(p) > 0$. The price is raised until it reaches a level p' such that for at least one bidder, $s^{-i}(p') > 0$. Now any bidder i for whom $s^{-i}(p') > 0$ is sold $s^{-i}(p')$ units at a price of p'. The price is raised again until it reaches a level p'' such that for at least one bidder the residual supply is greater—that is, $s^{-i}(p'') > s^{-i}(p')$. Now each such bidder is sold $s^{-i}(p'') - s^{-i}(p')$ units at a price of p''. The price is raised again until the residual supply facing some bidder increases, and so on. Thus, objects are sold whenever there is a jump in any bidder's residual supply because one or more bidders reduce the amount they demand.[3] The pricing rule implicit here is the *same* as that in a Vickrey auction—each bidder pays the area under the residual supply function he faces up until the point that the residual supply intersects his demand function.

The workings of the auction are illustrated in Figure 12.4. In addition to the three demand functions from the previous section, the residual supply functions facing the bidders are depicted. When the price is zero, all $s^{-i}(0) = 0$ and remain zero at low prices. When the price reaches 20, there is a jump in the residual supply facing bidder 1 since $s^{-1}(20) = 1$, whereas $s^{-2}(20)$ and $s^{-3}(20)$ are still zero. Bidder 1 is thus sold one unit at a price of $p' = 20$. The price is raised further and no change occurs until it reaches 24, when there is another jump in the residual supply facing bidder 1 since $s^{-1}(24) = 2$. For the other bidders, the residual supply is still 0. Bidder 1 is thus sold another unit at a price of $p'' = 24$. The next change occurs at $p''' = 28$ and now the residual supply facing bidder 1 jumps to $s^{-1}(28) = 3$ and that facing bidder 3 jumps to $s^{-3}(28) = 1$. Both bidders 1 and 3 are sold one unit each at a price of $p''' = 28$. Finally, when the price reaches 32, there are jumps in the residual supply functions facing both bidders 2 and 3: $s^{-2}(32) = 1$ and $s^{-3}(32) = 2$. Each is sold one unit each at a price of $p'''' = 32$. All six units have now been sold, so the auction is over.

Another way to formulate the workings of the Ausubel auction is to think of each unit of demand as a "claim" on a unit. When the price is low, the number of units claimed exceeds the total supply, so no units are awarded. As the price rises, the number of units claimed decreases until the number of units claimed by other bidders is less than the supply. A bidder is then said to have "clinched" a unit since, regardless of what happens in the remainder of the auction, there is at least one unit that is not claimed by the other bidders.[4]

Figure 12.5 summarizes the relationships between the three sealed-bid formats for multiunit auctions and their open counterparts. As noted earlier, all the equivalences are *weak*—in general, they hold only if values are private, so the information conveyed in open formats is not useful. The figure also shows the single-unit antecedents of the multiunit auctions. Despite appearances, the uniform-price auction is not the appropriate extension of the single-unit second-price auction—it does not inherit the strategic and economic properties of the second-price auction. The Vickrey auction does and is, in fact, the appropriate extension.

---

[3]At any price, the residual supply jumps by at most one unit unless more than one bidder reduces his demand or some bidder reduces his demand by more than one unit. Both require that there be some ties in the bid vectors.

[4]Toward the end of the baseball season, a team is said to have "clinched" its division if its won-lost record is such that regardless of what happens in the remainder of the season, it will finish first.

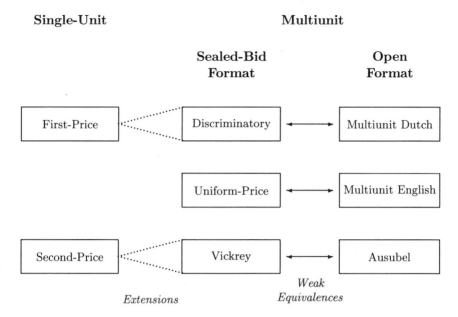

FIGURE 12.5. Extensions and Equivalences of Auction Formats

Outline of Part II

In this chapter we introduced three basic auction formats for the sale of multiple, identical units. In Chapter 13 we study equilibrium bidding behavior in the three auctions in a setting with independent private values. Bidding strategies cannot be explicitly derived, except in some special cases, so instead we highlight some basic strategic considerations in each of the three auctions. The analysis centers on the question of the efficiency of the different formats. Chapter 14 is then concerned with the question of revenue. It derives the revenue equivalence principle in the multiple object context and illustrates its use.

Chapter 15 concerns the sequential sale of multiple, identical units in a series of first- or second-price auctions, again in a private values setting. Chapter 16 concerns the sale of non-identical objects with particular emphasis on situations where the objects are complements. Chapter 17 then addresses some issues arising from interdependent values in a multiple object context.

Chapter Notes

Government securities are sold all over the world by means of discriminatory auctions. The U.S. Treasury has used discriminatory auctions since 1929 to sell short-term securities—called treasury *bills*—with maturities of 13, 26 and 52 weeks. Prior to the early 1970s, medium-term securities—

called treasury *notes*—with maturities of 2, 3, 5 and 10 years and long-term securities—called treasury *bonds*—with a maturities of more than 10 years, were sold at fixed prices set by the Treasury. Since the early 1970s these have also been sold by means of auction, typically using discriminatory pricing rules. In 1992, however, the treasury began to sell 2- and 5-year notes under uniform-price rules. This was intended as an experiment to see if, as argued by many economists, uniform-price auctions would reduce borrowing costs for the government and to ascertain the pros and cons of a switch to the uniform-price rules for selling all government securities, bills, notes, and bonds alike. A comparison of the data resulting from the two formats, however, does not show a clear advantage of one auction method over the other. A report by the U.S. Department of the Treasury (1998) summarizes the empirical findings.

In the United Kingdom electricity generators bid to sell their output on a daily basis. Since 1990 these electricity auctions were conducted using uniform-price rules, but in early 2000 the format was changed—in a direction opposite to that contemplated by the U.S. Treasury—to a discriminatory format. Note that electricity auctions are procurement auctions—the bidders are sellers rather than buyers—but the framework of this chapter is easily adapted to this setting.

The Vickrey multiunit auction was proposed by Vickrey (1961) as an antidote to some of the problems associated with the discriminatory and uniform-price auctions, in particular, the inefficiency of the latter two formats. The next chapter undertakes a detailed examination of these three auctions with a view to comparing their performance in terms of efficiency. The Ausubel ascending price auction was proposed by Ausubel (1997).

We have modeled multiunit auctions as the sale of multiple discrete units of the same good. Alternatively, one may think of a fixed supply of some good, normalized to, say, one unit, but suppose that it is perfectly divisible. A bidder's demand function can then be assumed to be continuous—at any price it specifies the share of the overall supply that the bidder is willing to purchase. All of pricing rules defined in this chapter have straightforward extensions to such a model. The continuous specification does not affect any essential properties of the various auctions but, for some purposes, proves to be analytically convenient. Auctions in such a setting have been called *share auctions* by Wilson (1979), who compares the expected revenues from the uniform price and discriminatory auctions to the expected revenue from the sale of the overall supply as one unit.

The auctions introduced in this chapter are all standard—each awards the K objects to the K highest bids. An example of a *nonstandard* auction format is the *voucher auction* scheme used to privatize industrial enterprises in the former Soviet Union, especially Russia. Under this scheme, all citizens were eligible to receive vouchers with a given face value—10,000 rubles in Russia—and typically about 25% of the shares of an enterprise were sold to the public. Vouchers were freely tradable and any person interested in purchasing shares of a particular enterprise could bid an amount b_i in terms of these vouchers. The auction rules were of the "everybody wins" variety. If the amounts bid were $(b_1, b_2, \ldots, b_N)$, then bidder i received a share

$$\theta_i = \frac{b_i}{\sum_j b_j}$$

of the portion of the enterprise for sale. Thus, every bidder received a positive share equal to the ratio of his bid to the total amount bid for that enterprise (see Boycko *et al.*, 1996). Thus, there were no "losing" bidders in the sense defined in this chapter. Indeed, voucher auctions are equivalent to a lottery in the following sense. Think of b_i as the number of lottery tickets, each sold at a unit of currency, purchased by bidder i. If the "winner" of the lottery is chosen by picking a ticket at random, then θ_i represents the probability that i will have the winning ticket. While voucher auctions are clearly inefficient, equilibrium behavior in such auctions—and their equivalent lotteries—has not been fully explored to date.

13

Equilibrium and Efficiency with Private Values

The previous chapter outlined the workings of some auction formats for the sale of multiple units of the same good. These formats differed in the manner in which prices at which the units were sold were determined, and we now examine how the different pricing rules affect bidding behavior. As in the case of a single object, we begin by considering the different auctions in a model where bidders' values are private and independently distributed, and again as a first step, we assume that bidders are *ex ante* symmetric.

13.1 The Basic Model

There are K identical objects for sale and N potential buyers are bidding for these. Bidder i's valuation for the objects is given by a private *value vector* $\mathbf{X}^i = \left(X_1^i, X_2^i, \ldots, X_K^i \right)$, where X_k^i represents the *marginal* value of obtaining the kth object. The total value to the bidder of obtaining exactly $k \leq K$ objects is then the sum of the first k marginal values: $\sum_{l=1}^{k} X_l^i$. It is assumed that the marginal values are declining in the number of units obtained so that $X_1^i \geq X_2^i \geq \ldots \geq X_K^i$. Bidders are assumed to be risk neutral.

Bidders are symmetric—each $\mathbf{X}_i$ is independently and identically distributed on the set

$$\mathcal{X} = \left\{ \mathbf{x} \in [0, \omega]^K : \forall k, x_k \geq x_{k+1} \right\} \qquad (13.1)$$

according to the density function f.

In the previous chapter we inverted the vector of bids $\mathbf{b}^i$ submitted by a bidder to obtain the demand function d^i submitted by him (see (12.1)). We can similarly invert each bidder's valuation vector $\mathbf{x}^i$ to obtain his "true" demand function δ^i defined by

$$\delta^i(p) \equiv \max\{k : p \leq x_k^i\} \tag{13.2}$$

Sometimes it will be useful to think of each bidder as drawing a demand function at random.

Some special cases of the preceding model—involving restrictions on the probability distribution that values are drawn from—are of interest.

Limited Demand Model

It may be that even though K units are being sold, each bidder has use for at most $L < K$ units. In that case, the support of f is the set

$$\mathcal{X}(L) = \{\mathbf{x} \in \mathcal{X} : \forall k > L, x_k = 0\}$$

so that there is no value derived from obtaining more than L units. Value vectors are of the form $(x_1, x_2, \ldots, x_L, 0, 0, \ldots, 0)$ and we then suppose that each bidder submits a bid $\mathbf{b}^i$, which is also an L vector. In an extreme instance, each bidder has use for only one unit ($L = 1$), and we will refer to this case as one of *single-unit demand*. If bidders value more than one unit with positive probability, then we will refer to that as the case of *multiunit demand*. The single-unit demand model is of interest because equilibrium behavior there is analogous to equilibrium behavior in auctions where only a single object is sold and demanded. As we will see, this is not true with multiunit demand.

Multiuse Model

A second, analytically useful, restriction on the form of the density function f occurs if the value vector $\mathbf{X}$ consists of order statistics of independent draws from some underlying distribution. Specifically, suppose that each bidder draws $L \leq K$ values $Z_1, Z_2, \ldots, Z_L$ independently from some distribution F, and it is useful to think of these as the values derived from the object in different uses. If he obtains only one unit, then it is used in the best way possible, so his value for the first unit is $X_1 = \max\{Z_1, Z_2, \ldots, Z_L\}$. If he obtains a second unit, it is put to the second-best use possible, so the marginal value of the second unit, X_2, is the second-highest of $\{Z_1, Z_2, \ldots, Z_L\}$. The marginal value of the third unit, X_3, is the third-highest of $\{Z_1, Z_2, \ldots, Z_L\}$, and so on.

We now turn to an examination of equilibrium bidding behavior in the three sealed-bid auction formats outlined in the previous chapter: the discriminatory, uniform-price, and Vickrey auctions. Since we consider a private values environment, it is the case that any equilibrium in the sealed-bid environment is outcome equivalent to an equilibrium of the corresponding open auction. Thus, any equilibrium in the discriminatory auction is equivalent to an equilibrium in the multiunit Dutch auction, any equilibrium in the uniform-price auction to one in the multiunit English auction, and any equilibrium in the Vickrey auction to one in the Ausubel auction.

The Vickrey auction is the simplest from a strategic standpoint, so we begin our analysis there. Next we turn to the uniform-price and discriminatory formats.

13.2   Vickrey Auctions

Recall that in a *Vickrey* auction each bidder submits a K-vector of bids $\mathbf{b}^i$, and the K highest bids are awarded units. The total amount paid by a bidder who is awarded k^i units is

$$\sum_{k=1}^{k^i} c^{-i}_{K-k^i+k} \qquad (13.3)$$

where $\mathbf{c}^{-i}$ is the K-vector of competing bids obtained by rearranging in decreasing order the $(N-1)\,K$ bids b^j_k, of bidders j other than i, and selecting the first K of these. Recall that the residual supply function facing bidder i, denoted by s^{-i}, can be obtained from $\mathbf{c}^{-i}$ as in (12.3). It is useful to think of

$$p^i_k \equiv c^{-i}_{K-k^i+k}$$

as the price bidder i pays for the kth unit. Notice that, by definition, $p^i_1 \le p^i_2 \le \ldots \le p^i_{k^i}$.

Just as it is a weakly dominant strategy to bid one's value in a second-price auction of a single object, it is a weakly dominant strategy to "bid one's true demand function" in a multiunit Vickrey auction. Figure 13.1 illustrates why, for instance, it does not pay bidder 1 to submit a demand function d^1 that lies below his true demand function δ^1. When he reports truthfully, bidder 1 obtains $k^1 = 4$ units. If he were to report d^1, he would win only three units forgoing some surplus on the fourth unit. More generally, we have

Proposition 13.1 *In a Vickrey auction, it is a weakly dominant strategy to bid according to $\beta^V(\mathbf{x}) = \mathbf{x}$.*

Proof. Consider bidder i and the bids $\mathbf{b}^{-i}$ submitted by the other bidders. As before, let $\mathbf{c}^{-i}$ be a vector consisting of the K highest bids of the other bidders. Suppose further that when bidder i submits a bid $\mathbf{b}^i = \mathbf{x}^i$, he is awarded k^i units. According to the Vickrey pricing rule, his payment

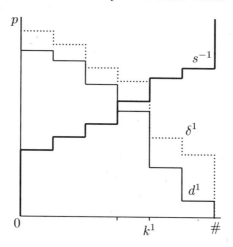

FIGURE 13.1. Dominant Strategy Property of Vickrey Auction

is given by (13.3) and it is the case that for all $k \leq k^i$, $x_k^i \geq c_{K-k^i+k}^{-i} = p_k^i$, whereas for all $k > k^i$, $x_k^i \leq c_{K-k^i+k}^{-i} = p_k^i$.

Now suppose bidder i were to submit a bid vector $\mathbf{b}^i \neq \mathbf{x}^i$ such that he is awarded the same number of units as when he submitted his true value vector $\mathbf{x}^i$; then the prices he pays for these units would be unaffected, as would his overall surplus—the total value less the sum of the prices paid.

If bidder i were to submit a $\mathbf{b}^i \neq \mathbf{x}^i$ such that he is awarded a greater number of units, say $l^i > k^i$, than if he were to submit his true value vector $\mathbf{x}^i$, then the prices he would pay for the first k^i units would be unchanged and, therefore, so would the surplus derived from these. For any unit $k > k^i$, however, the price p_k^i exceeds (or, at best equals) the kth marginal value x_k^i, so the surplus from these $l^i - k^i$ units would be negative (or at best, zero). As a result, the overall surplus would be lower (or at best, the same) than that if he were to bid truthfully.

Finally, if bidder i were to submit a $\mathbf{b}^i \neq \mathbf{x}^i$ such that he is awarded a smaller number of units, say $l^i < k^i$, as when he submitted his true value vector $\mathbf{x}^i$, then the prices he would pay for the first l^i units would be unchanged and therefore so would the surplus derived from these. But the surplus from any unit any unit $k < k^i$ was positive and is now forgone. Thus, by winning fewer units bidder 1's overall surplus would be lower than if he were to bid truthfully. ∎

It is important to observe that nowhere in the proof did we make use of the assumption that bidders were symmetric—Proposition 13.1 continues to hold even if bidders are asymmetric. An immediate consequence of the dominant strategy nature of the Vickrey auction is that the K objects are awarded in an efficient manner—they are awarded to the K highest values x_k^i. For future reference we record this observation as follows:

Proposition 13.2 *The Vickrey auction allocates the objects efficiently.*

The efficiency property of the Vickrey auction also extends to its open ascending-price counterpart, the Ausubel auction: It is an equilibrium strategy for a bidder to reduce his demand according to his *true demand function* δ^i, obtained by inverting his value vector $\mathbf{x}^i$. The resulting allocation is always efficient.

In the private value context, Vickrey auctions thus inherit the most important property of second-price auctions: It is a dominant strategy to bid truthfully and as a result, the allocations are efficient. While Vickrey auctions are always efficient, in some circumstances the outcome of a Vickrey auction may be deemed to be unfair. This is seen most easily in the context of a simple example. Suppose that there are two bidders with values $\mathbf{x}^1 = (10, 6)$ and $\mathbf{x}^2 = (9, 2)$. In a Vickrey auction each bidder bids his value vector so that each wins one unit. But notice that bidder 1 pays only $x_2^2 = 2$ for the unit he wins, whereas bidder 2 pays $x_2^1 = 6$. Thus, while bidder 1 attaches higher values to both units than does bidder 2, and indicates this by bidding truthfully, he ends up paying less than what bidder 2 pays. More generally, suppose there are two bidders i and j such that $\mathbf{x}^i \geq \mathbf{x}^j$ and the bids are such that i and j win the same number of units, say k. The vector of competing bids $\mathbf{c}^{-j}$ that j faces is at least as large as the vector of competing bids $\mathbf{c}^{-i}$ that i faces, so the amount that j pays for the k units that he wins is at least as large as the amount that i pays. Thus, in a Vickrey auction, if two bidders win the same number of units, then the one who indicates a willingness to pay more than the other will actually pay less.

What can be said about equilibrium behavior in the uniform-price and discriminatory auctions? Before addressing this question, we take a slight detour to examine the question of efficiency in general.

13.3   Efficiency in Multiunit Auctions

The requirement of efficiency restricts the form that equilibrium strategies can take. Consider any multiunit auction format in which bidders submit bid vectors $\mathbf{b}^i$ and the objects are awarded to the K highest bids—that is, a *standard auction*. As we have seen, the discriminatory, uniform-price and Vickrey auctions fall under this label.

Suppose that all bidders' value vectors $\mathbf{X}^i$ lie in the set $\mathcal{X}$ defined in (13.1) and that the density of $\mathbf{X}^i$, denoted by f, has full support. In any standard auction, the bidding strategy of a bidder, say i, is a function of the form $\boldsymbol{\beta}^i : \mathcal{X} \to \mathbb{R}_+^K$ satisfying, for all k, $\beta_k^i(\mathbf{x}^i) \geq \beta_{k+1}^i(\mathbf{x}^i)$.

Consider an equilibrium of some standard auction $(\beta^1, \beta^2, \ldots, \beta^N)$ and a particular realization of bidders' values $\mathbf{x}^1, \mathbf{x}^2, \ldots, \mathbf{x}^N$. In a standard auction, the K units will be awarded to the K highest of the $N \times K$ bids $\beta_k^i(\mathbf{x}^i)$, whereas efficiency demands that the K units be awarded to the K highest of the $N \times K$ marginal values x_k^i. For the equilibrium to allocate efficiently for *every* realization of the values, the ranking of the $N \times K$ bids $\beta_k^i(\mathbf{x}^i)$ must agree with the ranking of the $N \times K$ values x_k^i. In other words, efficiency requires that for all i, j and k, l,

$$x_k^i > x_l^j \text{ if and only if } \beta_k^i(\mathbf{x}^i) > \beta_l^j(\mathbf{x}^j) \tag{13.4}$$

The requirement in (13.4) has two implications. First, it must be that bidder i's bid on the kth object $\beta_k^i(\mathbf{x}^i)$ cannot depend on the value of, say, the lth object, x_l^i where $l \neq k$. Otherwise, with positive probability there are situations in which $\beta_k^i(\mathbf{x}^i)$ is the Kth highest of all the bids and some other bidder, say j, submits a bid $\beta_{k'}^j(\mathbf{x}^j)$, which is the $K + 1$st highest bid and this is just below $\beta_k^i(\mathbf{x}^i)$. Now there exists a change in x_l^i to $x_l^i - \varepsilon$ that affects i's bid so that $\beta_k^i(\mathbf{x}_{-l}^i, x_l^i - \varepsilon) < \beta_{k'}^j(\mathbf{x}^j)$ but ε is small enough so that the efficient allocation is unaffected. For such a change, the equilibrium allocation would be inefficient. Thus, we have argued that an implication of efficiency is that bidding strategies must be *separable*—the bid on the kth object can only depend on the kth marginal valuation.

A second implication is that the different components of the bidding strategy must be *symmetric* across both bidders and objects—that is, for all i, j and k, l, $\beta_k^i(\cdot) = \beta_l^j(\cdot)$. Otherwise, with positive probability there are situations in which the allocation will be inefficient; and this is for much the same reason why a first-price auction may not allocate a single object efficiently when there are asymmetries (see Chapter 4). In particular, if $i \neq j$, then there will be situations in which $x_k^i > x_l^j$, but $\beta_k^i(x_k^i) < \beta_l^j(x_l^j)$ and bidder i does not win an object he should have won on grounds of efficiency.

Together these imply that if an equilibrium is efficient then the bidding strategies must map values into bids using a single increasing function. The converse is also true—if values are mapped into bids using a single increasing function, then from (13.4) the equilibrium must be efficient. Finally, note that in a Vickrey auction, bids equal values, so values are mapped into bids using the identity function.

We summarize our findings as follows:

Proposition 13.3 *An equilibrium of a standard auction is efficient if and only if the bidding strategies are separable and symmetric across both bidders and objects—that is, there exists an increasing function β such that for all i and k,*

$$\beta_k^i(\mathbf{x}^i) = \beta(x_k^i)$$

13.4   Uniform-Price Auctions

We noted in the previous chapter that both the Vickrey and the uniform-price auctions were multiunit extensions of the single-unit second-price auction. As we have seen, the Vickrey auction inherits the dominant strategy property from the second-price auction and delivers efficient allocations. What of the uniform-price auction? This section explores the strategic properties of the uniform-price auction and finds that, in general, the uniform-price auction does not inherit the dominant strategy property of the second-price auction. In fact, the conditions required by Proposition 13.3 fail; as a result, the uniform-price auction is generally inefficient.

We begin by noting that in the independent private values setting studied here the uniform-price auction is known to have a pure strategy equilibrium. But a closed form expression for the strategies is not available, so we proceed indirectly. Rather than explicitly calculating equilibrium strategies—a difficult task even in specific examples—we will instead deduce some structural features that any equilibrium must have. These will then allow us to infer some important economic properties of the auction.

Recall that in a uniform price auction, bidder i wins exactly $k^i > 0$ units if and only if

$$b^i_{k^i} > c^{-i}_{K-k^i+1} \text{ and } b^i_{k^i+1} < c^{-i}_{K-k^i}$$

where $\mathbf{c}^{-i}$ is the vector of competing bids facing bidder i. The highest losing bid—the price at which all units are sold—is then just

$$p = \max\left\{ b^i_{k^i+1}, c^{-i}_{K-k^i+1} \right\}$$

Figure 13.2 illustrates the workings of the uniform-price auction when there are only two units for sale and bidder 1 submits a bid vector $\mathbf{b} = (b_1, b_2)$ (superscripts are omitted). If $b_2 > c_1$, and this occurs in the small triangular region to the left, bidder 1 wins both units and the price is c_1. If $b_1 < c_2$, and this occurs in the small triangular region to the right, bidder 1 does not win any units. In the remaining region he wins one unit and the price paid is $\max\{b_2, c_2\}$.

We begin with some simple observations regarding equilibrium bidding behavior. First, the bids cannot exceed marginal values—that is, for all i and k, $b^i_k \le x^i_k$. To see this, suppose that some bidder i bids an amount $b^i_k > x^i_k$. We claim that this is weakly dominated by the strategy of bidding $b^i_k = x^i_k$ (and if there is another bid, say b^i_{k+1}, such that $b^i_k \ge b^i_{k+1} > x^i_k$, then this is also reduced to x^i_k). If $b^i_k = p$, the price at which the units are sold, then bidder i is winning exactly $k-1$ units and reducing his bid to x^i_k can only improve his profits by possibly decreasing the price. If $b^i_k < p$, then reducing this bid to x^i_k makes no difference. If $b^i_k > p > x^i_k$, then bidder i is making a loss on at least one unit and decreasing b^i_k to x^i_k will reduce his loss—he will no longer win the units for which the price exceeded the

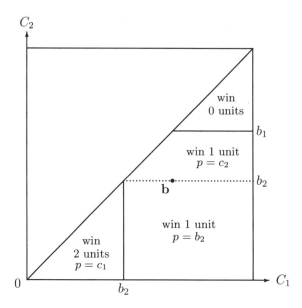

FIGURE 13.2. Outcomes in a Uniform-Price Auction with Two Units for Sale

marginal value. If $b_k^i > x_k^i > p$, then reducing his bid to x_k^i again makes no difference since he would still win the kth unit at the same price.

Second, the bid on the *first* unit must be the same as its value. Precisely, any strategy that calls upon a bidder to submit a bid $b_1^i < x_1^i$ is weakly dominated by a strategy in which $b_1^i = x_1^i$. To see this, suppose that $b_1^i < x_1^i$. If $p \geq x_1^i > b_1^i$, then bidder i is not winning any objects—all his bids are below the market-clearing price—and this would not change if he were to raise b_1^i to x_1^i. If $x_1^i > p \geq b_1^i$, then again bidder i is not winning any objects, but if he were to raise b_1^i to x_1^i, then he may win a unit and at a price that would be profitable. Finally, if $x_1^i > b_1^i > p$, then raising his bid to x_1^i makes no difference. Thus, we have argued that in a uniform-price auction it is a weakly dominant strategy for a bidder to bid truthfully for the first unit. Put another way, bidders do not have any incentive to shade their bids b_1^i for the first unit.

Bidders do have the incentive to shade their bids $b_2^i, b_3^i, \ldots, b_K^i$ for additional units, however, and this feature distinguishes the uniform-price auction from the Vickrey auction; in the latter, there is no incentive to shade bids for *any* of the units. Submitting a vector $\mathbf{b}^i \leq \mathbf{x}^i$, $\mathbf{b}^i \neq \mathbf{x}^i$ is equivalent to submitting a demand function d^i such that for some prices p the amount demanded $d^i(p)$ is lower than the true demand $\delta^i(p)$ (see (12.1) and (13.2)). Bid shading is thus sometimes referred to as *demand reduction*.

13.4.1   Demand Reduction

Let us look more closely at the case when there are only two units for sale—that is, $K = 2$. Further, suppose that the density of values f has full support on the set $\mathcal{X}$ defined in (13.1). Fix a symmetric equilibrium of the uniform-price auction $\beta = (\beta_1, \beta_2)$ that satisfies $\beta(\mathbf{0}) = \mathbf{0}$. Suppose that all bidders other than bidder 1, say, follow β. Suppose further that the marginal values bidder 1 assigns to the two units are given by $\mathbf{x} = (x_1, x_2)$ and bidder 1 bids $\mathbf{b} = (b_1, b_2)$. (Bidder indices are omitted so that we write b_k instead of b_k^1, and so on.) Let $\mathbf{c} = (c_1, c_2)$ be the competing bids facing bidder 1 and suppose that the distribution of the random variable $\mathbf{C}$ has a density on the set $\mathcal{X}$ given by $h(\cdot)$. Bidder 1's expected payoff is then given by

$$\Pi(\mathbf{b}, \mathbf{x}) = \int_{\{\mathbf{c}:c_1 < b_2\}} (x_1 + x_2 - 2c_1)\, h(\mathbf{c})\, d\mathbf{c}$$
$$+ \int_{\{\mathbf{c}:c_2 < b_1 \text{ and } c_1 > b_2\}} (x_1 - \max\{b_2, c_2\})\, h(\mathbf{c})\, d\mathbf{c}$$

The first term is bidder 1's payoff when he wins both units and the second term is his payoff when he wins only one unit. (See Figure 13.2.)

Let H_1 denote the marginal distribution of the higher competing bid C_1 and H_2 that of the lower competing bid C_2 with densities h_1 and h_2, respectively. Thus, $H_1(b_2) = \mathrm{Prob}[C_1 < b_2]$ is the probability that bidder 1 will defeat both competing bids and win two units. Similarly, $H_2(b_1) = \mathrm{Prob}[C_2 < b_1]$ is the probability that he will defeat the lower competing bid, so win *at least* one unit. The probability that he will win *exactly* one unit is then the difference $H_2(b_1) - H_1(b_2)$. Also, $H_2(b_2) - H_1(b_2) = \mathrm{Prob}[C_2 < b_2 < C_1]$ is the probability that the highest losing bid—the price at which the units are sold—is b_2. Using these facts, bidder 1's expected payoff can be rewritten as

$$\Pi(\mathbf{b}, \mathbf{x}) = H_1(b_2)(x_1 + x_2) - 2\int_0^{b_2} c_1 h_1(c_1)\, dc_1$$
$$+ [H_2(b_1) - H_1(b_2)]\, x_1$$
$$- [H_2(b_2) - H_1(b_2)]\, b_2 - \int_{b_2}^{b_1} c_2 h_2(c_2)\, dc_2$$

(Again, it may help to refer to Figure 13.2.)

Differentiating with respect to b_2 results in

$$\frac{\partial \Pi}{\partial b_2} = h_1(b_2)(x_2 - b_2) - [H_2(b_2) - H_1(b_2)] \tag{13.5}$$

and when $b_2 = x_2$, we determine that

$$\left. \frac{\partial \Pi}{\partial b_2} \right|_{b_2 = x_2} = -[H_2(x_2) - H_1(x_2)] < 0$$

since H_1 stochastically dominates H_2.

We have thus argued that a bidder can increase his payoff by shading his bid for the second unit—that is, the equilibrium bid for the second unit must be such that $b_2 < x_2$.

It is instructive to scrutinize the incentive to shade the bid for the second unit more closely. An increase in b_2 has two effects on a bidder's payoff. First, it increases the likelihood that the bidder will win the second object. To do this, b_2 must exceed the highest competing bid, c_1, and a small increase in b_2 raises the likelihood by $h_1(b_2)$. The gain from winning the second unit is just $(x_2 - b_2)$, so the first term in (13.5) represents the gain in expected payoff from raising the bid on the second unit slightly. The second effect is that an increase in b_2 raises the expected payment on the *first* unit (even though it does not affect the chances of winning it). This is because, with probability $H_2(b_2) - H_1(b_2)$, the amount bid on the second unit is the highest losing bid and hence determines the price paid for the first unit. The second term in (13.5) represents the resulting loss. When b_2 is close to x_2, the second effect dominates, so the bidder has an incentive to shade his bid.

In a uniform price auction, the shading of bids for units other than the first—demand reduction—results from the fact that, with positive probability, every bid other than that for the first unit may determine the price paid on all units. In other words, a bidder's own bids influence the price he pays. By contrast, in a Vickrey auction, a bidder's own bids determine how many units he wins but have no influence on the prices paid—each unit is purchased at a competing bid.

This situation occurs in the example presented in the previous chapter and is depicted in the middle panel of Figure 12.3 on page 169. The highest losing bid, and hence the market-clearing price, is bidder 1's bid for the fourth unit, b_4^1, and thus his own bid determines the amount he pays for the three units that he wins.

Two aspects of our analysis were special. First, we examined only the case when the number of units was two. The argument for demand reduction is quite general—considering more units only adds notational complexity—and applies no matter how many units are sold. Thus, no matter what K is, $\beta_1^i(x_1^i) = x_1^i$ and for all $k > 1$, $\beta_k^i(x_k^i) < x_k^i$. Figure 13.3 is a schematic portrayal of demand reduction when the number of units for sale is greater than two. Second, we assumed that the distribution of the competing bids facing a bidder admitted a density $h(\mathbf{c})$, so the distribution of bids did not have any mass points. This is not entirely innocuous since it rules out the possibility that for some open set of value vectors, the bids on some unit are constant. It turns out, however, that the demand reduction occurs even if the bidding strategies have mass points.

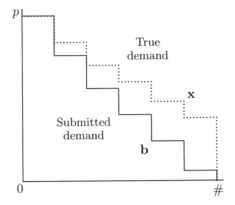

FIGURE 13.3. Demand Reduction in a Uniform-Price Auction

Proposition 13.4 *Every undominated equilibrium of the uniform-price auction has the property that the bid on the first unit is equal to the value of the first unit. Bids on other units are lower than the respective marginal values.*

Since the bidding strategies associated with different units are different— there is no shading on the first unit but there is on other units—by applying Proposition 13.3 we obtain the following:

Proposition 13.5 *Every undominated equilibrium of the uniform price auction is inefficient.*

Demand reduction (or bid shading) can be severe when the number of bidders is small relative to the number of units for sale. An extreme case of this phenomenon occurs in the following example.

Example 13.1 *There are two units for sale and two bidders with value vectors $\mathbf{X}$ that are identically and independently distributed according to the density function $f(x) = 2$ on $\mathcal{X} = \{\mathbf{x} \in [0,1]^2 : x_1 \geq x_2\}$.*

With this distribution of values, a symmetric equilibrium of the uniform-price auction is $\beta_1(x_1, x_2) = x_1$ and $\beta_2(x_1, x_2) = 0$. In every realization, each bidder wins one unit and the price is zero!

To see this, suppose that bidder 2 is following the strategy $\boldsymbol{\beta}$ as specified and bidder 1 with value vector $\mathbf{x}$ submits a bid vector $\mathbf{b} = (b_1, b_2) \gg \mathbf{0}$. As usual, let $\mathbf{c}$ denote the competing bids facing bidder 1—in this case, these are just the bids submitted by bidder 2—and we know that $\mathbf{c} = (y_1, 0)$ where $\mathbf{y}$ is bidder 2's value vector. Since $c_2 = 0$, bidder 1 is sure to win at least one unit. He wins only one unit if his low bid is a losing bid—that is, if $y_1 > b_2$ and in that case he pays b_2. He wins both units if his low bid of

b_2 exceeds the high bid of bidder 2, that is, if $y_1 < b_2$, and in that case the price he pays for each unit is y_1.

Let F_1 be the marginal distribution of X_1 with corresponding density f_1. Since $f(\mathbf{x}) = 2$ on $\mathcal{X}$, we know that $F_1(x_1) = (x_1)^2$ and $f_1(x_1) = 2x_1$ on the interval $[0, 1]$.

Bidder 1's expected payoff from bidding $\mathbf{b}$ when his values are $\mathbf{x}$ is simply

$$\Pi(\mathbf{b}, \mathbf{x}) = F_1(b_2)(x_1 + x_2) - 2\int_0^{b_2} y_1 f_1(y_1)\, dy_1$$
$$+ (1 - F_1(b_2))(x_1 - b_2)$$

where the first term is the payoff from winning both units and the second from winning only one unit.

Differentiating with respect to b_2 we obtain

$$\frac{\partial \Pi}{\partial b_2} = f_1(b_2)(x_2 - b_2) - 1 + F_1(b_2)$$
$$= 2b_2(x_2 - b_2) - 1 + (b_2)^2$$
$$= -(x_2 - b_2)^2$$
$$\leq 0$$

and this is strictly negative whenever $b_2 < x_2$. So it is optimal to set $b_2 = 0$ whatever the value of x_2.

In the example, demand reduction is so extreme that the equilibrium price is always zero and the two units are always split between the two bidders regardless of their values. The resulting inefficiency is clear. Finally, note that low revenue equilibria of this sort cannot arise if the number of bidders exceeds the number of units for sale. ▲

13.4.2   Single-Unit Demand

The inefficiency of the uniform-price auction does not result from the fact that multiple units are sold *per se* but rather from the fact that multiple units are demanded. Consider a situation in which $K > 1$ units are up for sale but each bidder has use for at most one unit—the case of single-unit demand. This is equivalent to supposing that the value vectors are drawn from the set

$$\mathcal{X}(1) = \{\mathbf{x} \in [0, \omega]^K : \forall k > 1, x_k = 0\}$$

Thus, f no longer has full support on $\mathcal{X}$. We already know that in a uniform-price auction it is weakly dominant to bid $b_1 = x_1$, and since the value of all additional units is zero, each bidder is bidding truthfully. Put another way, if all bidders have unit demand, there is no possibility that a winning bidder will influence the price paid, and hence there is no incentive for demand reduction. The upshot of this is that with single-unit demand the uniform-price auction is efficient.

13.5   Discriminatory Auctions

Recall that in a discriminatory or "pay-your-bid" auction, a bidder who is awarded $k^i \leq K$ units pays the sum of his first k^i bids, $b_1^i + b_2^i + \ldots + b_{k^i}^i$.

Once again we note that pure strategy equilibria are known to exist in a discriminatory auction when bidders have independent private values. When bidders are symmetric, as assumed in this chapter, a symmetric equilibrium is known to exist. No explicit characterization of the strategies is available, however, so, as in the previous section, we proceed indirectly by deducing properties that any equilibrium must satisfy.

It is obvious that there will be demand reduction in a discriminatory auction—to bid $b_k^i = x_k^i$ would ensure only that there is no gain from winning the kth object. To further understand the nature of equilibrium bids, let us look more closely at the two unit and two bidder case. Fix a symmetric equilibrium (β_1, β_2) of the discriminatory auction. First, notice that if the highest amount ever bid on the second unit is $\overline{b} = \max \beta_2(\mathbf{x})$, then it makes no sense for a bidder to bid more than $\overline{b}$ on the first unit. This is because any bid b_1 on the first unit that is greater than $\overline{b}$ will win with probability 1 and the bidder could do better by reducing it slightly. Thus, we have that in equilibrium

$$\max_{\mathbf{x}} \beta_1(\mathbf{x}) = \overline{b} = \max_{\mathbf{x}} \beta_2(\mathbf{x}) \tag{13.6}$$

Second, consider a particular bidder and let the random variable $\mathbf{C} = (C_1, C_2)$ denote the competing bids—that is, the bids of the other bidder. Let H_1 denote the marginal distribution of a bidder's high bid C_1 and let H_2 denote the marginal distribution of the other bidder's low bid C_2. Thus,

$$H_k(c) = \text{Prob}\left[\beta_k(\mathbf{X}) \leq c\right]$$

Since, for all $\mathbf{x}$, $\beta_1(\mathbf{x}) \geq \beta_2(\mathbf{x})$, it is clear that the distribution H_1 stochastically dominates the distribution H_2. As usual, let h_1 and h_2 denote the corresponding densities.

Suppose a bidder has values (x_1, x_2) and bids (b_1, b_2). He wins both units if $C_1 < b_2$ and the probability of this event is $H_1(b_2)$. He wins exactly one unit if $C_2 < b_1$ and $C_1 > b_2$ and the probability of this event is $H_2(b_1) - H_1(b_2)$. Thus, the expected payoff is

$$\begin{aligned} \Pi(\mathbf{b}, \mathbf{x}) &= H_1(b_2)(x_1 + x_2 - b_1 - b_2) \\ &\quad + [H_2(b_1) - H_1(b_2)](x_1 - b_1) \\ &= H_2(b_1)(x_1 - b_1) + H_1(b_2)(x_2 - b_2) \end{aligned} \tag{13.7}$$

The bidder's optimization problem is choose $\mathbf{b}$ to maximize $\Pi(\mathbf{b}, \mathbf{x})$ subject to the constraint that $b_1 \geq b_2$.

When the constraint $b_1 \geq b_2$ does not bind at the optimum, so that $b_1 > b_2$, the first-order conditions for an optimum are

$$h_2(b_1)(x_1 - b_1) = H_2(b_1) \tag{13.8}$$
$$h_1(b_2)(x_2 - b_2) = H_1(b_2) \tag{13.9}$$

Thus, we deduce that whenever $b_1 > b_2$, the bids are completely *separable* in the values—that is, β_1 does not depend on x_2 and β_2 does not depend on x_1.

When the constraint $b_1 \geq b_2$ binds at the optimum, so that $b_1 = b_2 \equiv b$, the first-order condition is

$$h_2(b)(x_1 - b) + h_1(b)(x_2 - b) = H_2(b) + H_1(b) \tag{13.10}$$

In this case, the bidder submits a "flat demand" function—bidding the same amount for the each of the two units. An examination of (13.7) reveals that if it is optimal to submit the flat demand bid b for the value vector $\mathbf{x} = (x_1, x_2)$ and also for the value vector $\mathbf{z} = (z_1, z_2)$, then it is optimal to submit the same flat demand bid b for any convex combination of the values $\lambda\mathbf{x} + (1 - \lambda)\mathbf{z}$, where $0 \leq \lambda \leq 1$.

13.5.1 Structure of Equilibria

Once again, we deduce some structural properties of equilibrium strategies without deriving the strategies explicitly. Indeed, unlike in the case of a single object, even if bidders are symmetric no closed form expression for the bidding strategies is available. This is because even symmetric bidders value different units of the same object differently. For example, when there are two units for sale to two bidders, bids on the first unit compete with rival bids on the second unit. Since the marginal distributions of the values are different, the gains and losses from, say, bidding higher on the first unit are different from those from bidding higher on the second unit.

Indeed, when the constraint $b_1 \geq b_2$ is not binding, the relevant first-order conditions, (13.8) and (13.9), that determine bidding strategies in a symmetric multiunit auction are the *same* as those that determine bidding strategies in an asymmetric single-object auction (see Chapter 4, especially (4.17) on page 47). The only difference is notational—the subscripts now index units—reflecting the fact that asymmetries across bidders have been replaced by asymmetries across different units of the same good. The two problems are not isomorphic, however. In the discriminatory auction, the constraint $b_1 \geq b_2$ binds some of the time—bidders submit flat demands with positive probability.

To see why, suppose for the moment that F_1 dominates F_2 in terms of the reverse hazard rate—that is, for all x,

$$\frac{f_1(x)}{F_1(x)} > \frac{f_2(x)}{F_2(x)}$$

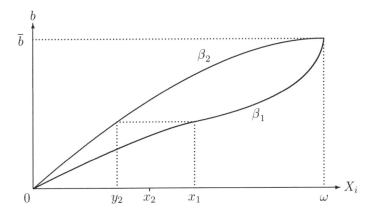

FIGURE 13.4. Illustration of the Necessity of Flat Demands

Suppose that (β_1, β_2) is a solution to the differential equations resulting from (13.8) and (13.9), that is, if we neglect the constraint that $b_1 \geq b_2$. Then we can deduce that for all $x \in (0, \omega)$, $\beta_2(x) > \beta_1(x)$, as shown in Figure 13.4. This is because Proposition 4.4 on page 48 applies to this situation unchanged—only the meaning of the subscripts is different—so the bids on the second unit will be more aggressive than bids on the first unit. But now for every $x_1 \in (0, \omega)$, if $x_2 > y_2 \equiv \phi_2(\beta_1(x_1))$, where ϕ_2 is the inverse of β_2, the constraint $b_1 \geq b_2$ surely binds and bidders must submit flat demands when that happens. Thus, we conclude that *bidders submit flat demands with positive probability.*

The assumption that F_1 dominates F_2 in terms of the reverse hazard rate is satisfied in the multi-use model outlined earlier. Suppose that each bidder first draws two values Z_1 and Z_2 independently from some distribution F—the values of the object in two different uses. If he obtains only one unit, then he uses it in the best way possible, so his value for the first unit is $X_1 = \max\{Z_1, Z_2\}$. The marginal value of the second unit is then $X_2 = \min\{Z_1, Z_2\}$. With this specification, F_1 and F_2 are just distributions of the highest and second-highest order statistics, respectively, and it is routine to verify that F_1 dominates F_2 in terms of the reverse hazard rate.

At the same time, it cannot be optimal for bidders to *always* submit flat demands. In particular, when the values (x_1, x_2) are close to $(\omega, 0)$, then the only possible flat demand bid (b, b) is close to $(0, 0)$. But an examination of (13.10) reveals that this is impossible, so that we must have that $b_1 > b_2$, that is, the submitted demand function is "downward sloping." Thus, we also conclude that *bidders submit downward sloping demands with positive probability.*

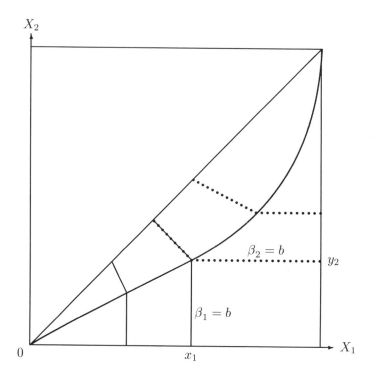

FIGURE 13.5. Equilibrium Bids in a Discriminatory Auction

Proposition 13.6 *Suppose that F_1 dominates F_2 in terms of the reverse hazard rate. In any equilibrium of the two-bidder, two-unit discriminatory auction, bidders submit flat demands if the difference in marginal values is small and submit downward sloping demands if the difference is large.*

Figure 13.5 illustrates Proposition 13.6 by delineating the set of values for which bidders submit flat demands (the region lying between the curve and the 45° line) and the set of values for which bidders submit downward sloping demands (the region lying below the curve). Points lying on the kinked solid lines are value pairs such that the bid on the first unit is a constant, and points on the kinked dotted lines are value pairs such that the bid on the second unit is a constant. Below the curve, the bids on the two units are separable, so the "iso-bid" curves for the first unit are vertical lines and for the second unit are horizontal lines. Above the curve, the same amount b is bid for both units, so the "iso-bid" curves are common, downward sloping lines and, as indicated by (13.10), have slope

$$-\frac{h_1(b)}{h_2(b)}$$

The iso-bid lines when flat demands are submitted are thus are not parallel and typically get flatter as the amount bid b increases. Given a value x_1 of the first unit, the bid on the first unit b exceeds the amount bid on the second unit as long as $x_2 \leq y_2$ (compare with Figure 13.4). Once $x_2 > y_2$ the constraint $b_1 \geq b_2$ binds and flat demands are submitted.

Given the features of equilibrium behavior highlighted above it is not surprising that the discriminatory auction is, in general, inefficient. The presence of flat demands and the fact that when downward sloping bidding on the second unit is more aggressive than on the first unit implies that the two units are not treated in symmetric fashion. Proposition 13.3 implies the following:

Proposition 13.7 *Every equilibrium of the discriminatory auction is inefficient.*

13.5.2   Single-Unit Demand

As in the case of the uniform-price auction, the general inefficiency of the discriminatory auction stems not from the multiplicity of units for sale but rather from the fact that bidders demand multiple units. Unlike the uniform-price auction, however, the discriminatory auction is efficient with single-unit demand only in the case where bidders are symmetric. This is not surprising since the single-unit first-price auction is also efficient only under the assumption of symmetry.

Suppose that there are N symmetric bidders, each of whom draws a single value independently from the same distribution F. A symmetric equilibrium of a discriminatory auction in which $K < N$ units are sold entails that each bidder follow the strategy

$$\beta(x) = E\left[Y_K^{(N-1)} \mid Y_K^{(N-1)} < x\right]$$

where $Y_K^{(N-1)}$ denotes the Kth-highest order statistic of $N-1$ draws from the distribution F.

The argument that this constitutes an equilibrium is the same as in Chapter 2, where $K = 1$. Since all bidders follow the same strategy, the K highest bids come from bidders with the K highest values; so with single-unit demand, the auction is efficient.

This chapter has focused on the efficiency of the various multiunit auctions. In the next chapter we turn to our other major concern—the revenue from the different auctions.

Chapter Notes

Vickrey (1961) first studied multiunit auctions and recognized that the discriminatory and uniform-pricing rules were inefficient. In fact, it is safe to say that this is the reason he proposed an entirely new pricing rule—which we now know by his name—that was efficient. He also recognized that the root cause of the inefficiency of the discriminatory and uniform-price auctions was not the multiplicity of units for sale but that bidders had multiunit demand.

There has been a lively debate regarding the merits of the various formats, mainly in the context of the auction of Treasury bills. The Treasury has traditionally used the discriminatory auction, but since the 1960s numerous economists have advocated a switch to the uniform-price format. The arguments in favor of the uniform-price auction have been made on many grounds—revenue, efficiency, strategic simplicity and susceptibility to collusion. Back and Zender (1993) summarize the debate and highlight the fact that many of the arguments that have been made are based on extrapolating properties of the two auctions from situations where bidders have single-unit demand to more general situations. As we have seen, and as Vickrey (1961) himself realized, the properties of these auctions in the context of single-unit demand do not extend to situations with multiunit demand. As a case in point, the strategic simplicity of the uniform-price auction with single-unit demand—it is a dominant strategy to bid one's value—does not extend to situations with multiunit demand—it is now advantageous to engage in demand reduction. The policy debate has concerned the relative merits of the discriminatory and uniform-price auctions; the attractive properties of the Vickrey auction seem to have been largely overlooked. We hasten to add, however, that these properties hold in a model with private values and such a specification does not seem the most natural in the context of Treasury bills.

The derivation of equilibrium bidding behavior in private value uniform-price auctions follows the work of Noussair (1995) and Englebrecht-Wiggans and Kahn (1998a). The example of low revenue equilibria in the uniform-price auction is taken from the latter paper. The analysis of equilibrium strategies in the discriminatory auction is, to a large extent, based on Englebrecht-Wiggans and Kahn (1998b). The issue of demand reduction has been studied in more detail by Ausubel and Cramton (1996).

In an important paper, Reny (1999) has shown that with independent private values, the discriminatory auction has a pure strategy equilibrium. In symmetric situations, there is a symmetric pure strategy equilibrium. Bresky (2000) extends Reny's work to show that a whole class of auctions—which includes both the uniform-price and discriminatory formats—has pure strategy equilibria, again in an independent private values setting that is possibly asymmetric.

We have argued that the discriminatory and uniform-price auctions are generally inefficient. Swinkels (1999) shows, however, that as the number of bidders gets arbitrarily large, the inefficiency in the discriminatory auction goes to zero. Essentially, in any equilibrium, once there are enough bidders, bidding behavior begins to resemble "price taking." Thus, the discriminatory auction is asymptotically efficient in the sense that the ratio of social surplus in equilibrium to the attainable social surplus approaches one. The rate at which the inefficiency goes to zero as the number of bidders increases may be slow, however, so the inefficiency may remain large even for a relatively large number of bidders. In a second paper, Swinkels (2001) studies a model in which the total supply is uncertain and derives results on the asymptotic efficiency of both the discriminatory and uniform-price auctions.

14
Some Revenue Considerations

The previous chapter focused on some properties of the equilibria of multiunit auctions and the consequences for the efficiency of the various formats. This chapter concerns the issue of revenue.

The revenue equivalence principle formed the cornerstone of the analysis of single object auctions in the independent private values setting. Its message was that if two auction formats resulted in the same equilibrium allocation, then the two auctions must result in the same expected payoffs and revenues. In its simplest form it ensured that if bidders are symmetric, then all standard single object auctions—in particular, the first- and second-price formats—resulted in the same expected revenue. This was because all of the standard auctions were efficient in the symmetric context. Indeed, we were able to use the revenue equivalence principle to derive equilibrium strategies in some unusual auction formats, for instance, third-price and all-pay auctions.

In this chapter we show that the revenue equivalence principle extends in a relatively straightforward manner to the multiple object environment. But we have already seen that even in symmetric settings, the standard multiunit auctions need not allocate in the same way and are not revenue equivalent. For instance, in Example 13.1, the revenue from a uniform-price auction was zero, whereas the revenue from the discriminatory or Vickrey auctions was positive. In some cases, however, it is possible to argue on *a priori* grounds that two multiunit auctions will allocate in the same way. The revenue equivalence principle then becomes a powerful tool—it can be used to derive equilibrium strategies—and in this chapter we illustrate its use in this manner.

14.1   Revenue Equivalence in Multiunit Auctions

Our basic setup is the same as in the previous chapter. Specifically, there are K identical objects for sale and N potential buyers are bidding for these. Bidder i's valuation for the objects is given by a K-vector $\mathbf{X}^i = \left(X_1^i, X_2^i, \ldots, X_K^i\right)$, where X_K^i represents the *marginal* value of obtaining the kth object and these are declining. We do allow for asymmetries among bidders. Thus, bidders' value vectors, while drawn independently from

$$\mathcal{X} = \left\{ \mathbf{x} \in [0, \omega]^K : \forall k, x_{k+1} \geq x_k \right\}$$

need not be identically distributed. Let bidder i's value vector $\mathbf{X}^i$ be distributed on $\mathcal{X}$ according to the density function f_i.

Fix an auction form A for allocating multiple units and fix an equilibrium $\boldsymbol{\beta} = (\boldsymbol{\beta}^1, \boldsymbol{\beta}^2, \ldots, \boldsymbol{\beta}^N)$ of A. Consider a particular bidder, say i, and suppose that other bidders $j \neq i$ follow the equilibrium strategies $\boldsymbol{\beta}^j$. Suppose that bidder i's value vector is $\mathbf{x}^i$ but he reports that it is $\mathbf{z}^i$—that is, he bids $\boldsymbol{\beta}^i(\mathbf{z}^i)$ instead of $\boldsymbol{\beta}^i(\mathbf{x}^i)$. Let $q_1^i(\mathbf{z}^i)$ denote the probability that bidder i will win the first unit when he bids $\boldsymbol{\beta}^i(\mathbf{z}^i)$, let $q_2^i(\mathbf{z}^i)$ denote the probability that he will win a second unit, and so on. In general, $q_k^i(\mathbf{z}^i)$ denotes the probability that he will win the kth unit.[1] If his value vector is $\mathbf{x}^i$, a bidder's gain from reporting that it is $\mathbf{z}^i$ can be written as

$$\sum_{k=1}^{K} q_k^i\left(\mathbf{z}^i\right) x_k^i = \mathbf{q}^i(\mathbf{z}^i) \cdot \mathbf{x}^i$$

where $\mathbf{q}^i(\mathbf{z}^i)$ is the K-vector of probabilities $q_k^i(\mathbf{z}^i)$.

Consider two different auction forms and fix equilibrium strategies in each. We will say that the two auction forms have the same *allocation rule* if the resulting probabilities $q_k^i(\mathbf{z}^i)$ in equilibrium are the same.

Let $m^i(\mathbf{z}^i)$ be the equilibrium expected payment in auction A by bidder i when he reports that his value vector is $\mathbf{z}^i$. Suppose that the auction is such that in equilibrium $m^i(0) = 0$. Bidder i's expected payoff is

$$\mathbf{q}^i(\mathbf{z}^i) \cdot \mathbf{x}^i - m^i(\mathbf{z}^i)$$

In equilibrium it is optimal to bid $\boldsymbol{\beta}^i\left(\mathbf{x}^i\right)$, so for all $\mathbf{z}^i$,

$$\mathbf{q}^i(\mathbf{x}^i) \cdot \mathbf{x}^i - m^i(\mathbf{x}^i) \geq \mathbf{q}^i(\mathbf{z}^i) \cdot \mathbf{x}^i - m^i(\mathbf{z}^i) \tag{14.1}$$

---

[1]For $k < K$, $q_k^i - q_{k+1}^i$ is the probability that bidder i will win exactly k units; q_K^i is the probability that bidder i will win all K units.

Now define

$$U^i(\mathbf{x}^i) \equiv \max_{\mathbf{z}^i} \left\{ \mathbf{q}^i(\mathbf{z}^i) \cdot \mathbf{x}^i - m^i(\mathbf{z}^i) \right\} \qquad (14.2)$$

to be the maximized payoff function and since U^i is the maximum of a family of affine functions—one for each $\mathbf{z}^i$—it is convex.

Notice that (14.1) can be rewritten as follows: for all $\mathbf{x}^i$ and $\mathbf{z}^i$,

$$U^i(\mathbf{z}^i) \geq U^i(\mathbf{x}^i) + \mathbf{q}^i(\mathbf{x}^i) \cdot (\mathbf{z}^i - \mathbf{x}^i) \qquad (14.3)$$

The inequality in (14.3), a consequence of equilibrium play, implies for all $\mathbf{x}^i$, the probability vector $\mathbf{q}^i(\mathbf{x}^i)$ is a *subgradient* of the payoff function U^i, which is convex, at the point $\mathbf{x}^i$. In other words, the vector $\mathbf{q}^i(\mathbf{x}^i)$ is perpendicular to the hyperplane that supports the function U^i at $\mathbf{x}^i$—the graph of the function U^i lies above the hyperplane.

So far we argued in a manner that is parallel to that presented in Chapter 5 (see, for instance, (5.5)), the only difference being that we now have multidimensional values—that is, value vectors. In the one-dimensional problem we were able to integrate q_i, the probability of winning the object, to obtain U_i. We wish to carry out a similar exercise here, and our next step serves to reduce the multidimensional problem to a single dimension.

Fix an arbitrary point $\mathbf{x}^i$ and define a function $V^i : [0, 1] \to \mathbb{R}$ by

$$V^i(t) = U^i(t\mathbf{x}^i)$$

so that $V^i(0) = U^i(\mathbf{0})$ and $V^i(1) = U^i(\mathbf{x}^i)$. Since $U^i : \mathcal{X} \to \mathbb{R}$ is convex and continuous, $V^i : [0, 1] \to \mathbb{R}$ is also convex and continuous. The function V^i is just a restriction of U^i to the line joining $\mathbf{0}$ to $\mathbf{x}^i$, so, while also convex, V^i is a function of only one variable.

A convex function of one variable is absolutely continuous and thus it is differentiable almost everywhere in the interior of its domain. Furthermore, every absolutely continuous function is the integral of its derivative, so we have

$$V^i(1) = V^i(0) + \int_0^1 \frac{dV^i(t)}{dt}\, dt \qquad (14.4)$$

Now suppose $t \in (0, 1)$ is such that V^i is differentiable at t. From (14.3),

$$\begin{aligned} V^i(t + \Delta) - V^i(t) &= U^i\big((t + \Delta)\mathbf{x}^i\big) - U^i(t\mathbf{x}^i) \\ &\geq \mathbf{q}^i(t\mathbf{x}^i) \cdot \Delta\mathbf{x}^i \end{aligned}$$

If $\Delta > 0$, then we get

$$\frac{V^i(t + \Delta) - V^i(t)}{\Delta} \geq \mathbf{q}^i(t\mathbf{x}^i) \cdot \mathbf{x}^i$$

and taking the limit as $\Delta \downarrow 0$ we obtain that

$$\frac{dV^i(t)}{dt} \geq \mathbf{q}^i(t\mathbf{x}^i) \cdot \mathbf{x}^i$$

On the other hand, if $\Delta < 0$, then taking the limit as $\Delta \uparrow 0$ we get the opposite inequality. Thus, if V^i is differentiable at $t \in (0, 1)$,

$$\frac{dV^i(t)}{dt} = \mathbf{q}^i\left(t\mathbf{x}^i\right) \cdot \mathbf{x}^i$$

Now substituting in (14.4) we obtain that for all $\mathbf{x}^i \in \mathcal{X}$:

$$U^i\left(\mathbf{x}^i\right) = U^i(\mathbf{0}) + \int_0^1 \mathbf{q}^i\left(t\mathbf{x}^i\right) \cdot \mathbf{x}^i \, dt \tag{14.5}$$

Thus, at any point $\mathbf{x}^i$, the payoff U^i is determined by the probabilities $\mathbf{q}^i$ up to an additive constant.

Since

$$m^i\left(\mathbf{x}^i\right) = \mathbf{q}^i\left(\mathbf{x}^i\right) \cdot \mathbf{x}^i - U^i\left(\mathbf{x}^i\right)$$

the expected payments in any two auctions with the same allocation rule are also the same. We have thus shown that the revenue equivalence principle holds for multiunit auctions as well.

Proposition 14.1 *The equilibrium payoff (and payment) functions of any bidder in any two multiunit auctions that have the same allocation rule differ at most by an additive constant.*

When each bidder, has use for at most one unit—the case of single-unit demand—the discriminatory and uniform-price auctions allocate efficiently. In this case, the revenue equivalence principle derived above can be applied, so the two auctions are revenue equivalent to the Vickrey auction.

With multiunit demands, only the Vickrey auction is generally efficient. In this case, the revenue equivalence principle provides little insight in determining the revenue from the discriminatory and uniform-price auctions relative to that from the Vickrey auction. Indeed, it is known that no general ranking of the revenues can be obtained—depending on the distribution of values one or the other auction may be superior. In specific instances, however, it is possible to argue on *a priori* grounds that all three auctions are efficient and in these instances the power of the revenue equivalence principle can be brought to bear. We now present such an example.

14.2 Revenue Equivalence with Multiunit Demand: An Example

Suppose that there are three units for sale ($K = 3$) and two bidders, each of whom wants at most two units ($L = 2$). Bidders' value vectors $\mathbf{X} = (X_1, X_2)$ are two-dimensional and are identically and independently distributed according to the density function f with support $\{\mathbf{x} \in [0,1]^2 : x_1 \geq x_2\}$.

Notice that the environment specified here has the feature that in any standard auction each bidder is assured of winning at least one unit. The Vickrey auction is, of course, efficient. In what follows, we will first argue, on *a priori* grounds, that the uniform-price auction also has an efficient equilibrium and we will then use the revenue equivalence principle to explicitly derive the equilibrium bidding strategies. We will analyze the discriminatory auction in the same way. The special structure given above is interesting because it represents one of the few known instances in which the equilibrium bidding strategies in the three multiunit auctions can be derived explicitly.

Let F_1 and F_2 denote the marginal distributions of X_1 and X_2, respectively, and let f_1 and f_2 be the corresponding marginal densities.

Vickrey Auction

In a Vickrey auction it is a dominant strategy for each bidder to bid truthfully—that is, to submit a bid vector $\mathbf{b}^i = \mathbf{x}^i$. The vector of competing bids that bidder i faces is

$$\mathbf{c}^{-i} = (x_1^j, x_2^j, 0)$$

where $j \neq i$. He is sure to win at least one unit, so he pays the third highest competing bid $c_3^{-i} = 0$ for this unit. He wins another unit if his value for the second unit exceeds bidder j's value for the second unit—that is, if $x_2^i > x_2^j$ and in that case pays the second-highest competing bid, $c_2^{-i} = x_2^j$, for this unit.

A bidder's expected payment when his value vector is $\mathbf{x} = (x_1, x_2)$ is therefore

$$
\begin{aligned}
m^{\mathrm{V}}(\mathbf{x}) &= \operatorname{Prob}\left[X_2 < x_2\right] E\left[X_2 \mid X_2 < x_2\right] \\
&= \int_0^{x_2} y f_2(y)\, dy
\end{aligned}
\tag{14.6}
$$

and notice that this is independent of x_1.

Example 14.1 *Suppose that X_1 and X_2 are the highest and second-highest order statistics, respectively, of two independent draws from a uniform distribution on $[0,1]$.*

In a Vickrey auction, the expected revenue of the seller is

$$E\left[R^{\mathrm{V}}\right] = E\left[Y_4^{(4)}\right] = \frac{1}{5}$$

where $Y_4^{(4)}$ is the lowest of four independent draws from the uniform distribution on $[0,1]$. ▲

Uniform-Price Auction

Recall that in a uniform price auction it is weakly dominant for each bidder to bid the value on the first unit. Thus, in any undominated equilibrium, $b_1^i = x_1^i$. It remains to determine the equilibrium bids on the second unit. Suppose that the bids on the second unit are determined by the increasing function $\beta_2 : [0,1] \to \mathbb{R}_+$ and in the interest of notational simplicity let us write $\beta \equiv \beta_2$. (Here we are postulating that the bids on the second unit are independent of the value of the first unit, and as we will see, this is indeed the case.) Now notice that if such an equilibrium exists, it will allocate efficiently. The reason is that once again each bidder is guaranteed to win at least one unit. A bidder will win a second unit only if $\beta(x_2^i) > \beta(x_2^j)$ and since β is increasing, $x_2^i > x_2^j$, so it is efficient for him to do so.

We can now use the revenue equivalence principle to deduce that in any such equilibrium of the uniform-price auction the expected payment of a bidder with value vector $\mathbf{x}$ is the same as in a Vickrey auction, so using (14.6) we obtain

$$
\begin{aligned}
m^{\mathrm{U}}(\mathbf{x}) &= m^{\mathrm{V}}(\mathbf{x}) \\
&= \int_0^{x_2} y f_2(y)\, dy
\end{aligned}
\tag{14.7}
$$

On the other hand, it is easy to see that the equilibrium expected payment of bidder 1 when his value vector is $\mathbf{x} = (x_1, x_2)$ is

$$
m^{\mathrm{U}}(\mathbf{x}) = \int_0^{x_2} 2\beta(y) f_2(y)\, dy + (1 - F_2(x_2))\,\beta(x_2)
\tag{14.8}
$$

The first term is the expected payment in the event that bidder i wins both units so that the highest losing bid, and hence the price, is $\beta(x_2^j)$. The second term derives from the event that bidder i wins only one unit, so the highest losing bid is his own bid for the second unit—that is, $\beta(x_2)$.

The revenue equivalence principle implies that if β is the equilibrium bidding strategy for the second unit, then it must satisfy: for all $z \in [0, \omega]$,

$$
\int_0^z y f_2(y)\, dy = \int_0^z 2\beta(y) f_2(y)\, dy + (1 - F_2(z))\,\beta(z)
$$

Differentiating with respect to z, we deduce that β must satisfy the differential equation

$$
z f_2(z) = \beta(z) f_2(z) + (1 - F_2(z))\,\beta'(z)
$$

together with the initial condition $\beta(0) = 0$. This can be rearranged as

$$
\beta'(z) = (z - \beta(z))\,\lambda_2(z)
\tag{14.9}
$$

where

$$\lambda_2(z) \equiv \frac{f_2(z)}{1 - F_2(z)}$$

is the hazard rate function associated with F_2. The solution to the differential equation (14.9) is

$$\beta(z) = \int_0^z y \lambda_2(y) \, dL(y \mid z) \tag{14.10}$$

where

$$L(y \mid z) = \exp\left(-\int_y^z \lambda_2(t) \, dt\right)$$

is the relevant integrating factor. (The reader may wish to refer to Proposition 6.3 on page 93.) The strategy β is increasing and the argument that this constitutes an equilibrium is straightforward.

We have thus shown that a symmetric equilibrium bidding strategy in the uniform-price auction is

$$\boldsymbol{\beta}^{\mathrm{U}}(x_1, x_2) = (x_1, \beta(x_2))$$

where β is defined in (14.10).

Example 14.1 (continued) X_1 and X_2 *are the highest and second-highest order statistics from a uniform distribution on* $[0, 1]$.

It may be verified that $\beta(z) = z^2$. The selling price is the lowest of the four bids submitted in total. Since three units are for sale, the expected revenue is

$$
\begin{aligned}
E\left[R^{\mathrm{U}}\right] &= 3E\left[\beta\left(Y_4^{(4)}\right)\right] \\
&= 3E\left[\left(Y_4^{(4)}\right)^2\right] \\
&= \frac{1}{5}
\end{aligned}
$$

where $Y_4^{(4)}$ is the lowest of four independent draws from the uniform distribution on $[0, 1]$. ▲

Discriminatory Auction

Once again, each bidder is assured of winning at least one unit. Now suppose that a bidder bids (b_1, b_2) such that $b_1 > b_2$. Reducing the bid on the first unit to $b_1 - \varepsilon > b_2$ does not affect a bidder's chances of winning the first unit—he wins it regardless of his bid—but increases his payoff since he pays less for this unit. Thus, it cannot be optimal to bid in a way that $b_1 > b_2$ and in equilibrium we must have $b_1 = b_2$. In other words, in any equilibrium of the discriminatory auction bidders always submit flat demand functions. Moreover, the amount bid is determined solely by the marginal value of the second unit, x_2.

Suppose that the bids on the second unit are determined by the increasing function $\beta_2 : [0, 1] \rightarrow \mathbb{R}_+$ and in the interest of notational simplicity let us once again write $\beta \equiv \beta_2$. Now notice that in this example, any equilibrium of the discriminatory auction with an increasing β is efficient. Suppose bidder i follows the equilibrium strategy of bidding the flat demand function $(\beta(x_2^i), \beta(x_2^i))$. He wins one unit for sure and wins a second unit if $\beta(x_2^i) > \beta(x_2^j)$. Since β is increasing, $x_2^i > x_2^j$, so it is efficient for i to win a second unit.

Since the equilibrium is efficient we can invoke the revenue equivalence principle to deduce that the expected payment of a bidder with value vector $\mathbf{x}$ in a discriminatory auction is the same as in a Vickrey auction. Using (14.6) we obtain

$$
\begin{aligned}
m^D(\mathbf{x}) &= m^V(\mathbf{x}) \\
&= \int_0^{x_2} y f_2(y)\, dy
\end{aligned}
\tag{14.11}
$$

On the other hand, we know that the expected payment in a discriminatory auction is

$$
m^D(\mathbf{x}) = \beta(x_2) + F_2(x_2)\,\beta(x_2)
\tag{14.12}
$$

The first term is the sure payment that the bidder will make for the first unit. The second term is the expected payment for the second unit, which he wins only if his value for the second unit x_2 exceeds the other bidder's value for the second unit. Since bidders submit flat demands, the amount paid for each unit is the same. From (14.11) and (14.12) we determine that

$$
\beta(x_2) = \frac{1}{1 + F_2(x_2)} \int_0^{x_2} y f_2(y)\, dy
\tag{14.13}
$$

The function β is increasing and the argument that this constitutes as equilibrium is straightforward.

Thus, we have shown that a symmetric equilibrium in the discriminatory auction is

$$
\boldsymbol{\beta}^D(x_1, x_2) = (\beta(x_2), \beta(x_2))
$$

where β is defined in (14.13).

Example 14.1 (continued) X_1 and X_2 are the highest and second-highest order statistics from a uniform distribution on $[0, 1]$.

The bidding strategy in the discriminatory auction is given by

$$\beta(z) = \frac{z^2 - \frac{2}{3}z^3}{1 + 2z - z^2}$$

The expected payment of a bidder with value x_2 for the second unit is

$$m^D(\mathbf{x}) = (x_2)^2 - \frac{2}{3}(x_2)^3$$

and the *ex ante* expected payment of a bidder is

$$m^D = \int_0^1 m^D(\mathbf{x})\, dx_2 = \frac{1}{10}$$

Since there are two bidders, the expected revenue of the seller in a discriminatory auction is twice the *ex ante* payment of each bidder and equals, as it must, $\frac{1}{5}$. ▲

Chapter Notes

The multidimensional revenue equivalence principle in Proposition 14.1 is due to Krishna and Perry (1998). It calculates the payoff $U^i(\mathbf{x}^i)$ by integrating the function $\mathbf{q}^i$ along the ray from $\mathbf{0}$ to $\mathbf{x}^i$ (as in (14.5)). It turns out, however, that the calculation does not depend on the particular path along which the integral is evaluated—it is path independent (see Krishna and Maenner, 2001). Specifically, for any smooth (continuously differentiable) path $\boldsymbol{\alpha} : [0, 1] \to \mathcal{X}$ such that $\boldsymbol{\alpha}(0) = \mathbf{0}$ and $\boldsymbol{\alpha}(1) = \mathbf{x}^i$,

$$U^i(\mathbf{x}^i) = U^i(\mathbf{0}) + \int_0^1 \mathbf{q}^i(\boldsymbol{\alpha}(t)) \cdot \mathbf{D}\boldsymbol{\alpha}(t)\, dt$$

Krishna and Maenner (2001) also show that the integral of a convex function does not depend on the particular selection from its subgradient mapping: The value of the integral would be the same if some selection other than $\mathbf{q}^i$ were used.

15

Sequential Sales

In all of the multiunit auctions considered thus far—the discriminatory, uniform-price, and Vickrey formats—all the units are sold at-one-go. In this chapter we examine situations in which the units are sold one-at-a-time in separate auctions that are conducted sequentially.

15.1   Sequential First-Price Auctions

Consider a situation in which the K identical items are sold to $N > K$ bidders using a series of first-price sealed-bid auctions. Specifically, one of the items is auctioned using the first-price format, and the price at which it is sold—the winning bid—is announced. The second item is then sold and again the price at which it is sold—the winning bid in the second auction—is announced. The third item is then sold, and so on.

We restrict attention to situations in which each bidder has use for at most one unit—the case of *single-unit demand*. We also suppose that bidders have private values and that each bidder's value X_i is drawn independently from the same distribution F on $[0, \omega]$. It is then natural to look for a symmetric equilibrium.

A bidding strategy for a bidder consists of K functions $\beta_1^{\mathrm{I}}, \beta_2^{\mathrm{I}}, \ldots, \beta_K^{\mathrm{I}}$ where $\beta_k^{\mathrm{I}}(x, p_1, p_2, \ldots, p_{k-1})$ denotes the bid in the kth auction given that the bidder's value is x and the prices in the $k - 1$ previous auctions were $p_1, p_2, \ldots, p_{k-1}$, respectively. All this assumes, of course, that the particular bidder has not already won an object and so is still active in the kth auction.

(From now on, if there is no ambiguity, the superscript "I" identifying the first-price format will be omitted.)

Notice that if the equilibrium strategies β_k are increasing functions of the value x, then the items will be sold in order of decreasing values. The first item will go to the bidder with the highest value, the second to the bidder with the second-highest value, and so on. In that case the K units will be allocated efficiently.

In what follows it will be convenient to think of the auctions as being held in different periods. Moreover, the auctions are assumed to be held in a short enough time—say, the same day—so that bidders do not discount payoffs from later periods.

15.1.1   Two Units

We begin by looking at a situation in which only two units are sold ($K = 2$), so a symmetric equilibrium consists of two functions (β_1, β_2), denoting the bidding strategies in the first and second periods, respectively. We conjecture that these are increasing and differentiable. The first-period bidding strategy is a function $\beta_1 : [0, \omega] \to \mathbb{R}_+$ that depends only on the bidder's value. The bid in the second period may depend on both the bidder's value and the price paid in the first auction, p_1. As usual, denote by $Y_1 \equiv Y_1^{(N-1)}$ the highest of $N - 1$ values, by $Y_2 \equiv Y_2^{(N-1)}$ the second-highest, and so on. Let F_1 and F_2 be the distributions of Y_1 and Y_2, respectively, and let f_1 and f_2 be the corresponding densities.

Since the first-period strategy β_1 is assumed to be invertible, the value of the winning bidder in the first period is commonly known; it is just $y_1 = \beta_1^{-1}(p_1)$. Thus, the second-period strategy can be thought of as a function $\beta_2 : [0, \omega] \times [0, \omega] \to \mathbb{R}_+$ so that a bidder with value x bids an amount $\beta_2(x, y_1)$ if $Y_1 = y_1$.

We are interested in equilibria that are sequentially rational—that is, equilibria with the property that following any outcome of the first-period auction, the strategies in the second period form an equilibrium. We begin with the second period.

Second-Period Strategy

Consider the second-period auction and the decision problem facing a particular bidder, say 1, whose value is x. Suppose all other bidders follow the equilibrium strategy $\beta_2(\cdot, y_1)$ and bidder 1 bids $\beta_2(z, y_1)$ in the second auction. Since the bidders competing against bidder 1 in the second auction have values $Y_2, Y_3, \ldots, Y_{N-1}$ and in equilibrium $Y_2 < y_1$, it makes no sense for bidder 1 to bid an amount greater than $\beta_2(y_1, y_1)$. His expected payoff in the second auction if he bids $\beta_2(z, y_1)$ for some $z \leq y_1$ is

$$\Pi(z, x; y_1) = F_2(z \mid Y_1 = y_1) \times [x - \beta_2(z, y_1)]$$

Differentiating $\Pi(z, x; y_1)$ with respect to z we obtain the first-order condition that in equilibrium, for all x,

$$f_2(x \mid Y_1 = y_1) [x - \beta_2(x, y_1)] - F_2(x \mid Y_1 = y_1) \beta_2'(x, y_1) = 0$$

where β_2' is the derivative of β_2 with respect to its first argument. Rearranging this results in the differential equation

$$\beta_2'(x, y_1) = \frac{f_2(x \mid Y_1 = y_1)}{F_2(x \mid Y_1 = y_1)} [x - \beta_2(x, y_1)] \tag{15.2}$$

together with the boundary condition $\beta_2(0, y_1) = 0$.

The probability that bidder 1 will win the second auction is the probability that Y_2, the second-highest of $N-1$ values, is less than z, conditional on the event that Y_1, the highest of $N - 1$ values, equals y_1. But because the different values are drawn independently, this is the same as the probability that $Y_1^{(N-2)}$, the highest of $N - 2$ values, is less than z, conditional on the event that $Y_1^{(N-2)} < y_1$. (See (C.6) in Appendix C for a formal demonstration.) This implies that the probability that bidder 1 will win the second auction is

$$
\begin{aligned}
F_2(z \mid Y_1 = y_1) &= F_1^{(N-2)}\left(z \mid Y_1^{(N-2)} < y_1\right) \\
&= \frac{F(z)^{N-2}}{F(y_1)^{N-2}} \tag{15.3}
\end{aligned}
$$

Now using (15.3) the differential equation (15.2) can be written as

$$\beta_2'(x, y_1) = \frac{(N - 2) f(x)}{F(x)} [x - \beta_2(x, y_1)]$$

or equivalently,

$$\frac{\partial}{\partial x} \left(F(x)^{N-2} \beta_2(x, y_1)\right) = (N - 2) F(x)^{N-3} f(x) x$$

Notice that the right-hand side of the preceding equation is independent of y_1 and hence of the price announcement. This means that β_2 is, in fact, independent of y_1; in other words, the *price announcements have no effect* on the equilibrium bids in the second period. The solution to the differential equation is

$$
\begin{aligned}
\beta_2(x) &= \frac{1}{F(x)^{N-2}} \int_0^x y d\left(F(y)^{N-2}\right) \\
&= E\left[Y_1^{(N-2)} \mid Y_1^{(N-2)} < x\right] \\
&= E[Y_2 \mid Y_2 < x < Y_1] \tag{15.4}
\end{aligned}
$$

where the last equality follows from (15.3). Thus, the complete bidding strategy for the second period is to bid $\beta_2(x)$ if $x \leq y_1$ and to bid $\beta_2(y_1)$ if $x > y_1$. The latter may occur if bidder 1 himself underbid in the first auction, say by mistake, causing someone else, with a lower value, to win. Even though this represents "off-equilibrium" behavior on the part of bidder 1 himself, recall that a strategy must prescribe actions in all contingencies.

The derivation of the strategy above is virtually the same as the derivation of the equilibrium bidding strategy in a first-price auction with symmetric private values (see Proposition 2.2 on page 17) and has been carried out using the necessary first-order conditions. Verifying the optimality of $\beta_2(x)$, and hence that β_2 constitutes a symmetric equilibrium in the second auction, is almost the same as in the case of a single-object first-price auction.

First-Period Strategy

In the first-period auction the decision problem facing a bidder is slightly more complex. Again let us take the perspective of bidder 1 with value x and suppose that all other bidders are following the first-period strategy β_1. Further, suppose that all bidders, including bidder 1, will follow β_2 in the second period, regardless of what happens in the first period.

The equilibrium calls on bidder 1 to bid $\beta_1(x)$ in the first stage, but consider what happens if he decides to bid $\beta_1(z)$ instead. If $z \geq x$, his payoff is

$$\Pi(z, x) = F_1(z)[x - \beta_1(z)] \\ + (N-1)(1 - F(z))F(x)^{N-2}[x - \beta_2(x)]$$

where the first term results from the event $Y_1 < z$, so that he wins the first auction with a bid of $\beta_1(z)$. The second term results from the event $Y_2 < x \leq z \leq Y_1$, so that he loses the first auction but wins the second. On the other hand, if $z < x$, his payoff is

$$\Pi(z, x) = F_1(z)[x - \beta_1(z)] + [F_2(x) - F_1(x)][x - \beta_2(x)] \\ + \int_z^x [x - \beta_2(y_1)]f_1(y_1)\,dy_1$$

where the first term again results from the event $Y_1 < z$. The second term results from the event $Y_2 < x < Y_1$, so that he loses the first auction but wins the second with a bid of $\beta_2(x)$. The third term results from the event $z < Y_1 < x$ so that he loses the first auction but wins the second with a bid of $\beta_2(Y_1)$.

The first-order conditions in the two cases are

$$0 = f_1(z)[x - \beta_1(z)] - F_1(z)\beta_1'(z) \\ - (N-1)f(z)F(x)^{N-2}[x - \beta_2(x)]$$

and

$$0 = f_1(z)[x - \beta_1(z)] - F_1(z)\beta_1'(z)$$
$$-f_1(z)[x - \beta_2(z)]$$

respectively. In equilibrium it is optimal to bid $\beta_1(x)$ and setting $z = x$ in *either* first-order condition results in the differential equation

$$\beta_1'(x) = \frac{f_1(x)}{F_1(x)}[\beta_2(x) - \beta_1(x)] \tag{15.5}$$

together with the boundary condition $\beta_1(0) = 0$. This can be rearranged so that

$$\frac{d}{dx}[F_1(x)\beta_1(x)] = f_1(x)\beta_2(x)$$

which has a solution

$$\beta_1(x) = \frac{1}{F_1(x)}\int_0^x \beta_2(y)f_1(y)\,dy$$
$$= E[\beta_2(Y_1) \mid Y_1 < x]$$
$$= E[E[Y_2 \mid Y_2 < Y_1] \mid Y_1 < x]$$
$$= E[Y_2 \mid Y_1 < x] \tag{15.6}$$

using (15.4).

Thus, we obtain the following:

Proposition 15.1 *Suppose bidders have single-unit demand and two units are sold by means of sequential first-price auctions. Symmetric equilibrium strategies are*

$$\beta_1^I(x) = E[Y_2 \mid Y_1 < x]$$
$$\beta_2^I(x) = E[Y_2 \mid Y_2 < x < Y_1]$$

where $Y_1 \equiv Y_1^{(N-1)}$ is the highest, and $Y_2 \equiv Y_2^{(N-1)}$ is the second highest, of $N-1$ independently drawn values.

15.1.2 More than Two Units

The construction underlying the equilibrium strategies in the two-unit case readily generalizes. So suppose that K units are sold in a sequence of K first-price auctions. The prices $p_1, p_2, \ldots, p_{k-1}$ in the first $k-1$ auctions are commonly known to the bidders in auction $k > 1$. In what follows, $Y_k \equiv Y_k^{(N-1)}$ denotes the kth highest of $N-1$ values, F_k denotes the distribution of Y_k, and f_k denotes the corresponding density.

As in the previous subsection, we will derive symmetric bidding strategies $(\beta_1, \beta_2, \ldots, \beta_K)$ by working backward from the last auction. So first consider the Kth auction—conducted in the last period. Following exactly the same reasoning as in the derivation of (15.4) leads to the conclusion that the bidding strategy in the last period is

$$\beta_K(x) = E[Y_K \mid Y_K < x < Y_{K-1}] \qquad (15.7)$$

Once again, the strategy in the last period does not depend on the price announcements.

Now consider the kth auction for some $k < K$. Given the detailed analysis of the two-unit case, we proceed somewhat heuristically.

Again let us take the perspective of bidder 1 with value x and suppose that all other bidders are following the kth period strategy β_k. Further, suppose that all bidders, including bidder 1, will follow the strategies $\beta_{k+1}, \beta_{k+2}, \ldots, \beta_K$ in the subsequent auctions.

The equilibrium calls on bidder 1 to bid $\beta_k(x)$ in the kth stage but consider what happens if he decides to bid slightly higher, say $\beta_k(x + \Delta)$. Now if $Y_k < x$, he would have won with his equilibrium bid $\beta_k(x)$ anyway, so the only consequence of his bidding higher is that he pays more than he would have. His expected payment increases by

$$F_k(x \mid Y_{k-1} = y_{k-1}) \times [\beta_k(x + \Delta) - \beta_k(x)] \qquad (15.8)$$

The expression in (15.8) thus represents the expected loss from bidding $\beta_k(x + \Delta)$ as opposed to $\beta_k(x)$. On the other hand, if $x < Y_k < x + \Delta$, he would have lost the kth auction with his equilibrium bid, whereas bidding higher results in his winning. Now there are two subcases. In the event that $Y_{k+1} < x < Y_k < x + \Delta$, he would have lost the kth auction but won the $k + 1$st. In the event that $x < Y_{k+1} < Y_k < x + \Delta$, however, he would have lost both the kth and the $k + 1$st auctions, and possibly won a later auction, say the lth for some $l > k + 1$. When Δ is small, however, the probability that $x < Y_{k+1} < Y_k < x + \Delta$ is very small—it is of second order in magnitude. Thus, the contribution to the expected gain from all events in which the bidder loses both the kth and the $k + 1$st auctions can be safely neglected when Δ is small. The overall expected gain from bidding $\beta_k(x + \Delta)$ is approximately

$$[F_k(x + \Delta \mid Y_{k-1} = y_{k-1}) - F_k(x \mid Y_{k-1} = y_{k-1})]$$
$$\times [(x - \beta_k(x)) - (x - \beta_{k+1}(x))] \qquad (15.9)$$

that is, it is the probability that $x < Y_k < x + \Delta$ times the difference in the equilibrium price paid tomorrow and the price paid today. Equating (15.8) and (15.9), dividing by Δ, and taking the limit as $\Delta \to 0$, we obtain the differential equation

$$\beta_k'(x) = \frac{f_k(x \mid Y_{k-1} = y_{k-1})}{F_k(x \mid Y_{k-1} = y_{k-1})} [\beta_{k+1}(x) - \beta_k(x)]$$

together with the boundary condition $\beta_k(0) = 0$. Now notice that as in (15.3),

$$
\begin{aligned}
F_k(x \mid Y_{k-1} = y_{k-1}) &= F_1^{(N-k)}\left(x \mid Y_1^{(N-k)} < y_{k-1}\right) \\
&= \frac{F(z)^{N-k}}{F(y_{k-1})^{N-k}}
\end{aligned}
$$

As before, the solution is independent of y_{k-1} and hence of the price announcements. The solution is

$$
\begin{aligned}
\beta_k(x) &= \frac{1}{F(x)^{N-k}} \int_0^x \beta_{k+1}(y) \, d\left(F(y)^{N-k}\right) \\
&= E\left[\beta_{k+1}\left(Y_1^{(N-k)}\right) \mid Y_1^{(N-k)} < x\right] \\
&= E\left[\beta_{k+1}(Y_k) \mid Y_k < x < Y_{k-1}\right] \qquad (15.10)
\end{aligned}
$$

An explicit solution to (15.10) can be obtained by working backward from the last period. Using (15.7), we deduce that

$$
\begin{aligned}
\beta_{K-1}(x) &= E\left[\beta_K(Y_{K-1}) \mid Y_{K-1} < x < Y_{K-2}\right] \\
&= E\left[E\left[Y_K \mid Y_K < Y_{K-1}\right] \mid Y_{K-1} < x < Y_{K-2}\right] \\
&= E\left[Y_K \mid Y_{K-1} < x < Y_{K-2}\right]
\end{aligned}
$$

and proceeding inductively in this fashion results in the solution for all k,

$$
\begin{aligned}
\beta_k(x) &= E\left[\beta_{k+1}(Y_k) \mid Y_k < x < Y_{k-1}\right] \\
&= E\left[E\left[Y_K \mid Y_{k+1} < Y_k\right] \mid Y_k < x < Y_{k-1}\right] \\
&= E\left[Y_K \mid Y_k < x < Y_{k-1}\right] \qquad (15.11)
\end{aligned}
$$

Thus, we obtain the following generalization of Proposition 15.1.

Proposition 15.2 *Suppose bidders have single-unit demand and K units are sold by means of sequential first-price auctions. Symmetric equilibrium strategies are given by*

$$
\beta_k^I(x) = E[Y_K \mid Y_k < x < Y_{k-1}]
$$

where β_k^I denotes the bidding strategy in the kth auction and $Y_k \equiv Y_k^{(N-1)}$ is the kth highest of $N-1$ independently drawn values.

Example 15.1 *Values are uniformly distributed on $[0, 1]$.*

In the last period, the equilibrium bidding strategy is

$$
\beta_K(x) = \frac{N-K}{N-K+1} x
$$

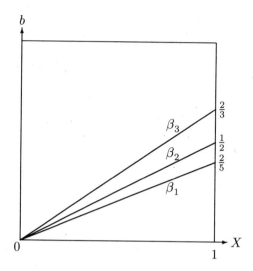

FIGURE 15.1. Equilibrium of Sequential First-Price Auction

Proceeding inductively, it may be verified that the bidding strategy in the kth first-price auction is

$$\beta_k(x) = \frac{N-K}{N-k+1}x$$

Figure 15.1 depicts the bidding strategies for the case of three objects $(K = 3)$ and five bidders $(N = 5)$. ▲

15.1.3 Equilibrium Bids and Prices

Some features of the equilibrium strategies are worth noting. First, for all k, $\beta_{k+1}(x) > \beta_k(x)$, that is, a bidder with value x who is active in the kth auction and fails to win, bids higher in the $k + 1$st auction. Informally, this is due to the deterioration of available supply relative to current demand. The higher bids from those who did not win in the previous period is, however, mitigated by the fact that there is one fewer bidder in this period. Indeed, the remaining bidders have smaller values than the winner of the previous round. Remarkably, the equilibrium is such that the two effects exactly offset each other and the prices in successive auctions show no trend. Precisely, the equilibrium price path is a *martingale*—at the end of the kth auction, the expected price in the $k + 1$st auction is the same as the realized price in the kth auction.

To see this, suppose that in equilibrium, bidder 1 with value x wins the kth auction. Then, absent any ties, it must be that

$$Y_{K-1} < \ldots < Y_k < x < Y_{k-1} < \ldots < Y_1$$

Now let the random variables P_k and P_{k+1} denote the prices in periods k and $k+1$, respectively. We know that the realized price in period k, $p_k = \beta_k(x)$. Moreover, the price in the $k+1$st period is the random variable $P_{k+1} = \beta_{k+1}(Y_k)$ and

$$
\begin{aligned}
E[P_{k+1} \mid P_k = p_k] &= E\left[\beta_{k+1}(Y_k) \mid Y_k < x < Y_{k-1}\right] \\
&= \beta_k(x) \\
&= p_k
\end{aligned}
$$

from (15.10). This establishes that the price path is a martingale. An implication of this property of the price path is that there are no opportunities for intertemporal arbitrage. For instance, if $E[P_{k+1} \mid P_k = p_k] < p_k$, then it would benefit bidders to decrease their bids on the current item with a view to waiting for the next item.

15.2 Sequential Second-Price Auctions

In this section we amend the model of the previous section so that the K items are sold using a series of second-price sealed-bid auctions. In all other respects, the model is the same. In particular, we suppose that, prior to bidding in a particular auction, the prices in all previous auctions are announced to all. And once again, we are interested in symmetric equilibrium strategies that are increasing. Instead of finding the equilibrium strategies directly, however, we will make use of the revenue equivalence principle.

15.2.1 Revenue Equivalence

If $\beta_1^{II}, \beta_2^{II}, \ldots, \beta_K^{II}$ is a symmetric increasing equilibrium, then, as in the case of sequential first-price auctions, the K units will be allocated efficiently. Indeed, the first unit will go to the bidder with the highest value, the second to the bidder with the second-highest value, and so on. This means that the two mechanisms—the sequential first- and second-price formats—are revenue equivalent (see Proposition 14.1 on page 202). Specifically, if $m^I(x)$ and $m^{II}(x)$ denote the expected payment by a bidder with value x in K sequential first- and second-price formats, respectively, then for all x,

$$
m^I(x) = m^{II}(x)
$$

Now define $m_k^I(x)$ to be the expected payment made in the kth auction by a bidder with value x when the items are sold by means of K first-price auctions. Define $m_k^{II}(x)$ in analogous fashion for the sequential second-price format. Clearly,

$$
m^I(x) = \sum_{k=1}^{K} m_k^I(x) \text{ and } m^{II}(x) = \sum_{k=1}^{K} m_k^{II}(x)
$$

While the revenue equivalence principle as such only guarantees that the overall expected payments in the two formats are the same, we claim that, in fact, for all k,

$$m_k^{\mathrm{I}}(x) = m_k^{\mathrm{II}}(x)$$

that is, the expected payment in the kth first-price auction is the same as the expected payment in the kth second-price auction. In other words, we claim that the two auctions are payment equivalent period by period. We argue by induction, starting with the Kth auction. Prior to the last auction, the information available to the remaining $N - K + 1$ bidders in either format is the same. For instance, bidder 1 knows his own value x, that his competitors have values $Y_{K+1}, Y_{K+2}, \ldots, Y_N$, and that $Y_K = y_K$. The revenue equivalence principle implies that $m_K^{\mathrm{I}}(x) = m_K^{\mathrm{II}}(x)$. Now consider the start of auction $K - 1$ and think of the remaining two formats as mechanisms for allocating *two* units. Once again the information available to the remaining $N - K + 2$ bidders is the same. For instance, bidder 1 knows his own value x, that his competitor have values $Y_K, Y_K, \ldots, Y_N$ and that $Y_{K-1} = y_{K-1}$. Once again, the revenue equivalence principle implies that

$$m_{K-1}^{\mathrm{I}}(x) + m_K^{\mathrm{I}}(x) = m_{K-1}^{\mathrm{II}}(x) + m_K^{\mathrm{II}}(x)$$

and since $m_K^{\mathrm{I}}(x) = m_K^{\mathrm{II}}(x)$, we have $m_{K-1}^{\mathrm{I}}(x) = m_{K-1}^{\mathrm{II}}(x)$. Proceeding inductively in this way establishes that for all k, $m_k^{\mathrm{I}}(x) = m_k^{\mathrm{II}}(x)$.

15.2.2   Equilibrium Bids

With the equality of the per-period expected payments in the sequential first- and second-price auctions in hand, we are ready to find the equilibrium bidding strategies in the latter. Clearly, in the last period it is a dominant strategy to bid one's value—that is,

$$\beta_K^{\mathrm{II}}(x) = x$$

and this is for the same reason that it is a dominant strategy in a single-unit second-price auction. Now notice that for any $k < K$, if bidder 1 with value x wins the kth auction, then it must be that

$$Y_{K-1} < \ldots < Y_k < x < Y_{k-1} < \ldots < Y_1$$

and the price he pays—the highest competing bid—is $\beta_k^{\mathrm{II}}(Y_k)$. Thus,

$$m_k^{\mathrm{II}}(x) = \mathrm{Prob}\left[Y_k < x < Y_{k-1}\right] \times E\left[\beta_k^{\mathrm{II}}(Y_k) \mid Y_k < x < Y_{k-1}\right]$$

On the other hand, in the first-price format a winning bidder pays his own bid, so

$$m_k^{\mathrm{I}}(x) = \mathrm{Prob}\left[Y_k < x < Y_{k-1}\right] \times \beta_k^{\mathrm{I}}(x)$$

But since $\beta_k^{\mathrm{I}}(x) = E\left[\beta_{k+1}^{\mathrm{I}}(Y_k) \mid Y_k < x < Y_{k-1}\right]$, from (15.11), the fact that the kth period expected payments are equal implies that

$$\mathrm{Prob}\left[Y_k < x < Y_{k-1}\right] \times E\left[\beta_k^{\mathrm{II}}(Y_k) \mid Y_k < x < Y_{k-1}\right]$$
$$= \mathrm{Prob}\left[Y_k < x < Y_{k-1}\right] \times E\left[\beta_{k+1}^{\mathrm{I}}(Y_k) \mid Y_k < x < Y_{k-1}\right]$$

Differentiating both sides of the equality with respect to x results in the identity

$$\beta_k^{\mathrm{II}}(x) = \beta_{k+1}^{\mathrm{I}}(x) \tag{15.12}$$

We have thus used the revenue equivalence principle to establish the following:

Proposition 15.3 *Suppose bidders have single-unit demand and K units are sold by means of sequential second-price auctions. Symmetric equilibrium strategies are given by*

$$\beta_K^{\mathrm{II}}(x) = x$$

and for all $k < K$,

$$\beta_k^{\mathrm{II}}(x) = \beta_{k+1}^{\mathrm{I}}(x)$$

where β_{k+1}^{I} is the $k+1$st period equilibrium bidding strategy in the sequential first-price auction format, derived in Proposition 15.2.

Example 15.2 *Values are uniformly distributed on $[0, 1]$.*

In the last period of a sequential second-price auction, it is a weakly dominant strategy to bid one's value, so

$$\beta_K(x) = x$$

Bidding strategies in earlier periods can be found using the strategies for the sequential first-price auction derived in Example 15.1 and applying the characterization obtained in Proposition 15.3. This results in

$$\beta_k(x) = \frac{N - K}{N - k} x$$

The bidding strategies are portrayed in Figure 15.2 for the case of three objects ($K = 3$) and five bidders ($N = 5$) and should be compared with the strategies for the sequential first-price auction in Figure 15.1. ▲

Again, some properties of the equilibrium bidding strategies are worth noting. First, for all k, $\beta_k^{\mathrm{II}}(x) > \beta_k^{\mathrm{I}}(x)$, that is, every bidder bids more in a second-price sequential auction than in its first-price counterpart. Second,

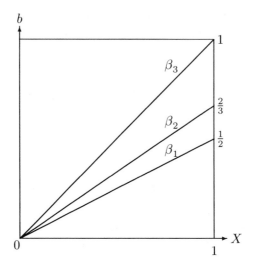

FIGURE 15.2. Equilibrium of Sequential Second-Price Auction

while it is a dominant strategy to bid one's value in the last period, this is not the case in earlier periods. This is because in any period $k < K$, there is an "option value" associated with not winning the current auction— the expected payoff arising from the possibility of winning an auction in some later period. In contrast to the case of a single-object, the strategies in a sequential second-price auction are optimal only if other bidders also adopt them. Third, the equilibrium price process in a sequential second-price auction is also a martingale. Suppose bidder 1 with value x wins in period $K - 1$. Then $Y_{K-1} < x < Y_{K-2}$ and the price in period $K - 1$ is the realization of the random variable $P_{K-1} = \beta_{K-1}^{II}(Y_{K-1})$. Let the realized price be $p_{K-1} = \beta_{K-1}^{II}(y_{K-1})$, where y_{K-1} is the realized value of Y_{K-1}. In the last period the bidder with value $Y_{K-1} = y_{K-1}$ will win and the price in the last period will be $P_K = \beta_K^{II}(Y_K) \equiv Y_K$ since it is weakly dominant to bid one's value in the last auction. Now

$$
\begin{aligned}
E\left[P_K \mid P_{K-1} = p_{K-1}\right] &= E\left[Y_K \mid Y_K < y_{K-1}\right] \\
&= \beta_{K-1}^{II}(y_{K-1}) \\
&= p_{K-1}
\end{aligned}
$$

In earlier periods, the martingale property of prices in a sequential second-price auction is a consequence of the corresponding property in a sequential first-price auction and the relationship between the two equilibrium strategies in Proposition 15.3.

Chapter Notes

Equilibria of sequential auctions were first derived by Milgrom and Weber (2000) in a paper written in 1982, but published only recently. The martingale property of prices with symmetric independent private values was derived there. They also studied sequential auctions in the interdependent value model with affiliated signals, extending their work in the single-object case (see Chapter 6). With the latter specifications, the price process is no longer a martingale. Prices have a tendency to drift upward—that is, $E[P_{k+1} \mid P_k = p_k] > p_k$—and the reason is that now price announcement carry valuable information. These results have also been reported by Weber (1983).

There is some evidence that in real-world sequential auctions—art and wine auctions, in particular—the prices tend to drift downward (Ashenfelter, 1989). Because the theoretical models predict either a (stochastically) constant or increasing price path, this fact has been dubbed the "declining price anomaly." McAfee and Vincent (1993) explore the theoretical implications of risk aversion on the part of bidders in sequential first- and second-price auctions. They find that symmetric equilibria exist and prices decline over time, but only if bidders' risk aversion *increases* with wealth. Increasing risk aversion leads to declining prices because the bidder who wins in the first period, say, has a higher value than those of the remaining bidders, so this bidder is more risk averse. Even though prices are expected to decline in the future, his greater aversion to risk offsets the incentive to wait for a random future price, which is lower on average. But since we typically expect risk aversion to decrease with wealth, this does not seem like a particularly compelling explanation of declining prices in sequential auctions.

Jeitschko (1999) offers a somewhat different explanation. He considers situations in which the number of units to be sold is not known to the bidders beforehand. For instance, suppose that the number of units to be sold is at most two but at the time of the first auction bidders are unsure whether or not a second unit will be sold at all. This means that the expected profits from the now uncertain second auction are lower than they would be if a second item were to be sold for sure. Arbitrage now drives up the price in the first auction, so prices decline. But this explanation, while interesting, is only partial at best. Declining prices are observed even when the number of units to be sold is announced beforehand, so there is no uncertainty in this regard. See, for example, the account of the auction for 24 satellite transponder leases reported in Weber (1983).

The results of this chapter were all derived under the restrictive assumption that all buyers have *single-unit demand*. A full treatment of sequential auctions with multiunit demands is problematic for reasons that are by now familiar—once a particular bidder has won the first unit his behavior and interests are different from those of the other bidders. In other words, even if bidders are symmetric *ex ante* multiunit demands introduce asymmetries in later auctions. There is one tractable case, however, as pointed out by Katzman (1999). Suppose only *two* units are for sale and these are sold by means of two second-price auctions. In the first stage, bidders are symmetric. In the second and last stage, even though they are no longer symmetric, each bidder has a dominant strategy to bid his or her value since no considerations regarding the future are necessary. Katzman (1999) is thus able to find a symmetric equilibrium of the two-stage second-price auction when bidders have multi- (that is, two-) unit demand.

16
Nonidentical Objects

In considering multiple object auctions we have thus far restricted attention to situations in which the objects are identical. Furthermore, we supposed that the marginal value of an additional unit declined with the number of units in hand. We now turn to the case where the objects, while related, are not identical.

16.1   The Model

Let $\mathcal{K}$ be a set of K distinct objects for sale and, as usual, let $\mathcal{N}$ be the set of buyers. Each buyer $i \in \mathcal{N}$ is assumed to assign a value $x^i(\mathcal{S})$ to each subset $\mathcal{S} \subseteq \mathcal{K}$. Subsets of $\mathcal{K}$ are called *packages* or *combinations*. Since there are K objects, the number of possible packages is 2^K. We can then think of a buyer's *value* as a 2^K-vector

$$\mathbf{x}^i = \left(x^i(\mathcal{S})\right)_{\mathcal{S} \subseteq \mathcal{K}}$$

We will suppose that $x^i(\emptyset) = 0$ and if $\mathcal{S} \subset \mathcal{T}$, then $x^i(\mathcal{S}) \leq x^i(\mathcal{T})$. The set of possible value vectors for i, $\mathcal{X}^i$, is assumed to be a closed and convex subset of the nonnegative orthant and $\mathbf{0} \in \mathcal{X}^i$. Notice that this is still a setting with private values.

Observe that the interpretation of the value vector is now somewhat different from that in the case of identical objects. With identical objects, the different components of $\mathbf{x}^i$ represented the *marginal* value of an additional unit. In the current specification, the component $x^i(S)$ represents the total value derived from a package S of the objects.

An *allocation* $\langle S^1, S^2, \ldots, S^N \rangle$ is an ordered collection of N packages, which forms a partition—that is, $\cup_{i \in \mathcal{N}} S^i = \mathcal{K}$ and for all $i \neq j$, $S^i \cap S^j = \emptyset$. The interpretation is, of course, that buyer i is allocated package S^i, so the requirement that an allocation be a partition amounts to saying that (i) every object must be allocated to some buyer, and (ii) no object can be allocated to more than one buyer. Let $\mathbb{K}$ denote the set of all allocations.

We adopt a mechanism design perspective and define an *allocation rule* $\mathbb{S} : \mathcal{X} \to \mathbb{K}$ as a function that assigns an allocation

$$\mathbb{S}(\mathbf{x}) = \langle S^1(\mathbf{x}), S^2(\mathbf{x}), \ldots, S^N(\mathbf{x}) \rangle$$

to each N-tuple of value vectors $\mathbf{x} = (\mathbf{x}^1, \mathbf{x}^2, \ldots, \mathbf{x}^N)$. As usual, a *direct mechanism* $(\mathbb{S}, \mathbf{M})$ consists of an allocation rule together with a payment rule.[1]

Given an allocation rule $\mathbb{S}$, let $q^i(S, \mathbf{z}^i)$ denote the probability that buyer i will be allocated the set of objects S when he reports his value vector as $\mathbf{z}^i$. Let

$$\mathbf{q}^i(\mathbf{z}^i) = (q^i(S, \mathbf{z}^i))_{S \subseteq \mathcal{K}}$$

be the 2^K-vector of allocation probabilities. Define $m^i(\mathbf{z}^i)$ to be buyer i's expected payment when reporting $\mathbf{z}^i$. His expected payoff from reporting $\mathbf{z}^i$ when his true value vector is $\mathbf{x}^i$ can then be written in the usual fashion as

$$\mathbf{q}^i(\mathbf{z}^i) \cdot \mathbf{x}^i - m^i(\mathbf{z}^i)$$

As in Chapter 5, a direct mechanism is said to be incentive compatible if truth-telling is an equilibrium—that is,

$$U^i(\mathbf{x}^i) \equiv \mathbf{q}^i(\mathbf{x}^i) \cdot \mathbf{x}^i - m^i(\mathbf{x}^i) \geq \mathbf{q}^i(\mathbf{z}^i) \cdot \mathbf{x}^i - m^i(\mathbf{z}^i)$$

The following "revenue equivalence" result then follows immediately.

Proposition 16.1 *The expected payoff (and payment) functions of a buyer in any two incentive compatible mechanisms with the same allocation rule differ by at most an additive constant.*

Proof. The proof is *identical* to that of Proposition 14.1. The only difference is that all the vectors are of size 2^K instead of size K. In particular, (14.5) holds—that is, for all $\mathbf{x}^i \in \mathcal{X}^i$,

---

[1] Notice that we are restricting attention to deterministic allocation rules. Given the concerns of this chapter, allowing for randomized rules would not affect what follows.

$$U^i(\mathbf{x}^i) = U^i(\mathbf{0}) + \int_0^1 \mathbf{q}^i(t\mathbf{x}^i) \cdot \mathbf{x}^i \, dt \tag{16.1}$$

and the conclusion of the proposition follows immediately. ∎

A mechanism $(\mathbb{S}, \mathbf{M})$ is said to be *individually rational* if for all i and $\mathbf{x}^i$, the expected payoff of buyer i is nonnegative—that is, if $U^i(\mathbf{x}^i) \geq 0$.

16.2   Efficient Allocations

Our first concern is with the possibility of achieving efficient allocations via an incentive compatible mechanism. The Vickrey-Clarke-Groves (VCG) mechanism, a natural extension of the Vickrey multiunit auction and already familiar from Chapter 5, provides a ready means of achieving efficiency. It is worthwhile to review its operation in the current context.

An allocation rule $\mathbb{S}$ is *efficient* if for every $\mathbf{x} \in \mathcal{X}$, the allocation $\mathbb{S}(\mathbf{x})$ maximizes *social welfare*—that is, the sum of buyers' values—over all allocations, so that

$$\mathbb{S}(\mathbf{x}) \in \arg \max_{\langle T^1, T^2, \dots, T^N \rangle} \sum_{i \in \mathcal{N}} x^i(T^i)$$

Define

$$W(\mathbf{x}) = \sum_{i \in \mathcal{N}} x^i(\mathcal{S}^i(\mathbf{x})) \tag{16.2}$$

to be the social welfare from an efficient allocation $\mathbb{S}(\mathbf{x})$ when the values are $\mathbf{x}$, and define

$$W^{-i}(\mathbf{x}) = \sum_{j \neq i} x^j(\mathcal{S}^j(\mathbf{x})) \tag{16.3}$$

to be the social welfare of individuals other than i from an efficient allocation $\mathbb{S}(\mathbf{x})$ when the values are $\mathbf{x}$.

The *VCG mechanism* is an efficient mechanism defined by the payment rule:

$$\begin{aligned} M^i(\mathbf{x}) &= \sum_{j \neq i} x^j(\mathcal{S}^j(\mathbf{0}, \mathbf{x}^{-i})) - \sum_{j \neq i} x^j(\mathcal{S}^j(\mathbf{x})) \\ &= W^{-i}(\mathbf{0}, \mathbf{x}^{-i}) - W^{-i}(\mathbf{x}) \end{aligned} \tag{16.4}$$

where, for all j, $\mathcal{S}^j(\mathbf{0}, \mathbf{x}^{-i})$ is the jth component of an efficient allocation $\mathbb{S}(\mathbf{0}, \mathbf{x}^{-i})$ that would result if i were to report $\mathbf{x}^i = \mathbf{0}$ (or equivalently, in many settings, if i were not present). Recall from Chapter 5 that the amount $M^i(\mathbf{x})$ buyer i pays in the VCG mechanism represents the *externality* that

i exerts on the other $N - 1$ agents by his presence in society. It is the difference between the welfare of the others "without him" and the welfare of the others "with him."

Fix some $\mathbf{x}^{-i}$, the values of agents other than i. In the VCG mechanism, the *ex post* payoff to i with value $\mathbf{x}^i$ when he reports that it is $\mathbf{z}^i$ is

$$x^i\left(\mathcal{S}^i\left(\mathbf{z}^i, \mathbf{x}^{-i}\right)\right) - M^i\left(\mathbf{z}^i, \mathbf{x}^{-i}\right) = W\left(\mathbf{z}^i, \mathbf{x}^{-i}\right) - W\left(\mathbf{0}, \mathbf{x}^{-i}\right) \qquad (16.5)$$

The second term is independent of the reported value $\mathbf{z}^i$, and by definition, the first term just represents the social welfare, so it is maximized by choosing $\mathbf{z}^i = \mathbf{x}^i$. Thus, "truth-telling" is a weakly dominant strategy in the VCG mechanism. *A fortiori*, the VCG mechanism is incentive compatible. Using (16.5) agent i's payoff in equilibrium (when $\mathbf{z}^i = \mathbf{x}^i$) is just $W(\mathbf{x}) - W(\mathbf{0}, \mathbf{x}^{-i})$—that is, the difference in social welfare when i reports $\mathbf{x}^i$ versus when he reports $\mathbf{0}$. Moreover, (16.5) implies that the payoff to a buyer with value vector $\mathbf{0}$, is 0 and for any $\mathbf{x}^i$ the expected payoff in the VCG mechanism is nonnegative. Thus, the VCG mechanism is also individually rational.

Now suppose that the value vectors $\mathbf{x}^i$ are independently distributed. The following result is a generalization of Proposition 5.5 on page 77 to the case of multiple objects. Its proof is identical to that of Proposition 5.5.

Proposition 16.2 *Among all mechanisms for allocating multiple objects that are efficient, incentive compatible and individually rational, the VCG mechanism maximizes the expected payment of each agent.*

The VCG mechanism not only achieves efficiency, but from the perspective of the seller, it does so in the most advantageous way. It raises the highest revenue among all efficient mechanisms. In the remainder of this chapter we turn to some practical matters.

16.3   Substitutes and Complements

We have said little about the nature of the objects being sold other than to say that they are not necessarily identical. Indeed, the results of the preceding section do not rely on any specific relationship among the set of objects.

In previous chapters we considered multiple object auctions in which the objects were different units of the same good. Different units of the same good are, of course, perfect substitutes and we assumed that the marginal value of a unit to a buyer declined with the number of units already in hand. Generalizing this property to the case of non-identical objects, we will say that the objects being sold are *substitutes* if the marginal value of obtaining a particular object A is smaller if the set of objects already in hand is "larger." Formally, buyer i considers the objects in $\mathcal{K}$ to be substitutes if for all $A \in \mathcal{K}$ and packages $\mathcal{S}$ and $\mathcal{T}$ not containing A, such that $\mathcal{S} \subset \mathcal{T}$,

$$x^i(\mathcal{S} \cup \{A\}) - x^i(\mathcal{S}) \geq x^i(\mathcal{T} \cup \{A\}) - x^i(\mathcal{T}) \qquad (16.6)$$

It can be shown that (16.6) is equivalent to requiring that for all packages $\mathcal{S}$ and $\mathcal{T}$,

$$x^i(\mathcal{S}) + x^i(\mathcal{T}) \geq x^i(\mathcal{S} \cup \mathcal{T}) + x^i(\mathcal{S} \cap \mathcal{T})$$

In particular, if $\mathcal{S} \cap \mathcal{T} = \emptyset$, then, since $x^i(\emptyset) = 0$, the inequality reduces to

$$x^i(\mathcal{S}) + x^i(\mathcal{T}) \geq x^i(\mathcal{S} \cup \mathcal{T})$$

so the substitute property implies that $x^i(\cdot)$ is a *subadditive* function over the set of packages. When we say that the objects in $\mathcal{K}$ are substitutes, we mean that all buyers consider them as such.

In analogous fashion, we will say that the objects are *complements* if the marginal value of obtaining a particular object A is larger if the set of objects already in hand is "larger." Formally, buyer i considers the objects in $\mathcal{K}$ to be complements if for all $A \in \mathcal{K}$ and packages $\mathcal{S}$ and $\mathcal{T}$ not containing A, such that $\mathcal{S} \subset \mathcal{T}$,

$$x^i(\mathcal{S} \cup \{A\}) - x^i(\mathcal{S}) \leq x^i(\mathcal{T} \cup \{A\}) - x^i(\mathcal{T}) \qquad (16.7)$$

This is equivalent to requiring that for all packages $\mathcal{S}$ and $\mathcal{T}$,

$$x^i(\mathcal{S}) + x^i(\mathcal{T}) \leq x^i(\mathcal{S} \cup \mathcal{T}) + x^i(\mathcal{S} \cap \mathcal{T}) \qquad (16.8)$$

In particular, if $\mathcal{S} \cap \mathcal{T} = \emptyset$, then we have

$$x^i(\mathcal{S}) + x^i(\mathcal{T}) \leq x^i(\mathcal{S} \cup \mathcal{T})$$

implying that $x^i(\cdot)$ is a *superadditive* function. Again, when we say that the objects in $\mathcal{K}$ are complements we mean that all buyers consider them as such.[2]

If both (16.6) and (16.7) hold, then the values are *additive*—that is, the value of any package $\mathcal{S}$ is simply the sum of the values of the individual objects in that package. In this case, it is useful to think of the different objects as being completely unrelated since the value derived from a particular object A does not depend on whether another object B is obtained or not.

---

[2] Functions satisfying (16.8) are said to be *supermodular*. In come contexts—in the theory of cooperative games—they are also called *convex*.

16.4 Bundling

In some circumstances it may be in the interests of the seller to *bundle* some or all the goods together—that is, to sell some objects only as part of a specific larger package. Specifically, the seller may partition the K objects in $\mathcal{K}$ into $L \leq K$ bundles $\mathcal{B}_1, \mathcal{B}_2, \ldots, \mathcal{B}_L$. The objects in any $\mathcal{B}_l$ must be sold to the same buyer. In effect, bundling forces the buyers to treat each $\mathcal{B}_l$ as a single object.

Once the seller has decided to bundle the objects, the only possible subsets that the buyers can obtain are those of the form $\cup \mathcal{B}_l$ and consequently only the values for these subsets are relevant. The VCG mechanism can then be used to allocate the bundles and given any partition of $\mathcal{K}$ into bundles it will allocate the bundles efficiently. Of course, full efficiency will not be achieved in general because social welfare may increase if some of the goods in a particular bundle are allocated to separate buyers. The VCG mechanism would, nevertheless, be constrained efficient—that is, welfare maximizing subject to the bundling constraint.

Is bundling advantageous for the seller? A striking example illustrating its benefits occurs when there are only two buyers.

Proposition 16.3 *Suppose there are two buyers ($N = 2$). In the VCG mechanism, the revenue to the seller from selling all the objects as a single bundle exceeds the revenue derived from bundling them in any other way.*

Proof. Let $\mathcal{B}_1, \mathcal{B}_2, \ldots, \mathcal{B}_L$ be a partition of $\mathcal{K}$ into L bundles. Suppose that in the VCG mechanism with the bundles it is constrained efficient to allocate set $\mathcal{S}^1$ to buyer 1 and $\mathcal{S}^2 = \mathcal{K} \setminus \mathcal{S}^1$ to buyer 2 where each $\mathcal{S}^i$ is a union of some bundles. Then, in particular we have

$$x^1\left(\mathcal{S}^1\right) + x^2\left(\mathcal{S}^2\right) \geq \max\left\{x^1\left(\mathcal{K}\right), x^2\left(\mathcal{K}\right)\right\} \qquad (16.9)$$

In the VCG mechanism buyer 1 would pay the externality he exerts on buyer 2—that is, $x^2\left(\mathcal{K}\right) - x^2\left(\mathcal{S}^2\right)$. Similarly, buyer 2 would pay $x^1\left(\mathcal{K}\right) - x^1\left(\mathcal{S}^1\right)$. The revenue accruing to the seller is

$$x^1\left(\mathcal{K}\right) + x^2\left(\mathcal{K}\right) - x^1\left(\mathcal{S}^1\right) - x^2\left(\mathcal{S}^2\right)$$

Now if the seller were to require that all the objects be sold as a single bundle—in this case, the VCG mechanism is equivalent to a second-price auction—then the revenue would be $\min\left\{x^1\left(\mathcal{K}\right), x^2\left(\mathcal{K}\right)\right\}$. But

$$\min\left\{x^1\left(\mathcal{K}\right), x^2\left(\mathcal{K}\right)\right\} \geq x^1\left(\mathcal{K}\right) + x^2\left(\mathcal{K}\right) - x^1\left(\mathcal{S}^1\right) - x^2\left(\mathcal{S}^2\right)$$

because of (16.9). Thus, the revenue from bundling all the objects as one is greater than the revenue from any other form of bundling. In particular, it is greater than the revenue from not bundling at all and selling the objects individually—that is, in the case of $L = K$.

As long as it is not efficient to allocate all the objects to one of the buyers—that is, the inequality in (16.9) is strict—selling the objects as a single bundle is strictly better for the seller. ∎

We have shown that with only two buyers, it is always better to sell the objects as a single bundle. Remarkably, this holds regardless of whether the objects are substitutes or complements.

One may reasonably conjecture that when there are more than three buyers it may not be advantageous to bundle if the objects are substitutes. An example shows that bundling may not be advantageous even when the objects are complements.

Example 16.1 *With three or more buyers, bundling may not be optimal.*

Suppose that there are two objects, A and B, and three buyers with values given in the following table.

	$\mathbf{x}^1$	$\mathbf{x}^2$	$\mathbf{x}^3$
A	8	4	7
B	4	7	1
AB	14	12	10

Notice that A and B are complements since for each buyer $x^i(AB) > x^i(A) + x^i(B)$.[3]

Without bundling, the efficient allocation is to give A to buyer 1 and B to buyer 2. The welfare from this allocation is 15 and this exceeds the welfare from any other allocation. If buyer 1 were not present, or equivalently if he reported $\mathbf{x}^i = 0$, then it would be efficient to give A to buyer 3 and B to buyer 2 for a total welfare $W^{-1}(\mathbf{0}, \mathbf{x}^{-1}) = 14$, so in the VCG mechanism buyer 1 would pay $W^{-1}(\mathbf{0}, \mathbf{x}^{-1}) - W^{-1}(\mathbf{x}^1, \mathbf{x}^{-1}) = 7$. If buyer 2 were not present, then it would be efficient to give both objects to buyer 1, so buyer 2 would pay $W^{-2}(\mathbf{0}, \mathbf{x}^{-2}) - W^{-2}(\mathbf{x}^2, \mathbf{x}^{-2}) = 14 - 8 = 6$. The total revenue in the VCG mechanism would be 13.

If A and B were sold as a single bundle, then it would go to buyer 1 and he would pay 12.

Thus, in this example it is better for the seller to sell the objects separately even though all buyers consider them to be complements. ▲

The distinguishing feature of the two-buyer case is that if one of the buyers is not present, the K objects must necessarily be awarded to the other buyer. As is apparent in the preceding example, this is not true once

---

[3]We write $x^i(AB)$ to denote $x^i(\{A, B\})$.

there are three or more buyers. A second feature of the two-buyer case is that bundling is advantageous for every realization of buyers' values, so this advantage holds no matter what the distribution of values. This is also special to the two-buyer situation. In general, whether or not bundling is advantageous depends on how buyers' values are distributed.

16.5   Some Computational Issues

The VCG mechanism is an effective means of achieving efficiency but it imposes a substantial computational burden on the buyers and the seller. First, each buyer is asked to submit a value for each subset S of $\mathcal{K}$ and thus the vector $\mathbf{x}^i$ that is submitted is of size 2^K. Second, the seller is asked to determine (i) an efficient allocation based on the submitted value vectors and (ii) each buyer's payment.

To find an efficient allocation the seller needs to solve the following integer programming problem: for all i and S choose variables $\theta^i(S) \in \{0, 1\}$ to maximize

$$\sum_{i \in \mathcal{N}} \sum_{S \subseteq \mathcal{K}} x^i(S) \theta^i(S) \tag{16.10}$$

subject to the constraints

$$\forall i, \ \sum_{S \subseteq \mathcal{K}} \theta^i(S) \ \leq \ 1 \tag{16.11}$$

$$\forall A, \ \sum_{S \ni A} \sum_{i \in \mathcal{N}} \theta^i(S) \ \leq \ 1 \tag{16.12}$$

where $S \ni A$ denotes that the sum is taken over all subsets $S \subseteq \mathcal{K}$ that contain the object A. If the variable $\theta^i(S) = 1$, then package S is allocated to buyer i. The objective function of the integer program is just the total value—the social welfare—derived from the allocation and its maximized value is just $W(\mathbf{x})$. The N constraints (16.11) ensure that each buyer is allocated at most one package. The K constraints (16.12) ensure that each object is allocated to at most one buyer. The total number of variables $\theta^i(S)$ is $N \times 2^K$. We will refer to this as the *allocation problem*.

Determining each buyer's payments in the VCG mechanism requires, in addition, that a similar allocation problem be solved once the buyer in question has been removed from the picture. If each buyer receives at least one object, then this means that N additional allocation problems, similar to the one above, need to be solved.

Since $\mathcal{K}$ is a finite set one could, in principle, list all possible allocations to find one that is optimal. As a practical method, however, this would be too cumbersome since even when relatively few objects are sold the number of possible allocations grows exponentially with the number of objects. While other, more efficient, algorithms can be used in specific circumstances, it is not known whether there is a general polynomial time algorithm—one in which the number of steps required to reach a solution grows as a polynomial function of the size of the problem. The allocation problem belongs to a class of problems computer scientists call *NP-hard*.

Of course, these theoretical measures of the underlying computational complexity are based on a general "worst-case" analysis. While it may not be possible to rule out that in some problems the number of steps grows exponentially, it may well be that in "typical" problems the number of steps is not prohibitively large. Conversely, even knowing that there is a polynomial algorithm does not ensure that it is practical; it may well be that the number of steps grows as a polynomial of high degree.

In many situations, there may be some natural structure that limits the set of packages that bidders consider valuable, thereby simplifying the allocation problem. Let us examine a few examples.

As a first step, notice that the allocation problem is simple in two extreme cases. First, if all the objects are identical so that as in Chapter 12 each buyer cares only about the number of objects he receives, then efficient allocations are relatively simple to determine. Second, if the objects are completely unrelated so that the value of a package is just the sum of the values of the objects in that package—the case of additive values— once again the allocation problem is relatively simple: each object can be efficiently allocated independently of how other objects are allocated.

A more interesting special case is the following. Suppose that the K objects can be linearly ordered as

$$A_1, A_2, A_3, \ldots, A_k, A_{k+1}, \ldots, A_K$$

and it is the case that these are complements but that for all buyers the values are strictly superadditive only among "adjacent" objects. Thus, for example, while the possibility that $x^i(A_1 A_2 A_3) > x^i(A_1 A_2) + x^i(A_3)$ is allowed, it is required that $x^i(A_1 A_2 A_4) = x^i(A_1 A_2) + x^i(A_4)$. In this case the allocation problems are computationally manageable. The reason is that the integer program specified above can be safely solved as a linear program. In other words, we can neglect the requirement that each $\theta^i(S)$ is either 0 or 1. The solution to the resulting linear program will automatically be such that the $\theta^i(S)$ will satisfy this requirement. Linear programming problems, unlike their integer programming counterparts, can of course be efficiently solved.

16.6 Budget Constraints

We saw in Chapter 4 that when bidders are subject to budget constraints, the first- and second-price auctions need not yield the same expected revenue. Here we briefly look at the effects of budget constraints on bidding behavior in multiple object auctions. Unlike in Chapter 4, however, we suppose that there is complete information regarding values and budgets. Thus, what follows is only meant to indicate some novel issues that arise in the multiple object context.

Suppose that there are two objects, A and B, and these are sold sequentially by means of two English auctions. Specifically, A is brought up for sale in the first auction, whose results are announced in public. After that, B is sold in a second auction. There are two buyers with values given in the following table.

	$\mathbf{x}^1$	$\mathbf{x}^2$
A	14	8
B	3	4
AB	16	12

Suppose further that these values are commonly known—there is *no* incomplete information regarding values.

In the first auction, since $x^1(A) > x^2(A)$, bidder 1 wins object A at a price of 8. In the second auction, bidder 2 attaches a greater value to object B than does bidder 1, so bidder 2 wins B at a price of 3. The total revenue accruing to the seller is 11.

Now suppose that bidder 1 has a budget of $w^1 = 13$ and bidder 2 has a budget of $w^2 = 11$. These budgets are inflexible—neither bidder can pay more than his budget—and suppose that these are also commonly known. Once again suppose that A and B are sold, in that order, by means of two separate English auctions. What constitutes equilibrium bidding behavior once budgets come into play?

First, consider the second auction, in which B is offered for sale. Bidding behavior in this auction is clear. Let $\widehat{w}^i$ be the amount of money bidder i has left over after the first auction is over and call this i's *residual budget*. The residual budget is just the original budget w^i less the amount, if any, that i spent in the first auction. It is clear that in the second auction, bidder i should stay in until the price reaches $p^i(B) \equiv \min\left\{\widehat{w}^i, x^i(B)\right\}$.

Now consider the first auction—that is, the one in which A is sold. The price cannot exceed 11 since that is bidder 2's budget. Moreover, as long as the current price $p \leq 11$, it is not in bidder 1's interest to drop out. This is because the largest profit he can make in the second auction is 3, and if $p \leq 11$, the profit from buying A at p exceeds this amount. Thus, bidder 1 is not the first to drop out. How high is bidder 2 willing to go? Bidder 2 values object A at $x^2(A) = 8$, but if he drops out at 8, this will leave bidder 1 with a residual budget of $\widehat{w}^1 = 13 - 8 = 5$, so bidder 2 will end up paying $\min\left\{\widehat{w}^1, x^1(B)\right\} = 3$ for B. But bidder 2 can reduce the price he pays in the second auction by staying in after the price in the first auction reaches 10. The longer he stays in, the more he depletes bidder 1's budget, thereby reducing the amount bidder 1 is able to bid in the second auction. Thus, it is in bidder 2's interest to stay in as long as possible—that is, until the price reaches 11. Moreover, bidder 2 is confident that bidder 1 will not drop out before then. By running up the price in this manner, bidder 2 is able to reduce bidder 1's residual budget to $13 - 11 = 2$, and this is the price bidder 2 would pay for B in the second auction. Thus, in equilibrium, bidder 1 would win A at a price of 11 and bidder 2 would then win B for 2. The total revenue of the seller is now 13.

An interesting aspect of equilibrium behavior in this situation is that it is rational to for bidder 2 to stay in the first auction past the point that the price exceeds his value, so he is no longer interested in winning A. The motive for doing this is to weaken bidder 1 for the second auction. Such *overbidding* can, of course, be rational only in multiple object auctions. This overbidding results in a higher revenue to the seller than if there were no budget constraints—the seller's revenue is 13 rather than 11. An increase in revenue resulting from the presence of budget constraints can also only arise in a multiple object setting.

Chapter Notes

Most of the material in this chapter is well known. Proposition 16.2 is just an extension of Proposition 5.5 from Chapter 5 and is due to Krishna and Perry (1998).

Circumstances in which bundling is advantageous for a monopolist have been the subject of extensive study in the literature on industrial organization. Proposition 16.3, showing that bundling is always advantageous when there are only two bidders, generalizes previous results on multiunit auctions obtained by Palfrey (1983), concerning additive values, and K. Krishna and Tranæs (2001), concerning more general valuations. Whether or not it is profitable to bundle has also been studied in the context of procurement. In that context, the issue is whether or not the buyer should award the contract to a single supplier—as a bundle—or conduct a "split-award auction," in which more than one supplier is used. Anton and Yao (1992) have studied circumstances in which it is optimal for the buyer to split the award between two suppliers. In their model the buyer does not commit beforehand to a particular course of action; rather the decision of whether or not to split the award is made once the bids are received. Chakaraborty (1999) studies a two-object model with additive values that are independently and identically distributed. He finds sufficient conditions so that it is profitable to bundle if and only if the number of buyers is less than some threshold N^*. To some extent, his results support the general intuition that bundling is profitable when there is a small number of buyers.

Armstrong (2000) and Avery and Hendershott (2000) show the advantages of bundling in a setting in which two objects are for sale and there are two-point values for each object. These papers show that the optimal auction in this setting displays bundling like features—the probability that a particular bidder will be allocated an object is larger if he has already been allocated the other one than if he has not. Unlike in the situation considered in this chapter, however, the seller need not commit to sell the objects as a bundle.

Issues surrounding the computational complexity of finding efficient allocations have been surveyed very nicely by de Vries and Vohra (2001). The computationally manageable example of linearly ordered objects with complementarities only among adjacent items is due to Rothkopf et al. (1998).

The question of how budget constraints affect equilibrium behavior in sequential multiple object auctions was first studied by Pitchik and Schotter (1988). The example showing that budget constraints may actually increase the seller's revenue is taken from a paper by Benoît and Krishna (2001). Both of these papers consider the issue in the context of models with complete information.

17

Multiple Objects and Interdependent Values

Our treatment of multiple object auctions has been confined to the case of private values. Even in this relatively simple setting, we saw that the question of efficiency was a delicate one. On the other hand, we also saw that the question of efficiency in single-object auctions with interdependent values was delicate as well. In this chapter we study multiple object auctions when buyers have interdependent values. As we will see, a combination of these two features only makes the attendant difficulties more acute, even insurmountable. In some sense we have reached the limits of what auction-like mechanisms can accomplish in terms of allocating efficiently, at least at a general level. It is perhaps fitting, therefore, that this is the last chapter.

It turns out that the problems associated with interdependence arise not from the multiplicity of the objects *per se* but rather from the multiplicity of signals that each buyer receives—that is, on the dimensionality of the available information. We begin by looking at situations in which there are multiple objects for sale but each buyer receives only a one-dimensional signal. We then look at the case of multidimensional information.

17.1   One-Dimensional Signals

Our basic setup is the same as in Chapter 10. Specifically, there are K identical objects for sale and N potential buyers. Prior to the sale, each buyer receives a one-dimensional signal $x^i \in \mathcal{X}^i \equiv [0, \omega^i]$. Buyer i's valuations for the objects depend on the signals $\mathbf{x} = \left(x^1, x^2, \ldots, x^N \right)$ received by all the buyers and the *marginal value* of obtaining the kth unit is determined by the function

$$v_k^i(\mathbf{x}) = v_k^i \left(x^1, x^2, \ldots, x^N \right)$$

We suppose that the marginal values for successive units decline so that for all $k < K$,

$$v_k^i(\mathbf{x}) \geq v_{k+1}^i(\mathbf{x})$$

and that a buyer's valuations respond nonnegatively to all signals—that is, for all i, j and k,

$$\frac{\partial v_k^i}{\partial x^j}(\mathbf{x}) \geq 0 \tag{17.1}$$

and positively to his own signal—that is, (17.1) holds with a strict inequality whenever $i = j$. We will write $\mathbf{v}^i(\mathbf{x}) = \left(v_1^i(\mathbf{x}), v_2^i(\mathbf{x}), \ldots, v_K^i(\mathbf{x}) \right)$ to denote the vector of marginal valuations of buyer i when the signals are $\mathbf{x}$.

The vector valuations $\mathbf{v}^1, \mathbf{v}^2, \ldots, \mathbf{v}^N$ are said to satisfy the multiunit *single crossing condition* if for all j, for all $i \neq j$, and for all k and l,

$$\frac{\partial v_k^j}{\partial x^j}(\mathbf{x}) > \frac{\partial v_l^i}{\partial x^j}(\mathbf{x}) \tag{17.2}$$

at every $\mathbf{x}$ such that $v_k^j(\mathbf{x})$ and $v_l^i(\mathbf{x})$ are equal and among the K highest of the $N \times K$ marginal values at $\mathbf{x}$.

We are interested in determining circumstances in which efficient allocations may be achieved. In this regard the importance of the single crossing condition has already been pointed out in the single object context.

17.1.1 An Efficient Direct Mechanism

Consider the following direct mechanism, obtained by combining elements from the generalized Vickrey-Clarke-Groves (VCG) mechanism for a single unit that was introduced in Chapter 10 and the Vickrey multiunit auction that was introduced in Chapter 12. Each buyer is asked to report his signal x^i. The K objects are then awarded efficiently relative to these reports—they are awarded to the K highest marginal values, when evaluated at the reported signals. Formally, given the signals $\mathbf{x}$, the $N \times K$ values $\{v_k^i(\mathbf{x}) : i = 1, 2, \ldots N; k = 1, 2, \ldots, K\}$ are computed and the K units are awarded to the K highest of these values—that is, if buyer i has $k^i \leq K$ of the K highest values, then i is awarded k^i units.

Fix the signals $\mathbf{x}^{-i}$ of the other buyers. For any signal z^i of buyer i define $\mathbf{c}^{-i}(z^i, \mathbf{x}^{-i})$ to be the vector of *competing bids* facing buyer i. This is obtained by rearranging the $(N-1)K$ values $v_k^j(z^i, \mathbf{x}^{-i})$ of buyers $j \neq i$ in decreasing order and selecting the first K of these. Thus, $c_1^{-i}(z^i, \mathbf{x}^{-i})$ is the highest of the others' values, $c_2^{-i}(z^i, \mathbf{x}^{-i})$ is the second-highest, and so on. Notice that the single-crossing condition (17.2) implies that for all i and k, l the function $v_k^i\left(\cdot, \mathbf{x}^{-i}\right)$ crosses any $c_l^{-i}\left(\cdot, \mathbf{x}^{-i}\right)$ at most once and when it does, the former has a greater slope than does the latter.

Suppose that when buyer i reports his signal as x^i and the others report $\mathbf{x}^{-i}$, he wins $k^i \leq K$ units. For any $k \leq k^i$, define

$$y_k^i(\mathbf{x}^{-i}) = \inf\left\{z^i : v_k^i\left(z^i, \mathbf{x}^{-i}\right) \geq c_{K-k+1}^{-i}\left(z^i, \mathbf{x}^{-i}\right)\right\}$$

to be the smallest signal for i that would result in his winning k units. By definition if $l < k$, then

$$y_l^i(\mathbf{x}^{-i}) \leq y_k^i(\mathbf{x}^{-i})$$

Also, if buyer i wins k^i units when he reports his true signal x^i, then

$$x^i \leq y_{k^i+1}^i(\mathbf{x}^{-i})$$

Now define

$$p_k^i = c_{K-k+1}^{-i}\left(y_k^i(\mathbf{x}^{-i}), \mathbf{x}^{-i}\right)$$

In the generalized VCG mechanism, i is asked to pay an amount

$$\sum_{k=1}^{k^i} p_k^i = \sum_{k=1}^{k^i} c_{K-k+1}^{-i}\left(y_k^i(\mathbf{x}^{-i}), \mathbf{x}^{-i}\right)$$

where as defined above, $y_k^i(\mathbf{x}^{-i})$ is the smallest signal for i that would result in his winning k units. A buyer who does not win any units does not pay anything.

As an illustration, consider the situation in Figure 17.1 in which buyer i's valuations for the first and second unit are depicted as functions of his own signal. The competing bids c_K^{-i} and c_{K-1}^{-i} are also depicted, again as functions of i's signal. The signals of other buyers are fixed at some $\mathbf{x}^{-i}$. Suppose that buyer i wins two units when he reports his signal as x^i. Thus, $v_2^i(x^i, \mathbf{x}^{-i}) > c_{K-1}^{-i}(x^i, \mathbf{x}^{-i})$, but $v_3^i(x^i, \mathbf{x}^{-i}) < c_{K-2}^{-i}(x^i, \mathbf{x}^{-i})$, so that he defeats two competing bids but not the third. To determine how much he should pay for the two units, first suppose his signal is 0. In that case, he would not win any units. Now raise i's signal until it reaches a level y_1^i such that he would just win a unit—that is, when $v_1^i = c_K^{-i}$. The price buyer i is asked to pay for the first unit is $p_1^i = c_1^{-i}(y_1^i, \mathbf{x}^{-i})$. Now raise his signal further until it reaches a level y_2^i such that he would just win two units—that is, when $v_2^i = c_{K-1}^{-i}$ and this occurs when i's signal is y_2^i. The price that buyer i is asked to pay for the second unit that he wins is $p_2^i = c_{K-1}^{-i}(y_2^i, \mathbf{x}^{-i})$.

Figure 17.2 portrays the same situation from a different perspective by emphasizing the relationship of the generalized VCG mechanism to the Vickrey multiunit auction. The left-hand panel shows buyer i's value

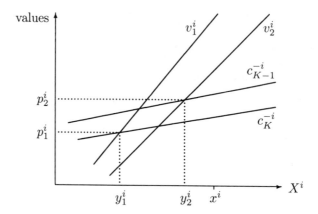

FIGURE 17.1. The Generalized VCG Mechanism for Multiple Units

vector—or equivalently, his true demand function—together with the vector of competing bids—or equivalently, the residual supply function facing buyer i. The demand function depends on i's signal but because values are interdependent, so does the residual supply function. As shown in the left-hand panel, buyer i wins two units. The price paid for the first unit is determined by finding the lowest signal such that his highest value v_1^i equals the lowest competing bid c_K^{-i}. As depicted in the middle panel of Figure 17.2, this occurs when $z^i = y_1^i$ and the buyer is asked to pay the amount $p_1^i = c_K^{-i}(y_1^i, \mathbf{x}^{-i})$ for the first unit. Now z^i is raised some more until it reaches a level such that he would win exactly two units. As depicted in the right-hand panel of the figure, this occurs when $z^i = y_2^i > y_1^i$ since we then have $v_2^i(y_2^i, \mathbf{x}^{-i}) = c_{K-1}^{-i}(y_2^i, \mathbf{x}^{-i})$ and, by the single crossing condition, $v_1^i(y_2^i, \mathbf{x}^{-i}) > c_K^{-i}(y_2^i, \mathbf{x}^{-i})$. The buyer is asked to pay an amount $p_2^i = c_{K-1}^{-i}(y_2^i, \mathbf{x}^{-i})$ for the second unit. Since $y_1^i < y_2^i < x^i$, at these prices, the buyer makes a positive surplus on each unit that he wins.

As in the Vickrey multiunit auction, the number of units that buyer i wins when he reports a signal z^i and the others report $\mathbf{x}^{-i}$ is equal to the number of competing bids that he defeats. Likewise, the prices that buyer i pays are determined by the competing bids he defeats. But the manner in which prices are determined needs to be amended in order to account for the fact that values are now interdependent. The original Vickrey pricing rule of asking buyers to pay the competing bids $c_l^{-i}(x^i, \mathbf{x}^{-i})$ that they defeat would, however, give them the incentive to report lower signals in an attempt to lower the prices they would have to pay. The incentives for truth-telling are restored by making the prices paid by a buyer independent of his own reported signal. This reasoning leads to the following result.

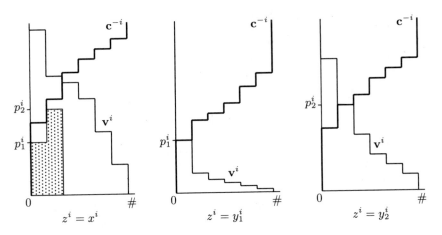

FIGURE 17.2. Prices in the Generalized VCG Mechanism

Proposition 17.1 *Suppose that signals are one-dimensional and the valuations* **v** *satisfy the multiunit single crossing condition. Then truth-telling is an efficient* ex post *equilibrium of the generalized VCG mechanism.*

Proof. Suppose that when all buyers report their signals **x** truthfully, it is efficient for buyer i to be awarded k^i objects. In other words, when evaluated at **x**, exactly k^i of his values $v_k^i(\mathbf{x})$ are among the K highest of all values.

By reporting his signal truthfully, buyer i pays for each of the k^i units an amount which is no greater than its true value, so makes a nonnegative profit. If he were to report a $z^i > x^i$, then he would win at least as many units as before. The prices for the first k^i units would remain the same as if he had reported $z^i = x^i$. For any additional units, however, the price paid would be too high, since for $k > k^i$,

$$y_k^i(\mathbf{x}^{-i}) > x^i$$

and the price paid would be

$$p_k^i = v_k^i\left(y_k^i(\mathbf{x}^{-i}), \mathbf{x}^{-i}\right) > v_k^i\left(x^i, \mathbf{x}^{-i}\right)$$

thus resulting in a loss. On the other hand, if he reports a $z^i < x^i$, then the number of units that he would win is at most what he would win by reporting $z^i = x^i$. For any of the units won the prices would be the same as before but he would forgo some surplus for units, say the k^ith unit, that he did not win. ∎

In the case of private values, the generalized VCG mechanism reduces to the Vickrey multiunit auction and, as we have seen, in that case it is a dominant strategy to report truthfully.

17.1.2 Efficiency via Open Auctions

When values are interdependent, information necessary to determine the values is dispersed among the bidders. To achieve efficiency, this information must emerge during an auction. In the context of a single object auction we saw that the English auction was quite remarkable in this regard—under relatively weak conditions the relevant information emerged in a way that resulted in efficiency. Specifically, in Chapter 9 we found that

1. With two bidders, the English auction had an efficient *ex post* equilibrium provided the single crossing condition was satisfied (see Proposition 9.1 on page 127).

2. With more than two bidders, the single crossing condition by itself was not enough. Stronger conditions—for instance, the average crossing condition—had to be invoked in order to guarantee that the English auction had an efficient *ex post* equilibrium (see Proposition 9.2 on page 131).

Here we explore the extent to which open ascending price auctions have analogous properties in the multiunit context.

Two Bidders

We first consider situations in which there are only two bidders. As noted above, when there was a single object for sale, the two-bidder English auction was efficient as long as the single crossing condition was satisfied (Proposition 9.1). In addition, with two bidders, the English auction was strategically equivalent to the sealed-bid second-price auction, so the latter was efficient as well. Now, with private values the multiunit analogues of the second-price and English auctions are the Vickrey and Ausubel auctions, respectively. The multiunit formats inherited all the relevant properties of their single unit counterparts and we wish to explore the extent to which the analogy can be pushed in the interdependent values environment.

It is instructive to begin by studying the sealed-bid Vickrey auction. When there are only two bidders, the K-unit Vickrey auction can be decomposed into K separate second-price auctions. This is because bidder 1 wins one unit if and only if his first bid, b_1^1, defeats the Kth bid of bidder 2, b_K^2. He wins a second unit if and only if his second bid, b_2^1, defeats the $K-1$st bid of bidder 2, b_{K-1}^2. In general, bidder 1 wins a kth unit if and only if his kth bid, b_k^1, defeats the $K-k+1$st bid of bidder 2, b_{K-k+1}^2. Moreover, the price bidder 1 pays for the first unit is just the defeated bid b_K^2, the price for the second unit is the defeated bid b_{K-1}^2, and so on. In particular, bidder 2's bids on units other than the $K-k+1$st unit do not affect the price that bidder 1 would pay were he to win a kth unit. A symmetric argument applies for bidder 2. Thus, we can think of the two-bidder

Vickrey auction as K separate second-price auctions: in the kth auction, bidder 1 with value v_k^1 competes with bidder 2 with value v_{K-k+1}^2. This insight leads to the following generalization of Proposition 9.1.

Proposition 17.2 *Suppose that there are two bidders and the valuations* **v** *satisfy the multiunit single crossing condition. Then there exists an ex post equilibrium of the Vickrey multiunit auction that is efficient.*

Proof. Fix a $k \le K$ and define $l = K - k + 1$. As in Chapter 9, the multiunit single crossing condition guarantees that there exist continuous and increasing functions ϕ_k^1 and ϕ_l^2 such that for all $p \le \min\{\phi_k^1(\omega^1), \phi_l^2(\omega^2)\}$, they solve the following pair of equations

$$
\begin{aligned}
v_k^1\left(\phi_k^1(p), \phi_l^2(p)\right) &= p \\
v_l^2\left(\phi_k^1(p), \phi_l^2(p)\right) &= p
\end{aligned}
\tag{17.3}
$$

Define $\beta_k^1 : [0, \omega^1] \to \mathbb{R}_+$ by $\beta_k^1 = \left(\phi_k^1\right)^{-1}$ and $\beta_l^2 : [0, \omega^2] \to \mathbb{R}_+$ by $\beta_l^2 = \left(\phi_l^2\right)^{-1}$. Notice that since for all k, $v_{k+1}^1 \le v_k^1$ and $v_{l-1}^2 \ge v_l^2$, the solutions satisfy the inequality $\beta_{k+1}^1 \le \beta_k^1$ and $\beta_{l-1}^2 \ge \beta_l^2$.

We claim that it is an equilibrium for bidder 1 to bid a vector

$$
\boldsymbol{\beta}^1(x^1) = \left(\beta_1^1(x^1), \beta_2^1(x^1), \dots, \beta_K^1(x^1)\right)
$$

when his signal is x^1 and for bidder 2 to bid a vector

$$
\boldsymbol{\beta}^2(x^2) = \left(\beta_1^2(x^2), \beta_2^2(x^2), \dots, \beta_K^2(x^2)\right)
$$

when her signal is x^2.

Suppose that with these bids, bidder 1 wins k^1 units and bidder 2 wins $K - k^1$ units. Consider a $k \le k^1$ and notice that we must have $p^1 \equiv \beta_k^1(x^1) > \beta_{K-k+1}^2(x^2) \equiv p^2$, that is, bidder 1's kth bid must have defeated bidder 2's $K - k + 1$st bid, and by the rules of the Vickrey auction, he pays p^2 for the kth unit. Now (17.3) implies that

$$
v_k^1\left(\phi_k^1(p^2), \phi_l^2(p^2)\right) = p^2
$$

where as usual, $l = K - k + 1$. Since $x^1 = \phi_k^1(p^1) > \phi_k^1(p^2)$ and $\phi_l^2(p^2) = x^2$,

$$
v_k^1(x^1, x^2) > p^2
$$

This implies that bidder 1 makes an *ex post* profit on the kth unit that he wins and since he cannot affect the price he pays, he cannot do better.

In addition, (17.3) also implies that

$$
v_l^2\left(\phi_k^1(p^1), \phi_l^2(p^1)\right) = p^1
$$

and since $\phi_l^2(p^1) > \phi_l^2(p^2) = x^2$ and $\phi_k^1(p^1) = x^1$,

$$v_l^2(x^1, x^2) < p^1$$

This implies that bidder 2 does not want to win the lth unit since the price would be too high. Thus, there exists an *ex post* equilibrium.

The equilibrium constructed here is efficient because from (17.3)

$$v_k^1\left(\phi_k^1(p^2), \phi_l^2(p^2)\right) = v_l^2\left(\phi_k^1(p^2), \phi_l^2(p^2)\right)$$

and again since $x^1 = \phi_k^1(p^1) > \phi_k^1(p^2)$ and $\phi_l^2(p^2) = x^2$,

$$v_k^1(x^1, x^2) > v_l^2(x^1, x^2)$$

because of single crossing. This means that the unit in question—which is, simultaneously, the kth unit for bidder 1 and the lth unit for bidder 2—is indeed awarded to the bidder who values it more. ∎

The reasoning in Proposition 17.2 applies to the Ausubel open ascending price auction as well. Recall that in the Ausubel auction the price rises and bidders indicate how many units they are willing to buy at the current price. A bidder is allocated a unit every time the residual supply from the other bidders increases. To find an equilibrium of the auction, let β^1 and β^2 be determined as above and consider the following pair of strategies. Both bidders' demands are K at a price of zero. For all $k \leq K$, bidder i reduces his demand from k to $k-1$ at the price $p_k^i = \beta_k^i\left(x^i\right)$. It is routine to verify that this constitutes an efficient *ex post* equilibrium of the Ausubel auction.

With two bidders, it appears that the single-unit results of Chapter 9 extend to the multiunit context in a relatively straightforward manner. The same is not true when the number of bidders is greater than two.

Three or More Bidders

There is no multiunit analog of Proposition 9.2. Once the number of bidders exceeds two, the Ausubel auction need not have an efficient equilibrium. Stringent restrictions on the valuation functions do not rectify the problem.

Example 17.1 *When there are three or more bidders and values are interdependent, the Ausubel open ascending price auction need not allocate efficiently. This may happen even if bidders have unit demands.*

Suppose that there are two units for sale ($K = 2$) and three bidders ($N = 3$), each of whom wants at most one unit of the good—this is the case of unit demand. The valuations are

$$
\begin{aligned}
v^1(x^1, x^2, x^3) &= x^1 + \alpha x^2 \\
v^2(x^1, x^2, x^3) &= x^2 \\
v^3(x^1, x^2, x^3) &= x^3
\end{aligned}
$$

and the signals X^i all lie in $[0, 1]$ and $\alpha \in (0, 1)$ is a parameter. Clearly, the single crossing condition is satisfied.

Consider an open ascending price auction. Since each bidder wants at most one unit of the good, the workings of the Ausubel auction are the same as the workings of the multiunit English auction. In other words, the price rises until one of the bidders drops out. At that stage, the total supply is equal to the total demand, so the auction is over. Thus, the two units are sold to the two remaining bidders at the price at which the first bidder drops out.

Each bidder need only decide when to drop out. Bidder 2 has private values, so it is weakly dominant for him to drop out when the price reaches his private value. The same is true for bidder 3. Suppose that there is an equilibrium in which bidder 1 follows an increasing and continuous strategy β^1, so he drops out when the price reaches $\beta^1\left(x^1\right)$.

First, suppose $\beta^1(0) = 0$. Now if the signals are such that $\alpha x^2 > x^3$, then it is efficient for bidders 1 and 2 to get one unit each. But if x^1 is close to zero, the continuity of β^1 implies that bidder 1 will drop out first, thereby leading to an inefficient outcome. Second, suppose $\beta^1(0) > 0$. Now if the signals are such that $x^2 < x^3$ and x^1 is small, it is efficient for bidders 2 and 3 to get one unit each. But if $x^2 < \beta^1(0)$, then bidder 2 will drop out first, again leading to an inefficient outcome. ▲

In a single-unit English auction the object is not awarded until all but one of the bidders have dropped out. This means that the winning bidder knows the signals of all bidders and hence his own value. This is not true in the multiunit analogue of the English auction. Some units are awarded *before* all the information has been revealed and it is this feature that leads to inefficiency. Thus, it seems that, except for the case of two bidders, the common auction formats are ill equipped to handle interdependent values in the multiunit context. All this is still under the somewhat uncomfortable assumption that while bidders have multiunit demands, their signals are one-dimensional. The state of affairs is even worse, however, if buyers' signals are multidimensional.

17.2   Multidimensional Signals

Now suppose that each buyer's information consists of an L-dimensional signal $\mathbf{x}^i = \left(x_1^i, x_2^i, \ldots, x_L^i\right)$ and that buyer i's valuations for the K objects depend on the $L \times N$ signals $\mathbf{x} = \left(\mathbf{x}^1, \mathbf{x}^2, \ldots, \mathbf{x}^N\right)$ received by all the buyers. For the moment we make no assumptions on L and K. The *marginal value* of obtaining the kth unit is determined by the function

$$v_k^i\left(\mathbf{x}\right) = v_k^i\left(\mathbf{x}^1, \mathbf{x}^2, \ldots, \mathbf{x}^N\right)$$

All signals are assumed to have a nonnegative effect on all values—that is, for all i, j and k, l,

$$\frac{\partial v_k^i}{\partial x_l^j} \geq 0$$

17.2.1 Single Object

Although we are concerned with multiple object auctions, the problems resulting from multidimensional signals are already apparent when only a single object is for sale. Thus, while buyers receive L dimensional signals $\mathbf{x}^i$, there is only a single object for sale whose value to i can be written as $v^i(\mathbf{x}) = v^i(\mathbf{x}^1, \mathbf{x}^2, \ldots, \mathbf{x}^N)$. The following example illustrates the fundamental nature of the difficulty in the simplest possible setting.

Example 17.2 *Suppose there is a single object for sale to one of two buyers. Buyer 1 receives a two-dimensional signal $\mathbf{x}^1 = (x_1^1, x_2^1)$, whereas buyer 2 is completely uninformed. Buyer 1's first signal determines his own value for the object, whereas his second signal determines buyer 2's value. Thus,*

$$\begin{aligned} v^1(\mathbf{x}^1) &= x_1^1 \\ v^2(\mathbf{x}^1) &= x_2^1 \end{aligned}$$

Clearly, efficiency requires that the object go to buyer 1 only if $x_1^1 \geq x_2^1$. We claim that there does not exist an incentive compatible mechanism that is efficient. The revelation principle ensures that it is enough to consider direct mechanisms.

Consider an efficient mechanism whose payment rule asks buyer 1 to make the payment $M^1(\mathbf{z}^1)$ when he reports $\mathbf{z}^1 = (z_2^1, z_2^1)$ (buyer 2 is completely uninformed). First, notice that M^1 must be constant for all $\mathbf{z}^1$ such that $z_1^1 > z_2^1$. Otherwise, then buyer 1 will report a signal $\mathbf{z}^1$ that minimizes his payment $M^1(\mathbf{z}^1)$ over all $\mathbf{z}^1$ such that $z_1^1 > z_2^1$. In the same way M^1 must be constant for all $\mathbf{z}^1$ such that $z_1^1 < z_2^1$. If not, then buyer 1 will report a signal $\mathbf{z}^1$ that minimizes his payment $M^1(\mathbf{z}^1)$ over all $\mathbf{z}^1$ such that $z_1^1 < z_2^1$. Thus, we conclude that there exist two payments m' and m'' (these could be positive or negative) such that

$$M^1(\mathbf{z}^1) = \begin{cases} m' & \text{if } z_1^1 > z_2^1 \\ m'' & \text{if } z_1^1 < z_2^1 \end{cases}$$

Suppose buyer 1's signal is $\mathbf{x}^1$. If he reports $z_1^1 > z_2^1$, he gets the object and pays m' so that his payoff is $x_1^1 - m'$. On the other hand, if he reports $z_1^1 < z_2^1$, he does not obtain the object, so his payoff is $-m''$. It is better to report $z_1^1 > z_2^1$ if and only if

$$x_1^1 \geq m' - m''$$

But this means that buyer 1's incentives to report $z_1^1 > z_2^1$ versus $z_1^1 < z_2^1$ do not depend on the signal x_2^1. But efficiency hinges precisely on a comparison of x_1^1 and x_2^1, so it is impossible to achieve. ▲

The reader may wonder—quite legitimately—whether the impossibility of achieving efficiency in the preceding example is not due to the failure of some sort of single crossing condition. In situations in which signals were one-dimensional, the single crossing condition—requiring that a buyer's signal have a greater impact on his own value than on others' values—was vital to the question of efficiency. In Example 17.2, however, buyer 1's second signal, x_2^1, has a greater impact on buyer 2's value than on his own. Consider the following, only slightly more complicated, example.

Suppose that both buyers receive two-dimensional signals $\mathbf{x}^i = \left(x_1^i, x_2^i\right)$ and that their respective values are

$$v^1(\mathbf{x}^1) = x_1^1 + x_2^1$$
$$v^2(\mathbf{x}^1) = x_1^2 + \alpha x_2^1$$

where $\alpha \in (0,1)$ is a parameter. Now each buyer's signals have a greater impact on his own value than on the value of the other buyer. But virtually the same argument as above shows that efficiency is impossible to achieve. Buyer 1 cares only about the sum of his own signals $x_1^1 + x_2^1$, so he cannot be induced to reveal more than that. Buyer 2's value, however, depends on buyer 1's second signal, x_2^1, alone. To determine who should win the object it is necessary to extract information regarding x_2^1 separately from that regarding the sum $x_1^1 + x_2^1$. Buyer 1, however, cannot be provided with the incentives to reveal x_2^1 separately from $x_1^1 + x_2^1$. As a result, efficiency cannot be attained.

More generally, consider a direct mechanism with a payment rule $\mathbf{M}$ in which truth-telling is an *ex post* equilibrium. Consider the signals $\mathbf{x}^{-i}$ of all buyers other than i. As in Chapter 10, we will say that buyer i is *pivotal at* $\mathbf{x}^{-i}$ if there exist signal vectors $\mathbf{y}^i$ and $\mathbf{z}^i$ such that $v^i(\mathbf{y}^i, \mathbf{x}^{-i}) > \max_{j \neq i} v^j(\mathbf{y}^i, \mathbf{x}^{-i})$ and $v^i(\mathbf{z}^i, \mathbf{x}^{-i}) < \max_{j \neq i} v^j(\mathbf{z}^i, \mathbf{x}^{-i})$. In other words, when the others' signals are $\mathbf{x}^{-i}$, i's signal determines whether or not it is efficient for him to get the object. Incentive compatibility requires that when his signal is $\mathbf{y}^i$, it is optimal for i to report $\mathbf{y}^i$ rather than $\mathbf{z}^i$, so that

$$v^i(\mathbf{y}^i, \mathbf{x}^{-i}) - M^i(\mathbf{y}^i, \mathbf{x}^{-i}) \geq -M^i(\mathbf{z}^i, \mathbf{x}^{-i})$$

Likewise, when his signal is $\mathbf{z}^i$, it is optimal to report $\mathbf{z}^i$ rather than $\mathbf{y}^i$, so that

$$-M^i(\mathbf{z}^i, \mathbf{x}^{-i}) \geq v^i(\mathbf{z}^i, \mathbf{x}^{-i}) - M^i(\mathbf{y}^i, \mathbf{x}^{-i})$$

Combining the two conditions results in

$$v^i(\mathbf{y}^i, \mathbf{x}^{-i}) \geq M^i(\mathbf{y}^i, \mathbf{x}^{-i}) - M^i(\mathbf{z}^i, \mathbf{x}^{-i}) \geq v^i(\mathbf{z}^i, \mathbf{x}^{-i})$$

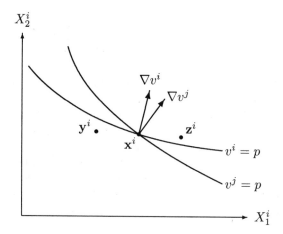

FIGURE 17.3. Efficiency with Multidimensional Signals

and so a necessary condition for incentive compatibility is

$$v^i(\mathbf{y}^i, \mathbf{x}^{-i}) \geq v^i(\mathbf{z}^i, \mathbf{x}^{-i})$$

that is, buyer i's value when he wins the object must be at least as high as when he does not. Put another way, keeping others' signals fixed, an increase in buyer i's value that results from a change in his own signal cannot cause him to lose if he were winning earlier. Once again we see that *ex post* incentive compatible mechanisms must be *monotonic* in values—an increase in the value resulting from a change in his own signal must increase the chances that a buyer wins. In Chapter 10, we saw that when signals were one-dimensional this monotonicity (see (10.1)), together with the requirement of efficiency, led to the single crossing condition. When signals are multidimensional, however, monotonicity in values can be reconciled with efficiency only in very exceptional circumstances. Let us see why.

Suppose that there exists an $\mathbf{x}^i$ such that for some buyer j, $v^i(\mathbf{x}^i, \mathbf{x}^{-i}) = v^j(\mathbf{x}^i, \mathbf{x}^{-i}) \equiv p$, say, and these values are the highest among all buyers. Consider, as in Figure 17.3, the level curves of v^i and v^j in the space of i's signals. If these intersect, and the slopes of the level curves at the point of intersection are different, then as depicted, we can find two signals $\mathbf{y}^i$ and $\mathbf{z}^i$ such that

$$p > v^i(\mathbf{y}^i, \mathbf{x}^{-i}) > v^j(\mathbf{y}^i, \mathbf{x}^{-i})$$

but

$$v^j(\mathbf{z}^i, \mathbf{x}^{-i}) > v^i(\mathbf{z}^i, \mathbf{x}^{-i}) > p$$

Efficiency requires that i win when the signal is $\mathbf{y}^i$ and lose when the signal is $\mathbf{z}^i$. But since $v^i(\mathbf{z}^i, \mathbf{x}^{-i}) > v^i(\mathbf{y}^i, \mathbf{x}^{-i})$, it is the case that buyer i

wins when his value is $v^i(\mathbf{y}^i, \mathbf{x}^{-i})$ but loses when his value increases to $v^i(\mathbf{z}^i, \mathbf{x}^{-i})$, thereby violating the monotonicity property of incentive compatible mechanisms. Thus, we have argued that as long as the level curves $v^i = p$ and $v^j = p$ intersect, efficiency is impossible. The following result summarizes our findings.

Proposition 17.3 *Suppose there exists an efficient direct mechanism in which truth-telling is an ex post equilibrium. If buyers' signals are multi-dimensional, then at any $\mathbf{x}^i$ such that $v^i(\mathbf{x}^i, \mathbf{x}^{-i}) = v^j(\mathbf{x}^i, \mathbf{x}^{-i})$ and these are maximal, it must be that*

$$\nabla v^i(\mathbf{x}^i, \mathbf{x}^{-i}) = \nabla v^j(\mathbf{x}^i, \mathbf{x}^{-i})$$

where ∇v^i and ∇v^j denote the L-vectors of partial derivatives of v^i and v^j with respect to i's signals (the gradients of v^i and v^j with respect to $\mathbf{x}^i$).

The necessary condition in the preceding proposition—the equality of the gradients—is a very strong requirement that is almost never satisfied; it is nongeneric in the sense that a slight perturbation in the valuation functions will cause it to be violated. The essential difficulty is that a buyer's payment—a one-dimensional instrument—can only be used to extract one-dimensional information from the buyer. The information that can be extracted concerns the *value* of the buyer, rather than his *signal* and information concerning i's value alone is, in general, insufficient to decide the efficiency question when values are interdependent. The one exception occurs when buyer i's signals affect all buyers' values in the same manner so that the relevant information can effectively be reduced to a one-dimensional variable. Otherwise, such a reduction is impossible, and as a result, so is efficiency.

Another way to understand Proposition 17.3 is to note that in the present context monotonicity requires that the following multidimensional version of single crossing hold. Suppose $v^i(\mathbf{x}^i, \mathbf{x}^{-i}) = v^j(\mathbf{x}^i, \mathbf{x}^{-i})$ and $\mathbf{t}^i \neq \mathbf{0}$ is such that the directional derivative of v^i with respect to $\mathbf{x}^i$ in the direction $\mathbf{t}^i$ is positive—that is,

$$\nabla v^i(\mathbf{x}^i, \mathbf{x}^{-i}) \cdot \mathbf{t}^i > 0$$

In other words, i's utility increases if his signal $\mathbf{x}^i$ increases in the direction $\mathbf{t}^i$. Monotonicity now requires that for any such $\mathbf{t}^i$,

$$\nabla v^i(\mathbf{x}^i, \mathbf{x}^{-i}) \cdot \mathbf{t}^i > \nabla v^j(\mathbf{x}^i, \mathbf{x}^{-i}) \cdot \mathbf{t}^i \tag{17.4}$$

that is, the change in i's value must be greater than the change in j's value. But as is clear from Figure 17.3, this cannot hold if the level curves of v^i and v^j intersect: if we let $\mathbf{t}^i = \mathbf{z}^i - \mathbf{x}^i$, then (17.4) is violated. In this sense, the appropriate single crossing condition cannot be generically satisfied once signals are multidimensional.

17.2.2   Multiple Objects

It is not surprising that the impossibility result from the previous section extends to the multiple object setting. But there is an important exception—the case of additively and informationally *separable* valuations.

Separability and Efficiency

Suppose that K distinct objects, labeled $A, B, C, \ldots$, and so on, from a set $\mathcal{K}$ are for sale. Each buyer receives a K-dimensional signal

$$\mathbf{x}^i = \left(x_A^i\right)_{A \in \mathcal{K}}$$

with the interpretation that x_A^i is the one-dimensional information received by buyer i that pertains to object A. Buyers' valuations for the different objects are *informationally separable*—that is, the value of an object $A \in \mathcal{K}$ to buyer i is of the form

$$v_A^i(x_A^1, x_A^2, \ldots, x_A^N)$$

In other words, the value to i of obtaining object A depends on the signals of all buyers that pertain only to object A, and not on signals x_B^j, say.

We also need that for each $A \in \mathcal{K}$, the valuations $v_A^1, v_A^2, \ldots, v_A^N$ satisfy the *single crossing* condition.

Suppose further that there are no complementarities and that the valuations are *additively separable*—the value derived from obtaining particular bundle of objects is simply the sum of the values of the individual objects in that bundle. Thus, for instance, the value of the bundle $\{A, B\}$ to buyer i is simply

$$v_A^i(x_A^1, x_A^2, \ldots, x_A^N) + v_B^i(x_B^1, x_B^2, \ldots, x_B^N)$$

The separable model, albeit special, may be quite natural in some settings. Suppose that the objects being sold are the rights to conduct business in different regions of a country. For instance, object A may be a license awarding exclusive rights to supply local telephone services in area A. Each buyer may have some information x_A^i concerning demand conditions in area A. In that case, as a first approximation, it is not unnatural to suppose that a buyer's value for license A depends only on information concerning demand conditions in region A and not on demand conditions in another region, say B.

The virtue of the separable specification is that the problem of allocating the objects efficiently neatly decomposes into K separate problems: the objects can be efficiently allocated one at a time. Object A should be allocated to the buyer who derives the largest benefit from it—that is, to the buyer with the largest value of $v_A^1, v_A^2, \ldots, v_A^N$—and this allocation does not depend in any way on other values v_B^i. Similarly, object B should be allocated to the buyer with the largest value of $v_B^1, v_B^2, \ldots, v_B^N$ regardless of the values v_A^i. This in turn means that the allocation of object A depends only on the signals x_A^i that pertain to A, the allocation of object B depends only on the signals x_B^i that pertain to B, and so on.

The separable specification also implies that the mechanism design problem can likewise be decomposed into K separate problems, each with one-dimensional signals. We can then use K generalized VCG mechanisms for allocating single objects as in Chapter 10. In particular, each buyer is asked to report his signal $\mathbf{x}^i$. Object A is awarded to the buyer with the highest value v_A^i for A when evaluated at the reported signals $x_A^1, x_A^2, \ldots, x_A^N$ of all buyers that pertain to A. If buyer i is awarded object A, then he pays $v_A^i(y_A^i(\mathbf{x}_A^{-i}), \mathbf{x}_A^{-i})$ where $y_A^i(\mathbf{x}_A^{-i})$ is defined by

$$y_A^i(\mathbf{x}_A^{-i} = \inf \left\{ z_A^i : v_A^i(z_A^i, \mathbf{x}_A^{-i}) \geq \max_{j \neq i} v_A^j(z_A^i, \mathbf{x}_A^{-i}) \right\}$$

Truth-telling is an *ex post* equilibrium in each mechanism in isolation and the separable specification guarantees that no buyer can gain from simultaneously misreporting more than one signal. Thus, in the separable model an efficient allocation of multiple objects can be attained via the generalized VCG mechanism.

Proposition 17.4 *Suppose buyers' valuations for K different objects are additively and informationally separable. Then truth-telling is an efficient ex post equilibrium of the generalized VCG mechanism.*

In the separable model the K objects would also be efficiently allocated in a sequence of English auctions. This assumes, of course, that the valuations for each object A are such that an efficient equilibrium exists. This would be satisfied, for instance, if for each A, the valuations satisfied the average crossing condition introduced in Chapter 9.

In general, the valuations need not be separable and buyers' valuations for object A, say, may depend on both x_A^i and x_B^i. In that case, the arguments leading up to Proposition 17.3 imply that efficiency cannot be attained.

Chapter Notes

Much of the material in this chapter originates in the paper by Maskin (1992) who recognized that the possibility of attaining efficiency hinged on the dimensionality of buyers' signals. Maskin (2001) is a more up-to-date survey of the area.

Proposition 17.2, demonstrating the efficiency of the Vickrey auction when there are only two bidders with one-dimensional signals, was derived by Perry and Reny (2001). They also observed that this result does not hold once there are three or more bidders with multiunit demand. Example 17.1, showing that with three or more bidders open auctions are inefficient even with single-unit demand, is due to Morgan (2001, private communication).

Maskin (1992) was the first to show the impossibility of allocating efficiently if buyers have multidimensional information. Proposition 17.3 is based on an impossibility result in Dasgupta and Maskin (2000). Jehiel and Moldovanu (2001) have extended these results in many directions. The interpretation of the impossibility result as a necessary failure of single crossing is due to Reny (2001, private communication).

Part III

Appendices

Appendix A
Continuous Distributions

Given a random variable X, which takes on values in $[0, \omega]$, we define its cumulative *distribution function* $F : [0, \omega] \to [0, 1]$ by[1]

$$F(x) = \text{Prob}\,[X \leq x] \tag{A.1}$$

the probability that X takes on a value not exceeding x. By definition, the function F is nondecreasing and satisfies $F(0) = 0$ and $F(\omega) = 1$ (if $\omega = \infty$, then $\lim_{x \to \infty} F(x) = 1$). In this book we always suppose that F is increasing and continuously differentiable.

The derivative of F is called the associated probability *density function* and is usually denoted by the corresponding lowercase letter $f \equiv F'$. By assumption, f is continuous and we will suppose, in addition, that for all $x \in (0, \omega)$, $f(x)$ is positive. The interval $[0, \omega]$ is called the *support* of the distribution. When (A.1) holds we will say that X is distributed according to the distribution F or, equivalently, according to the density f.

If X is distributed according to F, then the *expectation* of X is

$$E\,[X] = \int_0^\omega x f(x)\,dx$$

---

[1] We will allow for the possibility that X can take on any nonnegative real value. In that case, with a slight abuse of notation, we will write $\omega = \infty$.

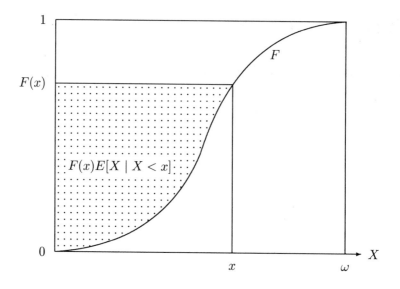

FIGURE A.1. Conditional Expectation

and if $\gamma : [0, \omega] \to \mathbb{R}$ is some arbitrary function, then the expectation of $\gamma(X)$ is analogously defined as

$$E\left[\gamma\left(X\right)\right] = \int_0^\omega \gamma\left(x\right) f\left(x\right) dx$$

Sometimes the expectation of $\gamma(X)$ is also written as

$$E\left[\gamma\left(X\right)\right] = \int_0^\omega \gamma\left(x\right) \, dF(x)$$

The *conditional expectation* of X given that $X < x$ is

$$E\left[X \mid X < x\right] = \frac{1}{F(x)} \int_0^x tf(t) \, dt$$

and so

$$
\begin{aligned}
F(x)E\left[X \mid X < x\right] &= \int_0^x tf(t) \, dt \\
&= xF(x) - \int_0^x F(t) \, dt \qquad (A.2)
\end{aligned}
$$

which is obtained by integrating the right-hand side of the first equality by parts. The formula in (A.2) shows that $F(x)E\left[X \mid X < x\right]$ is the shaded area lying above the curve F in Figure A.1.

Hazard Rates

Let F be a distribution function with support $[0, \omega]$. The *hazard rate* of F is the function $\lambda : [0, \omega) \to \mathbb{R}_+$ defined by

$$\lambda(x) \equiv \frac{f(x)}{1 - F(x)}$$

If F represents the probability that some event will happen before time x, then the hazard rate at x represents the instantaneous probability that the event will happen at x, given that it has not happened until time x. The event may be the failure of some component—a lightbulb, for instance—and hence it is sometimes also known as the "failure rate." Notice that as $x \to \omega$, $\lambda(x) \to \infty$.

Since

$$-\lambda(x) = \frac{d}{dx} \ln(1 - F(x))$$

if we write

$$F(x) = 1 - \exp\left(-\int_0^x \lambda(t)\, dt\right) \tag{A.3}$$

then this shows that any arbitrary function $\lambda : [0, \omega) \to \mathbb{R}_+$ such that for all $x < \omega$,

$$\int_0^x \lambda(t)\, dt < \infty$$

and

$$\lim_{x \to \omega} \int_0^x \lambda(t)\, dt = \infty \tag{A.4}$$

is the hazard rate of some distribution; in particular, that defined by (A.3). The fact that $\lambda(x) \geq 0$ ensures that F is nondecreasing and (A.4) ensures that $F(\omega) = 1$.

If for all $x \geq 0$, $\lambda(x)$ is a constant, say $\lambda(x) \equiv \lambda > 0$, then (A.3) results in the *exponential distribution*

$$F(x) = 1 - \exp(-\lambda x)$$

whose expectation $E[X] = 1/\lambda$.

Closely related to the hazard rate is the function $\sigma : (0, \omega] \to \mathbb{R}_+$ defined by

$$\sigma(x) \equiv \frac{f(x)}{F(x)}$$

sometimes known as the *reverse hazard rate.*[2] Since

$$\sigma(x) = \frac{d}{dx} \ln F(x)$$

---

[2] In some applications this is also referred to as the inverse of the *Mills' ratio.*

if we write

$$F(x) = \exp \left(- \int_x^\omega \sigma(t)\, dt \right) \tag{A.5}$$

then this shows that any arbitrary function $\sigma : (0, \omega) \to \mathbb{R}_+$ such that for all $x > 0$,

$$\int_x^\omega \sigma(t)\, dt < \infty$$

and

$$\lim_{x \to 0} \int_x^\omega \sigma(t)\, dt = \infty \tag{A.6}$$

is the reverse hazard rate of some distribution; in particular, that defined by (A.5). The fact that $\sigma(x) \geq 0$ ensures that F is nondecreasing and (A.6) ensures that $F(0) = 0$.

Jointly Distributed Random Variables

Let X and Y be two random variables taking on values in $[0, \omega_X]$ and $[0, \omega_Y]$, respectively. We will say that X and Y have the *joint density* $f :$ $[0, \omega_X] \times [0, \omega_Y] \to \mathbb{R}_+$ if for all $x' < x''$ and $y' < y''$

$$\text{Prob}\, [x' \leq X \leq x'' \text{ and } y' \leq Y \leq y''] = \int_{y'}^{y''} \int_{x'}^{x''} f(x, y)\, dx\, dy$$

We will then say that X and Y are jointly distributed according to f. We will assume that f is continuous and positive on $(0, \omega_X) \times (0, \omega_Y)$.

The *marginal density* of X is

$$f_X(x) = \int_0^{\omega_Y} f(x, y)\, dy$$

and the marginal density of Y is similarly defined. The random variables X and Y are *independent* if and only if

$$f(x, y) = f_X(x) \times f_Y(y)$$

For any $x > 0$, the *conditional density* of Y given that $X = x$ is

$$f_Y(y \mid X = x) = \frac{f(x, y)}{f_X(x)}$$

and for any $x > 0$, the *conditional expectation* of Y given that $X = x$ is defined as

$$E[Y \mid X = x] = \int_0^{\omega_Y} y f_Y(y \mid X = x)\, dy$$

Let us denote by $E\left[Y \mid X\right] : \left[0, \omega_X\right] \to \mathbb{R}_+$ the function of X whose value at $X = x$ is $E\left[Y \mid X = x\right]$. The function $E\left[Y \mid X\right]$ is then also a random variable and it is meaningful to speak of its expectation. Using the preceding definitions, it can be verified that

$$E_X\left[E_Y\left[Y \mid X\right]\right] = E_Y\left[Y\right]$$

This identity is sometimes known as the "law of iterated expectation."

Extensions to an arbitrary finite number of random variables are straightforward.

Notes on Appendix A

The material on continuous random variables is quite standard and can be found in any reasonable book on probability theory. Ross (1989) has presented a concise treatment of the relevant concepts and results.

Appendix B
Stochastic Orders

There are numerous senses in which one distribution F may "dominate" or may be "greater than" another distribution G and each induces a partial order over the space of all distributions.[1] In this appendix we discuss some of these notions, called *stochastic orders*, that play an important role in auction theory.

For the sake of convenience, we assume that all distributions being compared have the same support, say $[0, \omega]$. As usual, we allow for the possibility that the support is the nonnegative portion of the real line.

First-Order Stochastic Dominance

Given two distribution functions F and G, we say that F (first-order) *stochastically dominates* G if for all $z \in [0, \omega]$,

$$F(z) \leq G(z) \tag{B.1}$$

If the random variables X and Y are distributed according to F and G, respectively, and (B.1) holds, then we will also say the X stochastically dominates Y.

Now suppose $\gamma : [0, \omega] \rightarrow \mathbb{R}$ is an increasing and differentiable function. If X stochastically dominates Y, and these have distribution functions F

---

[1]A partial order is reflexive and transitive. It need not be complete.

and G, respectively, then

$$E\left[\gamma\left(X\right)\right] - E\left[\gamma\left(Y\right)\right] = \int_0^\omega \gamma\left(z\right)\left[f\left(z\right) - g\left(z\right)\right] dz$$

and integrating by parts, we obtain

$$E\left[\gamma\left(X\right)\right] - E\left[\gamma\left(Y\right)\right] = -\int_0^\omega \gamma'\left(z\right)\left[F\left(z\right) - G\left(z\right)\right] dz \geq 0$$

since $\gamma' > 0$ and $F \leq G$. In particular, $E\left[X\right] \geq E\left[Y\right]$.

Hazard Rate Dominance

Suppose that F and G are two distributions with hazard rates λ_F and λ_G, respectively. If for all x, $\lambda_F\left(x\right) \leq \lambda_G\left(x\right)$, then we say that F *dominates* G *in terms of the hazard rate*. This order is also referred in short as hazard rate dominance.

If F dominates G in terms of the hazard rate, then (A.3) immediately implies that

$$F\left(x\right) = 1 - \exp\left(-\int_0^x \lambda_F(t)\, dt\right) \leq 1 - \exp\left(-\int_0^x \lambda_G(t)\, dt\right) = G\left(x\right)$$

and hence F stochastically dominates G. Thus, hazard rate dominance implies first-order stochastic dominance.

Reverse Hazard Rate Dominance

Suppose that F and G are two distributions with reverse hazard rates σ_F and σ_G, respectively. If for all x, $\sigma_F\left(x\right) \geq \sigma_G\left(x\right)$, then we say that F *dominates* G *in terms of the reverse hazard rate*. This order is also referred to as reverse hazard rate dominance, in short.

If F dominates G in terms of the reverse hazard rate, then (A.5) immediately implies that

$$F\left(x\right) = \exp\left(-\int_x^\omega \sigma_F(t)\, dt\right) \leq \exp\left(-\int_x^\omega \sigma_G(t)\, dt\right) = G\left(x\right)$$

and hence, again, F stochastically dominates G. Thus, reverse hazard rate dominance also implies first-order stochastic dominance.

Likelihood Ratio Dominance

The distribution function F *dominates* G *in terms of the likelihood ratio* if for all $x < y$,

$$\frac{f(x)}{g(x)} \leq \frac{f(y)}{g(y)} \tag{B.2}$$

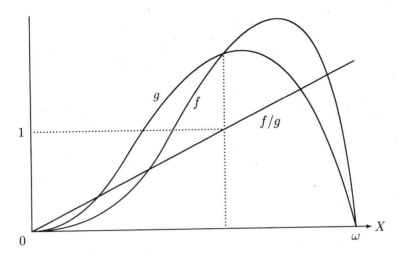

FIGURE B.1. Likelihood Ratio Dominance

or equivalently, if the ratio f/g is nondecreasing in x. We will refer to this order as likelihood ratio dominance. See Figure B.1 for an illustration. As shown, if F dominates G in terms of the likelihood ratio, then f and g can "cross" only once.

Likelihood ratio dominance is, of course, equivalent to the following: for all $x < y$,

$$\frac{f(y)}{f(x)} \geq \frac{g(y)}{g(x)}$$

This implies that for all x,

$$\int_x^\omega \frac{f(y)}{f(x)}\, dy \geq \int_x^\omega \frac{g(y)}{g(x)}\, dy$$

so that

$$\frac{1 - F(x)}{f(x)} \geq \frac{1 - G(x)}{g(x)}$$

which is the same as

$$\lambda_F(x) \leq \lambda_G(x)$$

Thus, likelihood ratio dominance implies hazard rate dominance.

Similarly, by writing (B.2) as follows: for all $x < y$,

$$\frac{f(x)}{f(y)} \leq \frac{g(x)}{g(y)}$$

and integrating, we obtain

$$\int_0^y \frac{f(x)}{f(y)}\, dx \leq \int_0^y \frac{g(x)}{g(y)}\, dx$$

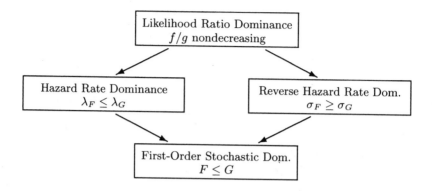

FIGURE B.2. Different Notions of Stochastic Ordering

so that for all y,

$$\frac{F(y)}{f(y)} \leq \frac{G(y)}{g(y)}$$

which is the same as: for all y,

$$\sigma_F(y) \geq \sigma_G(y)$$

Thus, likelihood ratio dominance also implies reverse hazard rate dominance.

We have already shown that hazard rate dominance and reverse hazard rate dominance both imply first-order stochastic dominance. Figure B.2 summarizes the relationships among the four notions of stochastic orders considered so far.

Mean-Preserving Spreads

A fifth notion of stochastic order is useful in comparing distributions with the same mean.

Suppose X is a random variable with distribution function F. Let Z be a random variable whose distribution conditional on $X = x$, $H\left(\cdot \mid X = x\right)$ is such that for all x, $E\left[Z \mid X = x\right] = 0$. Suppose $Y = X + Z$ is the random variable obtained from first drawing X from F and then for each realization $X = x$, drawing a Z from the conditional distribution $H\left(\cdot \mid X = x\right)$ and adding it to X. Let G be the distribution of Y so defined. We will then say that G is a *mean-preserving spread* of F.

As the name suggests, while the random variables X and Y have the same mean—that is, $E\left[X\right] = E\left[Y\right]$—the variable Y is "more spread-out" than X since it is obtained by adding a "noise" variable Z to X.

Now suppose $U : [0, \omega] \rightarrow \mathbb{R}$ is a concave function. Then we have

$$
\begin{aligned}
E_Y [U(Y)] &= E_X [E_Z [U(X + Z) \mid X = x]] \\
&\leq E_X [U(E_Z [X + Z \mid X = x])] \\
&= E_X [U(X)]
\end{aligned}
$$

where the inequality follows from the assumption that U is concave.

This fact is used to define another notion of order between distributions with the same mean. Given two distributions F and G with the same mean, we say that F *second-order stochastically dominates* G if for all concave functions $U : [0, \omega] \rightarrow \mathbb{R}$,

$$
\int_0^\omega U(x) f(x) \, dx \geq \int_0^\omega U(y) g(y) \, dy
$$

We have shown that if G is a mean-preserving spread of F, then F second-order stochastically dominates G. The converse is also true—although we omit a proof of this fact here—and so the two notions are equivalent.

Second-order stochastic dominance is also equivalent to the statement that for all x,

$$
\int_0^x G(y) \, dy \geq \int_0^x F(x) \, dx
$$

with an equality when $x = \omega$. Again, we omit a proof of this fact.

Notes on Appendix B

A comprehensive discussion of the various notions of stochastic orders and their relationships can be found in Shaked and Shanthikumar (1994). This book contains a very useful collection of results that had hitherto been scattered about in the literature and, as a result, had been somewhat inaccessible.

Appendix C
Order Statistics

Let $X_1, X_2, \ldots, X_n$ be n independent draws from a distribution F with associated density f. Let $Y_1^{(n)}, Y_2^{(n)}, \ldots, Y_n^{(n)}$ be a rearrangement of these so that $Y_1^{(n)} \geq Y_2^{(n)} \geq \ldots \geq Y_n^{(n)}$. The random variables $Y_k^{(n)}$, $k = 1, 2, \ldots, n$ are referred to as *order statistics*.

Let $F_k^{(n)}$ denote the distribution of $Y_k^{(n)}$, with corresponding probability density function $f_k^{(n)}$.

When the "sample size" n is fixed and there is no ambiguity, we will economize on notation and write Y_k instead of $Y_k^{(n)}$, F_k instead of $F_k^{(n)}$ and f_k instead of $f_k^{(n)}$.

We will typically be interested in properties of the highest and second-highest order statistics, Y_1 and Y_2.

Highest Order Statistic

The distribution of the highest order statistic Y_1 is easy to derive. The event that $Y_1 \leq y$ is the same as the event: for all k, $X_k \leq y$. Since each X_k is an independent draw from the same distribution F, we have that[1]

$$F_1(y) = F(y)^n \tag{C.1}$$

---

[1] We write $F(y)^n$ to denote $(F(y))^n$.

The associated probability density function is

$$f_1(y) = nF(y)^{n-1}f(y)$$

Observe that if F stochastically dominates G (for all x, $F(x) \leq G(x)$) and F_1 and G_1 are the distributions of the highest order statistics of n draws from F and G, respectively, then F_1 stochastically dominates G_1.

Second-Highest Order Statistic

The distribution the second-highest order statistic Y_2 can also be easily derived. The event that Y_2 is less than or equal to y is the union of the following disjoint events: (i) all X_k's are less than or equal to y, and (ii) $n-1$ of the X_k's are less than or equal to y and one is greater than y. There are n different ways in which (ii) can occur, so we have that

$$
\begin{aligned}
F_2(y) &= \underbrace{F(y)^n}_{(i)} + \underbrace{nF(y)^{n-1}(1 - F(y))}_{(ii)} \\
&= nF(y)^{n-1} - (n-1)F(y)^n \quad\quad\quad\quad \text{(C.2)}
\end{aligned}
$$

The associated probability density function is

$$f_2(y) = n(n-1)(1 - F(y))F(y)^{n-2}f(y) \quad\quad\quad\quad \text{(C.3)}$$

Again, it can be verified that if F stochastically dominates G and F_2 and G_2 are the distributions of the second-highest order statistics of n draws from F and G, respectively, then F_2 stochastically dominates G_2.

Relationships

Observe that

$$
\begin{aligned}
F_2^{(n)}(y) &= nF(y)^{n-1} - (n-1)F(y)^n \\
&= nF_1^{(n-1)}(y) - (n-1)F_1^{(n)}(y)
\end{aligned}
$$

and so

$$f_2^{(n)}(y) = nf_1^{(n-1)}(y) - (n-1)f_1^{(n)}(y) \quad\quad\quad\quad \text{(C.4)}$$

This immediately implies that

$$E[Y_2^{(n)}] = nE[Y_1^{(n-1)}] - (n-1)E[Y_1^{(n)}]$$

Also note that

$$
\begin{aligned}
f_2^{(n)}(y) &= n(n-1)(1 - F(y))F(y)^{n-2}f(y) \\
&= n(1 - F(y))f_1^{(n-1)}(y) \quad\quad\quad\quad \text{(C.5)}
\end{aligned}
$$

Joint and Conditional Distributions of Order Statistics

Even though $X_1, X_2, \ldots, X_n$ are independently drawn, the order statistics $Y_1^{(n)}, Y_2^{(n)}, \ldots, Y_n^{(n)}$ are not independent. The joint density of $\mathbf{Y} = (Y_1^{(n)}, Y_2^{(n)}, \ldots, Y_n^{(n)})$ is

$$f_{\mathbf{Y}}^{(n)}(y_1, y_2, \ldots, y_n) = n! f(y_1) f(y_2) \ldots f(y_n)$$

if $y_1 \geq y_2 \geq \ldots \geq y_n$ and 0 otherwise. From this it is routine to deduce that the joint density of the first and second order statistics is

$$f_{1,2}^{(n)}(y_1, y_2) = n(n-1) f(y_1) f(y_2) F(y_2)^{n-2}$$

if $y_1 \geq y_2$ and 0 otherwise.

The density of $Y_2^{(n)}$ conditional on $Y_1^{(n)} = y$ is

$$
\begin{aligned}
f_2^{(n)}\left(z \mid Y_1^{(n)} = y\right) &= \frac{f_{1,2}^{(n)}(y, z)}{f_1^{(n)}(y)} \\
&= \frac{n(n-1) f(y) f(z) F(z)^{n-2}}{n f(y) F(y)^{n-1}} \\
&= \frac{(n-1) f(z) F(z)^{n-2}}{F(y)^{n-1}}
\end{aligned}
$$

if $y \geq z$ and 0 otherwise. On the other hand, the density of $Y_1^{(n-1)}$ conditional on the event $Y_1^{(n-1)} < y$ is

$$
\begin{aligned}
f_1^{(n-1)}\left(z \mid Y_1^{(n-1)} < y\right) &= \frac{f_1^{(n-1)}(z)}{F_1^{(n-1)}(y)} \\
&= \frac{(n-1) f(z) F(z)^{n-2}}{F(y)^{n-1}}
\end{aligned}
$$

Thus,

$$f_2^{(n)}\left(\cdot \mid Y_1^{(n)} = y\right) = f_1^{(n-1)}\left(\cdot \mid Y_1^{(n-1)} < y\right) \tag{C.6}$$

Order Statistics for Symmetric Nonindependent Random Variables

Suppose that the random variables $X_1, X_2, \ldots, X_n$ are distributed on $[0, \omega]^n$ according to the joint density function f and that f is a symmetric function of its arguments. Let $Y_1^{(n)}, Y_2^{(n)}, \ldots, Y_n^{(n)}$ be the random variables obtained by rearranging $X_1, X_2, \ldots, X_n$ in decreasing order so that $Y_1^{(n)} \geq Y_2^{(n)} \geq \ldots \geq Y_n^{(n)}$.

To determine the joint density of $\mathbf{Y} \equiv (Y_1^{(n)}, Y_2^{(n)}, \ldots, Y_n^{(n)})$, first notice that the support of $\mathbf{Y}$ is the set $\{\mathbf{y} \in [0, \omega]^n : y_1 \geq y_2 \geq \ldots \geq y_n\}$. Since f is symmetric, if $g_{\mathbf{Y}}$ is the joint density of $\mathbf{Y}$, then

$$g_{\mathbf{Y}}(y_1, y_2, \ldots, y_n) = \begin{cases} n! f(y_1, y_2, \ldots, y_n) & \text{if } y_1 \geq y_2 \geq \ldots \geq y_n \\ 0 & \text{otherwise} \end{cases}$$

To see why this is correct, fix a $\mathbf{y} \in [0, \omega]^n$ such that $y_1 \geq y_2 \geq \ldots \geq y_n$. The "event" $\mathbf{Y} = \mathbf{y}$ occurs as long as some permutation of the variables $\mathbf{X}$ equals $\mathbf{y}$. There are $n!$ such permutations and since the density of $\mathbf{X}$ is symmetric, the preceding formula results.

Notes on Appendix C

A basic discussion of order statistics can be found in any standard text on probability theory. The books by David (1969) and Arnold *et al.* (1992) contain more specialized treatments.

    We caution the reader that the terminology and notation in these and other specialized texts is different from that employed in auction theory. We have denoted the *highest* of $X_1, X_2, \ldots, X_n$ by $Y_1^{(n)}$, the *second-highest* by $Y_2^{(n)}$, and so on. In statistics it is conventional to call the *smallest* of $X_1, X_2, \ldots, X_n$ as the "first" order statistic, the *second-smallest* as the "second" order statistic and so on., and these are denoted, respectively, by $Y_1^{(n)}, Y_2^{(n)}$, and so on. (or some similar notation)—in other words, the order is reversed. The definitions and results in statistics texts like those mentioned here need to be read with some care to account for these differences in terminology and notation.

Appendix D
Affiliated Random Variables

Suppose that the random variables $X_1, X_2, \ldots, X_n$ are distributed on some product of intervals $\mathcal{X} \subset \mathbb{R}^n$ according to the joint density function f. The variables $\mathbf{X} = (X_1, X_2, \ldots, X_n)$ are said to be *affiliated* if for all $\mathbf{x}', \mathbf{x}'' \in \mathcal{X}$,

$$f(\mathbf{x}' \vee \mathbf{x}'') f(\mathbf{x}' \wedge \mathbf{x}'') \geq f(\mathbf{x}') f(\mathbf{x}'') \tag{D.1}$$

where

$$\mathbf{x}' \vee \mathbf{x}'' = (\max(x_1', x_1''), \max(x_2', x_2''), \ldots, \max(x_n', x_n''))$$

denotes the component-wise maximum of $\mathbf{x}$ and $\mathbf{x}'$, and

$$\mathbf{x}' \wedge \mathbf{x}'' = (\min(x_1', x_1''), \min(x_2', x_2''), \ldots, \min(x_n', x_n''))$$

denotes the component-wise minimum of $\mathbf{x}'$ and $\mathbf{x}''$. (See Figure D.1.) If (D.1) is satisfied, then we also say that f is affiliated.[1]

Suppose that the density function $f : \mathcal{X} \to \mathbb{R}_+$ is strictly positive in the interior of $\mathcal{X}$ and twice continuously differentiable. Using (D.1), it is easy to verify that f is affiliated if and only if, for all $i \neq j$,

$$\frac{\partial^2}{\partial x_i \partial x_j} \ln f \geq 0 \tag{D.2}$$

---

[1] A function g is said to be *supermodular* if $g(\mathbf{x}' \vee \mathbf{x}'') + g(\mathbf{x}' \wedge \mathbf{x}'') \geq g(\mathbf{x}') + g(\mathbf{x}'')$. Thus, f is affiliated if and only if $\ln f$ is supermodular; in other words, f is *log-supermodular*.

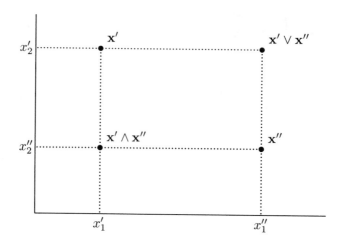

FIGURE D.1. Component-Wise Maxima and Minima

In other words, the off-diagonal elements of the Hessian of $\ln f$ are nonnegative.

Suppose that the random variables $X_1, X_2, \ldots, X_n$ are symmetrically distributed and, as in Appendix C, define $Y_1, Y_2, \ldots, Y_{n-1}$ to be the largest, second largest, $\ldots$, smallest from among $X_2, X_3, \ldots, X_n$. From (D.1) it follows that if g denotes the joint density of $X_1, Y_1, Y_2, \ldots, Y_{n-1}$, then

$$g(x_1, y_1, y_2, \ldots, y_{n-1}) = (n-1)! f(x_1, y_1, \ldots, y_{n-1})$$

if $y_1 \geq y_2 \geq \ldots \geq y_{n-1}$ and 0 otherwise. Now it immediately follows that

- If $X_1, X_2, \ldots, X_n$ are symmetrically distributed and affiliated, then $X_1, Y_1, Y_2, \ldots, Y_{n-1}$ are also affiliated.

Two Variables

We now present some special, but important, results concerning affiliation between two variables.

Suppose the random variables X and Y have a joint density $f : [0, \omega]^2 \to \mathbb{R}$. If X and Y are affiliated, then for all $x' \geq x$ and $y' \geq y$,

$$f(x', y)f(x, y') \leq f(x, y)f(x', y')$$

or equivalently that

$$\frac{f(x, y')}{f(x, y)} \leq \frac{f(x', y')}{f(x', y)} \tag{D.3}$$

Let $F(\cdot \mid x) \equiv F_Y(\cdot \mid X = x)$ denote the conditional distribution of Y given $X = x$ and, as usual, let $f(\cdot \mid x) \equiv f_Y(\cdot \mid X = x)$ denote the corresponding density function. Then (D.3) is equivalent to

$$\frac{f(y' \mid x) f(x)}{f(y \mid x) f(x)} \leq \frac{f(y' \mid x') f(x')}{f(y \mid x') f(x')}$$

and so

$$\frac{f(y \mid x')}{f(y \mid x)} \leq \frac{f(y' \mid x')}{f(y' \mid x)} \tag{D.4}$$

Thus, we determine that if X and Y are affiliated, then for all $x' \geq x$, the *likelihood ratio*

$$\frac{f(\cdot \mid x')}{f(\cdot \mid x)}$$

is increasing and this is referred to as the *monotone likelihood ratio property*.

In the language of Appendix B, (D.4) implies that for all $x' \geq x$, $F(\cdot \mid x')$ *dominates* $F(\cdot \mid x)$ *in terms of the likelihood ratio*. Likelihood ratio dominance was the strongest stochastic order considered in Appendix B and the results derived there immediately imply that if X and Y are affiliated, then the following properties hold:

- For all $x' \geq x$, $F(\cdot \mid x')$ dominates $F(\cdot \mid x)$ in terms of the *hazard rate*; that is,

$$\lambda(y \mid x') \equiv \frac{f(y \mid x')}{1 - F(y \mid x')} \leq \frac{f(y \mid x)}{1 - F(y \mid x)} \equiv \lambda(y \mid x)$$

  or equivalently, for all y, $\lambda(y \mid \cdot)$ is nonincreasing.

- For all $x' \geq x$, $F(\cdot \mid x')$ dominates $F(\cdot \mid x)$ in terms of the *reverse hazard rate*; that is,

$$\sigma(y \mid x') \equiv \frac{f(y \mid x')}{F(y \mid x')} \geq \frac{f(y \mid x)}{F(y \mid x)} \equiv \sigma(y \mid x)$$

  or equivalently, for all y, $\sigma(y \mid \cdot)$ is nondecreasing.

- For all $x' \geq x$, $F(\cdot \mid x')$ (first-order) *stochastically dominates* $F(\cdot \mid x)$; that is,

$$F(y \mid x') \leq F(y \mid x)$$

  or equivalently, for all y, $F(y \mid \cdot)$ is nonincreasing.

All of these results extend in a straightforward manner to the case where the number of conditioning variables is more than one. Suppose $Y, X_1, X_2, \ldots, X_n$ are affiliated and let $F_Y(\cdot \mid \mathbf{x})$ denote the distribution of Y conditional on $\mathbf{X} = \mathbf{x}$. Then, using the same arguments as above, it can be deduced that for all $\mathbf{x}' \geq \mathbf{x}$, $F_Y(\cdot \mid \mathbf{x}')$ dominates $F_Y(\cdot \mid \mathbf{x})$ in terms of the likelihood ratio. The other dominance relationships then follow as usual.

Conditional Expectations of Affiliated Variables

Suppose X and Y are affiliated. The fact that $F(y \mid \cdot)$ is nonincreasing implies in turn that the expectation of Y conditional on $X = x$, $E[Y \mid X = x]$, is a nondecreasing function of x. In other words, the "regression line" of Y against X has nonnegative slope. Thus, X and Y are nonnegatively correlated.

Also, the same fact implies that if γ is a nondecreasing function, then $E[\gamma(Y) \mid X = x]$ is a nondecreasing function of x. More generally,

- If $X_1, X_2, \ldots, X_n$ are affiliated and γ is a nondecreasing function, then for all i,

$$E[\gamma(\mathbf{X}) \mid x_1' \le X_1 \le x_1'', x_2' \le X_2 \le x_2'', \ldots, x_n' \le X_n \le x_n'']$$

is a nondecreasing function of x_i' and x_i''.

Notes on Appendix D

The affiliation inequality in (D.1) is known as a version of *total positivity* in the statistics literature (Karlin and Rinott, 1980). More specifically, a vector random variable $\mathbf{X}$ that satisfies (D.1) is said to be "MTP$_2$" (*multivariate total positivity*) and the implications of this have been extensively studied. Closely related is the notion of *association* and the "FKG inequality" (see Shaked and Shanthikumar, 1994). The term "affiliation" appears to have been coined by Milgrom and Weber (1982) and the appendix to their paper is a convenient reference for results useful in auction theory.

Appendix E
Some Linear Algebra

This appendix derives an auxiliary result used in the proof of Proposition 9.2 in Chapter 9.

Matrices with Dominant Averages

An $n \times n$ matrix $\mathbf{A}$ satisfies the *dominant average* condition if in every column the off-diagonal terms are less than the average of the column,

$$\forall i \neq j, \ a_{ij} < \frac{1}{n} \sum_{k=1}^{n} a_{kj} \tag{E.1}$$

and the average of each column is positive,

$$\forall j, \ 0 < \frac{1}{n} \sum_{k=1}^{n} a_{kj} \tag{E.2}$$

Observe that if $\mathbf{A}$ satisfies the dominant average condition and $\mathbf{A}^i$ is obtained by deleting the ith row and ith column of $\mathbf{A}$, then $\mathbf{A}^i$ also satisfies the condition. This is because if from any column an entry that is less than the average is deleted, then the average of the remaining entries increases.

Let $\mathbf{e}^i \in \mathbb{R}^n$ denote the ith unit vector and let $\mathbf{e} = \sum_{i=1}^{n} \mathbf{e}^i$ denote the vector of 1's. Although the same symbols will be used for different n, the sizes of these vectors will be apparent from the context.

Lemma E.1 *Suppose* $\mathbf{A}$ *is an* $n \times n$ *matrix that satisfies the dominant average condition. Then there exists a unique* $\mathbf{x} \gg \mathbf{0}$ *such that*

$$\mathbf{A}\mathbf{x} = \mathbf{e} \tag{E.3}$$

We first show that there is a strictly positive solution to (E.3). The proof is by induction on n.

Step 1: For $n = 1$, the fact that there is a strictly positive solution is immediate. Now suppose that the result holds for all matrices of size $n - 1$.

Let $\mathbf{A}$ be an $n \times n$ matrix. Define $\mathbf{A}^i$ to be the $(n-1) \times (n-1)$ matrix obtained from deleting the ith row and the ith column of $\mathbf{A}$. From the induction hypothesis, for each $i = 1, 2, \ldots, n$, there exists an $\mathbf{x}^i \gg \mathbf{0}$ such that

$$\mathbf{A}^i \mathbf{x}^i = \mathbf{e}$$

which is the same as: for all $k \neq i$,

$$\sum_{j \neq i} a_{kj} x_j^i = 1 \tag{E.4}$$

Let

$$\sum_{j \neq i} a_{ij} x_j^i = c_i \tag{E.5}$$

Step 2: Adding the $n - 1$ equations (E.4) with (E.5) results in

$$\sum_{j \neq i} \left(\sum_{k=1}^{n} a_{kj} \right) x_j^i = (n - 1) + c_i > 0$$

which is positive because of (E.2) and the fact that $\mathbf{x}^i \gg \mathbf{0}$. But now (E.1) implies that

$$
\begin{aligned}
c_i &\equiv \sum_{j \neq i} a_{ij} x_j^i \\
&< \sum_{j \neq i} \left(\frac{1}{n-1} \sum_{k \neq i} a_{kj} \right) x_j^i \\
&= \sum_{k \neq i} \left(\frac{1}{n-1} \right) \left(\sum_{j \neq i} a_{kj} x_j^i \right) \\
&= 1
\end{aligned}
$$

using (E.4). Thus, $(n - 1) + c_i > 0$ and $c_i < 1$.

Step 3: Since $(n - 1) + c_i > 0$ and $c_i < 1$, for all i, $\frac{1}{1-c_i} > \frac{1}{n}$, so

$$\sum_{i=1}^{n} \frac{1}{1 - c_i} > 1 \tag{E.6}$$

Now let $\mathbf{y}^i \in \mathbb{R}_+^n$ be the vector obtained by appending 0 in the ith coordinate to $\mathbf{x}^i \in \mathbb{R}_{++}^{n-1}$. Then (E.4) and (E.5) can be compactly rewritten as follows: for all i,

$$\mathbf{A}\mathbf{y}^i = \mathbf{e} - (1 - c_i)\,\mathbf{e}^i$$

Dividing through by the positive quantity $(1 - c_i)$ results in

$$\mathbf{A}\left(\frac{1}{1 - c_i}\mathbf{y}^i\right) = \frac{1}{1 - c_i}\mathbf{e} - \mathbf{e}^i$$

Adding the n such equation systems, one for each i yields

$$\mathbf{A}\left(\sum_{i=1}^n \frac{1}{1 - c_i}\mathbf{y}^i\right) = \left(\sum_{i=1}^n \frac{1}{1 - c_i}\right)\mathbf{e} - \mathbf{e}$$

or equivalently,

$$\mathbf{A}\sum_{i=1}^n \frac{1}{K\,(1 - c_i)}\mathbf{y}^i = \mathbf{e}$$

where $K = \left[\left(\sum_{i=1}^n \frac{1}{1-c_i}\right) - 1\right] > 0$ from (E.6). Since each $\mathbf{y}^i \geq \mathbf{0}$ with only the ith component equal to zero, and $(1 - c_i) > 0$ we determine that

$$\mathbf{x} = \sum_{i=1}^n \frac{1}{K\,(1 - c_i)}\mathbf{y}^i \gg \mathbf{0}$$

is a solution to the system (E.3).

Thus, there is a strictly positive solution to (E.3).

Step 4: We now verify that the solution is unique by arguing that $\det \mathbf{A} \neq 0$, and hence $\mathbf{x} = \mathbf{A}^{-1}\mathbf{e}$. Again, the proof is by induction on n.

For $n = 1$ it is immediate that the solution is unique. Now suppose that for all matrices of size $n - 1$, there is a unique solution to the system. Let $\mathbf{A}$ be of size n and let $\mathbf{x} \gg \mathbf{0}$ be such that $\mathbf{A}\mathbf{x} = \mathbf{e}$.

If $\mathbf{A}$ is singular, then there exists a column, say the kth, which is a linear combination of the other $n - 1$ columns—that is, for all $j \neq k$ there exists a z_j such that

$$\forall i, \; a_{ik} = \sum_{j \neq k} a_{ij}z_j \tag{E.7}$$

and since $a_{kk} > 0$, not all the z_j can be zero.

Of course, (E.3) is equivalent to

$$\forall i, \; \sum_{j=1}^n a_{ij}x_j = 1$$

and substituting from (E.7) yields that

$$\forall i, \ \sum_{j \neq k} a_{ij} (z_j x_k + x_j) = 1 \tag{E.8}$$

As before, let $\mathbf{A}^k$ be the $(n-1) \times (n-1)$ matrix obtained from $\mathbf{A}$ by eliminating the kth row and the kth column of $\mathbf{A}$. From the induction hypothesis, there exists a unique $\mathbf{y} \gg \mathbf{0}$ such that $\mathbf{A}^k \mathbf{y} = \mathbf{e}$, which is equivalent to

$$\forall i \neq k, \ \sum_{j \neq k} a_{ij} y_j = 1 \tag{E.9}$$

Since the solution is unique, comparing (E.9) and the equations in (E.8) for $i \neq k$ implies that $\forall j \neq k$, $z_j x_k + x_j = y_j$, and the kth equation in (E.8) can be rewritten as

$$\sum_{j \neq k} a_{kj} y_j = 1 \tag{E.10}$$

Step 5: Now adding the $n-1$ equations in (E.9) and dividing by $n-1$ results in

$$\sum_{j \neq k} \left(\frac{1}{n-1} \sum_{i \neq k} a_{ij} \right) y_j = 1 \tag{E.11}$$

But (E.1) implies that

$$\forall j, \ a_{kj} < \frac{1}{n-1} \sum_{i \neq k} a_{ij} \tag{E.12}$$

and since $y_j > 0$, (E.12) implies that

$$\sum_{j \neq k} a_{kj} y_j < 1$$

contradicting (E.10). Thus, $\mathbf{A}$ is not singular and $\mathbf{A}\mathbf{x} = \mathbf{e}$ has a unique solution. ∎

The dominant average condition may be weakened as follows. An $n \times n$ matrix $\mathbf{A}$ satisfies the *dominant weighted average* condition if there exist positive weights $\lambda_1, \lambda_2, \ldots, \lambda_n$ with $\sum_i \lambda_i = 1$ such that

$$\forall i \neq j, \ a_{ij} < \sum_{k=1}^{n} \lambda_k a_{kj}$$

and

$$\forall j, \ 0 < \sum_{k=1}^{n} \lambda_k a_{kj}$$

The conclusion of Lemma E.1 follows under this weaker condition.

Suppose $\mathbf{A}$ is a matrix that satisfies the *dominant diagonal* condition and for all $i \neq j$, $a_{ij} \leq 0$. Then $\mathbf{A}$ satisfies the dominant weighted average condition.

Appendix F
Games of Incomplete Information

Auction theory models the decision problems collectively facing bidders in an auction as a game of incomplete information. This appendix contains definitions of some conceptual tools that are used throughout the book. It is intended only as a sketch of the relevant material. The reader should consult one of the references mentioned in the notes at the end of this appendix for a more complete treatment.

A *game* G consists of (i) a set $\mathcal{N}$ of players; (ii) for each player $i \in \mathcal{N}$ a nonempty set $\mathcal{A}_i$ of actions; and (iii) for each player $i \in \mathcal{N}$ a payoff function $u_i : \times_j \mathcal{A}_j \to \mathbb{R}$. A *Nash equilibrium* of a game G is a vector $\mathbf{a}^* \in \times_j \mathcal{A}_j$ of actions such that for all i and $a_i \in \mathcal{A}_i$,

$$u_i(\mathbf{a}^*) \geq u_i(a_i, \mathbf{a}^*_{-i})$$

In a game of incomplete information, a player's payoff depends not only on the actions of other players but also on information that is only partly known to the player. Because of this each player evaluates strategies on the basis of expected payoffs conditional on the information available to the player.

Formally, a *game of incomplete information* Γ consists of (i) a set $\mathcal{N}$ of players; (ii) for each player $i \in \mathcal{N}$ a nonempty set $\mathcal{A}_i$ of actions; (iii) for each player $i \in \mathcal{N}$ a set of signals $\mathcal{X}_i$; (iv) for each player $i \in \mathcal{N}$ a payoff function $u_i : \times_j \mathcal{A}_j \times_j \mathcal{X}_j \to \mathbb{R}$; (v) a probability distribution f over the product set of signals $\times_j \mathcal{X}_j$. A (pure) *strategy* for player i is a function $\alpha_i : \mathcal{X}_i \to \mathcal{A}_i$ mapping signals into actions.

This formulation postulates the following timing of events. First, the signals $\mathbf{X}$ are drawn according to f and player i is told the realization $X_i = x_i$ of his signal. Second, armed with the knowledge that $X_i = x_i$ each player chooses an action a_i. Finally, based on the signals $\mathbf{x}$ of all the players and their actions $\mathbf{a}$, payoffs are realized.

In the context of auctions the set of players is, of course, the set of bidders. An action corresponds to a bid. The signals encode the information available to bidders prior to the auction. A bidding strategy maps this information into bids.

Dominant Strategies

A strategy α_i is said to (weakly) *dominate* α'_i if for all $\mathbf{x} \in \mathcal{X}$ and all $\mathbf{a}_{-i}$,

$$u_i(\alpha_i(x_i), \mathbf{a}_{-i}, \mathbf{x}) \geq u_i(\alpha'_i(x_i), \mathbf{a}_{-i}, \mathbf{x})$$

with a strict inequality for some $\mathbf{x}$ and $\mathbf{a}_{-i}$.

The strategy α_i is *dominant* if it (weakly) dominates every other strategy α'_i. If every player has a dominant strategy α^*_i, then we will refer to $\boldsymbol{\alpha}^*$ as a *dominant strategy equilibrium*.

A strategy α_i is *undominated* if there does not exist another strategy α'_i that dominates it.

Bayesian-Nash Equilibria

A (pure strategy) *Bayesian-Nash equilibrium* of a game of incomplete information Γ is a vector of strategies $\boldsymbol{\alpha}^*$ such that for all i, for all $x_i \in \mathcal{X}_i$ and for all $a_i \in \mathcal{A}_i$,

$$E\left[u_i(\boldsymbol{\alpha}^*(\mathbf{X}), \mathbf{X}) \mid X_i = x_i\right] \geq E\left[u_i\left(a_i, \boldsymbol{\alpha}^*_{-i}(\mathbf{X}_{-i}), \mathbf{X}\right) \mid X_i = x_i\right] \quad \text{(F.1)}$$

where $\boldsymbol{\alpha}^*(\mathbf{x}) = (\alpha^*_i(x_i))_{i \in \mathcal{N}}$ denotes the vector of actions of all players and $\boldsymbol{\alpha}^*_{-i}(\mathbf{x}_{-i}) = (\alpha^*_j(x_j))_{j \neq i}$ denotes the vector of actions of the other players. Suppose α_i is some alternative strategy. Then for all i and x_i (F.1) holds for $a_i = \alpha_i(x_i)$. Taking the expectation of both sides with respect to x_i implies that if $\boldsymbol{\alpha}^*$ is a Bayesian-Nash equilibrium, then for all i and all strategies α_i,

$$E\left[u_i(\boldsymbol{\alpha}^*(\mathbf{X}), \mathbf{X})\right] \geq E\left[u_i\left(\alpha_i(X_i), \boldsymbol{\alpha}^*_{-i}(\mathbf{X}_{-i}), \mathbf{X}\right)\right] \quad \text{(F.2)}$$

The inequality in (F.1) says that for all i, the strategy α^*_i is optimal against $\boldsymbol{\alpha}^*_{-i}$ when evaluated at the *interim* stage—that is, when players know their own signals, whereas the inequality in (F.2) says that α^*_i is optimal against $\boldsymbol{\alpha}^*_{-i}$ when evaluated at the *ex ante* stage—that is, before players know their own signals. As we have argued, interim optimality implies *ex ante* optimality. Conversely, *ex ante* optimality implies that interim optimality holds almost surely—that is, if (F.2) holds, then (F.1) can fail only for x_i in a set whose probability is zero.

In this book the term *equilibrium* of a game of incomplete information is always taken to mean "Bayesian-Nash equilibrium."

Ex Post Equilibria

An *ex post equilibrium* is a Bayesian-Nash equilibrium $\boldsymbol{\alpha}^*$ with the property that for all i, for all $\mathbf{x} \in \mathcal{X}$ and all a_i,

$$u_i\left(\boldsymbol{\alpha}^*(\mathbf{x}), \mathbf{x}\right) \geq u_i\left(a_i, \boldsymbol{\alpha}^*_{-i}(\mathbf{x}_{-i}), \mathbf{x}\right)$$

In other words, an *ex post* equilibrium $\boldsymbol{\alpha}^*$ is a Bayesian-Nash equilibrium with the additional requirement that even if all players' signals $\mathbf{x}$ were known to a particular bidder i, it would still be optimal for him to choose $\alpha_i^*(x_i)$, that is, i would not suffer from any regret. Put another way, for all $\mathbf{x}$, the actions $(\alpha_i^*(x_i))_{i \in \mathcal{N}}$ constitute a Nash equilibrium of the game $G(\mathbf{x})$ in which each player $i \in \mathcal{N}$ chooses an action a_i from $\mathcal{A}_i$ and has the payoff function $u_i(\cdot, \mathbf{x})$. Finally, an *ex post* equilibrium $\boldsymbol{\alpha}^*$ is robust in the sense that it is independent of the probability distribution f of signals. Precisely, if $\boldsymbol{\alpha}^*$ is an *ex post* equilibrium when the signals are distributed according to the distribution f, then it is also an *ex post* equilibrium when the signals are distributed according to some $g \neq f$.

Every dominant strategy equilibrium is an *ex post* equilibrium, and by definition, every *ex post* equilibrium is a Bayesian-Nash equilibrium. Thus, we have

$$\begin{array}{ccc} \text{Set of Dominant} & \subseteq & \text{Set of } Ex\ Post \\ \text{Strategy Equilibria} & & \text{Equilibria} \end{array} \subseteq \begin{array}{c} \text{Set of Bayesian-} \\ \text{Nash Equilibria} \end{array}$$

A Bayesian-Nash equilibrium $\boldsymbol{\alpha}^*$ is said to be an *undominated equilibrium* if for all i, α_i^* is undominated.

Notes on Appendix F

Strategic situations in which players are unsure about some aspect of the game—the set of available strategies, the payoffs, or what other players believe about them—are called games of incomplete information. The conceptual underpinnings for such games were developed by Harsanyi (1967/1968) who argued first that all uncertainty faced by a player can be summarized as a single variable, called his "type," and, second, that the prior distribution over the vector of types is common to all the players. According to Harsanyi (1967/1968), all differences in what players know and believe about each other should stem from differences in their private information—their types—alone and not from differences in their initial beliefs. Harsanyi's conception thus allows a game of incomplete information to be reformulated as a game of imperfect information—one in which only players' information differs—and these can be analyzed along conventional lines. The term *Bayesian-Nash* equilibrium of a game of incomplete information then refers to a *Nash* equilibrium of the resulting imperfect information game.

As mentioned in the preface, Vickrey's (1961) model of auctions as games was already along these lines. In particular, Vickrey (1961) implicitly assumed that the joint distribution of values was commonly known to all bidders.

More detailed discussions of these issues may be found in the game theory textbooks by Fudenberg and Tirole (1991) and Osborne and Rubinstein (1994).

The notion of dominance used in this book involves *ex post* payoffs—a strategy dominates another only if it is never worse against any vector of actions of other players in any circumstances and sometimes strictly better. An alternative weaker notion involves *interim* payoffs—a strategy $\alpha_i(\cdot)$ dominates $\alpha_i'(\cdot)$ in the interim sense if, when evaluated according to expected payoffs conditional on a player's own signal, $\alpha_i(\cdot)$ is never worse than $\alpha_i'(\cdot)$ against any $\boldsymbol{\alpha}_{-i}$ and strictly better against some $\boldsymbol{\alpha}_{-i}$.

The notion of *ex post* equilibrium has been used in many contexts by different authors under different rubrics. It is the same as the notion of "uniform incentive compatibility" introduced by Holmström and Myerson (1983). In the auction context, its use appears to originate in the work of Crémer and McLean (1985). Maskin (1992) refers to an *ex post* equilibrium as a "robust" Bayesian-Nash equilibrium.

Appendix G
Existence of Equilibrium in First-Price Auctions

In this appendix we explore the issue of the existence of a pure strategy Bayesian-Nash equilibrium in first-price auctions. Our setting is one of independent private values. Of course, when bidders are symmetric, an equilibrium in closed form can be derived as in Proposition 2.2 on page 17. But when bidders are asymmetric, such a closed form solution is not readily available and we are thus interested in determining whether an equilibrium exists at all. For example, in Chapter 4, we studied some properties of equilibria in this setting (see Proposition 4.4 on page 48, for instance) but assumed that there was an equilibrium in which bidders' strategies were increasing functions of their values. We also computed equilibrium strategies explicitly for the case when there were two bidders with uniformly distributed values over differing supports.

The question of whether an equilibrium exists in general—regardless of the distributions or the number of bidders—is somewhat involved. Most of the difficulties stem from the fact that bidders' payoffs in an auction are discontinuous in the amounts bid. For instance, in a two-bidder first-price auction, if bidder 1 bids b_1, then his payoff is zero as long as $b_2 > b_1$, but is typically positive if $b_2 = b_1$. Standard results on the existence of equilibrium in games assume that players' payoff functions are continuous, so these cannot be directly applied. Moreover, even under the assumption of continuity, these results usually conclude only that a *mixed* strategy equilibrium—in which players randomize—exists.

In this appendix we outline a method of proof that separates the problem into two components. In the first, and key, step it is assumed that bidders may only bid in discrete amounts—there is some minimum bid increment, say, one cent. Somewhat remarkably with this restriction, it is possible to formulate the question of existence of equilibrium in a way that standard tools can be brought to bear on the problem. Thus, it is possible to show that with discrete bids, there exists a *pure* strategy equilibrium in which each bidder's strategy is a nondecreasing function of his or her value (see Proposition G.1). The second step shows that a limit of these equilibria, as the minimum bid increment shrinks, is a pure strategy equilibrium of the auction in which bids are not restricted. In the interests of space, here we do not prove the second step; rather we only indicate some of the attendant difficulties.

Equilibrium with Discrete Bids

Suppose that there are N bidders with independently distributed values. Bidder i's value X_i is distributed over the interval $\mathcal{X}_i = [0, \omega_i]$ according to the distribution function F_i with associated density f_i.

Let $\omega = \max_i \omega_i$. Fix an integer T and define

$$\mathcal{B}^T = \left\{ \frac{t}{T}\omega : t = 0, 1, \dots, T \right\}$$

to be the finite set of allowable bids. Thus, there is a minimum bid increment of ω/T. In what follows, we will use the notation

$$b^t \equiv \frac{t}{T}\omega$$

A strategy for bidder i in an auction with discrete bids is a function $\beta_i : \mathcal{X}_i \to \mathcal{B}^T$. Fix the strategies β_j of bidders $j \neq i$ and let $H_i(b^t)$ denote the probability that i will win with a bid of b^t. Formally, for $t = 0, 1, \dots, T$,

$$H_i(b^t) = \text{Prob}\left[\max_{j \neq i} \beta_j(X_j) \leq b^{t-1} \right]$$
$$+ \frac{1}{k+1} \text{Prob}\left[\max_{j \neq i} \beta_j(X_j) = b^t \right] \tag{G.1}$$

where k is the number of *other* bidders who bid exactly b^t. The first term comes from events in which i is the outright winner. The second term comes from events in which there is more than one bid at b^t and the winner is determined at random from among those with the highest bid. Because bids are discrete, ties occur with positive probability. Notice that $H_i(\cdot)$ is a nondecreasing function.

A bid $b_i \in \mathcal{B}^T$ is a *best response* at x_i by bidder i if it maximizes his expected payoff against β_{-i}, that is, if for all $b \in \mathcal{B}^T$,

$$H_i(b_i)(x_i - b_i) \geq H_i(b)(x_i - b) \tag{G.2}$$

Denote by $BR_i(x_i)$ the set of best responses at x_i.

Lemma G.1 *For any* β_{-i} *and* $0 < x_i' < x_i''$,

$$\min BR_i\left(x_i''\right) \geq \max BR_i\left(x_i'\right)$$

Proof. Let $b_i' = \max BR_i\left(x_i'\right)$. By definition, for all $b < b_i'$ such that $b \in \mathcal{B}^T$,

$$H_i\left(b_i'\right)\left(x_i' - b_i'\right) \geq H_i\left(b\right)\left(x_i' - b\right)$$

which can be rearranged as

$$\left(H_i\left(b_i'\right) - H_i\left(b\right)\right)x_i' \geq H_i\left(b_i'\right)b_i' - H_i\left(b\right)b \qquad \text{(G.3)}$$

Now notice that for all $b < b_i'$ we must have $H_i\left(b_i'\right) - H_i\left(b\right) > 0$. Since H_i is nondecreasing, $b < b_i'$ implies that $H_i\left(b_i'\right) - H_i\left(b\right) \geq 0$, but if $H_i\left(b_i'\right) - H_i\left(b\right) = 0$, then b_i' cannot be a best response—a bid of $b < b_i'$ has the same chances of winning while it decreases the amount bid if bidder i wins.

Now (G.3) implies that for $x_i'' > x_i'$, for all $b < b_i'$ such that $b \in \mathcal{B}^T$,

$$\left(H_i\left(b_i'\right) - H_i\left(b\right)\right)x_i'' > H_i\left(b_i'\right)b_i' - H_i\left(b\right)b$$

Thus, when the value is x_i'', it is strictly better to bid b_i' than to bid a smaller amount. This implies that any best response when the value is x_i'' is at least as large as b_i', so $\min BR_i\left(x_i''\right) \geq b_i'$. ∎

A bidding strategy for bidder i, $\beta_i : \mathcal{X}_i \rightarrow \mathcal{B}^T$ is said to be a *best response against* $\boldsymbol{\beta}_{-i}$ if for all x_i, $\beta_i\left(x_i\right)$ is a best response when his value is x_i.

The import of Lemma G.1 is that if the strategy $\beta_i : \mathcal{X}_i \rightarrow \mathcal{B}^T$ is a best response, then it is a nondecreasing function with a finite number of discontinuities—it is a "step function." Thus, we can find T points in $[0, \omega_i]$, say $\alpha_i^1 \leq \alpha_i^2 \leq \ldots \leq \alpha_i^T$ such that

$$\beta_i\left(x_i\right) = b^t \text{ if } \alpha_i^t < x_i < \alpha_i^{t+1} \qquad \text{(G.4)}$$

where by convention, we set $\alpha_i^0 \equiv 0$ and $\alpha_i^{T+1} \equiv \omega_i$. Note that we have said nothing about what happens at the points α_i^t themselves—$\beta_i\left(\alpha_i^t\right)$ is either b^{t-1} or b^t—but since there are only a finite number of such points, the bids at these points do not affect a bidder's expected payoff. Thus, except perhaps at a finite number of points, any β_i that is a best response is completely determined by the vector $\boldsymbol{\alpha}_i = \left(\alpha_i^1, \alpha_i^2, \ldots, \alpha_i^T\right)$. In other words, any β_i that is a best-response—and hence a step function—can be represented by a finite dimensional object, the vector $\boldsymbol{\alpha}_i$.

Given a bidding strategy β_i that is nondecreasing, if $\boldsymbol{\alpha}_i$ is such that (G.4) holds, we will write $\boldsymbol{\alpha}_i \leftrightarrow \beta_i$ to denote that β_i can be equivalently represented by $\boldsymbol{\alpha}_i$ and vice versa. In that case, we will refer to $\boldsymbol{\alpha}_i$ itself as the "bidding strategy" of bidder i.

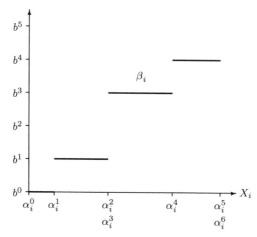

FIGURE G.1. A Best Response with Discrete Bids

See Figure G.1 for an illustration when $T = 5$. In the figure, there is no x_i such that $\beta_i(x_i) = b^2$, so $\alpha_i^2 = \alpha_i^3$. Similarly, there is no x_i such that $\beta_i(x_i) = b^5$, so $\alpha_i^5 = \alpha_i^6 \equiv \omega_i$.

Given the strategies $\boldsymbol{\alpha}_{-i} = (\boldsymbol{\alpha}_j)_{j \neq i}$ of the other bidders, let $\Gamma_i(\boldsymbol{\alpha}_{-i})$ denote the set of best response strategies for bidder i, consisting of vectors $\boldsymbol{\alpha}_i \in [0, \omega_i]^T$. By this we mean, of course, that there is a β_i that is a best response to $\boldsymbol{\beta}_{-i}$ and $\boldsymbol{\alpha}_i \leftrightarrow \beta_i$ and for all $j \neq i$, $\boldsymbol{\alpha}_j \leftrightarrow \beta_j$. The mapping $\Gamma_i(\cdot)$ assigns to every element in $\times_{j \neq i} [0, \omega_j]^T$ a subset of $[0, \omega_i]^T$ and we will refer to it as bidder i's *best-response correspondence*. Some properties of a bidder's best response correspondence will prove useful.

First, note that for all $\boldsymbol{\alpha}_{-i}$, the set of best responses $\Gamma_i(\boldsymbol{\alpha}_{-i})$ is a convex set. This is equivalent to saying that if some b_i is a best response at x_i' and also at x_i'', then for all $\lambda \in [0, 1]$ it is also a best response at $\lambda x_i' + (1 - \lambda) x_i''$ and this follows trivially from (G.2).

Second, note that if $(\boldsymbol{\alpha}_i^n, \boldsymbol{\alpha}_{-i}^n)$ is a sequence converging to $(\boldsymbol{\alpha}_i, \boldsymbol{\alpha}_{-i})$ and for all n, $\boldsymbol{\alpha}_i^n \in \Gamma_i(\boldsymbol{\alpha}_{-i}^n)$, then $\boldsymbol{\alpha}_i \in \Gamma_i(\boldsymbol{\alpha}_{-i})$. For all n and j let β_j^n be such that $\boldsymbol{\alpha}_j^n \leftrightarrow \beta_j^n$ and let β_j be such that $\boldsymbol{\alpha}_j \leftrightarrow \beta_j$. Let $H_i^n(\cdot)$ be defined according to (G.1) when bidders $j \neq i$ use strategies β_j^n and similarly, let $H^i(\cdot)$ be defined according to (G.1) when bidders $j \neq i$ use strategies β_j. Since $\boldsymbol{\alpha}_{-i}^n \to \boldsymbol{\alpha}_{-i}$, we have that for all $j \neq i$, $\beta_j^n \to \beta_j$, so $H_i^n(\cdot) \to H_i(\cdot)$ at every point of $\mathcal{B}^T$. Now it is routine to verify that if for all n, β_i^n is a best response to $\boldsymbol{\beta}_{-i}^n$, and $(\beta_i^n, \boldsymbol{\beta}_{-i}^n) \to (\beta_i, \boldsymbol{\beta}_{-i})$, then β_i is a best response to $\boldsymbol{\beta}_{-i}$. This establishes that $\boldsymbol{\alpha}_i \in \Gamma_i(\boldsymbol{\alpha}_{-i})$.

Kakutani Fixed Point Theorem. Let $\mathcal{Z}$ be a nonempty, compact and convex set and let Γ be a correspondence that maps every element $\mathbf{z} \in \mathcal{Z}$ to a nonempty subset of $\mathcal{Z}$. The Kakutani *fixed point theorem* states that if (i) Γ is *convex valued*—that is, for all $\mathbf{z}$, $\Gamma(\mathbf{z})$ is convex, and (ii) Γ has a *closed graph*—that is, $(\mathbf{y}^n, \mathbf{z}^n) \to (\mathbf{y}, \mathbf{z})$ and for all n, $\mathbf{y}^n \in \Gamma(\mathbf{z}^n)$ implies that $\mathbf{y} \in \Gamma(\mathbf{z})$, then there exists a $\mathbf{z}^*$ such that $\mathbf{z}^* \in \Gamma(\mathbf{z}^*)$. Such a $\mathbf{z}^*$ is called a fixed point of Γ.

Existence of Equilibrium. In our context, we can define $\mathcal{Z} = \times_i [0, \omega_i]^T$ and $\Gamma(\boldsymbol{\alpha}) = \times_i \Gamma_i (\boldsymbol{\alpha}_{-i})$ where each Γ_i is i's best response correspondence. As argued above, Γ is convex valued and has a closed graph. The Kakutani fixed point theorem then implies that there exists an $\boldsymbol{\alpha}^*$ such that $\boldsymbol{\alpha}^* \in \Gamma(\boldsymbol{\alpha}^*)$. If we define β_i^* as in (G.4), that is, $\boldsymbol{\alpha}_i^* \leftrightarrow \beta_i^*$, then $\boldsymbol{\beta}^* = (\beta_1^*, \beta_2^*, \ldots, \beta_N^*)$ constitutes an equilibrium of the first-price auction with discrete bids. We have thus established the following:

Proposition G.1 *Suppose all bids must lie in the set $\mathcal{B}^T$. Then there exists an equilibrium of the first-price auction in which all bidders follow nondecreasing strategies.*

Taking Limits

In the previous section, bidders were restricted to use strategies with a minimum bid increment of ω/T. We argued that with this restriction, for all T, there exists a pure strategy equilibrium, say $\boldsymbol{\beta}^*(T)$, in which each bidder's strategy is a nondecreasing function of his or her value. Here we are interested in examining what happens as the restriction is removed—that is, as T approaches infinity. A detailed treatment of this question is somewhat involved, so we only indicate the path to be followed.

First, it can be shown that there exists a subsequence of pure strategy equilibria $\boldsymbol{\beta}^*(T)$ that converges to a vector of strategies, say $\boldsymbol{\beta}^*$, in the auction in which bids are unrestricted. Moreover, the convergence is uniform almost everywhere. The strategies in $\boldsymbol{\beta}^*$ are, of course, all nondecreasing also.

Second, it can be argued that $\boldsymbol{\beta}^*$ constitutes an equilibrium of the auction with unrestricted bids. If for all i, the limiting strategy β_i^* were strictly increasing, this would follow immediately. This is because, in that case, ties would occur with probability zero. The argument that this is indeed the case uses the fact that the sequence $\boldsymbol{\beta}^*(T)$ converges to $\boldsymbol{\beta}^*$ uniformly almost everywhere and is rather involved. The interested reader may consult the readings mentioned in the notes that follow.

Notes on Appendix G

This appendix is based on the work of Athey (2001), in which she establishes a general result for the existence of pure strategy equilibria in games with incomplete information. The key insight is that as long as the conclusion of Lemma G.1 holds, the arguments leading up to Proposition G.1 can be applied unchanged and hence an equilibrium exists. A consequence of her result is that a pure strategy equilibrium can be shown to exist under a wide variety of circumstances, for example, with risk aversion or affiliated private values. For asymmetric interdependent values with affiliated signals, however, this technique is applicable to only the case of two bidders. (In some work that is ongoing as this was written, Reny and Zamir (2001, private communication) have extended this to an arbitrary number of bidders.)

Other papers that establish the existence of an equilibrium in first-price auctions using discrete approximation techniques—either by discretizing the set of values or, as above, the set of possible bids—include Lebrun (1996) and Maskin and Riley (2000b). Reny (1999) establishes a general existence result for a class of discontinuous games. This can also be applied to first-price auctions.

Jackson and Swinkels (2001) exhibit some very general existence results in private value settings by using somewhat different techniques. Their approach is to show that an equilibrium exists in an auxiliary game in which tie-breaking is endogenously chosen and then to show that the tie-breaking rule is, in fact, irrelevant.

An alternative approach is to write down a set of necessary conditions that a pure strategy equilibrium in increasing strategies must satisfy. For instance, if there are only two bidders, the necessary first-order conditions are, as derived in (4.18) on page 47, are that the inverse bidding strategies ϕ_1 and ϕ_2 must satisfy for $i = 1, 2$, and $j \neq i$,

$$\phi'_j(b) = \frac{F_j\left(\phi_j(b)\right)}{f_j\left(\phi_j(b)\right)} \frac{1}{\left(\phi_i(b) - b\right)} \tag{G.5}$$

together with the boundary conditions that for $i = 1, 2$, $\phi_i(0) = 0$. The fundamental theorem of differential equations provides sufficient conditions for the existence and uniqueness of the solution to such a system. A difficulty with this approach is that precisely where the boundary condition holds—at $b = 0$—the right-hand side of (G.5) has a $\frac{0}{0}$ form, so it is undefined. This means that the fundamental theorem of differential equations, which requires that the right-hand side satisfy a Lipschitz condition at the boundary point, cannot be directly applied. These difficulties can be overcome, however, as shown by Plum (1992) and Lebrun (1999).

References

Amann, E., and W. Leininger (1995): "Expected Revenue of All-Pay and First-Price Sealed-Bid Auctions with Affiliated Signals," *Zeitschrift für Nationalökonomie*, **61**, 273–279. ⟨110⟩[1]

Anton, J., and D. Yao (1992): "Coordination in Split Award Auctions," *Quarterly Journal of Economics*, **107**, 681–707. ⟨234⟩

Armstrong, M. (2000): "Optimal Multi-Object Auctions," *Review of Economic Studies*, **67**, 455–481. ⟨234⟩

Arnold, B., N. Balakrishnan, and H. Nagaraja (1992): *A First Course in Order Statistics*, New York, NY: Wiley. ⟨268⟩

Arrow, K. (1979): "The Property Rights Doctrine and Demand Revelation under Incomplete Information," in M. Boskin (ed.), *Economics and Human Welfare*, New York, NY: Academic Press, 23–39. ⟨82⟩

Ashenfelter, O. (1989): "How Auctions Work for Wine and Art," *Journal of Economic Perspectives*, **3**, 23–36. ⟨221⟩

d'Aspremont, C., and L. A. Gérard-Varet (1979a): "Incentives and Incomplete Information," *Journal of Public Economics*, **11**, 25–45. ⟨82⟩

---

[1] The numbers in the angled brackets following each entry indicate the pages on which a reference is made to this item.

d'Aspremont, C., and L. A. Gérard-Varet (1979b): "On Bayesian Incentive Compatible Mechanisms," in J.-J. Laffont (ed.), *Aggregation and Revelation of Preferences*, Amsterdam: North-Holland, 269–288. ⟨82⟩

Athey, S. (2001): "Single Crossing Properties and the Existence of Pure Strategy Equilibria in Games of Incomplete Information," *Econometrica*, **69**, 861–889. ⟨288⟩

Ausubel, L. (1997): "An Efficient Ascending-Bid Auction for Multiple Objects," mimeo, University of Maryland, June. ⟨176⟩

Ausubel, L. (2001): "A Generalized Vickrey Auction," *Econometrica*, forthcoming. ⟨150⟩

Ausubel, L., and P. Cramton (1996): "Demand Reduction and Inefficiency in Multi-Unit Auctions," mimeo, University of Maryland, July. ⟨196⟩

Avery, C. (1998): "Strategic Jump Bidding in English Auctions," *Review of Economic Studies*, **65**, 185–210. ⟨102⟩

Avery, C., and T. Hendershott (2000): "Bundling and Optimal Auctions of Multiple Products," *Review of Economic Studies*, **67**, 483–497. ⟨234⟩

Back, K., and J. Zender (1993): "Auctions of Divisible Goods: On the Rationale for the Treasury Experiment," *Review of Financial Studies*, **6**, 733–764. ⟨196⟩

Baye, M., D. Kovenock, and C. de Vries (1993): "Rigging the Lobbying Process: An Application of the All-Pay Auction," *American Economic Review*, **83**, 289–294. ⟨36⟩

Bikhchandani, S., and J. Riley (1991): "Equilibria in Open Common Value Auctions," *Journal of Economic Theory*, **53**, 101–130. ⟨124⟩

Benoît, J-P., and V. Krishna (2001): "Multiple Object Auctions with Budget Constrained Bidders," *Review of Economic Studies*, **68**, 155–179. ⟨234⟩

Birulin, O. (2001): "Inefficient Ex-Post Equilibria in Efficient Auctions," mimeo, Penn State University, May. ⟨124⟩

Boycko, M., A. Shleifer, and R. Vishny (1996): *Privatizing Russia*, Cambridge, MA: MIT Press. ⟨177⟩

Bresky, M. (2000): "Equilibria in Multi-Unit Auctions," mimeo, CERGE, Czech Republic, October. ⟨196⟩

Bulow, J., and P. Klemperer (1996): "Auctions versus Negotiations," *American Economic Review*, **86**, 180–194. ⟨82⟩

Bulow, J., and J. Roberts (1989): "The Simple Economics of Optimal Auctions," *Journal of Political Economy*, **97**, 1060–1090. ⟨81⟩

Capen, E., R. Clapp, and W. Campbell (1971): "Competitive Bidding in High-Risk Situations," *Journal of Petroleum Technology*, **23**, 641–653. ⟨102⟩

Cassady, R. (1967): *Auctions and Auctioneering*, Berkeley, CA: University of California Press. ⟨9⟩

Chakraborty, I. (1999): "Bundling Decisions for Selling Multiple Objects," *Economic Theory*, **13**, 723–733. ⟨234⟩

Che, Y-K., and I. Gale (1998): "Standard Auctions with Financially Constrained Bidders," *Review of Economic Studies*, **65**, 1–22. ⟨59⟩

Clarke, E. (1971): "Multipart Pricing of Public Goods," *Public Choice*, **2**, 19–33. ⟨82⟩

Crémer, J., and R. McLean (1985): "Optimal Selling Strategies Under Uncertainty for a Discriminating Monopolist when Demands are Interdependent," *Econometrica*, **53**, 345–361. ⟨150, 282⟩

Crémer, J., and R. McLean (1988): "Full Extraction of the Surplus in Bayesian and Dominant Strategy Auctions," *Econometrica*, **56**, 1247–1257. ⟨150⟩

Dasgupta, P., and E. Maskin (2000): "Efficient Auctions," *Quarterly Journal of Economics*, **115**, 341–388. ⟨140, 250⟩

David, H. (1969): *Order Statistics*, New York: Wiley. ⟨268⟩

de Vries, S., and R. Vohra (2001): "Combinatorial Auctions: A Survey," mimeo, TU München and Northwestern University, January. ⟨234⟩

Engelbrecht-Wiggans, R., and C. Kahn (1998a): "Multi-Unit Auctions with Uniform Prices," *Economic Theory*, **12**, 227–258. ⟨196⟩

Engelbrecht-Wiggans, R., and C. Kahn (1998b): "Multi-Unit Pay-Your-Bid Auctions with Variable Rewards," *Games and Economic Behavior*, **23**, 25–42. ⟨196⟩

Engelbrecht-Wiggans, R., P. Milgrom, and R. Weber (1983): "Competitive Bidding and Proprietary Information," *Journal of Mathematical Economics*, **11**, 161–169. ⟨124⟩

Fudenberg, D., and J. Tirole (1991): *Game Theory*, Cambridge, MA: MIT Press. ⟨x, 282⟩

Graham, D., and R. Marshall (1987): "Collusive Behavior at Single-Object Second-Price and English Auctions," *Journal of Political Economy*, **95**, 1217–1239. ⟨162⟩

Griesmer, J., R. Levitan and M. Shubik (1967): "Toward a Study of Bidding Processes, Part IV—Games with Unknown Costs," *Naval Research Logistics Quarterly*, **14**, 415–434. ⟨59⟩

Groves, T. (1973): "Incentives in Teams," *Econometrica*, **41**, 617–631. ⟨82⟩

Gupta, M., and B. Lebrun (1999): "First Price Auctions with Resale," *Economics Letters*, **64**, 181–185. ⟨60⟩

Haile, P. (2000): "Auctions with Private Uncertainty and Resale Opportunities," *Journal of Economic Theory*, forthcoming. ⟨60⟩

Harsanyi, J. (1967/1968): "Games of Incomplete Information Played by 'Bayesian' Players, Parts I, II, and III," *Management Science*, **14**, 159–182, 320–334, and 486–502. ⟨282⟩

Harstad, R., J. Kagel, and D. Levin (1990): "Equilibrium Bid Functions for Auctions with an Uncertain Number of Bidders," *Economics Letters*, **33**, 35–40. ⟨36⟩

Harstad, R., and D. Levin (1985): "A Class of Dominance Solvable Common-Value Auctions," *Review of Economic Studies*, **52**, 525–528. ⟨102⟩

Hendricks. K., and H. Paarsch (1995): "A Survey of Recent Empirical Work Concerning Auctions," *Canadian Journal of Economics*, **28**, 403–426. ⟨10⟩

Hendricks, K., and R. Porter (1989): "Collusion in Auctions," *Annales d'Économie et de Statistique*, **15/16**, 217–230. ⟨162⟩

Hendricks, K., R. Porter, and C. Wilson (1994): "Auctions for Oil and Gas Leases with an Informed Bidder and a Random Reservation Price," *Econometrica*, **62**, 1415–1444. ⟨10⟩

Holmström, B., and R. Myerson (1983): "Efficient and Durable Decision Rules with Incomplete Information," *Econometrica*, **51**, 1799–1820. ⟨282⟩

Holt, C. (1980): "Competitive Bidding for Contracts under Alternative Auction Procedures," *Journal of Political Economy*, **88**, 433–445. ⟨59⟩

Izmalkov, S. (2001): "English Auctions with Reentry," mimeo, Penn State University, August. ⟨140⟩

Jackson, M., and J. Swinkels (2001): "Existence of Equilibrium in Single and Double Private Value Auctions," mimeo, California Institute of Technology, October. ⟨288⟩

Jehiel, P., and B. Moldovanu (2001): "Efficient Design with Interdependent Values," *Econometrica*, **69**, 1237–1259. ⟨250⟩

Jeitschko, T. (1999): "Equilibrium Price Paths in Sequential Auctions with Stochastic Supply," *Economics Letters*, **64**, 67–72. ⟨221⟩

Kagel, J. (1995): "Auctions: A Survey of Experimental Research," in J. Kagel and A. Roth (eds.), *Handbook of Experimental Economics*, Princeton, NJ: Princeton University Press, 501–585. ⟨10⟩

Kagel, J., and D. Levin (1993): "Independent Private Value Auctions: Bidder Behaviour in First-, Second- and Third-Price Auction with Varying Numbers of Bidders," *Economic Journal*, **103**, 868–879. ⟨36⟩

Karlin, S., and Y. Rinott (1980): "Classes of Orderings of Measures and Related Correlation Inequalities, I: Multivariate Totally Positive Distributions," *Journal of Multivariate Analysis*, **10**, 467–498. ⟨272⟩

Katzman, B. (1999): "A Two Stage Sequential Auction with Multi-Unit Demands," *Journal of Economic Theory*, **86**, 77–99. ⟨222⟩

Klemperer, P. (2000): "Why Every Economist Should Learn Some Auction Theory," forthcoming in M. Dewatripont, L. Hansen, and S. Turnovsky (eds.), *Advances in Economics and Econometrics*, Cambridge, U.K.: Cambridge University Press. ⟨9⟩

Kreps, D. (1990): *A Course in Microeconomic Theory*, Princeton, NJ: Princeton University Press. ⟨ix⟩

Krishna, K., and T. Tranæs (2001): "Allocating Multiple Units," forthcoming, *Economic Theory*. ⟨234⟩

Krishna, V. (2000): "Asymmetric English Auctions," mimeo, Penn State University, September. ⟨140⟩

Krishna, V., and E. Maenner (2001): "Convex Potentials with an Application to Mechanism Design," *Econometrica*, **69**, 1113–1119. ⟨207⟩

Krishna, V., and J. Morgan (1997): "An Analysis of the War of Attrition and the All-Pay Auction," *Journal of Economic Theory*, **72**, 343–362. ⟨110⟩

Krishna, V., and M. Perry (1998): "Efficient Mechanism Design," mimeo, Penn State University, April. ⟨82, 207⟩

Laffont, J-J., H. Ossard, and Q. Vuong (1995): "Econometrics of First-Price Auctions," *Econometrica*, **63**, 953–980. ⟨10⟩

Landsberger, M., and B. Tsirelson (2000): "Correlated Signals against Monotone Equilibria," mimeo, University of Haifa, April. ⟨124⟩

Lebrun, B. (1996): "Existence of an Equilibrium in First Price Auctions," *Economic Theory*, **7**, 421–443. ⟨288⟩

Lebrun, B. (1999): "First Price Auctions in the Asymmetric *N* Bidder Case," *International Economic Review*, **40**, 125-142. ⟨288⟩

Levin, D., and J. Smith (1996): "Optimal Reservation Prices in Auctions," *Economic Journal*, **106**, 1271–1283. ⟨124⟩

Lucking-Reiley, D. (2000): "Vickrey Auctions in Practice: From Nineteenth-Century Philately to Twenty-First-Century E-Commerce," *Journal of Economic Perspectives*, **14**, 183–192. ⟨9⟩

Mailath, G., and P. Zemsky (1991): "Collusion in Second Price Auctions with Heterogeneous Bidders," *Games and Economic Behavior*, **4**, 467–486. ⟨162⟩

Marshall, R., M. Meurer, J.-F. Richard, and W. Stromquist (1994): "Numerical Analysis of Asymmetric First Price Auctions," *Games and Economic Behavior*, **7**, 193–220. ⟨59⟩

Mas-Collel, A., M. Whinston, and J. Green (1995): *Microeconomic Theory*, Oxford: Oxford University Press. ⟨ix⟩

Maskin, E. (1992): "Auctions and Privatization," in H. Siebert (ed.), *Privatization*, Kiel: Institut fur Weltwirtschaften der Universität Kiel, 115–136. ⟨140, 249, 282⟩

Maskin, E. (2001): "Auctions and Efficiency," mimeo, Institute for Advanced Study, Princeton, May. ⟨249⟩

Maskin, E., and J. Riley (2000a): "Asymmetric Auctions," *Review of Economic Studies*, **67**, 413–438. ⟨59⟩

Maskin, E., and J. Riley (2000b): "Equilibrium in Sealed High Bid Auctions," *Review of Economic Studies*, **67**, 439–454. ⟨288⟩

Matthews, S. (1987): "Comparing Auctions for Risk Averse Buyers: A Buyer's Point of View," *Econometrica*, **55**, 633–646. ⟨36, 59⟩

Matthews, S. (1995): "A Technical Primer on Auction Theory I: Independent Private Values," Discussion Paper No. 1096, Center for Mathematical Studies in Economics and Management Science, Northwestern University, May. ⟨9⟩

McAfee, P., and J. McMillan (1987a): "Auctions and Bidding," *Journal of Economic Literature*, **25**, 699–738. ⟨9⟩

McAfee, P., and J. McMillan (1987b): "Auctions with a Stochastic Number of Bidders," *Journal of Economic Theory*, **43**, 1–19. ⟨36⟩

McAfee, P., and J. McMillan (1992): "Bidding Rings," *American Economic Review*, **82**, 579–599. ⟨162⟩

McAfee, P., J. McMillan, and P. Reny (1989): "Extracting the Surplus in a Common Value Auction," *Econometrica*, **57**, 1451–1460. ⟨150⟩

McAfee, P., and P. Reny (1992): "Correlated Information and Mechanism Design," *Econometrica*, **60**, 395-421. ⟨150⟩

McAfee, P., and D. Vincent (1993): "The Declining Price Anomaly," *Journal of Economic Theory*, **60**, 191–212. ⟨221⟩

Milgrom, P. (1981): "Rational Expectations, Informations Acquisition, and Competitive Bidding," *Econometrica*, **49,** 921–943. ⟨102, 124⟩

Milgrom, P. (1985): "The Economics of Competitive Bidding: A Selective Survey," in L. Hurwicz, D. Schmeidler, and H. Sonnenschein (eds.), *Social Goals and Social Organization: Essays in Memory of Elisha Pazner*, New York, NY: Cambridge University Press. ⟨9⟩

Milgrom, P. (1987): "Auction Theory," in T. Bewley (ed.), *Advances in Economic Theory: Fifth World Congress*, Cambridge, U.K.: Cambridge University Press, 1–32. ⟨9, 28⟩

Milgrom, P., and R. Weber (1982): "A Theory of Auctions and Competitive Bidding," *Econometrica*, **50**, 1089–1122. ⟨102, 110, 124, 272⟩

Milgrom, P., and R. Weber (2000): "A Theory of Auctions and Competitive Bidding, II," in P. Klemperer (ed.), *The Economic Theory of Auctions*, Cheltenham, U.K.: Edward Elgar. ⟨221⟩

Myerson, R. (1981): "Optimal Auction Design," *Mathematics of Operations Research*, **6**, 58–73. ⟨28, 36, 81, 150⟩

Myerson, R., and M. Satterthwaite (1983): "Efficient Mechanisms for Bilateral Trading," *Journal of Economic Theory*, **28**, 265–281. ⟨82⟩

Noussair, C. (1995): "Equilibria in a Multi-Object Uniform Price Sealed Bid Auction with Multi-Unit Demands," *Economic Theory*, **5**, 337–351. ⟨196⟩

Ortega Reichert, A. (1968): *Models for Competitive Bidding under Uncertainty*, Ph.D. Dissertation (Technical Report No. 8), Department of Operations Research, Stanford University. ⟨102, 124⟩

Osborne, M., and A. Rubinstein (1994): *A Course in Game Theory*, Cambridge, MA: MIT Press. ⟨x, 282⟩

Palfrey, T. (1983): "Bundling Decisions by a Multiproduct Monopolist with Incomplete Information," *Econometrica*, **51**, 463–484. ⟨234⟩

Perry, M., and P. Reny (1999): "On the Failure of the Linkage Principle in Multi-Object Auctions," *Econometrica*, **67**, 885–890. ⟨124⟩

Perry, M., and P. Reny (2001): "An Ex-Post Efficient Auction," *Econometrica*, forthcoming. ⟨249⟩

Pitchik, C., and A. Schotter (1988): "Perfect Equilibria in Budget-Constrained Sequential Auctions: An Experimental Study," *Rand Journal of Economics*, **19**, 363–388. ⟨234⟩

Plum, M. (1992): "Characterization and Computation of Nash Equilibria for Auctions with Incomplete Information," *International Journal of Game Theory*, **20**, 393–418. ⟨59, 288⟩

Reny, P. (1999): "On the Existence of Pure and Mixed Strategy Nash Equilibria in Discontinuous Games," *Econometrica*, **67**, 1029–1056. ⟨196, 288⟩

Riley, J., and W. Samuelson (1981): "Optimal Auctions," *American Economic Review*, **71**, 381–392. ⟨28, 36⟩

Robinson, M. (1985): "Collusion and the Choice of Auction," *Rand Journal of Economics*, **16**, 141–145. ⟨162⟩

Ross, S. (1989): *Introduction to Probability Models*, San Diego, CA: Academic Press. ⟨257⟩

Rothkopf, M., A. Pekec, and R. Harstad (1998): "Computationally Manageable Combinatorial Auctions," *Management Science*, **44**, 1131–1147. ⟨234⟩

Royden, H. (1968): *Real Analysis*, New York, NY: Macmillan Publishing Company. ⟨82⟩

Shaked, M., and G. Shanthikumar (1994): *Stochastic Orders and their Applications*, San Diego, CA: Academic Press. ⟨263, 272⟩

Swinkels, J. (1999): "Asymptotic Efficiency for Discriminatory Private Value Auctions," *Review of Economic Studies*, **66**, 509–528. ⟨197⟩

Swinkels, J. (2001): "Efficiency of Large Private Value Auctions," *Econometrica*, **69**, 37–68. ⟨197⟩

U.S. Department of the Treasury (1998): *Uniform-Price Auctions: Update of the Treasury Experience*, Office of Market Finance, Washington D.C., October (available online at http://www.treasury.gov/domfin). ⟨176⟩

Vickrey, W. (1961): "Counterspeculation, Auctions and Competitive Sealed Tenders," *Journal of Finance*, **16**, 8–37. ⟨ix, 9, 28, 36, 59, 82, 176, 196⟩

Vickrey, W. (1962): "Auctions and Bidding Games," in *Recent Advances in Game Theory*, Princeton Conference Series, **29**, Princeton, NJ: Princeton University Press, 15–27. ⟨28, 36⟩

Weber, R. (1983): "Multiple Object Auctions," in R. Engelbrecht-Wiggans, M. Shubik, and R. Stark (eds.), *Auctions, Bidding and Contracting: Uses and Theory*, New York, NY: New York University Press, 165–191. ⟨221⟩

Wilson, R. (1967): "Competitive Bidding with Asymmetrical Information," *Management Science*, **13**, 816–820. ⟨124⟩

Wilson, R. (1969): "Competitive Bidding with Disparate Information," *Management Science*, **15**, 446–448. ⟨102⟩

Wilson, R. (1977): "A Bidding Model of Perfect Competition," *Review of Economic Studies*, **44**, 511–518. ⟨102⟩

Wilson, R. (1979): "Auctions of Shares," *Quarterly Journal of Economics*, **94**, 675–689. ⟨176⟩

Wilson, R. (1993): "Strategic Analysis of Auctions," in R. Aumann and S. Hart (eds.), *Handbook of Game Theory*, Amsterdam: North-Holland. ⟨9⟩

Wilson, R. (1998): "Sequential Equilibria of Asymmetric Ascending Auctions: The Case of Log-Normal Distributions," *Economic Theory*, **12**, 433–440. ⟨140⟩

Wolfstetter, E. (2001): "Third- and Lower-Price Auctions," mimeo, Humboldt University. ⟨36⟩

Index